Discovered in China more than 2,000 years ago, tofu has long served as East Asia's most important family of soybean foods. Lending itself to a wide variety of forms, an almost endless variation of uses, tofu adapts easily to Western recipes and is versatile enough to become an essential ingredient in many favorite Western dishes.

Here is everything you need to know about tofu in a beautifully illustrated book that explores tradition, techniques of making tofu in the modern kitchen, nutritional benefits and a tempting array of recipes that include dishes from the East and West. A protein food that makes fullest use of the earth's nutritional resources, tofu offers a revolutionary yet simple approach to meeting the world's critical food requirements.

"The most important book on food ever published for vegetarians—if not for all the world. Clear prose and beautiful illustrations take you step by step through tofu making at home.... *Buy this book!*"
The Vegetarian Alternative

"Awakened the West to the wonders of Tofu."
The New York Times

"Among the recent tofu cookbooks put out for the American cook to date, *The Book of Tofu*...is the most complete and useful."
Cuisine

"Delicious, easy-to-follow recipes...meticulous...fascinating...highly recommended."
Library Journal

"A seminal work."
The Washington Post

Also by William Shurtleff and Akiko Aoyagi
Published by Ballantine Books:

THE BOOK OF MISO

THE BOOK OF
TOFU

PROTEIN SOURCE OF THE FUTURE...NOW!

Volume I
Condensed and Revised

William Shurtleff
and
Akiko Aoyagi

Illustrated by Akiko Aoyagi

BALLANTINE BOOKS • NEW YORK

For Suzuki Shunryu roshi (1906-1971)
Zen master and friend

Library of Congress Catalog Card Number: 74-31629

ISBN 0-345-35181-9

This edition published by arrangement with Autumn Press, Inc.

Printed in Canada

First Ballantine Books Edition: January 1979
Seventeenth Printing: May 1990

Cover Illustration: A Traditional Tofu Shop Based On Kyoto's Yuba Han, By Akiko Aoyagi

Contents

Preface   vii
Acknowledgments   xiii
1. Protein East and West   1
2. Tofu as a Food   14
3. Getting Started   33
    Favorite Tofu Recipes   56
4. Soybeans   58
5. Fresh Soy Puree   76
6. Okara (Soy Pulp)   87
7. Curds & Whey   101
8. Tofu & Firm Tofu   110
9. Deep-fried Tofu   215
    Deep-fried Tofu Cutlets   253
    Deep-fried Tofu Burgers & Treasure Balls   261
    Deep-fried Tofu Pouches   270
10. Soymilk   288
11. Silken Tofu   311
12. Grilled Tofu   325
13. Frozen & Dried-frozen Tofu   339
14. Fermented Tofu   358
15. Yuba   367

Appendix A: Tofu Restaurants in Japan   379
Appendix B: Tofu Shops and Soy Dairies
    in the West   392
Appendix C: Varieties of Tofu in East Asia   402
Appendix D: Table of Equivalents   406
Bibliography   407
Glossary   413
Index   421

Preface

After returning to America from my first visit to Japan, a summer practicing Zen meditation, I had the good fortune to meet Shunryu Suzuki *roshi,* head abbot of the Tassajara Zen Mountain Center. Moved by his example, I joined the Tassajara community, nestled in the wild beauty of the Santa Lucia mountains near Big Sur, California. Working as a cook in the Center's fine kitchens. I grew to appreciate the value of our natural food diet and soon came to feel that the utterly simple way of life and practice that this man brought to the West was the most wonderful gift I had ever received.

After two and a half years at Tassajara, I spoke to Suzuki roshi about returning to Japan to continue practicing meditation, study the culture and language from which his teaching emerged, and learn more of the art of Buddhist vegetarian cookery. He encouraged me in my desire to help bring more of the East to the West, and I soon found myself a penniless student in Kyoto. It was thus out of necessity that I first made tofu—pronounced TOE-fu and also known in the West as soybean curd—a part of my daily diet, grateful that it was both nutritious and inexpensive.

Akiko and I met not long thereafter and quickly found that we shared an interest in the traditional life-styles and arts of the Far East. She was working as a designer and was also a good cook. Knowing that I was intrigued by tofu, she prepared me many of her favorite recipes using each of Japan's seven different types of tofu. One evening, through a mutual friend who considers himself a tofu connoisseur, we received our first introduction to the world of tofu haute cuisine at one of Japan's oldest and most renowned tofu restaurants. The dinner was composed of twelve small dishes, each artistically presented and each featuring tofu in one of its many forms. Here, indeed, was tofu like we had never tasted it before: that evening *The Book of Tofu* was born.

We soon began to explore the realm of tofu cookery in earnest. Each morning we walked to our neighborhood tofu shop—one of the 38,000 scattered throughout Japan—and bought our supply for the day, always freshly prepared. I had never imagined that tofu could be coaxed into such a range of forms and textures, nor that it could combine harmoniously with so many different foods and flavors. Our low-calorie meals grew richer in protein and more deliciously varied, while our food bill remained as low as ever.

At first our repertoire was largely Japanese. We began to visit tofu restaurants throughout Japan, enjoying what seemed like an endless variety of tofu dishes served in elegant but simple settings: next to a garden in autumn colors, by a pond with its symphony of cicadas, or in a quiet temple overlooking a garden of white sand raked into wavelike eddies. Whenever possible, we met with the head cook at these restaurants and stood at his elbow watching, taking notes, trying to absorb the subtleties of his art as he prepared each of his specialties. Later, we tried each of these recipes at home—sometimes over and over again—until we were satisfied with the results. We then grew bolder and began experimenting with tofu in traditional Western-style dishes. Akiko's creative touch yielded delicious tofu dips and puréed dressings, egg dishes and casseroles, salads and soups, barbequed tofu, and deep-fried tofu burgers.

As word of our special interest spread throughout the neighborhood, the master of our local tofu shop invited us to visit him early one morning to watch the tofu-making process first hand. We were deeply impressed with the feeling of alertness and care in his work. His movements were precise and graceful, joined in an effortless rhythm that, at times, flowed like a dance. A true master, he held in highest esteem the traditional, natural way and the spirit of fine craftsmanship. Working in an attractive, compact shop attached to his home, he used only natural ingredients to prepare the tofu he sold from his shop window and throughout the neighborhood. Like the traditional swordmaker or potter, his daily life was a practice, a spiritual path or, as the Japanese say, a Way. It was obvious that his work was more than a means of economic livelihood. For him, the joy of fine craftsmanship was its own fulfillment and reward.

I returned again and again to watch this master at work. Finally I asked to become his disciple and apprentice. Over a period of more than a year, he gradually taught me the techniques of making tofu in the traditional way.

This man urged us to record the methodology and, if possible, the spirit of his art both for Westerners seeking meaningful work and for future generations of Japanese who might someday wish to rediscover the rewards of fine craftsmanship presently obscured by modern industrial values and the "economic miracle." Throughout my apprenticeship, Akiko and I were encouraged to scour Japan to seek out every traditional tofu master we could find. To do so, we spent the warm months travelling up and down the islands, carrying backpacks and the tools necessary for our study. Often spending the night in temples, we met many Zen masters and practiced meditation with their students. And on many mornings, under a sky full of stars, Akiko and I wound our way to the one lighted shop on the sleeping streets of Japan's towns or cities to join a tofu master at his work.

Traditional tofu makers had often spoken to us with nostalgia and praise of the fine tofu once made in farmhouses throughout the country. To locate this legendary tofu and learn the secrets of its preparation, we backpacked early one spring into the remotest parts

of Japan. We learned the traditional art from grand-
mothers in the mountainous back country while, to
our surprise, the members of Banyan Ashram—a
farming and meditation community on tiny Suwanose
Island—taught us a remarkably simple way of making
tofu unknown to even the more professional craftsmen
with whom we studied.

As we continued our work, several simple facts
came together to broaden our perspective. The writings of nutritionists, ecologists, and experts studying
world food and population problems convinced us
that a meat-centered diet makes very inefficient use
of the earth's ability to provide mankind with protein.
It soon seemed to us imperative that the West learn
to use soybeans directly as a source of inexpensive,
high-quality protein, as people in East Asia have been
doing for thousands of years. Here, where density of
population has long posed serious problems, tofu is
the most important and most popular way of transforming soybeans into a delicious food. Yet how unfortunate it seemed that there were fewer tofu shops
in the combined countries and continents of India,
Africa, South America, Russia, Canada, Europe, and
America, than within the space of one-half square mile
in Tokyo, Taipei, Seoul, or Peking.

We also came to feel that the tofu shop, requiring
a minimum of energy resources, technology, and capital, could serve as a model for decentralized home or
cottage industries throughout many parts of the developing and developed worlds. With this thought in
mind, we took to studying shops in Japan and Taiwan
which, we felt, combined the best of both traditional
and modern techniques, making possible the large-
scale production of good-quality tofu at relatively low
cost. We also visited Japan's largest and most modern
tofu factories to study their production-line methods
in detail.

Traditional tofu masters have a saying that there
are two things they will not show another person:
how to make babies and how to make tofu. But to

our continual surprise, these men invited us in—sometimes hesitatingly at first—to observe them at work and ultimately opened their hearts and homes to us in a way that was a continual source of inspiration to our research. We returned again and again to our favorite shops, each time with new questions, each time able to understand things we had not noticed or grasped before. Perceiving the sincerity of our intention to transmit the fundamentals of their craft to the West, they ended up sharing secrets with us that they would never have dreamed of revealing to their compatriots. We only hope that our efforts here do justice to their kindness, and to the care and patience they showed us in making sure that we *really* understood.

A rhythm emerged between our research in the field, writing, art work, and daily meditation which nurtured our growing book. Over a period of almost three years, we prepared and enjoyed more than 1,200 tofu dishes. This book contains only the 250 recipes which seem to us best suited to Western tastes. Each recipe uses only natural foods and none requires the inclusion of meat.

As our work neared its completion, both Akiko and I realized that perhaps our finest teacher had been tofu itself. Like water that flows through the worlds, serving as it moves along, tofu joyfully surrenders itself to the endless play of transformation. Pierced with a skewer, it sizzles and broils above a bed of live coals; placed in a bubbling, earthenware pot over an open fire, it snuggles down next to the mushrooms and makes friends; deep-fried in crackling oil, it emerges crisp and handsome in robes of golden brown; frozen all night in the snow under vast mountain skies, it emerges glistening with frost and utterly changed. All as if it knew there was no death to die, no fixed or separate self to cling to, no other home than here.

A true democrat in spirit, tofu presents the same face to rich and poor alike. Placed before nobility in East Asia's finest haute cuisine, it is humble and unpretentious. Served up as peasant fare in rustic farmhouses, it is equally at home. Though unassertive, it is indispensable in the diet of more than one billion people. Holding to simplicity, it remains in harmony with all things, and people never tire of its presence. Through understatement and nuance, it reveals its finest qualities.

Since earliest times, the people of East Asia have honored tofu in poem and proverb. Known as "meat of the fields" and "meat without a bone," tofu has provided them with abundant sustenance. In yielding and offering itself up, it seems to find its perfect balance in the greater dance. In the coming decades and centuries, tofu could nurture people around the world. To this end, we wish to send it on its way in the four directions.

Tokyo, Japan
March 1975

Acknowledgments

WE WOULD like to thank the following people for their help in making this book: Mr. Toshio Arai, who gave us hundreds of hours of his time, taught us the traditional art and practice of making tofu, and prepared the tofu we ate and enjoyed each day; Mr. Shinji Morii, master of Morika, one of Japan's oldest and most famous tofu shops; Mr. Koryu Abe, Japan's foremost tofu historian; Mr. Hiroyoshi Masuda and his father, masters of one of Kamakura's finest traditional tofu shops; Ms. Kisa Asano and Mr. Mankichi Nagai, head craftspeople at two of Kyoto's oldest and finest yuba shops; Mr. Kiyoichi Oya, vice president of the Japanese National Tofu Union and president of the Tokyo Tofu Union; Mr. Tokuji Watanabe, director of the National Food Research Institute in Tokyo and one of the world's foremost authorities on tofu; Mr. Takichi Okumura, owner of Tokyo's renowned Sasa-no-yuki restaurant, and his head chefs, Mr. Sugita and Mr. Fushimi; Mr. Shigemitsu Tsuji, master and chief chef at Kyoto's Nakamura-ro restaurant, famous throughout Japan as a lecturer and writer on Japanese cuisine and tofu, and author of a recent book on tofu cookery; Mr. Toshio Yanaihara, author of many works on tofu and head of a large Japanese cooking school; Messrs. Scott Sawyers, Lloyd Reid, and Jack Yamashita of the American Soybean Association in Japan; Dr. Harry W. Miller, the West's foremost authority on soymilk and pioneer in the field of using soybeans as foods; Mr. Teisuke Yabuki, president of the Luppy Soymilk Company; Mmes. Ito Kidoguchi, Kazuko Ozawa, and Minoru Watanabe, all in their seventies, who first taught us how to make farmhouse tofu; the members of Banyan Ashram who taught us how to make tofu coagulated with sea water and introduced us to the riches of their simple way of life; Mr. Kyo Ko, owner of Fukyo-dofu, Tokyo's largest manufacturer of Chinese-style tofu; Dr. Shiro Kudo of Asahimatsu and Dr. Tadashi Honma of Misuzu, Japan's two largest producers of dried-frozen tofu; Messrs. Itaro Hayashi, Ei Tamura, Daisaburo Noma and Kinjiro Sugai, each masters of fine traditional tofu shops at which we studied; Messrs. Shotaro Yoshikawa and Minoru Narahara; two leaders of Japan's movement to return to the use of natural nigari coagulant; Mr. Kiyoshi Takato, manager of one of Japan's largest and most modern tofu factories; and tofu makers throughout Taiwan, Korea, and America who gave generously of their time and experience.

Finally, we would like to give special thanks to our parents for their aid and encouragement, to Mr. Tyler Smith for his editorial suggestions, and to our publisher, Nahum Stiskin, whose faith and support were with us from the first conception of this book until its completion.

1

Protein East and West

FOR OVER TWO millennia in China and 1,000 years in Japan, soybeans have served as one of the most important sources of protein. In countries such as these, where people have long had to live with the problem of overpopulation, soybeans have been prized for their remarkable ability to produce over 33 percent more protein from an acre of land than any other known crop and *twenty* times as much usable protein as could be raised on an acre given over to grazing beef cattle or growing their fodder (Fig. 1). It is thus easy to understand why meat protein is a great deal more expensive than soy protein and why, as population pressure on the land increases, it seems inevitable that more and more farmers all over the world will be planting soybeans. Their "protein efficiency" is the first and, perhaps, primary reason why soybean foods have played such a key role in the daily diet of the people of East Asia.

Not only is the protein yield of soybeans high in terms of quantity—soybeans contain about 35 percent protein, more than any other unprocessed plant or animal food—it is also excellent in terms of quality. Soy protein includes all of the eight essential amino acids in a configuration readily usable by the human body. It is now becoming common knowledge that there is no essential difference between plant and animal proteins. From the body's point of view, the amount of usable protein contained in ½ cup of soybeans is no different from that contained in 5 ounces of steak. And inexpensive soybean foods contain no cholesterol, almost none of the relatively indigestible

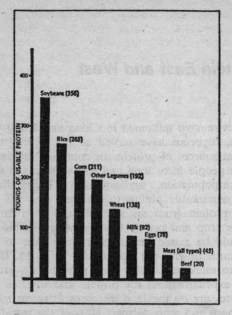

Fig. 1. Per-acre Yields of Usable Protein from Different Food Sources

Source: Calculated from USDA per-acre yield statistics (1971-74) and WHO/FAO/UNICEF Protein Advisory Group Bulletin #6, 1971.

saturated fats found in most animal foods, and an extremely low ratio of calories to protein. These basic facts, now scientifically well documented, have been understood intuitively throughout East Asia since earliest times.

But just as Westerners prefer to transform whole kernels of wheat into breads, pasta, and other foods made from flour, so have the people of East Asia preferred to transform whole soybeans into other forms. Since long before the Christian era, men and women throughout Asia have participated in a vast experiment to find simple yet effective ways of creating soy protein foods that are versatile, easily digestible, and, above all, delicious. Centuries of creative endeavor have yielded three great products which now serve as the cornerstones of East Asian nutrition and cuisine: *tofu, miso* (fermented soybean paste), and *shoyu* (natural soy sauce). Whereas miso and shoyu are essentially high-protein seasonings, tofu is a food that can serve as the backbone of a diet in much the same way that meat and dairy products are now used in the dietary pattern of the West. The development of traditional technologies and methods for transforming soybeans directly into these foods may someday be regarded as one of East Asia's greatest contributions to mankind, and a major step in the direct utilization by man of the earth's bounty of protein.

Today, throughout much of Asia, tofu is by far the most important way of using soybeans as a daily food. Indeed tofu is as much a part of Oriental culture, language, and cookery as is bread in the West. In America, a country with twice the population of Japan, there are 19,000 bakeries and the average annual consumption of bread is 73 loaves per person. The tofu made in Japan's 38,000 tofu shops provides the average Japanese with about seventy 12-ounce cakes each year. And there are an estimated 150,000 tofu shops in China, 2,500 in Taiwan, 11,000 in Indonesia, 1,400 in North and South Korea, and still more in the Philippines, Thailand, and Vietnam.

America's Soy Protein Tragedy

Now imagine how strange it would seem if, in the world's largest wheat producing country, most of the people had never tasted bread. Yet no less unusual is the present situation in America, the world's largest producer of soybeans, where the majority of people have not yet tasted, seen, or even heard of tofu.

America now produces about two-thirds of the world's soybeans. They are one of our largest and most important farm crops, second only to corn (and ahead of wheat!) in total dollar value, and third in total acreage. The 47 million tons of soybeans harvested in 1975 is enough to provide every person in the United States with 165 pounds of pure, high-quality protein. If all of this protein were used directly as food—in the form of tofu, for example—it would be sufficient to fulfill the average adult protein requirement of every American for about 3 years! And if the protein obtainable from one year's harvest of America's soybeans were distributed equally among all people on the planet, it would fulfill about 25 percent of their yearly protein requirements, according to even the most conservative Western standards.

But the tragedy of our present situation is that less than 15 percent of America's non-exported soy protein ever reaches human beings: 1½ percent directly in soybean foods and about 13 percent indirectly in the form of meat and dairy products.

What happens to all the rest? To understand the answer to this question we must first recognize that, while in East Asia soybeans have traditionally been used to make tofu and other soybean foods, in the West they have been viewed primarily as an oilseed. Almost all of America's non-exported soybeans are shipped to huge modern factories where their oil is extracted in a continuous, automated process. The largest and most important piece of machinery employed is a counter-current hexane solvent extractor, capable of handling over 4 million pounds of soybeans per day. Soy oil, which contains no protein, is degummed, refined, bleached, deodorized, and winterized by industro-chemical processes and then sold as cooking or salad oil. Some of the oil is hydrogenated to produce margarine and vegetable shortenings. The defatted soybean meal, a byproduct of the oil extraction process, contains about 2½ times as much protein by weight as steak.

Now, *where* does this protein go? In America, about 95 percent of all non-exported soy protein ends up as feed for livestock, and of this, 77 to 95 percent is irretrievably lost in the process of animal metabolism. In addition, we feed livestock 78 percent of all our grain, most of which could be used directly as food. American farmers use more of their soybeans and grain as fodder than farmers in any other country. These losses, creating the appearance of scarcity in the midst of actual plenty, are a direct result of our failure to understand and make use of the soybean's great potential as a food. For if the total protein available from these crops were utilized directly by human beings, it could make up an estimated 90 percent of the world's protein deficiency.

The process described above, inherent in the Western meat-centered diet, is the cause of our immense protein waste. In *Diet for a Small Planet*, Frances Moore Lappé shows how we use the cow as a protein factory in reverse: we feed it from 14 to 21 pounds of protein from sources that could be used directly as food, and we obtain only 1 pound of protein from the meat. In this highly inefficient process, only 5 to 7 percent of the total protein consumed by a feedlot steer or cow is returned for human consumption as meat. Likewise only 12 percent is returned by a hog as pork, 15 percent by a chicken as meat and 22 percent as eggs, and 23 percent by a cow as milk. In her appeal for a more rational use of the earth's bounty, Ms. Lappé urges Westerners to get off the "top" of the food chain and begin to utilize sources of high-quality, non-meat protein.

Although Americans make up only 6 percent of the world's population, they account for 30 percent of its total meat consumption. The per capita American consumption of beef, pork, and poultry presently runs about 254 pounds per year, or 316 grams per day. This is about 5 times the world average and 15 times the average intake for people in East Asia. In order to produce this much meat, American farmers plant an astounding 50 percent of their total acreage in feed crops, and U.S. livestock are fed 120 million tons of feed-grains each year. Consequently, the average

American now consumes the equivalent of 2,000 pounds of grain and soybeans annually, roughly 90 percent of which is in the form of meat, poultry, and eggs. But in developing countries—where most grains and soybeans are used directly as food—the average person consumes only about 400 pounds of grain per year. Hence the birth of one meat-eating American has the same effect on world food resources as the birth of *five* children in India, Africa, or South America. On the other hand, a reduction in American meat consumption of only 10 percent could free 12 million tons of soybeans, corn, wheat, and other grains, enough to meet the annual grain requirements of 60 million people in less developed countries.

Worldwide Protein Crisis

It is now generally conceded that the world is facing a serious food crisis. More precisely, it is a protein crisis, and not one that is likely to go away or even become less critical during the coming decades. We have watched regional famines spread and become more frequent, and experts are no longer as optimistic as they once were about the "Green Revolution" with its high-yielding strains of "dwarf" hybrid wheats and rices, whose primary advantage is their responsiveness to large doses of chemical fertilizers. Obtaining high yields from the "miracle" seeds requires large amounts of increasingly expensive energy, energy to make chemical fertilizers and pesticides, and to run irrigation pumps and farm machinery. The high costs of these "inputs" has bankrupted many small farmers in third-world countries or forced them to sell their farms to the wealthy landed elite. Moreover, farm mechanization on the increasingly large farms has left large numbers of farm workers without jobs and caused mass migration to city slums. Recent important studies by the International Labor Organization and the United Nations Institute for Social Development show

that in a wide range of developing countries the Green
Revolution has helped to widen the gap between the
rich and poor and to aggravate the problem of hunger.

It is now estimated that more than one-fourth of
the world's four billion people (including 450 million
children equalling more than twice the population of
the United States!) confront hunger or famine during
at least some part of each year. In many developing
countries, according to United Nations statistics, 25
percent to 30 percent of all children never see their
fourth birthday, largely due to malnutrition. And many
who do survive are permanently damaged physically
and mentally because of the lack of sufficient protein
in their diet. These facts so boggle the mind that most
of us are simply unable or unwilling to face them. But
this crucial problem of our age *must* be faced and
understood *now*, for each of us can begin *today* to
contribute directly to its solution.

The food crisis is continually aggravated by two
basic trends that all experts agree must be reversed as
rapidly as possible. The first trend, understood since
the time of Malthus, is that linear increases in food
production fall farther and farther behind exponen-
tial increases in population. In the less developed
countries, the amount of food available to each person
is steadily decreasing. With the world's population
doubling every 35 years and expanding onto what is
now farmland, and with most of the earth's good-
quality land already under intensive cultivation, the
cost of farming previously unused land on mountain
sides or in deserts and jungles grows increasingly expensive. And hungry people are the least able to pay
these costs.

The second trend, which is just now beginning to
be recognized, concerns the relationship between af-
fluence and the consumption of basic foods. As people
develop a higher standard of living, they generally
desire a larger proportion of meat and other animal
protein in their diet (Fig. 2). During the past 12
years, cattle herds have increased 30 percent in the

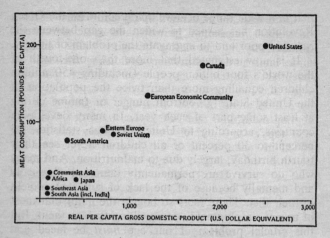

Fig. 2.   World Meat Consumption vs. Income
Source: U.S. Dept. of Agriculture

United States and 28 percent throughout the rest of
the world. During the same period per-capita livestock
meat consumption has increased 22 percent in the
United States, 26 percent in France and Canada, 30
percent in Russia, 33 percent in West Germany, 94
percent in Italy, and an astonishing 364 percent in
Japan. (Japan, however, still has the lowest annual
per capita meat consumption of any of the above
countries; its 51 pounds per year is only 20 percent
of top-ranking America's 254 pounds.) Since more
than 14 pounds of fodder protein are needed to produce 1 pound of protein from beef, a small increase
in demand for meat leads to enormous increases in
the indirect consumption of soy and grain proteins.
This results in a sharp decrease in the amounts of
these foods available for human consumption, especially in poorer countries. In addition, rising demand
for soybean and grain fodders pushes up their prices,
creating a vicious cycle that further aggravates the
shortages in poorer countries.

To reverse the first trend, every effort must be made to reduce population growth and raise agricultural productivity by increasing per-acre yields, bringing more land under cultivation, and using this land for essential high-protein food crops (rather than cash crops such as coffee, tobacco, cocoa, and tea, which have little or no nutritional value). One hope for the coming decades is that developing countries with suitable topography and climate will follow the lead of Brazil in realizing the tremendous economic and nutritional potential of soybeans. From a mere 650,000 tons in 1968, Brazil's soybean production soared to 10.5 million tons in 1974, a *sixteenfold* increase in only 6 years. Having recently surpassed China to become the world's second largest soybean producer, Brazil is now working to boost production to 15 million tons by 1980 and hopes eventually to overtake first-place America. With exports totaling almost 1 billion dollars annually, soybeans have now surpassed coffee as Brazil's chief export crop, and the government is actively encouraging farmers to turn their coffee plantations into soybean farms.

(At the same time, however, industrialized nations are now becoming increasingly aware of the limits and dangers of conventional agricultural methods to create an ever-expanding food supply. Intensive use of pesticides and chemical fertilizers, the two main factors responsible for the great postwar jump in agricultural output, and attempts to clear more and more land for agricultural use are beginning to place such heavy stresses on the planet's basic ecosystems that they could easily create environmental problems of a greater magnitude than the food problems they are now intended to solve.)

While most Westerners—and particularly those not involved in agriculture—can participate directly in the reversal of the first trend only through family planning, every Westerner can participate in a very vital and immediate way to reverse the second trend, and thereby actively help to relieve the suffering that afflicts millions of our fellow human beings around the world. We can and must make more efficient use of the food presently available on the planet. And we must understand clearly the fact, often overlooked in discussing world food shortages, that there is presently more than enough food and protein for all the people in the world. The extremely complex problem of distributing this food in a just and compassionate way, avoiding large-scale misuse of its great nutritional potential, demands our fullest attention. Not the earth's natural limitations but the wisdom with which we use the earth's bounty will determine whether or not there is sufficient food for all human beings during the coming decades.

Most experts agree that to make fullest use of the protein we now have, the citizens of the world's affluent, industrialized nations will have to make basic changes in their eating habits. Most important, they will have to start eating less meat—especially beef. All of man's food comes initially from plant sources and, in fact, 70 percent of the world's protein is still consumed directly from plants. By rediscovering the wisdom inherent in traditional dietary patterns that make use of non-meat protein sources, we can free millions of tons of high-quality soy and grain protein to be used directly as food. (Since, according to various government estimates, the average American now receives from 12 to 45 percent more protein than his body can even use, Americans can perhaps most easily reduce their consumption of expensive protein foods.) In a world where the affluent nations appear to many as islands of plenty in a sea of hunger, each of us must make a personal effort to rectify this dangerous imbalance. We can begin by working to make best use of our ample protein supplies.

Hopefully, more and more people, recognizing that a meat-centered diet squanders the earth's food resources, will turn to nutritionally and ecologically viable alternatives—such as tofu. Many have already found that a meatless diet, low in saturated fats and cholesterol, makes sense in terms of good health, mental alertness, and a general feeling of physical well being. For many more people, the determining forces may well be primarily economic: skyrocketing meat prices. The basic inefficiencies of land use inherent in meat production have led food experts and economists to predict that in the coming decades, the prices of most meats could rise to the point where only the very rich could afford them. Yet whether we are moved by economic, ecological, religious or health considerations, or by a feeling of identification with the millions of hungry people around the world, each of us can help solve the world food problem by starting now to change the way we eat.

The Growing Importance of Soy Protein

One thing is virtually certain: Over the coming years, we can expect soy protein to play an increasingly important role in our daily lives. Although scientists continue to explore futuristic high-yielding sources such as single cell proteins (SCP, including yeasts, bacteria, and molds), microalgae (such as chlorella, spirulina, and scenedesmus), and leaf proteins and synthetics, which may eventually prove to be safe, economically feasible, and acceptable to the consumer, most experts now consider soybeans to be the most realistic and promising source of low-cost, high-quality protein available in large enough quantities to meet human needs on a worldwide scale. Hence, throughout the world, there is great interest in finding ways of using soybeans directly as a source of protein. In the United States, where 70 percent of all food protein presently comes from animal sources and only 30 percent from plants, major food research firms estimate that within 10 to 20 years these figures will be reversed. And the most rapid increase is, of course, seen in the use of soy protein. Whereas an estimated 150,000 tons of the latter were used directly in U.S.

foods in 1972, it is predicted that more than *twelve* times this amount will be used by 1980.

Although these figures sound promising, an examination of their actual relevance to the world food crisis seems to suggest several problems. We must remember that the total amount of soy protein now used directly as food in the U.S. is still extremely small—only about 1½ percent of the total available from the domestic crop. Most of this protein is used in the form of plain or defatted soy flour (containing 40 to 52 percent protein), which is purchased primarily by the food industry and used in small amounts as a conditioner, extender, emulsifier, or moisture retainer in canned foods, baked goods, and processed meats. The presence of this soy additive is usually acknowledged only in small print on the label, and the word "soy" is often carefully omitted. Some soy flour is sent to developing countries in food supplements as part of America's worldwide nutritional aid program. Yet it is not expected that these ways of using soy protein will be of major importance during the coming decades.

Rather, experts in the food industry foresee the use of advanced Western technology to create a wide range of new, synthetic soybean foods. Many of these are already available: protein concentrates, isolates, spun proteins and, most important, textured vegetable proteins. The latter, extruded from defatted soybean meal (or whole soy flour) in highly sophisticated factories, are generally added as extenders to ground or processed meat products in order to lower their cost (and levels of saturated fats) while raising their protein content and improving their cooking qualities. Spun proteins, composed of tiny fibers or monofilaments of almost pure protein, are used to make imitation livestock products and meat analogs. By compressing the protein fibers to simulate the fibrous texture of meat, and adding the appropriate flavorings and colorings, food technologists are able to create imitation bacon, ham, sausages, beef, chicken, and a wide variety of new high-protein snacks. Many of these fabricated products are now available in Western supermarkets. For relatively affluent Westerners, such foods can provide protein which is somewhat less expensive than that found in meat, while also helping to make more efficient use of domestic soy protein. Yet it is now clearly understood that the technology for producing these foods is far too complex and costly to be of use in developing countries where hunger is most acute. And to the growing number of Westerners interested in natural foods, these highly refined products are bound to be of limited appeal.

As a clear and practical alternative, we must turn our attention to traditional East Asian methods for transforming soybeans into foods; methods that recognize food to be man's most direct link with the nurturing earth and which bind season and soil, man and food into a holistic, organic cycle. Each of the seven basic types of tofu can be made in any Western kitchen, or in small, decentralized enterprises using technology on a human scale and employing a minimum of energy. The tofu shop can be adopted as easily in Bangladesh, Brazil, and Nigeria as in the industrialized or "post industrial" societies of the West.

In tofu shops now located throughout America, craftsmen have already begun making tofu available at reasonable prices. We believe these shops are situated at an historic crossroads, and that they can and will make an invaluable contribution to the betterment of life on our planet during the years ahead.

2

Tofu as a Food

NUTRITIONALLY, the various types of tofu—there are seven in Japan and even more in China—have much the same importance for the people of East Asia that dairy products, eggs, and meat have for us in the West. (In Figures 3 and 4, tofu products are listed and illustrated in the approximate order of their availability in the U.S.) When looking for alternate sources of protein and when considering the benefits of a meatless way of eating, many people ask: "What will we use to replace meat?" Some experiment with eggs and dairy products, or with soybeans and grains. The traditional answer throughout East Asia has been tofu.

Before replacing all or part of the meat in our diet with less expensive protein from another source, most nutrition-conscious people will want to have enough sound, factual information to make this important decision with complete confidence. We feel that the following facts show tofu to be a truly remarkable food. And tofu's excellent nutritional record, extending over a period of thousands of years in China and Japan, gives practical substantiation to the findings of modern research.

Rich in High Quality Protein

The value of any food as a protein source depends on two factors: the *quantity* of protein in the food and the *quality* of that protein. Quantity is usually expressed as a simple percentage of total weight. By comparing the following figures, it can be seen that the highest percentages of protein are found in plant rather than animal foods:

Food	Percent Protein by Weight
Dried-frozen tofu	53
Yuba, dried	52
Soy flour (defatted)	51
Soy flour (natural)	40
Soybeans (whole, dry)	35
Cheeses	30
Fish	22
Chicken	21
Beef (steak)	20
Cottage cheese	20
Deep-fried tofu pouches	19
Deep-fried tofu burgers	15
Whole-wheat flour	13
Hamburger	13
Eggs	13
Firm tofu	11
Deep-fried tofu cutlets	10
Tofu	8
Brown rice (uncooked)	8
Milk (whole dairy)	3

Source: *Food Composition Tables* (Japan, 1964), *Composition of Foods* (USA, 1964), and Lappé, *Diet for a Small Planet* (1975)

Fig. 3. Tofu Products Available in the West

Name Used in This Book	Other Names	Description	Where Sold *	How Sold
Tofu	Soybean Curd	Reguar, medium-firm Japanese-style tofu	N,J,C,S,T	12- to 21-ounce cakes water-packed in plastic tubs or cartons; also canned
Firm Tofu	Toufu, Dow-foo, Bean Cake	Chinese-style firm tofu	N,J,C,S,T	Two or more 6-ounce cakes water-packed in plastic tubs
Silken Tofu	Kinugoshi, Soft or Custard Tofu, Shui Dow-foo, Sui-toufu	Soft Japanese-style tofu	N,J,C,S,T	12- to 20-ounce cakes water-packed in plastic tubs or cartons
Deep-fried Tofu Cutlets	Thick Agé, Nama-agé, Atsu-agé, Raw-fried Tofu	Deep-fried cakes of firm tofu	N,J,C,S,T	Cakes or slices of 5 ounces or less, dry-packed in plastic cartons or tubs; also sold in small triangles and cubes
Deep-fried Tofu Burgers	Ganmo, Ganmodokl	Deep-fried tofu patties containing minced vegetables	J	3½-ounce patties or 2-ounce balls dry-packed in plastic bags; or canned
Deep-fried Tofu Pouches or Puffs	Aburagé, Agé or Agé Puffs	A hollow pouch or puff of deep-fried tofu	N,J,C,S,T	Three ½- to 1-ounce pieces dry-packed in a cellophane bag

Hollow Deep-fried Tofu Cubes	Hollow Agé Puffs, Dow-foo Bok, Yu-toufu	Chinese-style, hollow 1½-inch cubes of deep-fried tofu	N,J,C,S,T	15 cubes, each ⅓ ounce, dry-packed in a cellophane bag
Soymilk	Tou-chiang, Tonyu, Soyalac	Regular or flavored with honey or carob	N,J,C,S,T	1-pint glass, paper, or plastic containers
Tofu Pudding	Fresh Soybean Pudding, Soft Tofu Curds	Soft curds of soymilk	N,J,C,S,T	1-pound portions in plastic tubs
Wine-fermented Tofu	Toufu-ru, Fuyu, Chinese Cheese, Bean Curd Cheese	Chinese-style soft cubes of fermented tofu in brining liquor	C	White varieties in 1-pint bottles; red varieties in small cans
Grilled Tofu	Yaki-dofu	A cake of firm tofu which has been grilled or broiled	J	10-ounce cakes water-packed in plastic tubs; or canned
Dried-frozen Tofu	Kori-dofu, Koya-dofu	Very lightweight cakes of tofu which have been frozen and then dried	J,S	Five to ten 1-ounce cakes in an airtight carton
Instant Powdered Tofu	Dehydrated Instant Tofu	Do-it-yourself, instant homemade tofu	J,S	A foil-wrapped package of powdered soymilk accompanied by a small package of coagulant

Name Used in This Book	Other Names	Description	Where Sold *	How Sold
Okara	Soy Pulp, Tofu Lees, Unohana	Insoluble portions of the soybean remaining after filtering off soymilk	J,T	8- to 16-ounce portions in plastic bags, balls, or mounds
Dried Yuba	Bean Curd Sheets	A high-protein film made from soymilk	J,C	4- to 8-ounce portions in paper or cellophane bags
Soymilk Curds	Oboro	Unpressed soft curds of coagulated soymilk	T	Available directly from tofu shops by special order
Pressed Tofu	Toufu-kan, Dow-foo Gar	Chinese-style small cakes of very firmly pressed tofu	C	Three 4-ounce cakes sealed in a plastic pouch
Savory Pressed Tofu	Wu-hsiang Toufu-kan, Flavored Soybean Cake	Pressed tofu seasoned with soy sauce and spices	C	Three 4-ounce cakes sealed in a plastic pouch

* N = Natural and health food stores   J = Japanese food markets   C = Chinese food markets
   S = Supermarkets, and co-op markets   T = Available at most tofu shops by special request

Furthermore, we notice that dried-frozen tofu and *yuba* (a close relative of tofu) contain the highest percentages of protein found in any natural foods in existence. Moreover, the top five protein sources are all derived from soybeans. The data presented in Figure 5 show the percentages of protein and other nutrients in the various types of tofu now available in the West.

Fig. 4. Tofu Products Available in the West

Fig. 5. Composition of Nutrients in 100 grams of Tofu

Type of Tofu	Food Energy Calories	Moisture %	Protein %	Fat %	Carbohydrates (incl. fiber) %	Fiber %
Tofu	72	84.9	7.8	4.3	2.3	0
Firm Tofu	87	79.3	10.6	5.3	2.9	0
Silken Tofu	53	88.4	5.5	3.2	1.7	0
Deep-fried Tofu Cutlets	105	79.0	10.1	7.0	2.8	0
Deep-fried Tofu Burgers	192	64.0	15.4	14.0	5.2	0.1
Deep-fried Tofu Pouches	346	44.0	18.6	31.4	4.6	0.1
Soymilk	42	90.8	3.6	2.0	2.9	0.02
Wine-fermented Tofu	175	52.0	13.5	8.4	14.8	1.2
Grilled Tofu	82	83.0	8.8	5.1	2.1	0
Dried-frozen Tofu	436	10.4	53.4	26.4	7.2	0.2
Okara	65	84.5	3.5	1.9	9.2	2.3
Dried Yuba	432	8.7	52.3	24.1	11.9	0
Pressed Tofu and Savory Pressed Tofu	182	61.6	22.0	11.0	6.1	0.1
Dry Soybeans	392	12.0	34.3	17.5	31.2	4.5

Note: Regular Japanese tofu varies in protein content from 6 to 8.4, and in water content from 87.9 to 83.9 percent; the mineral data above refer to tofu (and silken tofu) coagulated with calcium sulfate. Silken tofu and the rich soymilk prepared at tofu shops vary in protein from 4.9 to 6.3, and in water content from 89.7 to 87.4 percent. Commercially-distributed soymilk varies in protein from 3.6 to 5.8, and in water content from 90.8 to 88.2 percent. Deep fried tofu cutlets prepared with nigari often

Ash	Calcium	Sodium	Phosphorus	Iron	Vit. B_1 (Thiamine)	Vit. B_2 Riboflavin)	Niacin
%	Mg	Mg	Mg	Mg	Mg	Mg	Mg
0.7	146	6	105	1.7	0.02	0.02	0.5
0.9	159	7	109	2.5	0.02	0.02	0.6
1.2	94	23	71	1.2	0.02	0.02	0.3
1.1	240	15	150	2.6	0.02	0.02	0.5
1.4	270	17	200	3.6	0.01	0.03	1.0
1.4	300	20	230	4.2	0.02	0.02	0.5
0.5	15	2	49	1.2	0.03	0.02	0.5
11.6	165	458	182	5.7	0.04	0.18	0.6
1.0	180	15	120	1.9	0.02	0.02	0.4
2.6	590	18	710	9.4	0.05	0.04	0.6
0.9	76	4	43	1.4	0.05	0.02	0.3
3.0	270	80	590	11.0	0.20	0.08	2.0
1.9	377	16	270	4.4	0.05	0.05	0.6
5.0	190	3	470	7.0	0.50	0.20	2.0

contain up to 17.7 percent protein and only 58.7 percent water. Differences in composition depend primarily on the method of preparation, the type of coagulant, and the grade and protein content of the soybeans used.

Sources: *Food Composition Tables* (Japan, *1964*), *Food Composition Table for Use in East Asia* (FAO, 1972), *and Composition of Foods* (USDA, 1963)

Protein quality refers to the percentage of protein in a food that can be utilized by the body; it is usually expressed in terms of NPU (Net Protein Utilization), "biological value," or "protein score." The NPU of a food depends largely on the food's digestibility and on the degree to which the configuration of the eight essential amino acids making up the protein matches the pattern required by the body.

It is a common misconception that the protein found in animal foods is somehow basically different from (and superior to) plant protein. In fact, there is no basic difference. It is simply a question of degree. The higher the NPU of any food, the more completely the body is able to utilize that food's protein. The following figures show that, although animal foods tend to have the highest NPU ratings, a number of plant foods—including tofu—rank quite high on the scale:

Food	NPU (Percent)
Eggs	94
Milk, whole dairy	82
Fish	80
Cottage cheese	75
Brown rice	70
Cheeses	70
Wheat germ	67
Beef (steak and hamburger)	67
Oatmeal	66
Tofu	65
Chicken	65
Soybeans and soy flour	61
Peanuts	43
Lentils	30

(Source: Lappé, *Diet for a Small Planet*, 1975)

From the body's point of view, the protein in tofu is identical to the protein in chicken. Note that tofu has the fourth highest NPU of any plant food. It also has the highest NPU rating of all soybean products and all members of the protein-rich legume family. The soybean is the only legume which is a "complete protein," that is, one containing all of the eight essential amino acids. And the amino acid analysis of tofu is remarkably similar to that of most animal protein (including casein milk protein).

By combining the two sets of figures given above we can compare the true value of various protein sources. Regular tofu, for example, contains 7.8 percent protein, 65 percent of which is actually usable by the body. Thus, a typical 8-ounce (227 gram) serving of tofu can supply us with 227 x .65 x .078 or 11.5 grams of *usable* protein. This is a full 27 percent of the daily adult male protein requirement of 43.1 grams. The same amount of usable protein could be supplied by 3¼ ounces of steak (at a much higher price), 5½ ounces of hamburger, 1⅔ cups of milk, 2 eggs, or 2 ounces of (firm or hard) cheese.

High Protein Complementarity

Tofu is an excellent food to use in combining proteins since it contains an abundance of lysine, an essential amino acid that is deficient in many grain products. Most grains, on the other hand, are well endowed with the sulfur-containing amino acids methionine and cystine, the limiting amino acids in soybeans (Fig. 6). Thus soy and grain proteins, having exactly the opposite strengths and weaknesses, complement each other. By serving foods such as tofu and whole-grain bread or rice at the same meal and combining them in the correct ratio, we are able, in effect, to "create" new protein at no extra cost. The NPU of the resultant combination is considerably higher than that of either of the individual foods and, therefore, the total usable protein is much greater than if the foods were served at separate meals. Applying this principle of protein complementarity in planning our

Fig. 6. The Amino Acid Composition of Tofu Compared with the FAO/WHO Reference Pattern (expressed in mg per gram of nitrogen)

Amino Acids	FAO/WHO Pattern[1]	Tofu[2]	Tofu as Percent of FAO/WHO Pattern
Methionine-Cystine	220	156	71
Threonine	250	178	71
Valine	310	264	85
Lysine	340	333	98
Leucine	440	448	102
Isoleucine	250	261	104
Phenylalanine-Tyrosine	380	490	129
Tryptophan	60	96	160
Total	2250	2226	

Note: Amino acids in shortest supply in tofu are listed first.
Sources:
[1] *Provisional Amino Acid Scoring Pattern*, Technical Report Series 552 of WHO, 1973;
[2] *Food Composition Table for Use in East Asia*, FAO, 1972; tofu data based on two studies, one by B. R. Standahl, "Amino Acids in Oriental Soybean Foods," *Journal of the American Dietetic Association*, Vol. 50, No. 5. (1967)

daily meals allows us to make fullest use of the earth's abundant protein supplies. For example, by serving only 3½ ounces of tofu together with 1¼ cups brown rice, we obtain 32 percent more protein than if we served these foods separately. Thus, tofu's unique amino-acid composition makes it not only a basic protein *source,* but also a truly remarkable protein *booster.* As the figures below show, the use of even small amounts of tofu combined with grains and other basic foods (in the ratios indicated) can produce large increases in usable protein. Herein lies the key to tofu's value as an essential daily accompaniment to the grain-centered diet, the way of eating characteristic of virtually all traditional societies since earliest times.

Furthermore, the use of whole grains together with soy products creates a "protein-sparing effect": the body uses the grain carbohydrates as its source of fuel or energy and allows the protein to fulfill its basic function of tissue growth and repair.

Each of the following combinations provides exactly 50 percent of the daily adult male requirement of usable protein, or the equivalent of that found in 4½ ounces of (uncooked) steak. (All quantities of grains refer to the raw, uncooked product.)

Combination	Percent Increase
1 cup whole-wheat flour, 1½ tablespoons sesame butter, 3 ounces tofu	42
1 cup whole-wheat flour, 4½ ounces tofu	32
1¼ cups brown rice, 3½ ounces tofu	32
3 tablespoons each peanut and sesame butter. 4 ounces tofu	25
3/8 cup each whole-wheat flour and brown rice, 1¼ tablespoons peanut butter, 6¾ ounces tofu	24
¾ cup cornmeal, 1 cup milk, 5 ounces tofu	13

(Adapted from: *Diet for a Small Planet*)

The protein-rich combinations of tofu with whole-wheat flour suggest a variety of tofu (and nut butter) sandwiches or deep-fried tofu burgers, noodle or bulgur wheat dishes, and even *chapati, taco,* or pizza preparations. The traditional East Asian combination has, of course, been with rice.

Easy to Digest

While many high-protein foods, such as meats, dairy products, and beans, are quite difficult for some people to digest, tofu, prepared by a process that carefully removes the crude fiber and water-soluble carbohydrates from soybeans, is soft and highly digestible. Indeed, with a digestion rate of 95 percent, it is by far the most digestible of all natural soybean foods, and is much more digestible than cooked whole soybeans (68%). Thus, tofu can be an excellent food for babies, elderly adults, and people with digestive problems. The Chinese say that sages, yogis, and monks, who rely for sustenance on nothing but the mists of heaven and the fresh morning dew, are particularly fond of tofu as their third choice.

An Ideal Diet Food

Tofu is also the ideal diet food. A typical 8-ounce serving contains only 147 calories. An equal weight of eggs contains about 3 times as many calories, and an equal weight of beef about 4 to 5 times as many. Perhaps more important, next to soybean sprouts, tofu has the lowest ratio of calories to protein found in any known plant food. One gram of total protein costs you only 9 calories, and 1 gram of usable protein only 12 calories. The only animal foods which have a lower ratio are some types of fish and seafoods. Because of its low carbohydrate content, tofu is widely recommended for starch-restricted diets by doctors throughout East Asia. While providing 27 percent of your daily protein requirements, an 8-ounce serving of tofu costs you only 5 grams of carbohydrate and less than 7½ percent of the recommended daily adult requirement of 2,200 calories.

Low in Saturated Fats and Cholesterol

Tofu is unique among high protein foods in being low in calories and saturated fats and entirely free of cholesterol. And in this fact may be its greatest potential importance as a key to good health and long life. There is now a near consensus among doctors on the contributive role of animal fats and cholesterol to heart disease, the number-one health problem in the United States. It is well known that most doctors recommend a reduction in the consumption of animal foods as the first step in the treatment of heart disease, high blood pressure, arteriosclerosis, and atherosclerosis. Yet the standard American diet contains one of the world's highest proportions of saturated fats and cholesterol, since Americans presently obtain about 70 percent of all their protein from animal foods. And many low-carbohydrate reducing diets, because they depend on a large intake of meat, eggs, dairy products, and fish, result in an even larger intake of saturated fats and cholesterol. (The latter, present in all animal foods, is never found in tofu or other plant foods.) Moreover, the problem is becoming increasingly more serious as the proportion of saturated fats in the diet continues to rise: during the past 20 years, per capita American consumption of beef has more than doubled, while poultry consumption has increased by 150 percent. It is largely for these reasons that the American Heart Association now recommends that Americans cut their per capita meat consumption by one third while further reducing their intake of beef and pork in favor of poultry, which is lower in saturated fats.

Cross-cultural studies seem to indicate a clear relationship between low intake of animal fats and freedom from the heart and circulatory diseases mentioned above. The Japanese, for example, blessed with one of the world's lowest rates of these diseases, obtain only 39 percent of their protein from animal sources—primarily fish which are relatively low in saturated fats—and have about one-eighth the intake of saturated fats of most Americans. In China, where only 10 percent of the protein comes from animal sources, the cholesterol level is less than half that of most Americans. And observers have reported that the healthy, long-lived Hunzas rely on animal foods for only 1½ percent of their protein intake.

There is also a clear correlation between problems of overweight and the intake of animal foods high in saturated fats. Large-scale studies among Americans show that people practicing a meatless way of eating

are 20 pounds below the national average weight, and
that people following a standard meat-centered diet
are 12 to 15 pounds above their ideal weight. Tests
taken throughout the world likewise show that in societies with relatively low meat consumption (such as
Japan), the people more closely approach their ideal
weight.

Using tofu in place of livestock products as a basic
protein source is an easy way to greatly reduce total
intake of saturated fats and cholesterol. Regular tofu
contains only 4.3 percent vegetable-quality fats. These
are very low in saturated fats (15%), high in unsaturated fats (80%), and remarkably high in linoleic
acid, one of the most important polyunsaturated fatty
acids. By comparison, beef fat is high in saturated fats
(48%), low in unsaturated fats (47%), and contains only 9 percent linoleic acid. An essential fatty
acid, linoleic cannot be synthesized by the body and
must therefore be obtained directly from sources such
as soy products. Like natural lecithin, which is also
found in abundance in tofu's unrefined oils, linoleic
acid performs the vital functions of emulsifying, dis-
persing, and eliminating deposits of cholesterol and
other fatty acids which have accumulated in the vital
organs and blood stream. Soybeans, the best known
source of lecithin and linoleic acid, are used for the
extraction of these products now so popular in tablet
form at Western health food stores.

Rich in Minerals and Vitamins

Tofu is an excellent source of calcium, an essential
mineral for building and maintaining sound teeth and
bones, and one which is often deficient in the diets
of people who cannot afford dairy products. When
coagulated with calcium chloride nigari or calcium
sulfate—as is much of the tofu presently made in
America—regular tofu contains 23 percent, and silken
tofu 50 percent, more calcium by weight than dairy

milk. A standard 8-ounce serving of tofu, therefore, provides 38 percent of the average daily calcium requirement. As shown in Figure 5, tofu is also a good source of other minerals such as iron, phosphorus, potassium, and sodium, of essential B vitamins, and of choline and fat-soluble vitamin E.

A Health-giving Natural Food

Tofu is a traditional, natural food, prepared in essentially the same way today that it was more than one thousand years ago. Unlike so many high-protein foods, it has an alkaline composition which promotes long life and good health. In America, as in Japan, tofu is now a popular item in many natural and health food stores, and Japanese doctors regularly prescribe it (and soymilk) in curative diets for diabetes, heart disease, hardening of the arteries, and a variety of other circulatory problems. Except for the loss of crude soybean fiber, tofu is a whole food made from simple, natural ingredients. Whereas cow's milk is curdled or coagulated with an acid (rennet) to make cheese or curds, soymilk is generally coagulated with either *nigari* or calcium sulfate to make tofu. Nigari —also called bittern—is the mineral-rich mother liquor that remains after natural sea salt is extracted from sea water. Calcium sulfate, now generally used in its refined form, was traditionally prepared from ground, lightly roasted gypsum, which is found in abundance in the mountains of East Asia. Virtually all U.S. tofu is free of preservatives.

Backbone of the Meatless Diet

For the rapidly increasing number of Westerners who find that a meatless or vegetarian diet makes good sense, tofu can serve as a key source of protein just as it has since ancient times for the millions of people throughout East Asia practicing similar ways of eating.

Free of Chemical Toxins

Tofu—like other soybean products—is unique among high-protein, high-calcium foods in being relatively free of chemical toxins. It is well known that heavy metals, herbicides, and pesticides tend to concentrate in the fatty tissues of animals at the tops of food chains. Meat, fish, and poultry contain about 20 times more pesticide residues than legumes. Dairy foods, the next most contaminated group, contain 4½ times more. Since soybeans are an important legume feed crop at the base of the beef and dairy food chains, their spraying is carefully monitored by the Food and Drug Administration to keep the level of contamination at an absolute minimum.

Low in Cost

In addition to tofu's many fine qualities as a source of protein and basic nutrients, another endearing feature is its low cost. At the time of this writing, a typical 8-ounce serving of American-made tofu costs only 19½ cents. If the tofu is purchased directly from a tofu shop, the cost may be as low as 14 cents, and if the tofu is prepared at home, only 6½ cents! Store-bought tofu costs only 56 percent of the price of an equivalent weight of hamburger, 34 percent of chicken, and 15 percent of lamb rib chop. Furthermore, unlike most meats, a pound of tofu is a pound of tofu: no fat or bones. As the following figures show, the cost of one day's supply of usable protein (43.1 grams for an adult male) derived from or purchased in the form of tofu is relatively low compared with other common protein sources:

Food	Cost
Whole dry soybeans ($0.35/lb)	$0.16
Tofu, homemade (.13/lb)	.24
Whole eggs, medium (.66/doz)	.35
Tofu, Packaged Lactone Silken Tofu (in Japan; 5.5% protein [.15/lb])	.38
Tofu, dried-frozen (in Japan) (1.72/lb)	.47
Tofu, regular (in Japan) (.26/lb)	.49
Tofu, regular, at U.S. tofu shops (.28/lb)	.52
Hamburger, regular grind (.69/lb)	.56
Whole milk, nonfat (.35/qt)	.59
Cottage cheese, from skim milk (.60/lb)	.60
Tuna, canned in oil (1.30/lb)	.65
Tofu, regular, at U.S. supermarkets (.39/lb)	.74
Spaghetti (.51/lb)	.75
Swiss cheese, domestic (1.64/lb)	.83
Peanuts (1.02/lb)	.84
Cheddar cheese (1.70/lb)	.93
Whole-wheat bread (.59/lb)	1.02
Chicken, breast with bone (1.16/lb)	1.04
Pork loin chop, med. (1.29/lb)	1.36
Yogurt (.43/lb)	1.75
Porterhouse steak, choice grade w. bone (1.99/lb)	2.10
Lamb rib chop (2.59/lb)	3.14

(Source: Prices sampled at California and Tokyo supermarkets and tofu shops, Feb. 1975. Figures calculated from data in *Diet for a Small Planet*.)

Note that in Tokyo, where the cost of living is now higher than in the United States, the retail price of tofu is relatively low. As tofu becomes more popular in the West and the number of shops making it increases, we can expect similar price reductions due to greater competition, elimination of middlemen, and the economies of large-scale production and distribution.

Because tofu is inexpensive, it is a truly democratic food that can be enjoyed by people throughout the world, especially those whose nutritional needs are the greatest. In Taiwan, for example, a pound of tofu presently retails for about one-fourth the cost of tofu in America.

Easily Made at Home

Each of the different varieties of tofu can be prepared at home using utensils found in most kitchens and ingredients which are readily available. Homemade tofu will be ready in an hour, and the cost drops to about one-third the retail price. Like fresh bread warm from the oven, fresh tofu prepared at home has a richness and delicacy of flavor that is rarely matched by storebought varieties.

Quick & Easy to Use

Like yogurt, cottage cheese, or cheese, each of the different types of tofu is ready to eat and requires no further cooking. We find that most of our favorite ways of serving tofu are the simplest, sometimes taking less than a minute to prepare. For people who are often in a hurry and like their food ready instantly, this ease of use will, no doubt, add to tofu's appeal.

Versatile

Finally, tofu is so versatile that it can serve as an ingredient in almost the entire range of your favorite dishes and be used in the national cuisine of countries around the world. Perhaps no other food has such a wide range of interesting forms, textures, and flavors; each variety invites experimentation, ingenuity, and inventiveness. We have found again and again that tofu can transform even the simplest dishes into something completely new. Among the most adaptive of foods, it may be used in both virtuoso and supporting roles. Like the taste of water from a mountain stream or a breath of crisp autumn air, simple flavors are often the most satisfying. And because its simplicity is inexhaustible, tofu, in its many forms, can be enjoyed day after day, adding body and richness of flavor—as well as protein—to your daily meals.

3
Getting Started

THERE ARE presently more than 100 tofu shops in North America (see Appendix B). Since some of these are small Japanese or Chinese family-run operations, tofu products and their names vary slightly from shop to shop. Each shop prepares a number of varieties of fresh tofu each day and retails them through a rapidly growing number of food stores in its area. Larger shops often distribute their tofu up to 200 miles away. Tofu generally is available at reductions of about 25 percent if purchased directly from the tofu shop or if ordered unpackaged in bulk.

Look for fresh tofu in the refrigerated foods section of most markets. If your local market does not carry tofu, you may wish to give its management the name of the nearest tofu shop from which tofu can be ordered. In cities near tofu shops, good tofu cuisine is often served at Japanese, Chinese, and natural food restaurants.

Buying and Storing Tofu

What are the most important things to look for when buying tofu? First, try to buy tofu as soon as possible after it has been made; fresh tofu has by far the best flavor. In Japan, almost all tofu is served within one day after it is prepared. In the West, most fresh, packaged tofu now comes with a date stamped on the container indicating the date before which the tofu should be served. For regular tofu this date is 7 days, and for deep-fried tofu 10 days, after the tofu was made. Since many American tofu shops start work at 2

33

o'clock in the morning, their fresh tofu is often available in local food stores early the same day.

Next, look for the name of the tofu coagulant, which will be printed in small letters on the package. Traditional-style tofu will be made with a nigari-type coagulant (natural nigari, calcium chloride nigari, or magnesium chloride nigari) If the tofu is prepared with organically grown (Japanese-variety) soybeans and/or well water, so much the better. Almost all tofu made in America is free of preservatives and other chemical additives, but check the label to make sure.

When storing tofu (including firm, silken, and grilled varieties), keep in mind the following points:

• Keep tofu under constant refrigeration but do not allow it to freeze. See that it is not allowed to stand in a warm place before being refrigerated.

• If tofu was purchased water-packed and is not to be used right away, slit the top of the container along one edge and drain off the water. If you plan to serve the tofu within 24 hours, seal and refrigerate (without adding more water). If you are unable to serve the tofu until a later date, re-cover with cold water and refrigerate. Drain the tofu and add fresh water *daily*. It can be kept up to ten days in this way without spoiling, although naturally there will be some loss of flavor and texture. Since tofu keeps better when covered with plenty of water, you may wish to transfer the tofu from its small container to a pan or bowl containing several quarts of cold water; cover or seal the container before refrigerating.

• Always drain water-packed tofu briefly before use. For slightly firmer tofu, drain for several hours or overnight. Effective draining procedures are described on page 120.

• Tofu that is several days old can be refreshed by parboiling or deep-frying.

• Regular or deep-fried tofu can be stored indefinitely as homemade frozen tofu (p. 339).

When storing deep-fried tofu, simply refrigerate in an airtight container. Do not store under water.

Basic Recipes

The following stocks, sauces, toppings, dressings, rice and noodle dishes, and other basic preparations are often served with tofu. They play important supporting roles in tofu cookery, so we have grouped them all together here. They will be called for frequently in later recipes.

SOUP STOCKS AND BROTHS

The different varieties of fresh *dashi* (Japanese soup stock) serve as the basis for a wide variety of tofu preparations and are easily made from natural ingredients.

Number 1 Dashi *(Ichiban Dashi)*

MAKES 3 CUPS

3 cups water or Kombu Dashi
¼ to 1 cup bonito flakes (15 to 30 grams)

Heat the water until quite hot in a small saucepan. Add bonito flakes and bring to a boil. Turn off heat and allow to stand for 3 minutes, or until flakes settle; skim off foam. Filter the dashi through a (clothlined) strainer placed over a saucepan. Press flakes with the back of a spoon to extract remaining dashi, then reserve flakes. (Some cooks add fine-textured flakes to simmered broths, *nabe* dishes, and miso soups together with the dashi, or simply omit straining.)

Number 2 Dashi *(Niban Dashi)*

MAKES 2½ CUPS

2½ cups water
Bonito flakes and *kombu* reserved from Number 1 Dashi

Combine all ingredients in a small saucepan and bring just to a boil. Remove *kombu* immediately, then simmer for 1 more minute. Strain and allow to cool.

Two tablespoons of fresh bonito flakes may be added to the boiling water after removing the *kombu;* reduce heat to lowest point and simmer for 5 minutes before straining.

Kombu Dashi *(Kombu Stock)*

MAKES 3 CUPS

1 strip of *kombu,* about 3 by 7 inches, wiped lightly with a moistened, well-wrung cloth
3 cups water

Combine *kombu* and water in a saucepan and bring just to a boil. Turn off heat, remove *kombu,* and reserve for use in other cooking. Use dashi as required or, if preparing Number 1 Dashi proceed to add bonito flakes immediately.

Clear Broth *(Sumashi)*

MAKES 1½ CUPS

1½ cups Number 1 Dashi (p. 35) or Kombu Dashi (above)
1 teaspoon shoyu
½ teaspoon salt
½ teaspoon sake or *mirin* (optional)

Bring the dashi just to a boil over moderate heat. Reduce heat to low and stir in the shoyu, salt, and, if used, the sake or *mirin.* Proceed immediately to add the ingredients called for in the particular recipe in which the broth is used.

Sweetened Shoyu Broth

MAKES ½ TO ¾ CUP

In Japan, this preparation is widely used to season thinly sliced vegetables before using them in other recipes.

¼ to ½ cup dashi (p. 35), stock, or water
2 tablespoons shoyu
1 tablespoon honey
1 tablespoon sake or *mirin* (optional)

Bring all ingredients to a boil in a small saucepan. Add thinly sliced vegetables and return to the boil. Reduce heat to low, cover, and simmer, stirring until all liquid is absorbed or evaporated. If crispier vegetable pieces are desired, simmer for only 2 to 3 minutes. Drain off broth, reserving it for later use.

SHOYU DIPPING SAUCES

The following preparations are widely used with Chilled Tofu, Crisp Deep-fried Tofu, and Simmering Tofu.

Shoyu-Sesame-Gingerroot Dipping Sauce

¼ cup shoyu
1 teaspoon dark sesame oil
1 teaspoon lemon juice or vinegar
½ to 1 teaspoon grated gingerroot or powdered ginger
Dash of cayenne, Tabasco sauce, or 7-spice chili powder
2 teaspoons ground roasted sesame seeds or 1½ teaspoons honey

Combine all ingredients, mixing well. Delicious with fresh homemade tofu or Chilled Tofu. For variety, add or substitute 1 teaspoon crushed garlic or ½ teaspoon hot mustard.

Japanese Shoyu Dipping Sauces

SERVES 1

Pour 1½ teaspoons shoyu into a small (3-inch-diameter) dish. Stir in any of the following:

½ teaspoon grated gingerroot or juice pressed from grated
   gingerroot
¼ teaspoon grated *wasabi* or *wasabi* paste
¼ teaspoon crushed or minced garlic
½ teaspoon slivered *yuzu*, lemon, or orange peel
¼ teaspoon hot mustard
½ teaspoon sesame butter, *tahini*, or ground roasted sesame
   seeds
½ teaspoon nut butter (peanut, almond, cashew, etc.)
½ to 1 teaspoon orange, lemon, lime, or *yuzu* juice
1 to 3 tablespoons grated *daikon*

Mirin-Shoyu *(Wari-shita)*

MAKES ⅔ CUP

5 tablespoons dashi (p. 35) or soup stock
3 tablespoons shoyu
2 tablespoons *mirin*
2 teaspoons grated gingerroot

Combine ingredients in a small saucepan and bring
just to a boil. Serve hot or cold, garnished with grated
gingerroot.

Tosa-joyu *(Shoyu Dipping Sauce for Simmering Tofu)*

MAKES 1 CUP

¾ cup shoyu
3 tablespoons *mirin*

Combine ingredients in a small saucepan and bring
just to a boil.

MISO TOPPINGS

Five basic types of miso toppings are widely used in
tofu cookery: Sweet Simmered Miso, Miso Sauté, Special Miso Toppings, Finger Lickin' Miso, and regular
miso. All varieties make excellent toppings for Crisp
Deep-fried Tofu, Chilled Tofu, and many grain and
vegetable dishes. For many more recipes see *The Book
of Miso* [Autumn Press].

SWEET SIMMERED MISO (Nerimiso)

Nerimiso derives its name from the verb *neru* which means "to simmer, stirring constantly, until smooth and thick." Prepared by combining miso with honey or sugar, water or dashi, seasonings and/or sake, and in most cases, nuts, diced vegetables, or seafoods, some varieties—such as peanut, walnut, and *yuzu*—are sold commercially, but most are made at home or in Zen temple restaurants, where they are said to have originated.

Red Nerimiso

MAKES ½ CUP

This is the simplest and most basic form of Sweet Simmered Miso; all other recipes may be thought of as variations or elaborations on this fundamental theme. By adding different ingredients and seasonings (sesame, gingerroot, grated lemon rind, etc.) to those listed below, you can create a wide array of delicious toppings.

5 tablespoons red or barley miso
1½ to 2½ tablespoons honey
1 tablespoon water; or 1½ teaspoons each water and white wine (or sake or *mirin*)

Combine all ingredients in a small earthenware pot or a skillet and bring to a boil. Simmer for 2 to 3 minutes over low heat, stirring constantly with a wooden spatula or spoon, until mixture begins to thicken. Remove from heat and allow to cool to room temperature before serving. Cover and refrigerate unused portions.

White Nerimiso

MAKES 1¼ CUPS

This recipe, a specialty of Kyoto's 400-year-old Nakamura-ro restaurant, is used as the topping for Japan's most famous Tofu Dengaku. In springtime, ground *kinomé* is mixed with the miso, or individual sprigs of *kinomé* are used to garnish the Dengaku portions. The use of egg gives White Nerimiso a rich, smooth texture.

1 cup sweet white or ⅔ cup mellow white miso
3 tablespoons *mirin*
1½ tablespoons sake
1 egg yolk
3 tablespoons ground roasted sesame seeds or 1½ tablespoons sesame butter or *tahini*

Prepare as for Red Nerimiso.

Walnut Miso

MAKES 1 CUP

One of our favorite miso preparations, Walnut Miso is often served in Zen temple restaurants, and is sold commercially in Japan.

1 cup walnut meats, preferably large pieces
¼ cup red, barley, or akadashi miso
2 to 3 tablespoons honey or *mizuamé*
1 tablespoon water or 1½ teaspoons each water and white wine (or sake)

Prepare as for Red Nerimiso.

Peanut Miso

MAKES ½ TO ¾ CUP

½ to 1 cup whole (roasted) peanuts or ¼ cup peanut butter
¼ cup red, barley, or Hatcho miso
1½ to 3 tablespoons honey or *mizuamé*
2 tablespoons water; or 1 tablespoon each water and sake, wine, or *mirin*

Prepare as for Red Nerimiso.

Yuzu Miso

MAKES 1 CUP

This recipe comes from Tokyo's 370-year-old tofu restaurant, Sasa-no-Yuki, where the miso is served over

warm pieces of silken tofu and also sold in small
ceramic jars for home use.

½ cup (light) red or barley miso
6 to 6½ tablespoons sugar or 3 tablespoons honey
6 tablespoons water
½ teaspoon grated *yuzu* rind, or substitute 1 to 2 teaspoons
    grated lemon, lime, or orange rind

Prepare as for Red Nerimiso except add the *yuzu* rind
just before removing miso from heat.

Kinomé Miso *(Miso with Fresh Sansho Leaves)*

Also called *sansho* miso, this green and refreshingly
fragrant miso is a springtime favorite. When *kinomé,*
the fresh sprigs of the *sansho* tree, emerge early each
April, this miso is widely enjoyed as a topping for Tofu
Dengaku, in *aemono,* or on butter-fried mushrooms.

¼ cup (about 60) *kinomé* leaves (not sprigs)
5 tablespoons sweet white miso
1½ teaspoons honey
2 tablespoons water
1 teaspoon shoyu (optional)
1½ teaspoons *mirin* or sake (optional)
Dash of *sansho* pepper (optional)

Place leaves in a strainer, douse with boiling water,
and drain well. Grind leaves thoroughly in a *suribachi*
(or mortar), or mince with a knife. Combine the next
five ingredients in a small saucepan and prepare as for
Red Nerimiso. Add contents of saucepan and pepper,
if desired, to ground *kinomé* in *suribachi;* mix well.

MISO SAUTÉ *(Abura Miso)*

Originally a Chinese-style preparation featuring
fresh vegetables sautéed in sesame oil, Miso Sauté
serves as a delicious topping for brown rice or rice
porridge; fresh or cooked vegetable slices, and chilled
or deep-fried tofu. Refrigerated and well-sealed, un-

used portions will keep for up to 1 week. In each of the following recipes, up to one half of the oil may be sesame, which lends a nutty flavor and savory aroma. Experiment with other vegetables and nuts, or even with fruits.

Mushroom Miso Sauté

MAKES ½ CUP

2 tablespoons oil
10 mushrooms, thinly sliced
1 tablespoon red, barley, or Hatcho miso
1 teaspoon honey

Heat a skillet or wok and coat with the oil. Add mushrooms and sauté over medium heat for about 1 minute or until tender. Reduce heat to low, add miso and honey, and cook, stirring constantly, for about 1 minute more, or until mushrooms are evenly coated with miso. Allow to cool to room temperature before serving.

Other vegetables that may be substituted for the mushrooms include lotus root, kabocha, eggplant, sweet potato, burdock root, onion, and gingerroot.

Crumbly Tekka Miso

MAKES 1½ CUPS

The word tekka is composed of the Chinese characters for "metal" and "fire": this all-purpose condiment was traditionally simmered for a long time on a metal griddle or in a heavy iron pot. A favorite topping for brown rice, rice porridge, rice patties, and regular or deep-fried tofu, it is also served as is, as an hors d'oeuvre with sake, beer, or wine.

3 tablespoons sesame oil
½ cup minced burdock root, soaked in cold water for 15
minutes and drained
6 tablespoons minced carrot or slivered, reconstituted
kombu
¼ cup minced lotus root or whole peanuts
1 teaspoon grated gingerroot
¼ cup roasted soybeans (optional)
1 cup Hatcho, red, or barley miso
Dash of 7-spice chili powder (optional)

Heat a large skillet or wok and coat with the oil. Add burdock root and sauté over high heat for 1 minute. Reduce heat to medium, add carrot and lotus root, and sauté for 2 to 3 minutes. Mix in gingerroot, miso and, if used, soybeans and chili powder: sauté for 2 minutes more. Reduce heat to low and cook, stirring constantly with a wooden spatula, for 20 to 30 minutes, or until miso is crumbly and fairly dry. Allow to cool before serving. Refrigerate unused portions in an airtight container.

Sweetened Tekka Miso

MAKES 1¼ CUPS

The most popular form of *tekka* miso, this sweetened variety generally contains the same ingredients as Crumbly Tekka Miso plus honey; the miso is cooked only until smooth and firm.

1 tablespoon oil
⅔ cup thin rounds or matchsticks of burdock root, peeled,
soaked in cold water for 15 minutes, and drained
½ carrot, cut into matchsticks
½ cup diced or slivered lotus root (optional)
⅓ cup Hatcho, red, or akadashi miso
2 tablespoons honey
1 tablespoon sake or white wine
2 tablespoons ground roasted sesame seeds, sesame butter
or *tahini;* or ¼ cup poppy or hemp seeds
¼ cup roasted soybeans

Heat a wok or skillet and coat with the oil. Add burdock root and carrot, and sauté over medium-high heat for 3 or 4 minutes. Reduce heat to low, then stir in the next four ingredients and sauté for 3 or 4 minutes more. Stir in soybeans and remove from heat. Transfer to a bowl and allow to cool. Use as an all-purpose condiment or topping.

Spicy Korean Miso Sauté

MAKES ¾ CUP

2 tablespoons sesame oil
1 clove of garlic, crushed
1 tablespoon grated gingerroot
2 green peppers, minced
½ small onion, diced
Dash of minced red chili, Tabasco sauce, or 7-spice chili powder
3 tablespoons red, barley, or Hatcho miso
2 teaspoons soy sauce
1 tablespoon sake or white wine

Heat a wok or skillet and coat with the oil. Add the next five ingredients and sauté for 2 minutes. Stir in the miso, soy sauce, and sake, return just to the boil, and remove from heat. Allow to cool before serving. Delicious as a topping for fresh cucumber, celery, or tomato slices; for noodles or deep-fried tofu.

MIXED MISO (Awasé Miso)

These simple but delicious recipes, requiring no cooking, are quick and easy to prepare.

Mixed Red Miso Toppings

MAKES ABOUT ¼ CUP

Combine ¼ cup red, barley, or Hatcho miso with any one of the following, mixing well. Cover and refrigerate unused portions.

- Garlic: 2 cloves of garlic, grated or crushed
- Bonito: ¼ cup bonito flakes and, if desired, 1½ table-spoons *mirin*
- Umeboshi: 1½ tablespoons minced *umeboshi* salt plums (about 10) and, if desired, 2 tablespoons bonito flakes
- Wasabi: 1 teaspoon freshly grated *wasabi, wasabi* paste, or Western-style horseradish and, if desired, 1½ tea-spoons honey
- Gingerroot: 2 teaspoons grated gingerroot

Homemade Akadashi Miso

MAKES ¼ CUP

2 tablespoons Hatcho miso
2 tablespoons red or light-yellow miso
1 tablespoon honey or *mizuamé*
½ to 1 teaspoon shoyu

Combine all ingredients, mixing well. For a smoother texture, rub through a sieve.

Peking Duck Dipping Sauce
(Homemade T'ien Mien Chiang)

MAKES ½ CUP

¼ cup Hatcho miso
1½ teaspoons sesame oil
½ teaspoon vegetable oil
¾ teaspoon sake or white wine
1 teaspoon shoyu
1½ tablespoons honey
2 tablespoons water

Combine all ingredients, mixing until smooth. Refrigerate unused portions in a sealed container.

BROILED MISO (Yakimiso)

When broiled or grilled over an open fire, miso develops a delightful aroma and flavor, and in Japan, the use of cryptomeria or Japanese cedar *(sugi)* as the broiling plank imparts an additional subtlety to the fragrance.

Savory Broiled Miso

SERVES 1

Use 1 to 2 teaspoons of any of the following:
  A chunky, natural Hatcho, barley or red miso
  Any dark-colored Sweet Simmered Miso
  Any variety of Mixed Miso, especially varieties containing
    bonito flakes

If using a stove-top burner, charcoal brazier, or bed of live coals: Spread miso in a layer about ⅛ inch thick on a thin cedar plank, the lid of an earthenware bowl, in a clam or scallop shell, or in the concave surface of a large wooden or metal spatula or spoon. Holding the miso (with tongs) 1 to 2 inches above the open fire and moving it back and forth slowly, broil for 15 to 30 seconds (checking miso every 5 seconds) until it is fragrant and lightly speckled. If broiling miso on a lid, place lid on its matching (empty) cup or bowl to help retain miso fragrance. If using a shell, serve in the shell. Or scrape miso from the plank, spatula, or spoon into a small shallow dish. Serve immediately.

BASIC SAUCES

Each of these sauces may be served with a wide variety of different tofu preparations. They will all be called for in recipes throughout this book.

Onion Sauce

MAKES 3½ CUPS

This naturally sweet, rich brown sauce is prepared slowly like the basis for a French onion soup. Its basic form and many variations go well with a number of different types of tofu. For best results, make a large quantity at one time since the flavor improves after several days and re-warmings. It may be served hot or cold to equal advantage.

2 tablespoons oil
6 onions, thinly sliced
2 tablespoons shoyu; or 3 tablespoons red miso creamed in
　　¼ cup water
1 tablespoon butter

Heat a large casserole or heavy pot and coat with the oil. Add onions, cover, and simmer over low heat for about 2 to 3 hours, stirring thoroughly once every 10 minutes. When onions are a rich brown and very soft, mix in the butter and shoyu and simmer for 10 to 15 more minutes. (If using miso, return just to the boil, then remove from heat.) Serve hot or, for best flavor, allow to cool overnight and serve reheated or chilled the next day.

VARIATIONS

● To ½ cup chilled Onion Sauce add 1 to 2 tablespoons shoyu or miso. Serve as a topping for chilled or deep-fried tofu. For variety garnish with diced or grated cheese or thinly sliced onions.

● *Seasoned Onion Sauce with Nut Butters:* Thin your favorite nut butter with a small amount of water or stock and, if desired, some lemon or orange juice, and add to 2 parts Onion Sauce. Season with herbs, 7-spice chili powder, shoyu, or miso. Garnish with thinly sliced green onions or parsley. For variety add large chunks of nuts, diced cheese, or sprouts. Serve with Chilled Tofu or as a topping for any variety of deep-fried tofu.

Mushroom Sauce

FOR 2 TO 3 SERVINGS

1½ tablespoons butter
½ teaspoon minced garlic
1 tablespoon minced onion
½ teaspoon grated gingerroot
4 to 5 small mushrooms, thinly sliced
⅓ cup ketchup
1 tablespoon red miso (optional)
Dash of pepper

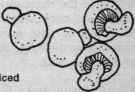

Melt butter in a skillet. Add garlic, onion, and ginger-root and sauté for about 1 minute. Add mushrooms and sauté for 2 more minutes. Add ketchup, miso, and pepper and sauté for 1 minute more. Serve with Tofu Burgers (p. 182), Okara Chapati (p. 96), Crisp Tortillas (p. 243), or as a topping for Chilled Tofu (p. 141).

White Sauce

MAKES 1 CUP

Also known as Cream- or Béchamel Sauce, this traditional Western favorite acquires a distinctive flavor and creaminess when seasoned with miso. Season lightly for use with vegetables (such as cauliflower or potatoes) and more prominently for use with tofu dishes. Numerous variations prepared with soymilk and containing tofu are given on page 310.

2 tablespoons butter or oil
2 tablespoons (whole-wheat) flour
1 cup milk (soy or dairy); or stock
3 to 4 teaspoons red miso; 2 to 2½ teaspoons shoyu;
  or ½ to ⅔ teaspoon salt
Dash of pepper, paprika, or cayenne
1 tablespoon minced parsley (optional)

Melt the butter (or heat the oil) in a skillet. Add flour and, stirring constantly, cook over low heat for 1 to 2 minutes, or until flour is well blended and its raw taste has vanished. Add ½ cup milk (or stock) a little at a time, continuing to stir, then mix in the miso and slowly add the remainder of the milk. Increase heat to medium and cook, whisking or stirring, for 3 to 4 minutes more, or until sauce develops a smooth, nicely thickened consistency. Stir in pepper and parsley and remove from heat.

Note: Many cooks prefer to heat the milk to just scalding before it is added. In this case, after sautéing flour, remove skillet from heat until flour stops bubbling. Then pour in the near-boiling milk. When it stops steaming, stir briskly until smooth and proceed as above.

Teriyaki Sauce

MAKES ⅔ CUP

Generally used in Japan to baste broiled fish, this savory sauce is now used by many Westerners with shish kebab and other barbequed preparations. Also good as a dip for fresh vegetables or a topping for deep-fried tofu.

¼ cup shoyu or 6 tablespoons red miso
3 tablespoons sake or white wine
3 tablespoons brown sugar
1 teaspoon grated gingerroot or 1½ teaspoons powdered
    ginger
2 cloves of garlic, crushed
1 tablespoon sesame or vegetable oil
¼ teaspoon dry mustard

Combine all ingredients, mixing well. Marinate foods (deep-fried tofu, green peppers, onions, tomatoes, etc.) for at least 1 hour before skewering and broiling. Use remaining sauce to baste.

Rich Gingerroot-Ankake Sauce

MAKES 1 CUP

⅔ cup dashi (p. 35), stock, or water
3 tablespoons shoyu
2 tablespoons natural sugar
2 teaspoons arrowroot or cornstarch, dissolved in 2 table-
    spoons water
2 teaspoons freshly grated gingerroot or gingerroot juice

Combine dashi, shoyu, and sugar in a small saucepan and bring to a boil. Stir in dissolved cornstarch and gingerroot and cook for about 1 minute until thick.

Korean Barbecue Sauce

MAKES ¼ CUP

2 tablespoons shoyu
2 teaspoons natural sugar
2 teaspoons sesame oil
1 tablespoon ground roasted sesame seeds or 1 teaspoon sesame butter or *tahini*
1 tablespoon diced leeks or onions
1 clove garlic, crushed
¼ teaspoon 7-spice chili powder or Tabasco sauce
Dash of pepper

Combine all ingredients, mixing well. Serve with Grilled Tofu Cutlets (p. 253), Grilled Tofu (p. 325), or any variety of deep-fried tofu.

Tomato & Cheese Sauce

MAKES 1¼ CUPS

2 tablespoons butter
1¼ cups chopped tomatoes
½ onion, minced
¾ cup grated cheese
½ teaspoon salt, 1 tablespoon shoyu, or 1½ tablespoons red miso
¼ teaspoon paprika
¼ teaspoon oregano or basil
Dash of pepper

Melt butter in a skillet. Add tomatoes and onions and sauté for 2 minutes. Cover, reduce heat to low, and simmer for 3 minutes. Uncover and continue simmering, stirring occasionally, for 15 minutes more, or until sauce is thick. Stir in remaining ingredients and remove from heat. Delicious served over deep-fried tofu.

Ketchup-Worcestershire Sauce

MAKES 6 TABLESPOONS

¼ cup ketchup
2 tablespoons Worcestershire sauce

Combine ingredients, mixing well. Serve with deep-fried tofu.

RICE, NOODLES, AND OTHER BASIC PREPARATIONS

Brown Rice

MAKES 4 CUPS

2 cups brown rice, rinsed and soaked overnight in 2⅔ cups
   water

In a heavy covered pot, bring water and rice to a boil over high heat. Reduce heat to low and simmer for 45 to 50 minutes or until all water is absorbed or evaporated. Uncover pot, remove from heat, and stir rice thoroughly with a wooden spoon. (If a slightly drier consistency is desired, transfer rice to a wooden bowl before stirring). Allow to cool for several minutes, then cover pot (or bowl) with a double layer of cloth until you are ready to serve.

To pressure cook: Rinse and drain 1 cup rice. Without soaking, combine in a pressure cooker with 1 cup water. Bring to pressure (15 pounds), reduce heat to low, and simmer for 25 minutes. Allow pressure to come down naturally for 10 to 15 minutes. Open pot and mix rice well. Allow to stand uncovered for 3 to 5 minutes, then cover with a cloth as above.

Brown Rice Porridge

SERVES 2 OR 3

Called *Congee* in China and *Okayu* in Japan, this is a popular main course at breakfast in many homes and temples. Easy to digest, rice porridge is considered the ideal food for sick people, and nursing mothers sometimes skim the creamy liquid from the porridge's surface to feed their babies as a breast milk supplement.

½ cup brown rice, rinsed and soaked overnight in 4½ cups
   water

Prepare as for brown rice, setting lid slightly ajar and simmering for about 90 minutes, or until rice develops a porridge-like consistency. Serve immediately, seasoned with Sesame Salt (p. 53) or salt- or miso-pickled vegetables. If desired, add crumbled *nori* and minced leeks.

Or combine 1¼ cups (leftover) cooked rice with 3½ cups water and, without soaking, proceed as above.

To pressure cook: Rinse and drain ½ cup rice. Without soaking, combine in a pressure cooker with 2½ cups water. Bring to pressure (15 pounds), reduce heat to low, and simmer for 45 minutes. Allow pressure to come down naturally for 10 to 15 minutes. Open pot and mix porridge well. Allow to stand uncovered for 3 to 5 minutes before serving.

Sushi Rice *(Rice in Vinegar Dressing)*

MAKES 2½ CUPS

1 cup (brown) rice, soaked in 1⅓ cups water overnight in a
    heavy 2- to 4-quart pot
Vinegar Dressing:
    2⅓ tablespoons (rice) vinegar
    1½ teaspoons honey
    2 teaspoons *mirin* (optional)
    ½ teaspoon salt

Bring soaked rice to a boil in a covered pot. Reduce heat to low and simmer for 40 to 50 minutes or until all water has been absorbed and rice is quite light and dry. (If using white rice, simmer for only 15 to 20 minutes.) Remove rice from heat and allow to stand for 5 minutes. Transfer hot rice to a large wooden bowl, platter, or other non-metallic container and immediately sprinkle on the dressing. With a wooden spoon, chopsticks, or a wide fork in one hand, and a fan or flat pot lid in the other, mix the rice vigorously while fanning to cool it as quickly as possible. Fan and stir for about 3 minutes, then allow rice to cool to room temperature.

Noodles

SERVES 2 OR 3

4½ to 5 ounces dry buckwheat or whole-wheat noodles (*soba* or *udon*)

Bring 2 to 3 quarts of water to a rolling boil over high heat. Scatter noodles slowly over surface of water and return to the boil. Lower heat until water is boiling actively but does not overflow. Cook uncovered for about 5 minutes, or until noodles are tender but not soft. Pour noodles into a colander placed in the sink and drain briefly, then transfer to a large container filled with circulating cold water. Stir noodles with chopsticks for several minutes until they cool to temperature of water, then transfer noodles back into colander; drain well and serve.

Sesame Salt *(Gomashio)*

MAKES ABOUT ½ CUP

2 teaspoons sea salt
5 tablespoons white or black sesame seeds

Heat a heavy skillet. Pour in the salt and roast, stirring constantly, for about 1 minute. Add the sesame seeds and roast until done. Grind the salt-sesame mixture in a *suribachi* (serrated mortar) or hand mill. Store in an airtight container.

Sweet Vinegared Gingerroot *(Gari)*

3 tablespoons vinegar
1 tablespoon honey
Dash of salt
1 piece of gingerroot peeled, sliced into paper-thin rounds (¼ cup), parboiled, drained, and patted dry with a towel

Combine the first three ingredients in a small saucepan and heat, stirring constantly, until quite hot. Now combine with the sliced gingerroot in a small bowl so that the gingerroot is fully immersed in the liquid. Cover and refrigerate overnight or for at least several hours. Serve with Inari-zushi, Sushi Rice, or other rice dishes.

Paper-thin Omelets

MAKES ABOUT 8

4 eggs
¼ teaspoon salt
1 teaspoon ground roasted sesame seeds (optional)
1 to 2 teaspoons oil

In a small bowl, combine eggs, ¼ teaspoon salt and sesame; mix well. Heat a small skillet and coat lightly with oil, pouring off any excess. Pour about one-eighth of the egg mixture into the skillet, swishing it around quickly so that it just covers the bottom of the pan. Cook over high heat for about 20 to 30 seconds on one side only to form a thin omelet. Transfer omelet to a plate and allow to cool. Prepare 8 omelets, oiling the pan lightly after every 3 or 4. Sliver to use as a garnish.

Tempura Batter

FOR 4 TO 6 SERVINGS

1 cup ice-cold water
1 egg yolk or whole egg
1¼ to 1½ cups (coarsely ground) unbleached white flour
½ teaspoon salt (optional)

In a mixing bowl, combine the water and egg yolk and beat well with a wire whisk or chopsticks. Sprinkle the flour and, if used, the salt evenly over the mixture. With a few quick strokes of the whisk (or a wooden spoon) lightly stir in the flour until all flour is moistened and large lumps disappear. (The presence of small lumps is alright.) Do not stir batter again after the initial mixing. Use as soon as possible and do not place too near the heat.

Mustard-Vinegar Miso Dressing *(Karashi Sumiso)*

MAKES ½ CUP

3 tablespoons sweet white miso
3 tablespoons vinegar
1½ teaspoons honey
1 teaspoon *mirin* (optional)
¼ teaspoon hot mustard

Combine all ingredients, mixing well.

Favorite Tofu Recipes

Among the many recipes in this book, there are certain ones we enjoy again and again, and like to serve to guests as an introduction to tofu cookery. Most take little time to prepare and use readily available ingredients. This chart gives suggestions for their use in a weekly menu. Our very favorite is Creamy Tofu Dressing (p. 143).

	Breakfast	Lunch	Dinner
Sun.	• Butter-fried Tofu with Fried Eggs (p. 171)	• Creamy Tofu Dressing (p. 143) with your favorite salad • Clubhouse Sandwich with Fried Tofu (p. 160)	• Tofu Cheese Soufflé (p. 175) • Tofu Guacamole (p. 148) with hors d'oeuvres
Mon.	• Tofu-Fruit Whips (p. 207) • Pan-fried Tofu (p. 178)	• Carrot, Raisin & Walnut Salad with Tofu (p. 155) • Tofu Burgers (p. 267) • Tofu Mayonnaise (p. 145)	• Tofu Spaghetti Sauce (p. 169) • Tofu Cheesecake (p. 210)
Tues.	• Fried Eggs with Deep-fried Tofu (p. 232)	• Tangy Tofu Cottage Cheese (p. 150) with your favorite salad • Crisp Deep-fried Tofu (p. 220)	• Tofu with Onion Sauce and Cheese (p. 179) • Sizzling Rice with Deep-fried Tofu (p. 241)

Wed.	• Iridofu (crumbled scrambled tofu) (p. 182)	• Chilled Tofu (p. 141) with Shoyu & Sesame Dipping Sauce (p. 37) • Homemade Soymilk (p. 299) with Honey & vanilla	• Buckwheat Noodle Gratin with Tofu (p. 177) • Tofu Cutlets with Pineapple Sweet & Sour Sauce (p. 238)
Thurs.	• Tangy Tofu & Prune Puree (p. 208)	• Curried Rice Salad with Tofu (p. 155) • Tofu Peanut Butter & Banana Spread (p. 148)	• Tofu Burgers with Mushroom Sauce (p. 177) • Tofu Strawberry Whip (p. 207)
Fri.	• Frozen Tofu Cutlets (p. 351)	• Fresh Fruit Salad with Tofu Whipped Cream (p. 157) • Deep-fried Tofu Sandwich with Lettuce & Tomato (p. 229)	• Fried Buckwheat Noodles with Deep-fried Tofu (p. 240) • Wine-fermented Tofu Dip with Curry (p. 365)
Sat.	• Breakfast Toast with Pan-fried Tofu (p. 161)	• Tofu Sour Cream (p. 152) • Onion Soup with Tofu Cutlets (p. 230)	• Grilled Tofu Cutlets with Korean Barbecue Sauce • Chunky Tofu & Pineapple Puree (p. 208)

4
Soybeans

WHOLE DRY soybeans are the essential ingredient in the tofu maker's art. Each evening, he concludes his daily cycle of work by measuring out 15 to 20 gallons of beans in a special wooden box made with precisely mitered corners and a brand of the gods of good fortune burned into one of its sides (Fig. 7). One of the gods is *Ebisu*, the deity of craftsmen, tradesmen, and fishermen; he symbolizes the hard worker who earns his living by honest toil. The other is *Daikoku,* the happy god whose wealth is so vast that he does not mind the rats nibbling at his bales of grain. The tofu maker washes the measured beans in a large cedar barrel bound together with hoops of brightly-polished brass, then sets them aside to soak overnight. He and the beans sleep under the same roof.

The story of tofu must begin with the story of soybeans. Officially known as *Glycine max* and botanically a member of the family Lequminosae (legumes), the soybean plant stands about 2 feet tall, has a slightly woody stem, and sprouts its leaves in groups of three. The leaves, stems, and pods are covered with soft brownish-green hairs, and the plant's seeds—soybeans —are borne in the pods which grow near the stalk in clusters of three to five (Fig. 8). Each pod usually contains two to three seeds. Fresh soybeans are similar in color and size to green peas. The mature, dried beans are usually yellow, tan, or beige, but some varieties are also black, brown, green, or bi-colored. American beans are slightly smaller and yellower than most Japanese varieties. They grow throughout the United States and well into Canada, but do best in states that border the Mississippi. The top four producers are Illinois, Iowa, Indiana, and Ohio. Planted from late April until mid June in rows about 40 inches apart, the fresh green beans are ready to eat as early as mid-July; the mature beans are harvested in September or October, after the leaves have fallen and the seeds have dried on the vine.

Two main types of legumes are oilseeds and pulses. Soybeans are oilseeds; they are not pulses. Soybeans are a legume that has a symbiotic relationship with *Rhizobia* bacteria, which form nodules on the plants' roots. *Rhizobia* capture nitrogen (the essential element in all protein) from the air and fix it in the soil, thereby greatly enhancing the soil's fertility. Hence, many of the first soybean plants grown in the United States were used simply as cover crops or "green manure"; even today, all farmers, after harvesting the beans, plow under the remainder of the plant to create nitrogen-rich humus soil. Easy to grow in small vegetable gardens or window boxes, the soybean plant is a favorite with organic and biodynamic gardeners, too, for much the same reason.

Where did the word "soybean" come from? The present-day Chinese call soybeans *ta-tou,* or "great beans." The Japanese pronounce the same written characters as *daizu.* It is obvious that neither of these words resembles the word "soy." But in a Chinese dictionary dating from about the beginning of the Christian era, soybeans are called *sou.* In addition, the Japanese pronounce the word for soy sauce (*chiang-yu*) as *shoyu.* The etymology of the English word may therefore be traced either to the Japanese word for soy sauce or to the ancient Chinese word for soybean.

The origins of the soybean plant are obscured by legend and the Oriental urge to endow all things worthy of respect with ancient ancestry. It is said that long ago, sages and wise rulers bestowed the bounty of soybeans upon the generations of mankind. The numerous myths, legends, and historical

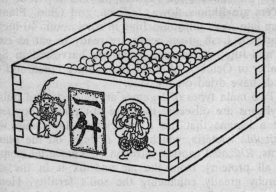

Fig. 7. A Soybean Measuring Box

accounts of its ancestry all reflect a common wish to honor the soybean for the service it has given to humanity.

In his excellent "On the Domestication of the Soybean," Hymowitz concludes that linguistic, literary, and genetic evidence seems to indicate that the soybean emerged as a domesticated plant in the eastern part of north China (probably in the area just south of present-day Peking) at least by the early Chou dynasty, about the 11th century B.C. The ancient ideographic character for soybeans, *shu*, first appears in the *Book of Odes* at this same time. There is no evidence of soybean remains in Neolithic sites prior to this time. However, legend has it that soybeans are one of the oldest crops grown by man, extensively cultivated and highly valued as a food for centuries before written records were kept.

In an eighteenth-century Chinese encyclopedia, the discovery of the soybean was attributed to two legendary characters, *Yu-hsiung* and *Kung-kung shih*, who were said to have lived more than five thousand years ago. But it is not clear whether they discovered beans in general or soybeans in particular. A more widely known theory states that in 2838 B.C., a legendary Chinese emperor named *Sheng nung* wrote a *Materia Medica* which describes the plants of China and includes a description of the soybean together with a long discourse on its medical properties. And in writings reported to be published as early as 2207 B.C., Chinese agricultural experts give detailed technical advice concerning soybean planting and soil preferences.

It is known from reliable historical sources that soybeans were cultivated in China before the Han Dynasty (206 B.C.-220 A.D.) and that they were used in processed form as food by the second century B.C., when the ruler Liu An of Huai-nan is said to have discovered the process for making tofu. According to the ten-volume *Chi'min Yaushu,* mankind's oldest encyclopedia of agriculture, compiled in the sixth century, soybeans were initially brought to China by the great Chinese explorer *Choken,* who was the first to make contact with Greece, Rome, and India, and to open the Silk Road.

The transmission of soybeans from northern China or Manchuria to Japan, probably via Korea, may have taken place sometime between the third and eighth centuries, concurrent with the spread of Buddhism. (The discovery of charred soybeans together with husked rice in Neolithic dwellings in Japan suggests that soybeans may actually have arrived in Japan long before the existence of written records.) The first mention of soybeans in Japan appears in the *Kojiki,* one of the nation's earliest and most famous documents, written in 712 A.D.; they are also mentioned in the equally famous *Nihonshoki* of 720 A.D. Records from the Nara period (710-794) show that soybean foods (such as miso and the progenitor of shoyu) were taxed by the government, and thus were an important part of the Japanese way of life even then.

Along with rice, wheat, barley, and millet, soybeans were included among China's venerated *mu-ku,* or Five Sacred Grains, as early as the beginning of the Christian era. Since soybeans are not technically a grain (they are a grain legume), some scholars believe that it was beans in general rather than the soybeans that were given this lofty title. Nevertheless, living close to the earth, the people of East Asia grasped the dependence of human life upon these basic crops. Their sense of the sacred grew out of a feeling of interrelationship—and gratitude—and determined their way of relating to soybeans and other essential foods.

The sense of the sacredness of soybean food is still alive in Japan today; here the words tofu, miso, and shoyu are commonly preceded in everyday speech by the honorific prefix o. Rather than saying tofu, most people say o-tofu, meaning "honorable tofu." And on the last day of winter, as determined by Japan's traditional lunar calendar, roasted soybeans play a key role in one of the country's most ancient and widely observed celebrations of ritual purification. In homes and temples throughout Japan, these fuku-mame or "beans of good fortune" are scattered by the handful in each room, then tossed through an open window into the cold night air with everyone chanting "Out with all evils; in with good fortune."

Today, the soybean has become the king of the Japanese kitchen. Indeed, the arrival of tofu, miso, and shoyu in Japan initiated a revolution in the national cuisine. Now when Japanese connoisseurs speak of these foods, they use many of the same terms we employ when evaluating cheeses or wines; traditional tofu master often say that the consummation of their art is but to evoke the fine flavors latent in the soybean. Again and again we have heard them declare that "only nigari can unfold the delicate nuances of sweetness and the fine, subtle bouquet in the best domestic beans." And when the new crop of soybeans arrives at tofu shops late each fall, ardent devotees sample the first tofu with the discrimination and relish of French vintners.

Many Japanese grow soybeans in their vegetable gardens and they are cultivated intensively along the

Fig. 8. The Soybean Plant

paths which separate one rice paddy from another. Varieties considered to have the finest flavors have been known for centuries by such names as "child of the white cranes" or "waving sleeves."

Except for Manchuria, the countries of East Asia have not traditionally pressed or crushed soybeans on a large scale to extract their oil. Nor have they generally baked, boiled, or ground the beans into flour. Using simple tools and processes, countless generations have discovered other ways of transforming soybeans into delicious foods. After almost 1,000 years of use in China, the soybean was transmitted to Japan. Over the period of another millennium, the Japanese modified each of the basic Chinese soybean foods and created a number of new ones. Finally, at the beginning of the present century, the Japanese made the first major commercial shipment of soybeans to the Western world. In its contact with the West's unique patterns of cooking, farming, and food-processing, the soybean entered a new phase in its long history.

A German botanist, Englebert Kaempfer, spent 3 years in Japan from 1690 to 1693 and was the first Westerner to study and write about Japanese soybean foods. The first small samples of seed soybeans arrived in the West as early as 1790 and were planted in England's Botanical Gardens. The fact that their arrival corresponded with the beginning of the industrial revolution was to have a profound effect on the way in which soybeans came to be used. In 1804 the soybean was first mentioned in American literature in *Willic's Domestic Encyclopedia*, and in 1854, the Perry Expedition brought two soybean varieties back from Japan. In 1908, when the first commercial shipment of soybeans from Asia to the West was received in England, they were processed for oil to be used in the manufacture of soap, while the meal was fed to dairy cattle. This pattern of use, so different from that in Asia, has remained basically unchanged up to the present time.

In America, the first soybeans were used as a forage crop and for green manure rather than as a food for people. The first small-scale processing of soybeans to obtain oil was begun in 1911. In 1920 the American Soybean Association was organized and by 1922 Decatur, Illinois, had become the center of soybean processing in the U.S. In 1923, Charles Piper and William Morse wrote *The Soybean*, the first comprehensive book in English on this subject. Showing great interest in all of the basic Oriental soybean foods, they studied their methods of preparation in detail and included a large number of recipes using them in Western-style cookery. With remarkable insight, they wrote in the preface to their classical study:

The importance of the soybean lies largely in the fact that the seeds can be produced more cheaply than those of any other leguminous crop. This is due to both its high yielding capacity and to the

ease of harvesting. These facts alone insure the
increasing importance of the crop in the future
when the land shall be called upon to yield its
maximum crop of food. There can be little doubt
that the soybean is destined to become one of the
major American crops. (p. v).

When Piper and Morse wrote these words, soybeans were still a relatively unknown commodity. It
was not until 1935 that the acreage of beans used for
oil extraction equalled that used for forage. Blessed
with expanses of territory well suited by climate and
soil quality for soybean production, and equipped
with a technology that has made it possible to produce a bushel of beans with less than 8 minutes labor,
the U.S. farmer was able by the 1950s to grow soybeans competitive price- and quality-wise with those
originating in the Orient. By 1973, the U.S. soybean
crop had reached the phenomenal figure of 1½ billion
bushels (47 million tons), a *twentyfold* increase in
size since 1940 and a 24 percent increase over the
previous year. Over the same period, the yield per
acre increased 68 percent to a high of 27 bushels.
Recent test plots have yielded as much as 60 to 100
bushels per acre, and experts feel that in the near
future a nationwide average of 40 bushels may be
possible. It is not likely that such large increases in
production and yield will ever again be duplicated by
soybeans or any other crop.

In the short space of two generations, America has
become the world's largest producer of soybeans, sup-
plying over 65 percent of the planet's total output.
The number-two producer, Brazil, supplies about 18
percent, and China about 13 percent. Argentina, Indonesia, Korea, Russia, and Canada also produce
fairly large crops. Soybeans are now the number one
U.S. farm export, and foreign demand is ever on the
rise. Worth an astounding 5 *billion* dollars in 1974
and accounting for more than 8 percent of our total
exports, soybean sales abroad generate a large pro-

portion of the foreign currency used to import oil and other basic raw materials.

Thus, a nutritional cornerstone of East Asian cuisine has emerged as the most important American cash crop. Called "meat of the fields" in Asia, soybeans are now known among American farmers as "gold from the soil." Nevertheless, as late as September 1973, the then president of the United States could make a statement—that made headlines throughout Japan—to the effect that he had never seen a soybean. A majority of adult Americans are reported to have first heard the word "soybean" less than ten years ago and many have never seen a soybean plant, nor tasted fresh (green) or whole dry soybeans, or soybean sprouts. Yet, having become so well established in our agriculture and economy, soybeans are now gradually becoming part of our language and culture. At least one relatively large-scale American farming enterprise, a Tennessee-based new-age community called *The Farm*, has taken the historic step of cultivating about 300 acres of them for use primarily as a food staple in the vegetarian diet of its members. *The Farm* is bound to be only the first of many as, over the coming years, the soybean becomes an ever-more integral part of our national cuisine.

Soy Protein Foods

In addition to the many types of tofu discussed in detail in this book, there are a number of other important soyfoods which we feel deserve mention.

Traditional Non-fermented Soyfoods

Whole Dry Soybeans, soybeans in their simplest and least expensive form, are widely available at natural and health food stores for 35 to 50 cents a pound; farmers sell their soybeans in bulk for 5 to 8 cents a pound. Most soybeans are the yellow type, but in

East Asia black soybeans are also popular. The larger-sized and slightly more expensive "vegetable" soybeans, bred from Japanese stock and rich in protein, are preferred by some to the smaller and more widely available U.S. "field" beans. Pressure-cooked for 30 minutes (and usually seasoned with miso or shoyu), all types go nicely in your favorite bean recipes as well as in dips, spreads, casseroles, and soyburgers.

Soynuts are now widely available at natural and health food stores in the West, generally sold in small bags or jars like roasted peanuts, in salted, unsalted, garlic, and barbecue flavors. Their good flavor, crisp-and-crunchy yet light texture, rich protein content (37% vs. 26% for roasted peanuts), and low cost have made them a popular snack, hors d'oeuvre, and delectable addition to "nut bars." They are made from select whole soybeans that are soaked overnight in water, drained briefly on toweling, then deep-fried ("oil roasted") at about 325°F for roughly 12 minutes.

Roasted Soybeans, a close relative of soynuts, are also widely available. Containing a remarkable 47 percent protein, they have been popular for centuries in Japan, where they are known as *iri-mame,* or the "beans of good fortune."

Fresh Green Soybeans are simply soybeans picked before they are mature. Steamed or simmered in the pods for 15 to 20 minutes until tender (they are never eaten raw because of the presence of soybean trypsin inhibitors, discussed in Chapter 5), then served lightly salted and chilled (usually in the pods), they are one of Japan's most popular summertime hors d'oeuvres. Containing 12 percent protein that is the highest in quality of any known soyfood (NPU-72 vs. 65 for tofu), they are a low-cost taste treat already sold canned in America and precooked in sausage-shaped plastic containers as *hitashi mame* in Japan. We predict they will become more popular than green peas in the West and soon be widely available at supermarkets and natural food stores.

Soy sprouts, made by sprouting soybeans, are one

of the world's finest diet foods. They contain fewer calories per gram of protein than any other known vegetable food. Inexpensive, tasty, and easily grown at home in 4 to 5 days, they make a nice addition to salads and sautéed preparations. To deactivate soybean trypsin inhibitors, they are always parboiled for 6 to 8 minutes, or lightly sautéed, before serving.

Natural Soy Flour and *Soy Grits* are made from whole dry soybeans that have been ground. The grits consist of flour too coarse to pass through a 100-mesh screen. Containing about 40 percent protein and 20 percent natural oils, soy flour makes a protein-enriching addition to breads, pasta, muffins, pancakes, tortillas, cakes, pastries, and other baked goods. It is used in amounts of about 10 to 20 percent by weight of total flour content.

Roasted Soy Flour, called *kinako* in Japanese, is made by grinding whole dry-roasted soybeans to yield a dark-tan flour. It has a nutty flavor and fragrance, contains over 38 percent protein, and is the key ingredient in a number of Japan's most popular natural-food confections. An excellent coffee substitute (coffee is also a bean), made from coarsely ground roasted soy flour, is now sold in America.

Traditional Fermented Soyfoods

Tempeh, Indonesia's most popular soy protein food, consists of tender-cooked soybeans bound together by a dense cottony mycelium of *Rhizopus* mold into compact, white cakes or patties about ¾-inch thick. Sold fresh, refrigerated or frozen, these cakes are usually sliced and fried until crisp and golden brown; their flavor and texture resemble those of southern fried chicken. Favorite Western recipes include Tempeh Burgers, Tempeh, Lettuce & Tomato Sandwiches, and Seasoned Crisp Tempeh. Topped with applesauce, they become tempeh chops; steamed and pureed, they make creamy dressings and spreads; crispy slices or cubes are wonderful as croutons in salads and soups, or added to pizza, stir-fried rice, casseroles, sauces, or tacos. Tempeh originated in Java prior to 1750 and today is prepared fresh each morning at 41,000 shops in Java alone (and at 8 shops in North America). Soy tempeh contains 19 percent protein and is the world's richest known source of vegetarian vitamin B_{12}. For details and many recipes, see our *Book of Tempeh* (Harper & Row).

Miso is a savory fermented seasoning made from soybeans, grain (rice or barley), salt, water, and *Aspergillus oryzae* mold starter. Miso's texture resembles that of a soft peanut butter and its many warm colors range from deep reddish browns through sunlight yellows. The six basic types are rice miso (including red miso and brown-rice miso), barley miso, soybean miso (including Hatcho miso), finger lickin' miso, sweet simmered miso, and modern misos (including akadashi miso and freeze-dried miso widely used in commercial instant miso soups). One of the basic staples and seasonings in every Japanese and Chinese kitchen, its range of flavors and colors, textures and aromas is at least as varied as that of the world's fine cheeses or wines. Prized for its almost unlimited versatility, it can be used like bouillon or a rich meat stock in soups or stews; like Worcestershire, soy sauce, or ketchup in sauces, dips, and dressings; like cheese in casseroles and spreads; like chutney or relish as a topping; or even as a pickling medium. The progenitor of miso, called *chiang,* originated in China prior to 722 B.C. and today miso is made at over 2,000 shops and factories in Japan—and at 6 shops in the United States. Containing an average of 13 percent protein and 13 percent salt, miso is generally used in quantities of 1 to 2 tablespoons at a time; for ½ teaspoon of salt or 2 teaspoons of shoyu you can substitute 1 tablespoon of red, barley, or Hatcho miso, or 2½ to 3 tablespoons of sweet miso. For details and over 400 recipes see our *Book of Miso* (Ballantine Books and Ten Speed Press).

Fig. 9. Miso

Fig. 10. Shoyu

Shoyu, or Japanese natural soy sauce, is now well known and widely available throughout the West. Made from equal parts soybeans and cracked roasted wheat, plus salt, water, and *Aspergillus sojae* mold starter, shoyu adds deep, rich, savory flavor to almost any dish, and its skillful use is truly the key to most tofu cookery. We use the Japanese name *shoyu* to distinguish this fine product from its low-quality American-made counterpart. The latter is a synthetic or chemical soy sauce, made *without fermentation* from hydrolyzed vegetable protein (defatted soy meal treated with acid), caramel coloring, corn syrup, salt, and water. It is generally sold under Chinese brand names and comprises two-thirds of all soy sauce sold in America today. Natural shoyu, imported to America and often sold as "tamari," (although real tamari is actually a completely different product made without the use of wheat), is made from whole soybeans aged in cedar vats at the natural temperature of the environment for at least one year; no preservatives are added. "Regular" shoyu, also a high quality product (produced mostly by Kikkoman in America), costs about two-thirds as much as natural shoyu; defatted soy meal is substituted for whole soybeans and the product is aged in epoxy-lined steel tanks in a slightly heated (75°F) room for about 6 months; it generally contains preservatives. Shoyu originated in Japan between 1561 and 1661 and its predecessor originated in China, probably 500 to 1000 years ago. In Japan 3,300 large shops and factories produce about 350 million gallons of shoyu a year. Kikkoman, the largest Japanese producer, accounts for about one third of the total. Containing 6.9 percent protein and 18 percent salt, 2 teaspoons of shoyu may be substituted for ½ teaspoon salt.

Natto, or fermented whole soybeans, is prepared (commercially or at home) by steaming soaked soybeans until they are tender, mixing them while still warm (104°F) with 10 to 20 percent of commercial natto or with natto starter (the bacterium *Bacillus subtilis* var. *natto*), then incubating the mixture in a polyethylene container at about 104°F for 15 to 24 hours. The dark-brown natto beans have a sticky-slippery surface so that, when lifted from a bowl, they form gossamer threads. Natto's flavor is strong and distinctive, with subtle ammonia overtones—some people love it, others don't. A whole food requiring no additional cooking, it is generally served as a topping for rice or noodles, sautéed with vegetables, or used in soups or Japanese salads (*aemono*). Natto originated in northeast Japan, probably over 1000 years ago; today it is prepared daily in more than 1,000 commercial shops and is widely available at Japanese food markets in the West. Cracked Natto (*hikiwari natto*), and Finger Lickin' Natto (*yukiwari natto*, containing rice koji and salt) are also popular in Japan. A close relative of natto from northern Thailand, called *thua-nao*, is sold as a savory cooked paste (containing salt, garlic, onion, and red chillies) or as sun-dried chips.

Soy nuggets, which include Japan's *Hamanatto* and *Daitokuji-natto*, are tasty traditional condiments or seasonings that look something like dark-brown to grayish-black raisins and have a savory, slightly salty flavor resembling that of mellow Hatcho (soybean) miso. We have chosen to give them English names, avoiding use of the term "natto," since they are totally unrelated to regular natto except that both are fermented soyfoods. The nuggets are inoculated with a mold (*Aspergillus oryzae*) rather than a bacterium and they are salty but not sticky. They originated in China over 2200 years ago. Sprinkled over rice or rice porridge, served as an hors d'oeuvre with green tea or sake, or used as an ingredient in miso soups or with cooked vegetables, they add zest to otherwise bland dishes. We sprinkle them over curry or spaghetti sauces, or fried eggs. Savory soy nuggets, the more popular of the two and a product of Hamamatsu city in central Japan, contain slivered gingerroot. Daitokuji Soy nuggets are a product of Daitokuji temple in Kyoto. We like both products, but prefer the savory soy nuggets since the Daitokuji Soy nuggets have a sharper, slightly saltier flavor. The Chinese progenitor of these products is called *tou-ch'ih*. In the Philippines, it is known as *tao-si*.

Modern Western Soyfoods

These products, developed in the West during the past several decades using high-level technology, are predicted to play an increasingly important role as meat substitutes and extenders in affluent countries.

Soy Flakes (or "microflaked soybeans") are made by running lightly dry-roasted whole soybeans through a roller miller to give a natural product which is easier and quicker to cook than whole soybeans.

Defatted Soy Flour and Grits, containing 50 to 52 percent protein, are prepared by cleaning, cracking, dehulling, and crushing soybeans to make soy flakes. Giant hexane solvent extractors remove the soybean oil then vaporize off the solvent, leaving defatted flakes which form the basis of all modern soy protein foods. Defatted soy flour consists of flakes ground fine enough to pass through a 100-mesh screen. (Grits do not pass through the screen.) The least expensive source of soy protein in the West and by far the most widely used as food (1 billion pounds in 1977), the flour is a key ingredient in protein-rich breads, diet foods, breakfast cereals, infant foods, processed and simulated meats, and confections. Large quantities are also sent to developing countries in food supplements such as CSM (corn-soy-milk mix) and WSB (wheat-soy blend) as part of America's worldwide nutritional aid program.

Soy Protein Concentrates, containing 70 percent protein, are made by removing the oil and soluble carbohydrates from defatted soy flakes. The tan-to-cream-colored powder is available in several particle sizes which cost about three times as much as the original soy flakes. Introduced in 1960, 70 million pounds were produced in 1977 for use in ground meats, breakfast cereals, and infant foods.

Soy Protein Isolates, containing 90 to 95 percent protein, were introduced in 1957. They are made by removing all non-protein constituents from defatted soy flakes, and cost about 7 to 8 times as much as the flakes. Eighty million pounds were produced in 1977. A cream-colored spray-dried powder with a bland flavor, isolates are now widely used in high-protein health food supplements, simulated dairy products such as coffee creams, whipped toppings, and frozen desserts (imitation ice cream), meat analogs and sausages, and in canned meats as binding agents. Some 70 percent of the soybean solids and 19 percent of the limiting amino acid methionine are lost in the process of making these isolates.

Spun Soy Proteins are made by dissolving or suspending soy protein isolates in alkalai, then extruding them through spinnerettes into an acid-salt bath to form tiny monofilament fibers. Introduced in 1957, they are now combined with ingredients such as wheat gluten, egg albumen, fats, flavoring, and coloring agents to form simulated meat items.

Textured Soy Proteins, containing about 52 percent protein, are made from defatted soy flour thermoplastically extruded under great pressure and heat to form small chunks. When hydrated these have a chewy meatlike texture and, when artificial colorings and flavorings are added, a meatlike flavor and appearance. Relatively inexpensive, TSP (also known by its Archer-Daniels Midland brand name TVP) is by far the most promising of the various new soy protein foods. The 140 million pounds produced in 1977 were used as extenders in ground and simulated meats, as imitation bacon bits, and in infant foods.

Textured Soy Concentrates, containing 70 percent protein, are made by the extrusion of soy concentrates. Introduced in 1975, they are still in the experimental stage with only 5 million pounds produced in 1977. They have a less beany flavor and produce less flatulence than TSP.

Soy Oil Products are the most widely used edible oils and fats in the United States, accounting for 65 percent of total oil consumption—a per capita usage of almost 31 pounds in 1975; of this, 44 percent was used as cooking and salad oils, 31 percent as vegetable shortenings, and 25 percent as margarine. Although it contains no protein, soy oil is rich in polyunsaturates and linoleic acid, and is very low in cost. The lecithin fraction of unrefined soy oil, widely sold in health food stores, is also used as an emulsifying, anti-spattering, and stabilizing agent.

5

Fresh Soy Puree

FRESH SOY PUREE, called gô in Japanese, is a white purée of well-soaked uncooked soybeans; it has the consistency of a thick pancake batter. It is interesting to note that the Japanese character for gô is also used to represent the verb *kureru* meaning "to give." This is appropriate, since gô is the source of each of the various tofu products (Fig. 11); it is the first transformation of whole soybeans in the alchemy of tofu-making. As in an archetypal image from the Chinese *Book of Changes,* the soft beans, heaped high, pass downward between heavy granite millstones. Turning slowly, the whispering stones merge the many bright-yellow soybeans into a cream-white, smooth purée, which flows over the sides of the lower, stationary stone and is caught in a large cedar tub. Nearby, in a massive black cauldron, boiling water awaits with the benediction of fire.

Soy purée is the only stage in the tofu making process where the entire soybean is still together; in the next step, the purée will be separated into *okara* and soymilk. Thus by using soy purée in cooking, we can enjoy the full range of the soybean's nutrients in their natural balance and completeness.

By soaking and grinding the soybean, we greatly reduce the amount of time and fuel required for its thorough cooking, just as it is quicker and more economical to cook rolled- rather than whole-grain oats. Moreover, unlike most other grains and pulses, soybeans contain substances called "soybean trypsin inhibitors" (SBTI), which obstruct the functioning of the pancreas-secreted trypsin enzyme essential for the di-

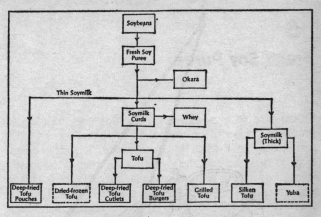

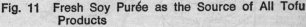

Fig. 11 Fresh Soy Purée as the Source of All Tofu Products

Fig. 12. Hand-turned Millstones

gestion of protein and the maintenance of proper growth. SBTI can—and must—be inactivated by cooking. Laboratory tests show that 70 to 80 percent of all SBTI present in the soybean must be destroyed if the

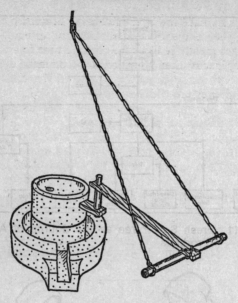

Fig. 13. Push-pull Millstones

Fig. 14. Motor-driven Millstones

body is to make use of the full array of nutrients in the
bean. They also show that soaking and grinding whole
soybeans greatly reduces the cooking time to attain this
level of inactivation. Nutritionists recommend that well-
soaked whole soybeans be simmered for four to six
hours or pressure cooked (at 15 pounds) for 20 to 30
minutes. Soy purée, however, need be simmered for
only 15 minutes or pressure-cooked for 10 if it is to be
used directly as a food (or be further processed into
soymilk), it requires as few as 7 to 10 minutes of simmering if it is to be made into tofu, since SBTI are contained in the soluble carbohydrates that dissolve in the
whey during the curding process.

To prepare soy purée with the best flavor and nutritional value, soak your soybeans for the correct length
of time, which varies with the air temperature as shown
in Figure 15. If tiny bubble have begun to form on the

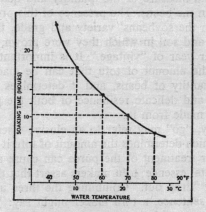

Fig. 15. Soaking Time for Soybeans

surface of the soak water, the beans have been soaked
too long. Examine the inside of a bean by breaking it
lengthwise into its two halves with your fingertips. If
the faces of the two halves are flat and the same color
in the center as at the edges, and if each half can be

easily broken crosswise into halves, the soaking time has been correct. However, if the faces of the two halves are slightly concave and a little more yellow at the center than at the edges, and if the halves are flexible and rubbery, the beans have not been soaked long enough.

After soaking, purée or grind the beans to a fine, smooth-textured consistency using an electric blender, a Corona hand mill, a juicer, a meat grinder with a fine attachment, an electric grain mill, a coffee mill, a mortar and pestle, or a *suribachi*. Most important, cook the fresh soy purée without delay, and do not overcook, lest some of the protein value be lost.

The word "gô" is used by Japanese tofu makers in three different ways. First, it refers to the white purée described above. Second, it is used to refer to a property of dry soybeans, similar to the gluten in wheat, which is a measure of the quantity and quality of the protein in the beans. The presence of this property depends on the soybeans' variety and grade, the region, climate, and soil in which they were grown, and their particular year of "vintage." It is important in determining the amount of tofu that can be made from a given quantity of beans, and it determines the cohesiveness and delicate resilience of both the purée and the tofu made from it.

Finally, "gô" may refer to an elusive essence of the purée which determines the amount of tofu it will yield. Improper treatment of the purée can cause a decrease in this vital essence; tofu makers assert that this gô can "fall" or "drop out." Combining the three usages into a single sentence, a tofu maker might say: "To make fine tofu, use soybeans containing good gô, grind them between slowly-turning stones to make smooth, fine-textured gô, and cook immediately, to prevent any of the essential gô from escaping"!

Since ancient times and until really quite recently, most Japanese kitchens were equipped with a pair of 10-inch-diameter, hand-turned millstones (Fig. 12). These were used to grind soybeans into gô during the preparation of farmhouse tofu or Gôjiru soup. On special occasions, they were used to grind whole grains into flour, roasted soybeans into *kinako,* or tender tea leaves into *matcha* used in the tea ceremony. In farmhouses where tofu was made regularly or in large quantities, and in traditional tofu shops throughout Japan and China, an interesting design was developed whereby large, heavy stones were turned using a push-pull system (Fig. 13). While one person worked the push-pull handle that revolved the upper stone, another ladled soaking soybeans into the stone's upper surface. Working in this way, it often took 1 or 2 hours for tofu makers to grind enough beans for a single cauldronful of tofu yielding 120 cakes. Work usually started as early as 2 o'clock in the morning and, during the summer, the beans were often ground and cooked in two separate batches each day to ensure freshness. In several of Kyoto's elegant old tofu and yuba shops where granite stones are still used, the stone floor near the base of the grinding platform is distinctly indented and worn smooth in the spots where many generations of fathers and sons pivoted their feet as they turned the great stones by hand.

While all of the fresh soy purée made in Japanese tofu shops is still ground between millstones, the great majority of the shops presently use relatively small, lightweight millstones that revolve more rapidly than the traditional, heavy stones. Some shops, however, have carefully preserved their beautiful heirloom millstones, mounting them vertically and driving them with a fanbelt and electric motor (Fig. 14). The tofu master must chisel the cutting grooves of both stones every three months to keep them sharp. Like the finest Western stone-burr mills or querns used for making stone-ground flours, these heavy stones yield soy purée, and hence tofu, of the finest quality.

It is interesting to note that although millstones have been used for more than 2,000 years in East Asia, the power to revolve them was traditionally provided entirely by man. It apparently never occurred to these

Fig. 16. Water-powered Millstones

Fig. 17. Wind-powered Millstones

craftsmen that natural forces—such as wind and water
—could be used as energy sources. Less than a century ago, most of the flour prepared in the West was
freshly ground each morning in stone mills powered by
either water wheels (Fig. 16) or windmills (Fig. 17).
The large stones were 3 to 4 feet in diameter and 12
inches thick, whereas we have never seen a Chinese

millstone larger than 17 inches in diameter and 5 inches thick.

The same basic principles used in making high-quality whole-grain flours are also applied in preparing soy purée. Each morning the tofu maker drains and rinses his well-soaked soybeans, then places them in a hopper above the grinder. He runs a slow trickle of water—often drawn from the shop's deep well—over the beans, down through the hopper and in between the stones to give his purée the desired thickness. The millstones revolve slowly and at medium pressure to ensure that the germ, skin, and body of the beans are smoothly blended, and to avoid overheating, which would cause the essential gô to escape. This way of grinding yields soy purée with a very fine grain; the latter, in turn, increases the tofu yield. It also helps to develop the natural cohesiveness or glutinous quality found in soybeans in much the same way that kneading develops gluten in bread.

Lest the essential gô escape, the purée should be used as soon as possible after it has been ground. Thus, in tofu shops it is scooped immediately into a cauldron of boiling water. Gô loses its potency the longer it sits unused and the tofu yield consequently declines.

In modern Japan, most of the purée made in tofu shops is used directly in the tofu-making process. Only occasionally do the more tradition-minded order it from the tofu shop for use in home cooking. Since most homes are now equipped with a blender, cooks can make their own.

Fresh soy purée can be added to soups or breads, or it can be sautéed with vegetables, mixed with diced foods and deep-fried, or used as a protein-rich base for casseroles and other baked dishes. Try using it in place of pre-packaged soy flour, meal, or grits in your favorite recipes; in most cases, cooking time will be reduced by 50 percent or more. This creamy-white, smooth purée invites imaginative experimentation to find new uses for a food that is rarely, if ever, mentioned in Western cookbooks.

Homemade Fresh Soy Purée

MAKES 2 CUPS

This purée has the consistency of a thick milkshake; its thicker counterpart described below is more like a paste. The two types may be used interchangeably in most recipes. (Note: 1 cup soybeans expands to about 2½ cups when soaked overnight.)

½ cup dry soybeans, soaked for 8 to 10 hours in 1 quart water
⅞ cup water

Rinse, then drain the beans in a colander. Combine beans and water in a blender and purée at high speed for about 3 minutes, or until smooth. Or, if a crunchier texture is desired, purée for only 1 minute.

Homemade Thick Soy Purée

MAKES 1¼ CUPS

½ cup dry soybeans, soaked for 8 to 10 hours in 1 quart water

Rinse, then drain the beans in a colander. Using a hand mill or meat grinder with a fine-blade attachment, grind beans to a smooth paste.

Gôjiru (Thick Miso Soup with Gô)

SERVES 4 TO 6

The most popular way of using gô in Japanese cookery, this famous wintertime soup is said to have originated in Japan's snowy northeast provinces.

2 tablespoons oil
1 onion, thinly sliced; or 1 leek cut into 2-inch lengths
½ carrot, cut into thin half moons
2 ounces deep-fried tofu, cut into thin strips
3 mushrooms, thinly sliced
2 inches *daikon*, cut into half moons; or ½ cup chopped celery
1 potato, sweet potato, yam, or taro, diced
2 cups Homemade Fresh Soy Purée
3½ to 4 cups water, stock, or dashi (p. 35)
5 to 6 tablespoons red miso or 3½ tablespoons shoyu

Heat a heavy pot and coat with the oil. Add the next six ingredients and sauté over medium heat for 5 to 10 minutes, or until potatoes are softened. Add soy purée and water, bring to a boil, and simmer uncovered for 10 to 15 minutes, stirring occasionally. Add miso thinned in a few tablespoons of the hot broth and simmer for 1 minute more. Serve immediately or, for a richer, sweeter flavor, allow to cool for about 6 hours.

Whole-wheat Bread with Gô

MAKES 6 LOAVES

This high protein bread has a delightfully moist texture and rich flavor. By properly combining soy and wheat proteins, we increase the total amount of usable protein by about 30 percent.

2 cups soybeans, soaked overnight in water, drained and rinsed
4 cups lukewarm water
2 tablespoons dried yeast
½ cup honey
12 cups whole-wheat flour, approximately
¼ cup oil
2½ tablespoons salt

Combine half the beans and 2 cups water in a blender; purée for about 3 minutes, or until smooth. Pour the purée into a large mixing bowl. Purée the remaining beans in the same way and add to the bowl together with honey, yeast, and 4 cups flour. Using a large wooden spoon, mix for about 5 minutes to form a smooth sponge. Cover bowl with a moist towel, and allow to stand for about 40 minutes in a warm place until sponge doubles in volume.

Add the oil and salt. Fold in about 2 cups flour at a time to form a smooth, firm dough. Turn dough out onto a well-floured bread board and incorporate the remaining flour while kneading. When dough has been kneaded 200 to 300 times and is fairly light and smooth-textured, place in a large, lightly oiled bowl, cover, and allow to double in volume. Punch down and allow to rise once again.

Preheat oven to 350°F. Turn dough out onto a lightly floured bread board and divide into 6 equal portions. Knead each portion about 20 times, shape into a loaf, and place into a lightly oiled bread pan. When the last loaf is in its pan, allow all loaves to rise for 5 to 10 minutes more. Bake for 40 to 50 minutes, or until nicely browned. Serve warm with butter.

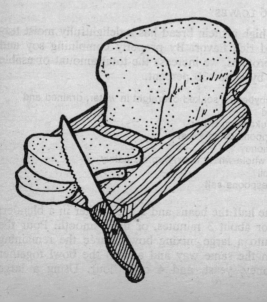

6

Okara (Soy Pulp)

AFTER SOYBEANS have been ground, the smooth purée is ladled into a cauldron of boiling water, returned to the boil, and simmered for 10 to 15 minutes. The contents of the cauldron are then ladled into a sturdy, coarsely-woven cloth sack set on a rack atop a curding barrel. The sack's mouth is twisted closed and the sack is pressed. In farmhouses a heavy millstone is set atop the sack; in tofu shops the sack is pressed either with a traditional lever (Fig. 18) or with a more modern hydraulic press or centrifuge. In each case liquid soymilk filters through the sack into the curding barrel, while the insoluble solids—called *okara* or soy pulp—remain in the sack. The soymilk is eventually made into tofu; the okara has its own special uses.

Okara is beige in color and has a crumbly, fine-grained texture, somewhat resembling cornmeal or freshly grated coconut. Some Westerners have remarked—only half in jest—that its appearance reminds them of moist sawdust. But the Japanese, in line with their ancient tradition of honoring even the simplest and most humble of foods, place the honorific prefix *o* before the word *kara,* which means "shell, hull, or husk." Thus *o-kara* means "honorable shell." In Chinese it is called "child of tofu lees" *(toufu cha-tsu),* "soy lees" *(tou-cha),* or "tofu's head" *(tou-to)* in contrast with the soft curds which are called the "tofu's brain." Trying to translate any of these words into descriptive English is almost impossible; terms such as "soy pulp, lees, grounds, mash, fines, residue, dregs," or the like hardly do justice to this fine food.

When the Japanese refer to okara as an ingredient in cooking, they often call it *unohana* after *Deutzia scabra,* a tiny white flower that grows in thick clusters

Fig. 18. A Traditional Lever Press

on briar bushes and blossoms in the spring (Fig. 19).
In 1869, the *haiku* poet Basho, on his last long trek
to the back country of northern Japan, wrote of
unohana in his journal:

> *Mounting towards the Shirakawa barrier*
> *"Autumnal winds" hummed in my ears,*
> *"The maple" stood imagined,*
> *But leaf-green branches haunting too.*
> *Against unohana white white briars,*
> *As if pushing through snow.*
> *(CID CORMAN translation)*

And indeed, okara deserves this sensitive treatment
and high evaluation for, when properly prepared, it is
a tasty and nutritious food which serves as an important ingredient in traditional Japanese cuisine. Okara
dishes are available in most delicatessens and at many
fine restaurants. Light and almost fluffy, okara absorbs
flavors well and gives body to sautéed vegetable dishes,
soups, casseroles, breads, and salads.

Fig. 19 Unohana

The most important constituent of okara is what nutritionists and doctors call "dietary fiber" and now consider to be an essential part of every well-balanced diet. Fiber, by definition, is indigestible. Composed of carbohydrates found in the outer bran layers of whole grains and the cell walls of natural vegetables and pulses, it passes unchanged through the human digestive tract performing two key functions: it provides the "bulk" or "roughage" necessary for regular bowel movements and the prevention of constipation; and it absorbs toxins (including environmental pollutants) and speeds their passage out of the body.

The recent re-evaluation of the importance of fiber-rich foods such as okara has resulted from the recognition of three dangerous trends in the dietary patterns of most industrialized nations: 1) our intake of dietary fiber is now only 20 percent of what it was one hundred years ago due both to the rapid rise in the consumption of sugar, meat, fats, and dairy products (all of which contain *no* fiber) and the decrease in the use of grains and vegetables; 2) a large proportion of the grains we do consume are in their refined, processed forms (such as white bread, rice, or pasta) which have been stripped of their fiber-rich (and nutritious) outer layers; 3) the average person has a steadily increasing intake of toxic substances from both food additives and the environment. Serving okara, therefore, allows us to make use of natural soybeans in the most holistic and health-giving way.

Containing about 17 percent of the protein in the original soybeans, okara itself consists of 3.5 percent protein by weight, or about the same proportion found in whole milk or cooked brown rice. While it is perhaps unfortunate that all of this protein is not transferred to tofu, its presence in okara is just that much more reason for utilizing this byproduct of the tofu-making process.

The tastiest and most nutritious okara is that removed in the process of making silken tofu, a variety made from very thick soymilk. Since this okara is pressed only once, it retains a great deal of the soymilk's flavor and nutrients, and has an obviously moist, cohesive texture. In the process of making regular tofu in tofu shops, soymilk is filtered through first a coarsely woven and then a finely woven sack. The small quantity of very fine-grained okara that collects in the second sack is usually pressed by hand (rather than with a press) so that it, too, retains a large portion of the soymilk taste and food value. During the winter months when the cold air ensures their freshness, both varieties are shaped into 4½-inch-diameter balls or sealed in small plastic bags to be sold for a few pennies per pound. Some tofu makers present okara to their customers free of charge as a token of appreciation for their patronage.

Before World War II, most tofu-shop okara was sold for use in cooking. Young apprentices at the shop were often allowed to cook the day's okara any way they wished and then sell their creations from door to door. At New Year's, okara croquettes and other tasty dishes, made and sold in this way, earned an impoverished apprentice a little pocket money.

In various parts of East Asia okara is inoculated with mold spores, pressed into the form of 1-inch-thick cakes, and incubated until it is bound together by the mycelium, creating a meatlike texture. The cakes are generally sliced and deep-fried or simmered with variout sauces or seasonings to make delicious entrees and side dishes. Indonesia's popular *okara tempeh* and *okara onchom* are two such products, inoculated respectively with *Rhizopus oligosporus* or *Neurospora intermedia* mold spores and incubated for 24 to 48 hours. Deep-fried, they have a nutty flavor, remarkably like that of southern fried chicken. Much of Indonesia's okara is wisely utilized in this way and fine okara tempeh is now produced by several tempeh shops in America. Another such product is *meitauza,* made in some parts of China by inoculating okara with *Actinomucor elegans* mold spores, and fermenting it for 10 to 15 days. After several hours of sun-drying, the cakes are cooked like tempeh and served as a nutritious flavoring agent.

In Japan, a typical tofu shop produces about 15 gallons of okara daily, or roughly 1 gallon for each gallon of dry soybeans used. But at most, only one gallon or so of this is retailed. The remainder is picked up daily at the shop by local dairymen who feed it to their cows to stimulate milk production and enrich the milk's nutrient content. In China, many tofu makers run small hog farms and use okara as their principal source of fodder. Okara also works well as an organic mulch and fertilizer, or as a free, high-protein pet food. (In Japan it is now used commercially in dried dog-and-cat foods.)

Nursing mothers have used okara for centuries to enrich their milk and stimulate its flow. It also serves as a traditional cure for diarrhea. Wrapped in a cloth and used to rub down the household woodwork, okara's natural oils coat and darken the wood, thus serving as a wax and polish.

At present in the United States, okara is available at some Japanese and Chinese groceries and, of course, at all tofu shops. But the easiest way to obtain okara is to prepare Homemade Tofu (p. 127) or Soymilk (p. 299). If you prepare enough tofu for two people, you will have as a byproduct about 1½ cups of okara, or enough for three to six servings.

Roasting or Parching Okara

The dry-roasting or parching called for in some recipes is meant to reduce okara's water content and give it a light, almost fluffy texture. When added to breads, muffins, cookies, or croquettes, roasted okara not only saves on flour but also gives much lighter results.

To roast using a skillet or wok, heat but do not oil the pan. Put in the okara and roast over low heat, stirring constantly with a wooden spoon or spatula, for about 3 minutes or until okara is light and dry but not browned.

When parching okara in an oven, spread the okara out on a large baking tin. Place in an unheated oven set at 350°F and heat for 5 to 10 minutes.

Homemade Okara

The okara which results as a byproduct from the preparation of homemade tofu, soymilk, or silken tofu is superior in taste, texture, and nutritional elements to that which is available from commercial tofu shops. It is also free. Since the okara is pressed by hand rather than mechanically, it retains the flavor and nutrition of the unpressed soymilk. The okara that remains after making soymilk is the tastiest and most nutritious, since

some of the thick soymilk always remains in it. Since
the okara from homemade tofu is generally separated
from the soymilk before the milk is thoroughly cooked
however, it is important that the okara be cooked
slightly longer than commercial okara, hence the cooking times in the recipes that follow.

To prepare homemade okara, refer to the recipes for
Homemade Tofu (p. 127) or Soymilk (p. 299).

Okara Scrambled Eggs

SERVES 3 OR 4

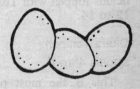

3 eggs
½ cup milk
¼ teaspoon salt
Dash of pepper
½ cup okara, firmly packed
1½ tablespoons butter

Combine the first four ingredients in a mixing bowl;
whisk or mix with a fork. Now stir in the okara. Melt
the butter in a skillet, add the egg-and-okara mixture,
and scramble over high heat for about 3 minutes or
until firm but not dry. Serve hot or cold.

Okara Burgers

MAKES 4 TO 5

1 cup okara
½ cup whole-wheat flour
1 egg, lightly beaten
¼ cup minced onion
¼ cup grated carrot
1 clove of garlic, minced or crushed
1 tablespoon shoyu
¼ teaspoon curry powder
Dash of pepper
Oil for deep-frying

Combine the first nine ingredients, mixing well, and
shape into patties. Heat the oil to 350°F in a wok,

skillet, or deep-fryer. Drop in patties and deep-fry until crisp and golden brown (p. 185). Serve as for Tofu Burgers (p. 267).

If deep-frying is inconvenient, patties may be fried or broiled. Also, try adding cooked brown rice.

VARIATIONS

• *Okara Fritters:* Add 6 tablespoons (soy) milk and 1 egg to the above ingredients. Drop by spoonfuls into the hot oil to deep-fry. Mix skimmings from oil back into batter after each batch has been deep-fried. Delicious topped with Tofu Mayonnaise (p. 145). Makes 12 to 14.

Okara Tempeh

SERVES 4 TO 6

This is the most popular way of using okara in Indonesia. The starter is available from The Farm, 156 Drakes Ln., Summertown TN 38483. Coarse-textured okara which has been pressed as firmly as possible to expel excess soymilk works best; it allows good air circulation during fermentation and gives a light, high-quality product.

2½ cups well-pressed okara
2 teaspoons vinegar
½ teaspoon tempeh starter (*Rhizopus oligosporus* mold spores) or ¼ cup minced fresh tempeh

Place okara in a preheated steamer and steam for 20 minutes, then spread steamed okara on a triple layer of paper toweling (or on a clean tray) and allow to cool to body temperature. Add vinegar and starter, mixing for 3 minutes, then spread to a depth of ½ to ¾ inch in a breadpan, baking tin, or in a Ziploc bag perforated with pinholes every ½ inch. Cover pan or tin with a sheet of aluminum foil perforated as above, and incubate at 88°F (31°C) for 22 to 26 hours. Cut into thin slices and deep-or-shallow fry. Serve with a sprinkling of shoyu.

Okara-Potato Pancakes

MAKES 5 TO 6

1 cup coarsely-grated mature potatoes
⅔ cup okara
3 eggs, lightly beaten
1 teaspoon salt
1½ 'tablespoons minced onion
1½ tablespoons whole-wheat flour
Oil for frying
Applesauce or butter

Place potato gratings in a cloth towel and wring towel to extract as much moisture from potatoes as possible. Combine in a bowl with the next five ingredients; mix well. Shape into ¼-inch-thick patties and fry in a well-oiled skillet on both sides until golden brown. Serve hot, topped with either applesauce or butter.

Okara Croquettes

MAKES 10

1 cup White Sauce (p. 48, use 1 teaspoon salt for seasoning)
2 teaspoons oil
½ onion, minced
2 tablespoons grated carrot
1 cup okara
¼ cup whole-wheat flour
1 egg, lightly beaten
⅔ cup bread crumbs or bread crumb flakes
Oil for deep-frying

Prepare White Sauce and set aside to cool. Heat a skillet and coat with the oil. Add onion and carrots, and sauté for 4 to 5 minutes, then add to the sauce together with the okara; mix well. Shape into (soft) cylinders 1 inch in diameter and 2½ inches long. Dust with flour, gently dip into egg, and roll in bread crumbs; set aside briefly to dry.

Heat oil to 350°F in a wok, skillet, or deep-fryer. Drop in croquettes and deep-fry until golden brown (p. 185). Serve hot or cold, as is or topped with Tofu Tartare Sauce (p. 147) or Creamy Tofu Dressing (p. 143).

Okara & Vegetable Sauté (Unohana no iri-ni)
SERVES 3 OR 4

This dish, sold ready-made in Japanese markets and delicatessens and prepared at fine restaurants, is the most popular way of serving okara in Japan. Most recipes call for carrots, *konnyaku, shiitake* mushrooms, leeks, and deep-fried tofu as the basic ingredients, but almost any other vegetables may be added or substituted. The flavor of this dish is substantially improved by allowing it to cool to room temperature. It is served as a side dish.

2 tablespoons oil (up to half of which may be sesame)
½ carrot, cut into matchsticks
2 onions or leeks, thinly sliced
1 cup okara, firmly packed
1½ cups water, stock, or dashi (p. 35)
1 to 1½ tablespoons honey
3 tablespoons shoyu
1 tablespoon sake or white wine

Heat a skillet or wok and coat with the oil. Add carrot slivers and sauté for about 2 minutes, then add onion slices and sauté until transparent. Mix in remaining ingredients and bring just to a boil. Reduce heat to low and simmer, stirring occasionally, for 10 to 15 minutes, or until most of the liquid has evaporated. Remove from heat and allow to cool to room temperature. Do not reheat to serve. For best flavor, refrigerate overnight or for at least 5 hours.

Okara Chapaties
MAKES 8

1¼ cups whole-wheat flour
½ cup okara, firmly packed
½ teaspoon salt
2 tablespoons water
1 tablespoon oil (optional)

Preheat oven to 350°F. Combine 1 cup flour with remaining ingredients in a large bowl, mixing well.

Knead for about 5 minutes to form a smooth dough. Divide dough into 8 parts and roll out each one on a floured board into a very thin 6-inch round. Place rounds on large baking trays and bake for 5 to 10 minutes, or until nicely browned. Allow to cool for at least 5 minutes, or until crisp. Serve topped with Mushroom Sauce (p. 47), butter, or a tofu spread (p. 147), or mounded with a salad or grain preparation.

To make *puri*, roll *chapati* dough into 4-inch rounds and deep-fry in 350°F oil. Turn after about 30 seconds and continue deep-frying until *puri* have puffed up and are golden brown.

Okara also may be used in waffles, cornmeal muffins, pie crusts, spoonbread, and all yeasted breads. Use 2 parts flour to 1 part packed okara.

Okara Whole-wheat Pancakes

MAKES 10

1¼ cups whole-wheat flour
1 tablespoon baking powder
1 teaspoon salt
1⅓ cups milk
¼ cup oil
2 tablespoons honey
½ teaspoon vanilla extract
3 eggs, separated into yolks and whites
¾ cup okara, lightly packed

Combine and sift the first three ingredients. In a separate container, combine the milk, oil, honey, vanilla, and egg yolks; mix well, then stir in okara. Beat egg whites until stiff. Lightly mix dry ingredients into wet ingredients, then fold in egg whites; avoid overmixing. Spoon batter in 6-inch rounds into a lightly oiled skillet and fry on both sides until golden brown. Serve with butter and either honey or maple syrup.

Wonderful Okara & Barley Flour Muffins

MAKES 12

1¼ cups barley flour
2 teaspoons baking powder
¼ teaspoon salt
1¼ cups milk
¼ cup honey
¼ cup oil
¼ teaspoon vanilla extract
¾ cup okara, lightly packed

Preheat oven to 400°F. Roast barley flour in a heavy skillet, stirring constantly, until well browned and fragrant. Cool briefly, then combine with baking powder and salt, mixing well. Combine the next four ingredients in a separate bowl, mix thoroughly, then stir in okara. Fold dry ingredients lightly into wet. Spoon batter to a depth of about ¾ inch into a lightly oiled muffin tin and bake for about 35 minutes or until well browned. Invert on a rack and cool thoroughly before serving.

For variety, omit roasting; use Japanese-style preroasted barley flour *(mugi-kogashi)* or the regular Western variety.

Soysage

SERVES 3 TO 4

Developed by The Farm in Tennessee, this recipe yields fried delicacies that taste remarkably like sausages. Double the recipe if you have a large pressure cooker; if you have no pressure cooker, use an oven.

1½ cups okara
¾ cup whole wheat flour
2 tablespoons shoyu
1 teaspoon wet mustard
½ teaspoon salt
¼ teaspoon oregano
¼ clove crushed garlic or ⅛ teaspoon garlic powder
Dash of pepper
1 to 5 tablespoons milk (soy or dairy) or water

Combine all ingredients but the milk or water, mixing well, then add just enough of the liquid to make a medium-firm dough. Oil the inside of several slender (sausage-shaped) tin cans, sturdy glasses, or cups (or an oven-proof bowl). Pack mixture into containers and cover with aluminum foil. Run about 1 inch of water into a pressure cooker, stand containers upright in water, and bring cooker to full pressure (15 pounds); simmer for 45 minutes. (Or stand containers in a tray of water and bake in a 350°F oven for 30 minutes.) Remove containers from cooker and allow mixture to cool until firm. Then remove sausages by inverting containers and shaking. Cut sausages into ¼-inch-thick rounds and fry on both sides in a well-oiled skillet. Serve as is, or topped with shoyu or ketchup-and-mustard. Also use in sandwiches. For variety try adding a little fennel, cayenne, honey, or allspice to the dough.

Or, omit the slicing and frying, and spread the cooked soysage like pâté.

Okara Granola

MAKES 1½ CUPS

This is our favorite okara recipe. Golden brown, crumbly, and slightly sweet, it has much the same nutty aroma as toasted wheat germ, for which it makes an excellent substitute. You may wish to prepare a large quantity and store it in sealed jars.

2 cups okara
4 to 5 tablespoons natural sugar or honey
2 tablespoons oil
1 tablespoons vanilla
⅛ teaspoon salt

Preheat oven to 350°F. Combine all ingredients, mixing well. Spread in a large, shallow pan and roast, stirring occasionally, for 50 to 60 minutes, or until nicely browned, crumbly, and fragrant. Serve with milk (try using the soymilk from which the okara was extracted) and top with raisins or fresh fruit. Also delicious as a topping for (soymilk) yogurt, a lightweight mix to take on hiking trips, or a substitute for bread crumbs in casserole toppings. Serve small portions; it expands!

For a crunchier texture and richer flavor, add ¼ cup any or all of the following: raisins, shredded coconut, toasted sunflower seeds or pine nuts, chopped almonds or walnuts, minced dates or apricots, toasted sesame seeds or wheat germ. Mix in these ingredients 5 minutes before the end of toasting. Use in any of the recipes in this book calling for crunchy granola.

Okara Doughnuts

MAKES ABOUT 10

⅔ cup okara, firmly packed
⅔ cup flour
1 egg, lightly beaten
1½ teaspoons baking powder
½ teaspoon salt
¼ cup raisins
3 to 6 tablespoons natural or brown sugar
½ teaspoon cinnamon
Oil for deep-frying

Combine the first eight ingredients in a bowl; mix well to form a dough. Roll out on a floured board and cut as for doughnuts. Heat the oil to 370°F in a wok, skillet, or deep-fryer. Slide in the doughnuts and deep-fry until golden brown (p. 185).

To make lighter doughnuts, roast the okara lightly (p. 91) before combining with ½ cup flour and 1 or 2 eggs.

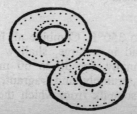

7

Curds and Whey

THE ART OF preparing homemade butter and cheese, and the vocabulary that went with it, are slowly disappearing from Western culture. But it was once commonly understood that when a solution of rennet—containing the enzyme rennin extracted from the membrane of the fourth stomach of unweaned calves, lambs, or kids—was added to cow's milk, or when the milk was left uncovered for several days in a warm place, it curdled, separating into a thin, watery liquid (whey) and soft white semi-solids (curds). The curds, primarily coagulated milk protein called "casein," could then be fermented and aged to make cheese, or churned to make butter.

Although many Westerners today have never seen or tasted curds, they were widely enjoyed by our forefathers and are still a common delicacy in countries such as India where they are served in curries and puddings with sliced bananas and oranges. When Yogananda, one of the first great Yoga masters to teach in the West, was considering a life of blissful meditation in solitude rather than one of working for the spiritual benefit of others, he was asked critically by his master: "Do you want the whole divine *channa* (curds) for yourself alone?" And the Indian saint, Ramakrishna, indicating how people tend to chit-chat aimlessly until something vital appears in their lives, once said: "When the curds, the last course, appear, one only hears the sound 'soop-soop' as the guests eat the curds with their fingers."

The process of making tofu curds from soymilk resembles that for making dairy curds from cow's or goat's milk. Soymilk can be curdled or coagulated with either a "salt" (such as nigari or magnesium chloride) or an acid (such as lemon juice or vinegar). When the coagulant is stirred into hot soymilk and the soymilk is allowed to stand undisturbed for several minutes, the milk separates into delicate, white curds and pale yellow whey.

Soymilk Curds

After stirring nigari into the soymilk in his large, cedar curding barrel, the tofu craftsman covers the barrel with a wooden lid and allows the nigari to begin its work. Slowly it coagulates the soy protein, which forms into curds and separates from the whey. After 15 or 20 minutes, the tofu maker rinses off a large, handsome bamboo colander and wraps its underside with cloth (Fig. 20). He sets this on the surface of the

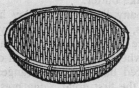

Fig. 20. A Bamboo Colander

mixture in the barrel and it slowly fills with whey. (The cloth keeps out the finer particles of curd.) The whey in the colander is ladled off and reserved for later use, and the colander is then weighted with a brick and replaced until it is again full (Fig. 21). This whey, too, is ladled off into a large wooden bucket where it forms a billowy head of foam (Fig. 22). When all the whey has been removed, only white curds remain in the barrel.

The Japanese refer to curds as *oboro*, meaning "clouded over, hazy, or misty." The same word is used

Fig. 21.   Weighting the Colander

Fig. 22.   Ladling Whey from Curds

in the translation of the Biblical passage "through a glass darkly," and for describing a moon half hidden in clouds. The term "oboro" is particularly appropriate when used in reference to the tofu-making process, for a container of curding soymilk looks like a translucent, amber sky filled with soft white clouds. Curds

made with nigari generally resemble cirrus clouds—
long, thin, and wispy. If stirred or handled too roughly,
they vanish. Curds made with calcium sulfate are more
substantial and billowing, like cumulonimbus.

Like the clouds it resembles in so many other ways,
oboro is transient; in a few moments it will be gone,
only to reappear as tofu. But before it vanishes or
changes form, it may be tasted. As soft as the most
delicate custard, warm fresh curds have the richness of
cream and a wonderful subtle sweetness.

When inviting guests to sample his *oboro,* the tofu
maker scoops up a small dipperful of curds, which he
empties carefully onto a bamboo pressing mat, allowing the curds to drain briefly. He then slides the curds
gently into a lacquerware bowl, seasons them with a
few drops of shoyu, and asks his guests to partake of
them while they are still warm. Many traditional masters have treated us to fresh curds in this way as we
watched them making tofu.

When curds are ladled into cloth-lined settling boxes
and pressed to make tofu, their fragile, almost insub-
stantial nature is given body and firmness. In most
shops the finished curds are then soaked in water for
several hours to firm and cool them, and thereby ensure maximum freshness. During the soaking, however,
some of the rich and subtly sweet flavor of the curds is
inevitably lost. Hence there are two simple ways to
make their full goodness available commercially: one
can either sell curds before they are pressed, or one can
refrain from soaking finished tofu in water. In Taiwan
and China, the warm curds themselves, called "flowers
of tofu," are sold from pushcarts by street venders
(Fig. 23). And many Chinese take a small pot or bowl
to the neighborhood tofu shop each morning to purchase these "flowers" for the family breakfast.

Almost all Japanese farmhouse tofu, and most commercial tofu in China and Taiwan, is allowed to cool
either in the settling box or on a wooden pallet. Since
these varieties of tofu are never soaked in water, their

Fig. 23. Selling Soymilk Curds

flavor remains closest to that of fresh curds. Home-made tofu can also be easily prepared in this way to keep it at its peak of flavor.

In Japan during the New Year's season, some tofu makers deliver warm curds from door to door. These are generally added to miso soups or seasoned with a little shoyu and any of the garnishes used for Chilled Tofu (p. 141). Curds are much more widely used in daily cookery in China than in Japan, being added there to noodle dishes, soups, and even sautéed vege-table dishes.

Many people may wonder why soymilk curds have never been fermented and aged in order to make Western-style cheeses. Research begun in the 1960s in California and Japan indicates that, in fact, tasty mild-flavored cheeses can be prepared inexpensively using bacteria from a dairy cheese starter and allowing well-pressed soymilk curds to ripen naturally for 3 to 9 weeks. These will soon be available commercially in flavors such as Cheddar (see Chapter 14).

In some parts of the United States, soymilk curds are now sold as Fresh Tofu Pudding, available in sealed polyethylene containers.

Whey

In the process of making tofu, whether at home or in a tofu shop, there are two inevitable byproducts: okara and whey. Containing valuable nutrients, both can be used in cooking. Whey is composed of 1 percent solids, 59 percent of which are proteins that were not solidified during the curding process. As shown in Figure 24, whey contains 9 percent of the protein originally found in the dry soybeans, plus much of the B vitamins and some of the natural sugars. It is produced in abundance whenever tofu is prepared; the curding process reduces 10 volumes of soymilk to about 1 part firmly-pressed curds and 9 parts whey. About 73.5 percent of the original soy protein and 50 percent of the solids (dry weight basis) are recovered in the final tofu. The main solids lost are water soluble carbohydrates, including oligosaccharides which are believed to cause flatulence or intestinal gas. The loss of these oligosaccharides is one factor that makes tofu so much more digestible than soybeans. However their presence in the whey together with an estimated 15 to 25 percent of the original soy nutrients makes the whey a mixed blessing.

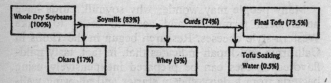

Fig. 24.   Percentage of Original Soybean Protein Contained in Byproducts of the Tofu-making Process

At tofu shops, where more than 15 to 20 gallons are produced each day, whey is used as an effective biodegradable soap. How does it work? During the curding process, some of the natural oils from the ground soybeans dissolve in the whey. These oils contain lecithin, which is well known for its ability to emulsify and dissolve fatty cholesterol deposits in the human bloodstream. In the same way, the lecithin in hot whey gently cuts through oils on anything it is used to wash and, when poured or stirred, forms a head of suds. The tofu maker carefully reserves the whey produced in his shop and uses it at the end of work each day to wash his tools. Both the deep-frying utensils and the barrels and dippers used for handling soymilk—which latter contains the natural oils found in soybeans—quickly become sparkling clean. On cold winter mornings, hot whey is also used to wash and warm the hands.

Some women use whey as a facial wash to remove oils and treat the complexion; others use it as a shampoo. It is also excellent for washing dishes, work clothes, or even fine silks. In Taiwan we noticed that many people come to tofu shops with a large pail to take home enough free "soap" to last for the day. In many homes it is used for washing and polishing wooden floors or woodwork, and for helping to give new woodwork a natural, seasoned look. Whey can also be used at home as a plant nutrient.

Like okara, warm whey is used to fatten livestock. Cows and horses are said to be able to gulp down a 3-gallon bucketful without taking a single breath. A tofu master in Kyoto told us how he offered a dray horse a pailful of whey one morning outside his shop. It seems that for years afterwards, whenever the horse passed, he stopped and refused to move until he was given his morning refresher.

Whey is collected in two different ways at tofu shops. First, as described above, it is ladled out of the curding barrel and reserved in a separate barrel or bucket. In addition, as it is pressed out of the tofu it is collected in the large wooden whey catch-box positioned underneath the forming boxes. If soymilk has been coagulated with just the right amount of nigari, its whey will have a transparent amber color and subtly sweet flavor. If too little coagulant is used, the whey will be cloudy due to the presence in it of uncoagulated soymilk proteins. If too much is used, the whey will be bitter. To preview the flavor of the tofu, many craftsmen therefore take a sip of whey as they begin to ladle it out of the curding barrel.

About 70 percent of the coagulant added to soymilk dissolves in and is separated off with the whey. Sometimes, therefore, when a little uncurdled soymilk remains in the bottom of the curding barrel, the tofu maker will solidify it by stirring in some warm whey.

We generally prefer to use the 9 to 10 cups of whey resulting from the preparation of Homemade Tofu (p. 127) as a soap for washing our utensils or as a source of nutrients for plants, the compost pile, or livestock. Some people use it in place of water or milk when making breads, pie doughs, and other baked goods, or as a tasty broth or soup stock. At last a soap so mild you can drink it!

Warm Soymilk Curds (Oboro-dofu)

Proceed as for Homemade Tofu (p. 127). Just after ladling the whey out of the cooking pot (i.e. before ladling the curds into the forming container), scoop curds by the ladleful from the firm upper layer in the pot. Carefully place each ladleful of curds into a soup bowl and allow to stand for 1 minute. Holding the curds with your fingertips, pour off any excess whey that may have accumulated in the bowl. Serve immediately as is or:

• Top warm curds with a few drops of shoyu, some whole or ground roasted sesame seeds and/or a dash of *sansho* pepper. Or serve with any of the dipping sauces, garnishes, or miso toppings used with Chilled Tofu (p. 141).

• Serve curds chilled, mixed with fresh fruit slices. Peaches, orange sections, or fruit cocktail are especially good.

• Serve as a dessert topped with a little maple syrup or honey, or as the Chinese dessert *toufu-hua,* topped with Sweet Peanut Sauce made by simmering together ¾ cup water, 3½ tablespoons unsalted peanuts, 1½ tablespoons natural sugar or honey, and ½ teaspoon shoyu.

• Serve ¼ to ½ cup fresh curds in each cup of your favorite miso soup (p. 165).

• Add curds to individual servings of tomato, onion, split pea or your favorite Western-style soups, then try seasoning lightly with shoyu or miso.

• Mix curds with lightly beaten eggs and stir into Chinese egg-flower soups.

• Gently stir curds into curry sauces or noodle dishes just before serving.

• Serve curds Chinese-style seasoned with soy sauce, minced garlic, chili powder, and sesame oil, or topped with Spicy Korean Miso Sauté (p. 44).

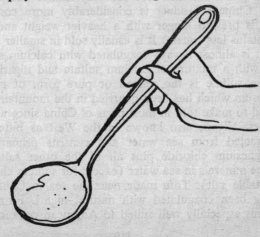

8

Tofu and Firm Tofu

THE TWO MOST POPULAR types of tofu in America (as well as in their respective countries) are Japanese-style tofu and Chinese-style firm tofu. Throughout this book we shall refer to the former as simply "tofu" or "regular tofu," and the latter as "firm tofu."

In Japan, tofu is also called *momen-goshi* ("cotton-filtered") to distinguish it from its popular counterpart *kinu-goshi* ("silken tofu"). In China, firm tofu is known in standard Mandarin, now the official language, as *toufu* (pronounced DOE-fu), but in Cantonese as *dowfu* or *daufu*.

Tofu: Regular and Firm

Regular and firm tofu are very similar except that the Chinese product is considerably more compact. (It is pressed longer with a heavier weight and thus contains less water.) It is usually sold in smaller cakes, and is almost always coagulated with calcium sulfate or with a mixture of calcium sulfate and nigari. Calcium sulfate is the refined or pure form of natural gypsum which has been quarried in the mountains and used to make tofu in most parts of China since ancient times. Nigari, also known in the West as bittern, is extracted from sea water and consists primarily of magnesium chloride plus all of the other salts and trace minerals in sea water (except for sodium chloride or table salt). Tofu made near the sea in China has long been coagulated with natural nigari. Firm tofu seems especially well suited to American cookery and

Fig. 25. Tofu

tastes. It has a more meaty texture and contains 25–35 percent more protein than Japanese tofu. Its firm, cohesive consistency allows it to keep its form well without additional pressing, making it ideal for use in frying, stir-frying, deep-frying, sautéeing, dicing in tossed salads (like cheese or ham), or puréeing to yield dressings, dips, spreads, sauces, or soups with an especially thick and creamy consistency. It is also very well suited for use in tropical or semitropical climates since its low water content helps it to stay fresh for up to several days without refrigeration or preservatives, and its firmness makes it easier to transport. Nine ounces of firm tofu can be substituted for 12 ounces of regular tofu in most recipes in this book.

Japanese-style tofu is prized for its softer, more delicate texture and, when made with nigari, its wonderful, subtly sweet flavor. Served on a hot summer's day as Chilled Tofu, it is a refreshing taste treat without equal. It also works very well in lighter dressings, fruit whips, mixed salads, desserts, and a host of other Western-style recipes described in this chapter. Although a little lower in protein than its Chinese counterpart, it is also lower in calories and makes for a lighter meal—more like yogurt or cottage cheese.

In addition to its specific uses described above, the word "tofu," like the word "bread" may also be used in a broader sense to refer to an entire family of foods;

seven basic types of Japanese tofu and some eighteen
types of Chinese tofu are described in the following
chapters and in Appendix C.

Name and Form

The word "tofu" has no exact equivalent in Western
cuisine and does not quite fit the English terms "soybean curd" and "soybean cheese" often used to describe it. Tofu is made *from* soybean curds just as
cheese is made *from* dairy curds: after ladling off whey
from the soymilk curds in his curding barrel, the tofu
maker scoops the curds into two cloth-lined wooden
forming boxes and tops them with a pressing lid and
heavy weight for about thirty minutes. During this time
the curds are firmed and made *into* tofu. The entire
tofu-filled box is then lifted into a tank of circulating
cold water (often well water), and inverted. Then the
box is lifted out, leaving the large (45-pound) block of
cloth-wrapped tofu resting on the bottom of the tank.
After the cloths are removed, a cutting board is slipped
under the tofu, and the tofu is cut under water into
individual small cakes. In Japan, tofu is generally
stored in the tank under water until it is sold; in China,
firmer "flats" to tofu may be placed uncut on wooden
pallets and taken to the marketplaces, where they are
then cut and sold. In either case, although the finished
product has the color and shape of a light cheese, it is
not fermented, aged, or ripened; hence the name "soybean cheese" is also inappropriate.

Tofu History in China

Of East Asia's three great soybean foods—tofu,
miso, and shoyu—only tofu has a theory associated
with its historical origin. According to ancient Chinese
and Japanese references, as well as to popular tradition, the method for preparing both soymilk and tofu
was discovered by Lord Liu An of Huai-nan in about

164 B.C. A famous scholar and philosopher, ruler and politician, Liu An is said to have been interested in alchemy and Taoist meditation. A close friend of many Taoist students, he may have undertaken his experiments with tofu as a way of introducing nutritious variety into their simple meatless diet. Historians believe that Liu An's tofu was probably coagulated with either nigari or seawater and had a firm texture similar to most of the tofu made in China today.

There are two basic theories which try to account for the discovery of tofu. Lord Liu An or earlier Chinese may have discovered the method for curding soymilk quite by accident. Since soybeans were considered one of the Five Sacred Grains, they were probably dried like other grains before being cooked. If later boiled, they would either be added to water whole, or first ground or mashed into a purée. If used in purée form, the result would be a thick "soup" that would have to be seasoned. If the cook added natural salt—which contains nigari—curds would soon form; the salt, intended as a seasoning, would have worked as a coagulant. The cook may later have decided to remove the fibrous okara from the purée to give the resulting curds a finer, more delicate texture. The next step, pressing, would have helped the food stay fresh longer and would have given it a texture firm enough to keep its form after being cut. The final result would then have been very similar to present-day tofu.

The second theory proposes that, since they did not generally raise cows or goats for milk, the Chinese were probably not familiar initially with the curding process; they may have learned it from the Indians in the south or the Mongols in the north, both of whom made curds and cheese. Advocates of the "importation theory" also note that the three other mild-flavored foods most favored by the Chinese—shark fins, swallow's nest, and trepang (sea slugs)—were also imported.

Tofu next appears in Chinese history about 800 years later. It is said that Bodhidharma, who lived in

China from about 520 to 528 and founded the Chinese *Ch'an* (Zen) school, engaged tofu in "Dharma combat" to probe tofu's understanding of the Buddha's way. Bodhidharma later praised tofu for its simplicity, its honest, straightforward nature, and its "lovely white robes."

The earliest existing document containing mention of tofu is the *Seiiroku,* written during the Sung Dynasty (960–1127), more than 1,000 years after the food's discovery. Numerous other books of this period refer to a work written about 60 to 100 B.C. (but no longer in existence) which contained the story of Lord Liu An and the earliest tofu. In a work of the late Sung Dynasty, there is a description of the menu served by a king to a prince, and tofu is included.

Tofu History in Japan

Tofu reached Japan during the eighth century and was probably brought from China by the numerous Buddhist monks and priests who were going back and forth between the two countries. Tofu is thought to have entered Japanese society through the upper classes, those who were connected with Chinese cultural and economic interchange, the court nobility, and the priesthood. Buddhist monks probably used tofu as a daily food in Japanese temples at a very early date. Emphasizing the value of a meatless diet, they were certainly a major factor in the early spread of tofu as a popular food. Some scholars believe that all of Japan's (and China's) earliest tofu shops were located within large temples or monasteries and were run by Buddhist priests and temple cooks.

During the Kamakura period (1185–1333), there was a large-scale movement to make Japanese Buddhism available to the common people. The five major Kamakura Zen temples each opened Buddhist vegetarian restaurants within their temple compounds, and existing records show that tofu was included on the menus. Laymen, having tasted tofu there for the first time, apparently learned from the monks how to prepare it, then opened their own shops in the capital cities of Kamakura and Kyoto. It was only later that tofu-making spread from the cities to the countryside.

During the Kamakura period, the new *samurai* ruling class practiced a simple, frugal, and down-to-earth way of life. These warriors greatly simplified the national cuisine by their example. It is said that tofu and miso replaced fresh river fish as the ruling shogun's prized delicacies, and that the samurai came to cherish deep-fried tofu pouches and tofu, particularly as ingredients in their breakfast miso soup. It was also at this time that farmers started growing soybeans on a large scale in Japan's cold, dry provinces.

During the Muromachi period (1336–1568) tofu spread throughout Japan and became a popular daily food at all levels of society. Many of the great tea masters of the period used tofu extensively in their Tea Ceremony Cookery, which helped to bring tofu into the world of Japanese haute cuisine and to introduce it to famous chefs and restauranteurs. Since most Japanese followed the Buddhist practice of refraining from eating the meat of "four legged animals," tofu was welcomed as a source of inexpensive and tasty protein. The Japanese went on to invent several new forms of the food, including dried-frozen tofu, deep-fried tofu burgers and pouches, grilled tofu, and silken tofu solidified with nigari.

As tofu became widely used in Japan, its basic character was gradually changed. In the hands of native craftsmen, tofu became softer, whiter, and more delicate in flavor. Farmhouse tofu alone retained some of the firmness and rich flavor of its Chinese predecessor.

When the Chinese Zen master, Ingen, came to Japan in 1661 he was surprised to find tofu unlike any he had known in China. In praise of this new food he composed an intricate yet simple proverb which is well known to this day. It described both the character of

Japanese tofu and that of a man who wishes to pass freely and peacefully through this fleeting, illusory world. The proverb went:

> *Mame de*
> *Shikaku de*
> *Yawaraka de*

Each line had a double meaning, allowing the poem to be read either:

Made of soybeans,	*or*	Practicing diligence,
Square, cleanly cut,		Being proper and honest
And soft.		And having a kind heart.

The word "tofu" first appears in a Japanese written document (the diary of Nakatomino Sukeshige) in 1183, where it is mentioned that tofu was used as a food offering at an altar. Mention is again made of it in a letter of thanks from the famous Buddhist priest Nichiren Shonin, written in 1239. The word "tofu" written with the present characters did not appear in Japan until the 1500s. The first Japanese "Book of Tofu" *(Tofu Hyaku Chin)* was written in 1782 and contained 100 tofu recipes culled from throughout Japan. A famous book in its day, it is still widely quoted.

Throughout its long history in Japan, tofu has appeared in numerous forms, some of which no longer exist. For example, when the Zen master Ingen, mentioned above, established the well-known Mampuku-ji temple south of Kyoto, he taught the monks and local tofu masters how to prepare Chinese-style Pressed Tofu. Although this very firm variety became popular during the next century, it is now prepared by only one shop in Japan and is featured in Zen Temple Cuisine only in restaurants near Mampuku-ji. A closely related type of firm tofu called *rokujo-dofu* was prepared by tying 5 pieces of pressed tofu together with rice straw (Fig. 70), then drying them in direct sunlight until they were dark brown and quite hard. Finely shaved, rokujo-dofu was used like bonito flakes; it is presently prepared only in Fukushima prefecture. A third variety of virtually extinct tofu was walnut tofu, prepared by mixing chunks of walnuts into soybean curds just before they were pressed. Chinese fermented tofu (called *nyufu* in Japan and *toufu-ru* in China) was transmitted to Japan in early times and became popular among the aristocracy, in temples, and in a few rural areas. Its strong flavor, however, led to its gradual decline; today it is rarely if ever seen.

As tofu became a part of the language and culture in both Japan and China, it came to be used in proverbs and sayings. In China, finding fault with a person is compared to "finding a bone in your tofu." When a Japanese wants to tell a person to "get lost," he may say "Go bump your head against the corner of a cake of tofu and drop dead." Or when speaking of something as being hopeless he might say "It's as futile as trying to clamp two pieces of tofu together."

Tofu became a part of the culture in other ways too. For example, in the Women's Mass for Needles, started 1600 years ago by the Emperor Nintoku and still practiced in Japan, a cake of tofu is placed on the household altar and all the needles that have been bent or broken during the year are thrust into it. Each needle is thought of as a living being whose body has been sacrificed in service, and the woman of the house, as an expression of her gratitude, gives it this soft resting place as a reward for its hard work.

Up until the start of World War II, virtually all Japanese tofu was prepared in small household shops from soy purée cooked over a wood fire in an iron cauldron and soymilk coagulated with natural nigari. Only after World War II did new coagulants (such as calcium sulfate) and ways of cooking (such as with pressurized steam) come into vogue. In recent years, large shops and factories have begun to mass-produce tofu; each 10½ ounce cake is water-packed in a polyethylene container, thermally sealed with a sheet of transparent film, and pasteurized by immersion for one hour in hot water to give a shelf life of up to 1 week. Distributed over an area of several hundred miles in refrigerated trucks, this tofu is sold in supermarkets and neighborhood grocery stores at a price slightly below that of the tofu sold in most neighborhood shops.

Today an estimated 90 percent of all the tofu in Japan is served in only *three* recipes, Chilled Tofu, Simmering Tofu, and Miso Soup, a fact that we find to be most unusual, given tofu's remarkable versatility. Most of the rest is served as Mabo-dofu, Dengaku, Iridofu, or Oden, recipes described in this chapter.

In recent years researchers in various parts of the world have found that tofu can also be made from protein-rich legumes other than the soybean: peanuts, winged beans (coagulated with calcium sulfate), and okra seeds (coagulated with lemon juice) may be but a few of the many possibilities.

The Great Leap Westward

About 900 years passed from the time of the discovery of tofu in China until its arrival in Japan. Another 1,200 years passed before it made the leap westward across the Pacific Ocean to America, where the first commercial tofu shops began operation in about 1900. Some of the largest shops began, strangely enough, during World War II in Japanese relocation camps. At Heart Mountain, Wyoming, for example, over 2,000 pounds of tofu were prepared daily by and for the Japanese there. Today, tofu shops are opening all across America (see Appendix B). Business is booming with sales increasing at about 25 percent a year. Quality, low cost tofu is available at many large supermarket chains as well as at natural food stores. The history of tofu in the West has really just begun, with an exciting start.

PREPARATORY TECHNIQUES

The following procedures are used regularly in cooking with tofu. Try to master them from the outset, since each gives the tofu a unique consistency and texture. The eight techniques listed below are in order of the amount of water each allows to remain in the tofu. Thus parboiling, the first technique, expels very little water, while crumbling rids the tofu of more than 65 percent of its moisture, leaving it very firm and containing more than 20 percent protein. Fig. 26 shows the effect of each technique on the weight, protein, and moisture content of a 12 ounce cake of tofu originally containing 7.8 percent protein and 84.9 percent water.

When fresh tofu is mashed or blended, 9 ounces yield 1 cup, and 12 ounces yield approximately 1½ cups.

Fig. 26. Effects of Preparatory Techniques on 1 Cake of Tofu

Preparatory Technique	Final Weight of 12 oz of Tofu (oz)	Percent Protein in Final Tofu (%)	Percent Reduction in Weight from Loss of Water (%)
Parboiling	11.5	8.0	3.5
Draining	10.0	8.5	17.0
Pressing	8.5	10.0	30.0
Squeezing	6.5	13.0	47.0
Scrambling	6.3	13.5	48.0
Reshaping	4.5	19.0	63.0
Crumbling	4.0	20.5	66.0
Grinding	4.0	21.0	67.0

Parboiling

This technique is used with both regular and silken tofu for at least four different purposes: 1) To warm the tofu before serving it topped with hot sauces; 2)

To freshen stored tofu that shows signs of spoiling; 3) To make the tofu slightly firmer so that when simmered in seasoned broths it absorbs flavors without diluting the cooking medium; 4) To impart to the tofu a slight cohesiveness desired when preparing *aemono* (Japanese-style tofu salads).

The addition of a small amount of salt to the water seasons the tofu slightly, imparts to it a somewhat firmer texture, and makes possible longer parboiling without the tofu developing an undesirably porous structure. (It is for these reasons that *kombu* or salt are generally added to the broth of Simmering Tofu and other *nabe* preparations.)

Because parboiling causes a slight loss in some of the tofu's delicate flavors, it should be used only when necessary.

• *Regular Parboiling:* Bring 1 quart water to a boil in a saucepan. Reduce heat to low and drop in tofu. Cover and heat for 2 to 3 minutes, or until tofu is well warmed. (For a firmer texture, cut tofu into 4 equal pieces before parboiling.) Lift out finished pieces with a slotted spoon.

• *Salted Water Method:* Bring 2 cups water to a boil in a saucepan. Add ½ teaspoon salt, drop in (uncut) 12-ounce cake of tofu, and return to the boil. Remove pan from heat and allow to stand for 2 to 3 minutes. Remove tofu, discarding water.

Draining

Draining or storing tofu out of water (for no more than 12 hours) gives it a fairly firm texture and also helps preserve its flavor, since its subtle natural sweetness is lost quite easily in water.

Place the tofu in a 1- or 2-quart flat-bottomed container. Cover well and refrigerate for 1 to 2 hours or, for a firmer texture, overnight.

If set on a small colander or folded towel placed

into the container beforehand, the tofu will drain even more thoroughly.

If two cakes are stacked one on top of the other, the one on the bottom will be almost as firm as if it were pressed (see below).

If the tofu was purchased in a sealed plastic tub, prick a tiny hole in bottom of tub, drain out any water, and place tofu and tub in container as described above.

Pressing

When pressing tofu, it is important to preserve the form and structure of the cake so that it may later be cut into thin slices. Tofu is fully pressed when it can be picked up and held vertically in the air without crumbling. Pressing time may be varied to suit the dish being prepared: light pressing preserves the tofu's softness for use in tossed salads, while lengthy pressing gives firmer, stronger tofu for use in deep-frying.

Because of its delicate texture and unique structure (which holds water in millions of tiny "cells") silken tofu must be handled very gently during pressing. Chinese-style firm tofu, because of its cohesive structure and low water content, may be used without further pressing in any recipe calling for pressed tofu. Pat its surface dry with a cloth before use.

• *Towel and Fridge Method:* Wrap the tofu firmly in a small terry-cloth or cotton towel folded into fourths (below), and set on a plate in a refrigerator for 1½ to

2 hours or overnight. To decrease the pressing time, drain the tofu beforehand, place a 2- or 3-pound weight on top of the tofu, and replace the damp towel with a dry one after about 30 minutes. Or cut the cake horizontally into halves before pressing and place in the towel as illustrated.

• *Slanting Press Method:* Wrap the tofu in a towel or bamboo mat *(sudare)* (or sandwich the tofu between bamboo mats) and place on a cutting board, tray, or large plate next to the sink; raise the far end of the board several inches. Set a 2- to 4-pound weight on the tofu and let stand for 30 to 60 minutes (below).

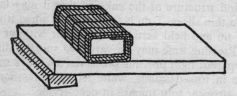

• *Sliced Tofu Method:* Cut the tofu crosswise into ½- to ¾-inch-thick slices and arrange on two towels placed on a raised cutting board (below). Cover the slices with a double layer of towels and pat lightly to ensure even contact. Allow to stand for 15 to 60 minutes. This method is commonly used when preparing tofu for deep-frying. For faster results, top with a cutting board and 5-pound weight and change the towels after 10 minute intervals.

Squeezing

This process results in a mashed tofu that is slightly cohesive and has a texture resembling that of cottage cheese.

Place drained, parboiled, pressed, or firm tofu at the center of a large dry dishtowel and gather its corners to form a sack. (Or use a tofu pressing sack if available.) Twist sack closed, then squeeze tofu firmly, kneading it for 2 or 3 minutes to expel as much water as possible (below). Squeeze lightly enough so that no tofu penetrates the sack. Empty the squeezed tofu into a mixing bowl.

Scrambling

This technique causes a further separation of tofu curds and liquid whey resulting in a texture similar to that produced by squeezing, but one which is slightly firmer and more crumbly.

Place tofu in an unheated skillet. Using a (wooden) spatula, break tofu into small pieces. Now cook over medium heat for 4 to 5 minutes, stirring constantly and breaking tofu into smaller and smaller pieces until whey separates from curds. Pour contents of skillet into a fine-mesh strainer; allow curds to drain for about 15 seconds if a soft consistency is desired, or for about 3 minutes for a firmer consistency. Spread curds on a large plate and allow to cool to room temperature.

Reshaping

This process yields a tofu cake having a very firm and cohesive consistency similar to that of natural cheese, or processed ham. Called *oshi-dofu,* or "Pressed Tofu," in Japan, it is used in recipes calling for pieces the size of French-fried potatoes which hold their shape during cooking or tossing.

The first method given below takes about twice as long as the second, but yields a tofu that retains more of its natural flavor and texture. The addition of salt that it calls for prevents the tofu from developing a somewhat elastic, web-like structure while also seasoning it. The second method yields a firmer structure that holds together better during sautéing. The tofu undergoes a slight loss in flavor that is not very noticeable if served with a well-seasoned sauce in the typical Chinese style.

• *Firm Seasoned Tofu:* Combine 24 ounces tofu and 1 teaspoon salt in a saucepan; mix well. Stirring constantly, cook over medium heat for about 4 minutes or until tofu begins to boil vigorously. Pour the tofu into a cloth-lined colander in the sink and allow to drain for several minutes. Transfer the cloth onto a cutting board and carefully fold the edges of the cloth over the tofu; shape the tofu into a cake about 5 inches square and 1 inch thick. Place a pan filled with 3 or 4 quarts of water on top of the cloth (below) and press for 1 to 2 hours in a cool place. Unwrap and cut as directed; or re-wrap in a dry towel and refrigerate for later use.

• *Very Firm Tofu:* Boil the tofu in unsalted water as when crumbling (see below). Drain tofu, then proceed as above, pressing the tofu for 30 to 60 minutes.

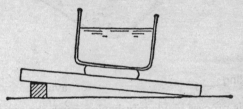

Crumbling

By reducing its water content to a minimum, we can obtain tofu with much the same texture as lightly sautéed, crumbly hamburger. Yet the tofu is slightly firmer, lighter, and fluffier, which makes it ideal for use in tossed salads, egg and grain dishes, spaghetti or curry sauces, and casseroles. (Silken tofu, too, can be crumbled, either by the method described below or by scrambling [p. 123] and then pressing as follows.)

Combine 12 ounces tofu and 1 cup water in a saucepan. With a wooden spoon or spatula, break the tofu into very small pieces while bringing the water to a boil. Reduce heat and simmer for 1 to 2 minutes. Place a colander in the sink and line with a large cloth (or a tofu pressing sack). Pour the contents of the pan onto the cloth, gather its corners to form a sack, then twist closed. Using the bottom of a jar or a potato masher, press the tofu firmly against the bottom of the colander to expel as much water as possible. Empty the pressed tofu into a large bowl and allow to cool for several minutes. Now break the tofu into very small pieces, using your fingertips or a spoon.

Grinding

This process yields tofu having much the same light, dry consistency as crumbled tofu, but with a texture that is finer and more uniform.

Using either regular or silken tofu, prepare reshaped or crumbled tofu (p. 125). Refrigerate tofu in a covered container until well chilled. Then, cutting into chunks if necessary, run through a meat grinder with a medium-fine attachment.

Homemade Tofu

If you find that fresh tofu is not available at a nearby store, try preparing your own at home using either whole soybeans or powdered soymilk. It's as enjoyable as baking bread—and considerably faster.

Homemade Tofu
MAKES 29 TO 39 OUNCES

We have found the following recipe, based on the traditional Japanese farmhouse method, to be easy to follow and virtually foolproof. The tofu will be ready 50 to 60 minutes after you start. One pound of soybeans yields about 3 to 4 pounds of tofu at a cost about one-third to one-fourth that of commercial tofu and less than one-half the cost (on a usable protein basis) of hamburger. Solidified with nigari, and served at its peak of freshness, homemade tofu contains a fullness of flavor and subtle sweetness seldom found in even the finest storebought varieties.

UTENSILS

To make fine homemade tofu, you will need the following common kitchen tools (Fig. 27):
A "cooking pot" with a lid (6 to 8 quarts)
A saucepan or teapot with lid (2 to 3 quarts)
A "pressing pot" or basin (6 to 10 quarts), the deeper the better
A large round-bottomed colander (that will rest in the mouth of the "pressing pot")
A "pressing sack" (see below) or a 2 foot square of coarsely woven cloth
An 18-inch square of cheesecloth, or a light cotton dishtowel of comparable dimensions
A "forming container" (see below) or flat-bottomed colander, preferably square or rectangular
A sturdy electric blender, food or grain mill, a

juicer (such as a champion) which can "purée" foods without separating juice and pulp, or a meat grinder

A long-handled wooden spatula or spoon
A rubber spatula
A sturdy 1-quart jar or potato masher
A 1-cup measuring cup
A set of measuring spoons
A fine-mesh strainer (wire or bamboo)
A shallow ladle or dipper about 1 inch deep and 3½ inches in diameter, or a large spoon

The use of a proper pressing sack and forming container, each easy to assemble, will make the work even easier. Both are now also widely available in commercial Tofu Kits (which also contain cheesecloth and nigari), sold at most natural food stores or mail ordered from The Soyfoods Center, P.O. Box 234, Lafayette, CA 94549.

• To make a pressing sack, obtain a piece of sturdy, coarse-weave linen or muslin cloth 15 by 36 inches. Each mesh opening should be big enough to poke a

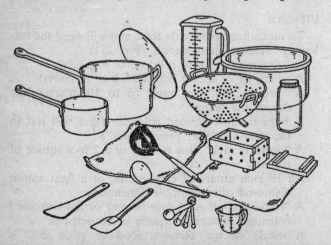

Fig. 27. Utensils for Making Tofu

pin through; too tight a weave will greatly reduce your tofu yield. Fold the cloth end to end, then sew the bottom and two-thirds of one side closed to give a sack 18 inches wide and 15 inches deep.

• The three containers shown in Fig. 28 can easily be made at home. Good inside dimensions are 4 by 7 by 4 inches deep. To make container (a) drill or use a hot skewer to pierce a number of ⅜-inch-diameter holes in the bottom, sides, and top as shown. (Or use a hammer and large nail to make similar holes from the inside out in a regular bread pan; file off any sharp edges.) Containers (b) and (c) have removable bottoms, allowing for easy removal of the tofu even if the container is not immersed in water. Good woods to use are Philippine mahogany, vertical-grain Douglas fir, pine, maple, cedar, or cherry. Join the sides with ring-shafted boat building nails, dowels, or rustproof screws. Drill ⅜-inch-diameter holes as shown. Fashion a flat wooden or plastic pressing lid (with or without holes) to fit down inside the box. To remove wood flavor and aroma from wooden boxes, scrub with a dilute solution of laundry bleach, rinse thoroughly, and dry in the shade (never in direct sunlight).

INGREDIENTS

Soybeans: The soybeans now sold at almost all natural- and health-food stores, most co-ops, and some supermarkets will make good tofu (p. 66). Beware of using soybeans that are more than one year old. They may yield a starchy-thick milk that clogs the pressing sack, has a poor flavor, and gives low tofu yields. Especially high-yielding soybeans are available from some tofu shops (see Appendix B).

Coagulants: All of the basic tofu coagulants listed below are readily available. We prefer to use nigari (bittern) since we find it gives tofu the best flavor: Natural nigari (the traditional Japanese coagulant), is now available at most natural food stores, and some

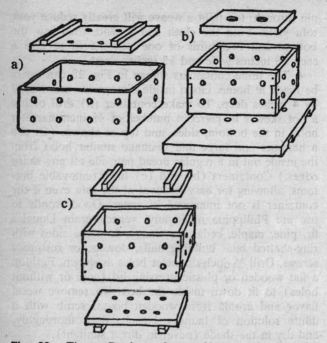

Fig. 28.   Three Designs for a Homemade Forming Container

tofu shops; liquid nigari can be prepared at home by placing moist natural sea salt in a sack hung over a pot and collecting the drippings. Refined nigari (magnesium chloride) or calcium chloride are available at your local school chemistry lab or from chemical supply houses. Seawater, which makes especially delicious tofu, can be gathered from clean stretches of ocean. Epsom salts or calcium sulfate (the refined form of gypsum, the earliest Chinese tofu coagulant) give somewhat higher bulk yields and a softer product by incorporating more water into the tofu. Lemon juice and vinegar, which are not used in tofu shops, give rather low yields of slightly granular, subtly tart tofu.

Thus your choice of coagulant depends on the type of tofu you want:

For subtly sweet, nigari tofu: 1½ teaspoons finely ground or moist (or 2 teaspoons coarse-granular) natural nigari, magnesium chloride, or calcilum chloride; or 1½ to 2½ teaspoons homemade liquid nigari; or 1½ cups seawater (freshly collected).

For mild, soft tofu use: 2 teaspoons Epsom salts (magnesium sulfate) or calcium sulfate; or 1½ tablespoons each calcium lactate and lemon juice (the latter being stirred into the soymilk just after the last of the calcium lactate has been added).

For subtly tart or sour tofu use: 4 tablespoons lemon or lime juice (freshly squeezed), or 3 tablespoons (cider) vinegar.

Method

1½ cups (275 grams) whole dry soybeans, washed, soaked in about 6 cups water for 10 to 12 hours; rinsed, and drained
16 cups water, approximately
Coagulant (see above)

1) Run 7½ cups (hot) water into cooking pot and 6 cups (hot) water into saucepan or tea kettle; cover both and bring to a boil over high heat. Meanwhile, place pressing pot in sink and set colander into pot. Moisten pressing sack (or 2-foot square of cloth) and line colander with sack, fitting mouth of sack over rim of colander. Moisten cheesecloth or light cotton dishtowel and use to line inside of forming container. Place container in or near sink, set atop a small bowl or pan if you wish to save the whey (Fig. 29a).

2) Divide drained beans into 2 squal portions. Combine 1 portion in a blender with 1 cup tap water, than add 1 cup boiling water from the saucepan (or 2 cups hottest tap water, about 175°F). Cover and purée at high speed for 1½ to 2 minutes, or until very smooth. (See that blender does not overheat.) Add

Fig. 29.   Preparing Homemade Tofu

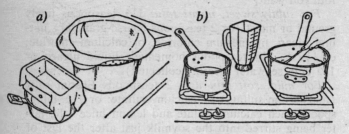

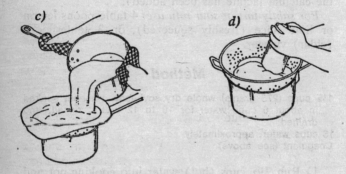

purée to water *boiling* in pot, then turn off heat under pot and re-cover. Purée the remaining soybeans with 2 cups hottest water and add to pot. Rinse out blender with ¼ cup (hot) water to retrieve any purée, and add to pot; fill blender with cold water to soak. (If using a food mill or juicer, grind beans without adding water, but increase water in cooking pot to 11½ cups.)

3) Stir purée briefly in cooking pot (Fig. b), then pour contents of pot into sack (Fig. c). Using a rubber spatula, retrieve any purée remaining in pot and transfer to sack. Quickly rinse out cooking pot with could water and return it to stove.

4) Twist closed mouth of sack. Using a glass jar or potato masher, press sack repeatedly against colander to extract as much soymilk as possible (Fig. d). Open

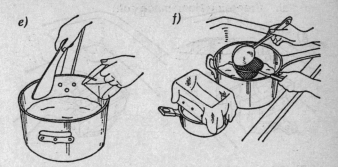

mouth of sack wide in colander, stir solids (okara) briefly, then measure out 3 cups boiling water from the saucepan and pour over okara. Stir again, twist closed sack, and again press repeatedly with jar. Now shake okara into one corner of sack, twist closed, and give a final strong pressing to extract any remaining soymilk. Pour soymilk into cooking pot; reserve okara for use in cooking.

5) Bring soymilk to a boil over high heat, stirring bottom of pot frequently, then reduce heat to medium and simmer for about 7 minutes. While simmering, measure coagulant into dry 1-cup measuring cup and set aside.

6) Remove pot from burner. Add water to coagulant in measuring cup (unless using sea water) until total volume equals 1 cup; stir until coagulant dissolves. Using wooden spoon or spatula, stir soymilk back and forth vigorously 5 or 6 times and, while stirring, pour in ⅓ cup coagulant solution. Stir 5 or 6 times more, making sure to reach bottom and sides of pot. Now stop spoon upright in soymilk and wait until liquid movement ceases; lift out spoon (Fig. e). Sprinkle another ⅓ cup coagulant solution over surface of soymilk, cover pot, and wait 2 to 3 minutes while curds form slowly—from the bottom up. Use this time to wash utensils, first in cold water.

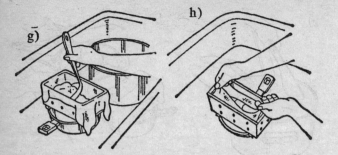

7) Stir remaining ⅓ cup coagulant solution. Uncover pot and, while very slowly stirring upper ½-inch-thick layer of curdling soymilk, sprinkle coagulant solution a little at a time over milky areas. (If soymilk has completely curdled, do not add more coagulant; proceed to step 8.) Cover pot and wait 3 minutes. (Wait 6 minutes if using Epsom salts or calcium sulfate.) Uncover and stir surface layer again for 20 to 30 seconds, then gently push spatula down edge of pot to the bottom in several places to free any soymilk that may be trapped below curds; stir again until all milky liquid curdles. Large delicate curds should now be floating like white clouds in the pale yellow whey.

(If any uncurdled milk liquid remains, dissolve one-fourth of the original amount of coagulant in ⅓ cup water and sprinkle over the uncurdled portions; stir gently until curdled.)

8) Place cooking pot in sink next to forming container. Gently press fine-mesh strainer partially into curds and whey so that only whey collects in strainer. Ladle all whey out of strainer and over cheesecloth in forming container so cloth clings smoothly to sides of container (Fig. f). Repeat until most whey is removed from curds, then set strainer aside.

9) Now gently ladle fragile curds—and any remaining whey—into forming container one layer at a time (Fig. g). Fold edges of cloth neatly over curds (Fig. h), place lid atop cloth, and set a 1½-to-3-pound

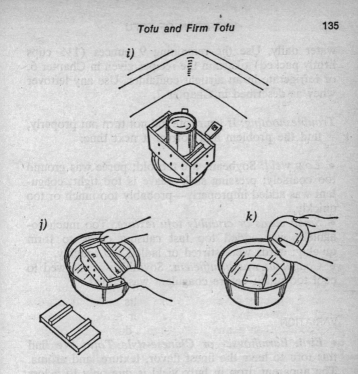

i)

j)

k)

weight on lid to press tofu for 15 minutes (Fig. i). (For firm tofu, use a 5-pound weight for 20 minutes.)

10) Fill a large basin or sink with cold water. Remove weight and lid, and submerge tofu-filled container in water (Fig. j). Slowly invert then lift out container, leaving cloth-wrapped tofu in water. Gently unwrap tofu under water, then cut cake crosswise into halves. Leave tofu in water for 3 to 5 minutes, until firm. Meanwhile, wash all pots and cloths. Then, using a small plate for support, lift out tofu cakes and drain them briefly (Fig. k).

To enjoy the flavor of the tofu itself, serve immediately as Chilled Tofu (p. 141). Tofu to be served later in the day should be refrigerated on a plate covered with plastic wrap; for storage up to 5 to 7 days, refrigerate tofu immersed in water and change the water daily. Use the remaining 9 ounces (1½ cups firmly packed) okara in the recipes given in Chapter 6, or refrigerate in an airtight container. Use any leftover whey as described in Chapter 7.

Troubleshooting: If your tofu did not turn out properly, find the problem and correct it next time.

- *Low yield:* Soybeans are too old; purée was ground too coarsely; pressing sack weave is too tight; coagulant was added improperly—probably too much or too quickly.
- *Small curds or crumbly tofu texture:* Too much coagulant was added too fast causing curds to form quickly; curds were stirred or ladled too roughly.
- *Coagulant was insufficient:* Soymilk was allowed to cool too much before coagulant was added.

VARIATION

- *Firm Farmhouse- or Chinese-style Tofu:* We find this tofu to have the finest flavor, texture, and aroma. The apparent drop in bulk yield is due only to a loss of water, not of protein or other nutrients.

Cook the puréed soybeans in a heavy iron pot over an open wood fire. Use a nigari-type coagulant and, if possible, new-crop, organically grown (Japanese) soybeans. Ladle the curds quickly and not too carefully into the forming container, and press for 30 minutes with a 5-pound weight. Then invert the container leaving the tofu resting on the lid. (Or lift off the sides of a farmhouse-style container [Fig. 30].) Remove the cloths and serve the tofu without immersing it in water.

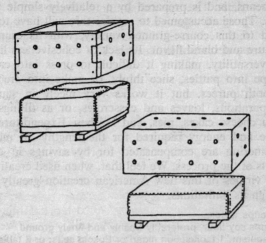

Fig. 30. Removing Tofo from a Farmhouse-style
Forming Container

Coarse-grained Soy-flour Tofu

MAKES 48 OUNCES

Here is America's first major contribution to the art
of tofu making—although it may actually be identical
to the earliest progenitor of Chinese tofu. Developed
by Frank and Rosalie Hurd (authors of the cookbook,
Ten Talents), Edith Cottrell (author of the *Oats, Peas,
Beans, and Barley* cookbook), and folks at The Farm
in Tennessee this product is fundamentally different
from most Oriental tofu in that it contains okara in the
final product and is prepared either from storebought
soy flour or freshly ground unsoaked soybeans. Its
virtues are that it can be prepared without use of an
electric blender, makes more complete use of the soy
nutrients and dietary fiber, gives a firm tofu with a
slightly (5 to 15%) higher yield per weight of dry

soybeans, and is prepared by a relatively simple process. Those accustomed to regular tofu will have to get used to this coarse-grained variety, with its crumbly texture and bland flavor. Its lack of cohesiveness limits its versatility, making it difficult to press into cakes, shape into patties, slice thinly, or make into creamy-smooth purées, but it works very nicely in sautéed preparations, loaves and casseroles, or as fillings for tofu cheese cakes, pies, and knishes. Expenditures of time and energy required for the lengthy 20 minute simmering are compensated for by savings in other parts of the process. We feel that, when used creatively, the virtues of this new American creation greatly outweigh its limitations.

19 cups water
4 cups soy flour, preferably freshly and finely ground
Coagulant: 1 tablespoon nigari or Epsom salts; or 6 table-
    spoons lemon juice or vinegar

Bring 18 cups water to a boil in a large pot. Add soy flour slowly, whisking to dissolve lumps and return to the boil. Reduce heat, and simmer, stirring bottom occasionally, for 20 minutes. Remove from heat and proceed to add coagulant dissolved in the remaining 1 cup water as explained in steps 6 and 7 of the basic recipe. Press the curds in the settling container with an 8- to 10-pound weight. Or, as The Farm folks do, transfer the unpressed curds directly into a pressing sack or dishtowel lining a colander set over a pot, then press and squeeze the contents; this gives the tofu a firm texture and rounded form. Refrigerate immediately or use in cookery.

VARIATION

• *Pressure-cooked Soy Flour Tofu:* Developed at The Farm, this method completely defies everything we know about making tofu—but it works. Bring 8 cups of water to a boil in a pressure cooker. Stir in 2 cups soy flour until no lumps remain, then mix in the coagulant: 1½ teaspoons nigari or calcium sulfate dissolved in ¼ cup water, or 3 tablespoons lemon juice or vinegar. Bring cooker to full pressure (15 pounds) and simmer for 7 minutes, then remove from heat and allow pressure to come down naturally. Open cooker and—voila: curds and whey. Proceed from step 8 in the basic recipe for Homemade Tofu. Makes 25 ounces.

Homemade Tofu (from Powdered Soymilk)
MAKES 20 TO 23 OUNCES

Tofu made from powdered soymilk is not quite as delicious as, and is somewhat more expensive than, tofu made from whole soybeans. However the process takes only about 35 minutes—as compared with 50 minutes when using whole soybeans—and is considerably easier since it is not necessary to grind the beans or remove and press the okara. One cup of powdered soymilk gives about the same yield as one cup of whole soybeans. Note that when using powdered soymilk, the whey which separates from the curds will be somewhat milkier than the whey from whole soybeans, even after the curds are well formed.

1 cup powdered soymilk
9 cups water
Coagulant; see any of the coagulants in the amounts listed in the recipe for Homemade Tofu (p. 127)

Combine powdered soymilk and water in a 1- to 1½-gallon pot. Whisk milk until well dissolved, then bring to a boil over high heat, stirring from time to time. Measure coagulant into a dry, 1-cup measuring cup and set aside. Reduce heat and simmer soymilk for 3 minutes. Add 1 cup water to coagulant and stir until dissolved. Proceed from step 6 as for Homemade Tofu.

Five-Color Tofu (Gomoku-dofu)
MAKES 21 OUNCES

Although no longer widely available in Japan, this

delicious tofu used to be prepared in traditional tofu shops on festive occasions or on special order. It was then usually deep-fried like tofu cutlets (p. 185). The deep-fried variety is still available in the food section of several of Japan's finer department stores.

Ingredients for Homemade Tofu (p. 127)

¼ cup grated carrot
¼ cup grated burdock root or minced lotus root
¼ cup minced mushrooms or cloud-ear mushrooms
¼ cup green beans, fresh corn, or ginkgo nuts, parboiled in lightly salted water

Prepare soymilk as in steps 1 through 5 of Homemade Tofu. After cooking soymilk for 5 minutes, stir in vegetables. Now proceed as for homemade tofu, steps 6 through 10. Serve as Chilled Tofu (p. 141) or, for best flavor, deep-fry and serve as Homemade Deep-fried Tofu Cutlets (p. 253).

VARIATIONS: (Use 2 to 4 tablespoons of each finely cut ingredient.)

• *Seashore Gomoku:* Hijiki, green *nori* flakes, bamboo shoots, sesame seeds, burdock root, and leeks.
• *Wild Mountain Vegetable Gomoku:* Osmund fern, cloud-ear mushroom, butterbur, and bamboo shoots.
• *Gohoji-dofu:* Use ¾ cup parboiled green soybeans.

TOFU QUICK AND EASY

In Japan, the quickest and easiest ways of serving tofu are also generally considered the most delicious. Here, in the preparation of food as in all the arts, simplicity is honored as the foundation of fine taste and beauty. The following dishes can be served at any meal and require no cooking at all.

Chilled Tofu *(Hiya-yakko)*
SERVES 1

Many connoisseurs maintain that this is the only recipe you need to know when using tofu. They are quick to add, however, that a creative cook can serve

Chilled Tofu in a different way each day of the year if full use is made of seasonal garnishes, subtly flavored dipping sauces, and richly seasoned toppings.

Chilled Tofu is at its best, though, on hot summer afternoons and balmy summer evenings. Both regular and silken tofu (p. 311) may be used in preparing it: silken tofu is preferred for its smooth, custard-like texture, and regular tofu for what many consider to be its more full-bodied flavor. Most important is the quality and freshness of the tofu itself.

It is said that this simple way of enjoying tofu first appealed to Japan's *yakko,* or lowest ranking samurai, about 300 years ago. A combination feudal retainer-servant-valet-and-footman, the yakko was not allowed to carry a sword, but was well known to the common folk because he marched at the very front of the procession whenever his lord made a public appearance. His prescribed uniform was a navy blue, waist-length coat with large square sleeves resembling heraldic banners. A distinctive 6- to 8-inch white square, the yakko's "crest" or "coat of arms," was dyed on the center of each sleeve. Since the color and shape of this square resembled the cubes of chilled tofu the yakko loved to eat, the new dish came to be known as "chilled yakko." And to this day, Japanese recipes call for cutting a 12-ounce cake of tofu into *yakko,* meaning 6 cubes. Chilled tofu is best cut and eaten with chopsticks since the cut surface is then better able to hold or absorb dipping sauces and garnishes.

6 to 8 ounces *fresh* tofu (regular or silken), chilled
1½ to 2 teaspoons shoyu, Shoyu Dipping Sauces (p. 37), Sweet Simmered Miso (p. 39), Finger Lickin' Miso or regular miso
Garnishes and Condiments (next page)

Place the tofu on a small plate or in a shallow bowl. If desired, cut tofu into 1-inch cubes.

If using shoyu or a shoyu dipping sauce, sprinkle it over the tofu and top with your choice of garnishes and/or condiments. Or serve the shoyu separately in a

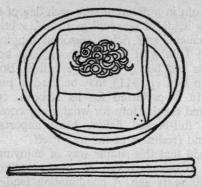

Fig. 31. Chilled Tofu

small dish and arrange the garnishes on a platter
nearby (Fig. 31). Invite each person to add garnishes
to the shoyu to taste.

If using miso or a miso topping, place a dab of the
miso on top of the tofu and serve without garnishes.

Garnishes and Condiments (in order of popularity):
    Thinly sliced leeks or onions, rinsed and pressed
    Grated or slivered gingerroot
    Crushed or minced garlic
    Bonito flakes
    Thin strips of *nori*
    7-spice chili powder
    Slivered *yuzu* peel
    Grated fresh *wasabi* or *wasabi* paste
    Wasabi pickled in sake lees
Popular Combinations:
    Gingerroot and leeks
    Bonito flakes, gingerroot, and leeks
    Nori and bonito flakes
    Hot mustard and bonito flakes
    Gingerroot, leeks, 7-spice chili powder, and bonito flakes

Iceberg Chilled Tofu

SERVES 1

6 to 8 ounces tofu, cut into 1-inch cubes
Shoyu or Shoyu Dipping Sauces (p. 37)
Garnishes and Condiments for Chilled Tofu (above)

Place the tofu cubes in a small serving bowl. Arrange 4 to 6 ice cubes around tofu, then add enough cold water to just cover tofu. Serve the shoyu or dipping sauce in a separate small dish accompanied by a variety of garnishes. Serve immediately to prevent tofu's subtle sweetness from being lost to the water.

Chilled Tofu with Applesauce & Granola

SERVES 2

6 ounces tofu, drained (p. 120) and chilled
¼ teaspoon salt
1 cup applesauce, chilled
½ cup raisins
Dash of cinnamon
¼ cup crunchy granola or nuts

Mash tofu together with salt. Mix in applesauce and raisins. Serve topped with cinnamon and granola.

TOFU DRESSINGS, SPREADS, DIPS, AND HORS D'OEUVRES

Using an electric blender, you can make a wide variety of Western-style tofu preparations in less than a minute. When blended or mashed, a 12-ounce cake of tofu makes about 1½ cups. Fresh or dried herbs make nice additions to many of these recipes.

Most of the following dressings plus Tofu Sour Cream can also be used with excellent results as sauces: spoon them over cooked vegetables just before serving. To prevent separation, do not reheat.

Creamy Tofu Dressings & Dips

MAKES 1 CUP

Here is a wonderful way to introduce tofu into your daily menu, served over salads like a thick Roquefort dressing, used as a dip with fresh carrot, celery, and jicama slices or potato chips, or even as a high-protein sandwich spread. Quick and easy to prepare, the possible variations are virtually unlimited. Each is thick, rich, and full of flavor, yet has only about one-fourth the calories of a typical mayonnaise-or-dairy-based dressing and is entirely free of cholesterol. The perfect answer for those who love creamy dressings but wish to avoid their typical oily qualities, saturated fats, and high cost. Several companies are now marketing a line of these dressings (shelf-life 2 months) in America.

6 ounces (⅔ cup) tofu, drained or pressed (p. 121) if desired; or firm tofu
1½ to 2 tablespoons lemon juice or vinegar
2 to 2½ tablespoons oil
¼ teaspoon salt
1 teaspoon shoyu, or 1½ teaspoons red miso, or ¼ teaspoon salt
Choice of seasonings (see below)

Combine all ingredients in a blender and purée for 20 seconds, or until smooth. (Or mash all ingredients and allow to stand for 15 to 30 minutes before serving.) If desired, serve topped with a sprinkling of minced parsley or a dash of pepper. Refrigerated in a covered container, these preparations will stay fresh for 2 to 3 days and their consistency will thicken—delectably. Can also be frozen.

SEASONINGS

Use any of the following (listed with our favorites first):

• *Garlic & Dill:* ½ to 1 clove of minced garlic and ¼ teaspoon dill seeds. Serve topped with a sprinkling of 1 tablespoon minced parsley. Also nice with only garlic.
• *Curry:* ½ teaspoon curry powder and 2 tablespoons minced onion. Top with a sprinkling of 1 tablespoon minced parsley.
• *Cheese & Garlic:* ¼ cup Parmesan or grated cheese and ½ clove of minced garlic (or ¼ onion). Serve topped with a sprinkling of minced parsley.

• *Roquefort:* In addition to the tofu use 1½ table-spoons lemon juice, 3 tablespoons oil, 1 tablespoon Roquefort cheese, ½ clove of garlic, ½ teaspoon salt, and ¼ teaspoon each fresh mustard and, if desired, pepper.

• *Onion:* ¼ cup diced onion. Excellent on all types of deep-fried tofu and with many vegetable dishes.

• *Gingerroot:* 1 teaspoon grated or 1½ teaspoons powdered gingerroot and a dash of 7-spice chili powder or Tabasco sauce. Try over tomato & cucumber salads. Top with a sprinkling of parsley.

• *Avocado:* 1 well-ripened avocado, peeled, seeded, and mashed. For tang, add a few drops of Tabasco and 2 tablespoons minced onion.

• *Carrot:* ¼ cup grated carrot and 2 teaspoons minced onion. Top with a sprinkling of parsley.

• *Sesame:* 2 tablespoons sesame butter or tahini and, if desired, 1 clove of crushed garlic.

• *Walnut:* ¼ cup each walnut meats and ketchup or tomato purée. Try over a salad of hard-boiled eggs, asparagus, and tomato wedges.

• *Pickle:* 2 small Western-style cucumber pickles. Nice over tomato wedges.

• *Herb:* ½ teaspoon fresh or dried herbs (oregano, marjoram, basil, caraway, etc.).

Tofu Mayonnaise

MAKES 1 CUP

At last a delicious mayonnaise that is easy to make at home—it takes less than a minute—is low in fats and calories, and is entirely free of cholesterol-rich eggs. Commercial mayonnaise, by comparison, must, by law, contain at least 80 percent fats—and most homemade varieties have even more. The following recipe, which serves 4 to 6, contains a total of only 466 calories, whereas an equal weight of commercial mayonnaise contains 1820 calories, or four times as many.

6 ounces tofu, drained and pressed (p. 121) if desired; or firm tofu
1½ to 2 tablespoons lemon juice or vinegar
2 tablespoons oil
½ teaspoon salt
Dash of pepper (optional)

Combine all ingredients in a blender and purée for about 20 seconds, or until smooth. Store as for Creamy Tofu Dressings (above).

Oil-free Tofu Dressings & Dips

MAKES 1¼ CUPS

Here is the answer for weight-watchers who love creamy dressings. If a blender is not available, simply mash ingredients together with a fork.

6 ounces tofu
1 tablespoon grated gingerroot
2½ teaspoons shoyu
1 tablespoon sesame butter, tahini, or ground roasted sesame seeds
1½ teaspoons honey

Combine all ingredients in a blender and purée until smooth. For variety, combine 6 ounces tofu with 3 tablespoons peanut butter, 1 tablespoon vinegar or lemon juice, and 1½ to 3 teaspoons honey.

Chinese-style Tofu-Sesame-Shoyu Dressing

MAKES 1½ CUPS

12 ounces tofu
2 tablespoons shoyu
2 teaspoons sesame oil
½ teaspoon honey
1 to 2 tablespoons minced leek, scallion, onion, or parsley
(optional)

Combine all ingredients, mashing well. Serve over tomato and cucumber slices.

Tofu Tartare Sauce

MAKES 2½ CUPS

1 cup minced Western-style cucumber pickles
8 ounces tofu
4 tablespoons oil
5 tablespoons lemon juice
1 teaspoon salt
½ teaspoon hot mustard
2 hard-boiled eggs
2 tablespoons diced onions
2 tablespoons minced parsley
2 tablespoons chopped green olives (optional)

Combine ¼ cup minced pickles with the next five ingredients and purée in a blender until smooth. Combine with the remaining pickles and other ingredients and mix well. Serve with deep-fried tofu and tofu croquettes. If desired, top with a sprinkling of parsley.

Tofu-Egg Spread

MAKES 1½ CUPS

12 ounces tofu, squeezed (p. 123)
2 hard-boiled eggs, diced
2 tablespoons oil
1 to 2 tablespoons lemon juice
½ teaspoon salt or 1 tablespoon red miso
2 tablespoons minced onion (optional)
1 tablespoon minced parsley

Combine the first six ingredients in a blender and purée
for 30 seconds. Garnish with the parsley and serve as
a sandwich spread.

Tofu, Peanut Butter & Banana Spread

SERVES 6 TO 8

12 ounces tofu
½ cup peanut butter (preferably unsalted)
1½ bananas
2 tablespoons lemon Juice
1 to 2 tablespoons honey

Combine all ingredients in a blender and purée until
smooth. (Or beat with a mixer in a large bowl.) Serve
as is on whole wheat bread, or top with nuts, raisins,
and thinly sliced bananas. Also delicious served simply
as a fruit purée.

Tofu Guacamole

MAKES 1½ CUPS

1 avocado, peeled and seeded
8 ounces tofu
3 tablespoons lemon juice
2 tablespoons oil
2 cloves of garlic, chopped or crushed
¾ teaspoon salt
2 teaspoons shoyu
¼ cup water

Combine all ingredients in a blender and purée until
smooth. (Or mash thoroughly with a fork; or whip.)
Delicious either as a dip or dressing. Try with tacos
or tortillas. Can be stored frozen.

Tofu Pickled in Miso (Tofu no Misozuké)

MAKES 6 OUNCES

   This preparation, salty and richly fragrant, has a
soft, cheeselike consistency resembling that of Chinese
fermented tofu.

12 ounces tofu, well pressed (p. 121)
Miso Bed:
    ½ cup red, barley, or Hatcho miso
    ½ teaspoon grated gingerroot
    ½ teaspoon sesame oil
    1 teaspoon sake or white wine
    Dash of 7-spice chili powder or Tabasco sauce

Cut pressed tofu crosswise into ½-inch-thick slices
and parboil for 3 minutes (p. 119); drain and allow
to cool to room temperature. Combine all ingredients
to make miso bed, mixing well. Place one-half the mixture into a shallow 1-quart container and smooth to
form an even layer. On this arrange the tofu slices,
cover with remaining miso mixture, and then with a
layer of plastic wrap spread over miso surface to keep
out air; allow to stand for 12 to 15 hours. Remove
tofu carefully from container and wipe off miso on
tofu surface with a damp cloth. Cut into ½-inch cubes
and serve with rice or, for best flavor and aroma, broil
on both sides until well browned before serving. Also
delicious as hors d'oeuvre.

Tofu Canapés

MAKES 16

16 slices of buttered bread or toast, each 1 by 3 inches
1½ tablespoons red miso or Walnut Miso (p. 40)
3 tablespoons sweet white, red, or Sweet Simmered Miso
    (p. 39)
12 ounces tofu, pressed (p. 121) and cut crosswise into 16
    slices
Canapé Toppings: Your choice of the following, thinly sliced:
    Hard-boiled eggs
    Cucumbers
    Tomatoes
    Green peppers
    Cheese
    Snow peas or green beans, parboiled
    Potatoes or sweet potatoes, steamed
    Carrots

Spread half of the bread pieces with red miso and half

with white miso. Cover each piece with a slice of tofu, and top with one slice of any of the canapé toppings. Pierce with foodpicks if desired.

If miso is unavailable, sprinkle the tofu and topping with a few drops of shoyu. Substitute crackers for the bread.

DAIRYLIKE TOFU PRODUCTS

In recent years, a growing number of people have begun to cut way back on their consumption of dairy products. Why? First, they are becoming very expensive. Second, many find they cause nasal congestion, are mucus forming and difficult to digest, and contain a relatively high level of chemical toxins. Third, for the growing number of Americans who are overweight or have high blood pressure, doctors are recommending the substitution of foods low in cholesterol, saturated fats, and calories. And, finally, we are increasingly understanding how commercial production of dairy products aggravates the world food crisis as we feed cattle large amounts of our finest grains and soy, which could be used directly by human beings.

Yet for many people, having to do without dairy products is difficult, if not a real struggle. Not only do they miss the rich dairy flavors, they may also find their culinary repertoire drastically restricted. If you are one of these people, your problems may now be over. Try the following recipes; we think you'll be surprised and delighted with the results . . . and the cost. See also Tofu Cheesecake (p. 210).

Tangy Tofu Cottage Cheese

SERVES 2

12 ounces tofu, well-drained or pressed (p. 121); or firm tofu
2 tablespoons oil or ¼ cup mayonnaise (tofu or egg)
2½ to 3 tablespoons lemon juice or vinegar
½ teaspoon salt or 2 teaspoons shoyu
1 clove of garlic, crushed or minced (optional)
Dash of pepper (optional)

Mash together all ingredients. Delicious on fresh vegetable salads.

VARIATIONS

● *Rich & Tangy:* Omit garlic and salt. Add 3 tablespoons red miso, 2 tablespoons minced parsley, and 1 tablespoon honey. If desired, top with a sprinkling of roasted sesame seeds.

● *Regular:* In addition to tofu use ½ teaspoon salt, 1 tablespoon oil, 1½ tablespoons lemon juice, and, if desired, a dash of pepper.

● *Sweetened:* In addition to the tofu use 2 tablespoons honey or natural sugar and, if desired, a dash of salt and ½ teaspoon vanilla extract. Nice with fresh fruit salads topped with raisins, slivered almonds, or sunflower seeds.

Tofu Whipped Cream or Yogurt

MAKES 1½ CUPS

This delicious fat-free preparation can be used like whipped cream or, as the basis of desserts, like yogurt.

12 ounces tofu
2 tablespoons honey
Pinch of salt
½ teaspoon vanilla extract

Combine all ingredients in à blender and purée until smooth. To serve as yogurt, top with a sprinkling of slivered almonds or walnut meats, shredded coconut, and raisins. Or reduce the sweetening by one-half and top with Okara Granola (p. 99).

Tofu Carob Frosties

MAKES 4

Dissolve 1 to 2 tablespoons carob (or cocoa) powder in an equal volume of cold (soy or dairy) milk, then add to the ingredients for Tofu Whipped Cream (above). Serve in cones or dessert dishes.

Tofu Sour Cream

MAKES 1½ CUPS

12 ounces tofu, parboiled (salted water method, p. 120) and
    squeezed (p. 123)
2 tablespoons lemon juice
¼ teaspoon salt

Combine all ingredients in a blender and purée until
smooth.

Tofu Cream Cheese

MAKES 1 CUP

Easily prepared at home, tofu cream cheese contains
no animal fats and costs about one-fourth as much as
its dairy counterpart. Use as you would dairy cream
cheese but do not reheat.

12 ounces tofu, squeezed (p. 123)
2 tablespoons oil
⅜ teaspoon salt
Dash of white pepper
1 teaspoon lemon juice (optional)

Combine all ingredients in a blender and purée until
smooth and thick.

Tofu Icing

MAKES 1 CUP

12 ounces tofu, squeezed (p. 123); or 1 cup Tofu Cream
    Cheese (above)
2 tablespoons honey
½ teaspoon vanilla
Dash of salt
2 tablespoons powdered milk (optional)
1½ teaspoons grated lemon or orange rind (optional)

Combine all ingredients in a blender and purée for 30
seconds; refrigerate until just before serving on cake
or cupcakes.

Tofu Ice Cream

SERVES 3 OR 4

18 ounces tofu, well chilled
3 tablespoons honey
¼ teaspoon vanilla extract
⅛ teaspoon salt

Combine 12 ounces tofu, honey, vanilla, and salt in a blender and purée for about 1 minute. Transfer to a covered container and place in the freezer overnight.

Purée remaining 6 ounces tofu in the blender until smooth. Cut the frozen tofu into small chunks. While puréeing at high speed, add a few chunks at a time to the tofu in the blender until all has been added and the mixture is smooth and thick. Serve immediately.

For variety, add toward the end of puréeing: 1 egg yolk, 2 to 4 tablespoons each chopped almonds or shredded coconut, and your choice of fresh or frozen fruits. Serve topped with chopped nutmeats. Or add 1 teaspoon powdered green tea (*matcha*) and 1 additional tablespoon honey; omit vanilla.

Banana-Tofu Shake

SERVES 3 TO 4

6 ounces (nigari) tofu
3 small frozen bananas, or fresh bananas and 3 ice cubes
1 tablespoon honey
¼ cup toasted wheat germ
¼ teaspoon nutmeg
¼ cup cold milk (soy or dairy)

Combine all ingredients in a blender and purée until smooth. Serve immediately. When milk is omitted, this preparation has the texture of banana ice cream.

TOFU IN SALADS

Tofu is a wonderful addition to almost any salad. Its soft texture complements the crisp crunchiness of fresh vegetables. And because tofu has so few calories per gram of protein, tofu salads can be enjoyed by weight-watchers.

Tofu can take at least 6 different forms when served in salads. Mashed or squeezed and lightly seasoned, it resembles cottage or ricotta cheese. Lightly drained and cubed, it can be used with or in place of croutons. Well-pressed and diced, it has the texture of soft cheese and goes well in marinated salads. Parboiled and crumbled, it may be used to keep a salad light. Reshaped and cut into thin strips, it has the consistency of firm cheese or ham. Finally, blended and seasoned, tofu can be turned into a variety of rich and creamy salad dressings.

Western-style Salads

We have divided the following tofu salads into Western and Japanese varieties depending on the type of dressing used and the method of preparation. Thus, a number of the Western salads—characterized by the use of a dressing containing oil and/or dairy products generally served over fresh, crisp greens and vegetable slices—also may contain typically Japanese ingredients.

Cauliflower Salad with Mashed Tofu

SERVES 4

1 small cauliflower
12 ounces tofu, mashed
2 ounces cheese, diced (optional)
¼ cup sunflower seeds (optional)
Caesar Dressing, or your favorite

Steam cauliflower for 10 minutes or until tender. Allow to cool, then separate into flowerets. Combine in a large bowl with remaining ingredients; toss lightly.

Or, marinate flowerets overnight in a well-seasoned oil and vinegar dressing.

Carrot, Raisin & Walnut Salad with Tofu

SERVES 4

6 ounces tofu, pressed (p. 121) and mashed; or 4½ ounces firm tofu
1 cup grated carrots, or diced apple or celery
½ cup raisins
½ cup (roasted) walnut meats, diced
1½ tablespoons red, barley, or Hatcho miso
1 teaspoon honey
1 teaspoon sake or white wine
2 tablespoons sesame butter
4 lettuce leaves (optional)

Combine all ingredients, mixing well. If desired, serve mounded on lettuce leaves. Also delicious in sandwiches and on toast.

Curried Rice Salad with Tofu

SERVES 6

18 ounces tofu, pressed (p. 121) and broken into very small pieces; or 13½ ounces firm tofu
2½ cups cooked Brown Rice (p. 51), chilled
3 tablespoons minced green onion or leek
2 tablespoons minced parsley
2 green peppers; one slivered and one cut into rings
Dressing:
   6 tablespoons oil
   ⅓ cup (rice) vinegar
   1 tablespoon lemon juice
   1 teaspoon curry powder
   ¼ teaspoon 7-spice chili powder
   1 clove of garlic, crushed
   ¾ teaspoon salt
   Dash of pepper
4 lettuce leaves
1 tomato, cut into wedges

Combine the first four ingredients with the slivered green pepper. Add dressing, mix lightly and, for best flavor, allow to stand for several hours. Serve mounded

on lettuce leaves in a large bowl; garnish with tomato
wedges and green pepper rings.

Lettuce and Tomato Salad with Mashed Tofu

SERVES 4

12 ounces tofu, mashed
Caesar or bleu cheese dressing
4 lettuce leaves
3 tomatoes, cut into wedges
2 cucumbers, cut into ovals
¼ cup sunflower seeds (optional)

Combine tofu and dressing in a bowl; mix well. Divide
lettuce leaves among 4 serving dishes. Place tomato
wedges and cucumber slices on top of lettuce, then top
with tofu-dressing mixture and a sprinkling of sunflower seeds.

Western-style Vinegared Shira-ae (Shirozu-ae)

SERVES 2

6 ounces tofu, pressed (p. 121) and mashed
1 tablespoon sesame butter or tahini
1 tablespoon lemon juice
1½ tablespoons vinegar
½ teaspoon salt or 1 tablespoon red miso
1 teaspoon sake or white wine
1 cucumber or small carrot, sliced into thin rounds
2 hard-boiled eggs, chopped
¼ cup walnut meats
¼ cup raisins
2 tablespoons minced cucumber pickles (optional)

Combine the first six ingredients, mixing until smooth.
Gently stir in the remaining ingredients and serve immediately.

Tossed Green Salad with Soft Tofu Cubes

SERVES 4

6 to 8 lettuce or Chinese cabbage leaves
1 tomato, cut into thin wedges
2 fresh mushrooms, thinly sliced
1 large cucumber, cut into thin ovals
1 green pepper, thinly sliced
1 hard-boiled egg, diced
¼ cup French Dressing
6 ounces tofu, drained (p. 120) and cut into ½-inch cubes
½ teaspoon salt
¼ cup sunflower seeds (optional)

Tear lettuce into salad-sized pieces and combine with the next five ingredients. Add the dressing and toss lightly. Now add the tofu cubes and season with salt; toss again. Serve topped with a sprinkling of sunflower seeds.

Fresh Fruit Salads with Tofu Dressings

• *Tofu Whipped Cream* (p. 305): Serve over any or all of the following: strawberries, thinly sliced apples, bananas, pears, peaches, or melon balls.
• *Tofu Cottage Cheese* (p. 150): Especially tasty as a filling for pear halves.
• *Sweetened Tofu Cottage Cheese* (p. 151): Serve in the same way as for Tofu Whipped Cream. Add a few drops of vanilla if desired. If using apples as the basis of the salad, top with raisins, slivered almonds or walnuts, sunflower seeds, and a sprinkling of toasted wheat germ and cinnamon. If using bananas, try the same toppings but substitute nutmeg for cinnamon.

Japanese-style Salads

In Japan, mixed foods served with a seasoned dressing are called *aemono*. Unlike most Western salads, which are made with vegetables in their raw state, these *aemono* salads are generally prepared with lightly cooked vegetables and served in tiny portions as an accompaniment to a main dish, which they are meant

to complement in color, texture, and taste. Most
aemono contain little or no oil, mayonnaise, or dairy
products. The dressing, generally prepared with vinegar (or lemon juice) and shoyu or miso, is often quite
sweet. *Aemono* are generally named after the dominant
seasonings in the dressing: Sesame Miso-ae, Mustard-
Vinegar Miso-ae, Walnut Miso-ae, etc.

Shira-ae with Miso and Kinome

SERVES 4

Shira-ae, or "white salad," is one of Japan's most
popular—and, in our opinion, most delicious—tofu
dishes. All varieties are at their best when chilled for
4 to 6 hours before serving. They are delicious used as
fillings for tofu pouches or as spreads for buttered toast
or sandwiches. Any of the following recipes may be
prepared without sugar, or with less than half the
amount ordinarily used. To make tangy *Shirozu-ae* (p.
156), add several tablespoons of vinegar or lemon
juice to your favorite variety of Shira-ae, and reduce
the amount of sugar slightly.

1 cake of *konnyaku,* cut into small rectangles and parboiled
1 carrot, cut into small rectangles
½ cup dashi (p. 35), stock, or water
½ teaspoon shoyu
½ teaspoon salt
1½ tablespoons honey
4 tablespoons ground roasted sesame seeds; or 2½ table-
    spoons sesame butter, or *tahini*
4 ounces tofu, parboiled and pressed (p. 121)
2 tablespoons sweet white miso or 1 tablespoon red miso
4 sprigs *kinome,* or substitute minced mint leaves

Combine the first five ingredients with 1 tablespoon
sugar in a small saucepan. Simmer until all liquid is
absorbed or evaporated, then allow vegetables to cool
to room temperature. To the sesame seeds in the *suribachi* add tofu, miso, and 2 tablespoons sugar; grind
together with a wooden pestle, then mix in the vegetables. Serve individual portions garnished with a sprig
of *kinome.*

Shira-ae with Sweet Potatoes and Konnyaku

SERVES 4 TO 6

½ small carrot, cut into matchsticks and parboiled
1 cake of *konnyaku*, cut into matchsticks and parboiled
3 tablespoons dried (cloud-ear) mushroom, reconstituted
      drained, and cut into thin strips
3 tablespoons sugar
2 tablespoons shoyu
6 tablespoons ground roasted sesame seeds; or
      3 tablespoons sesame butter, or *tahini*
¼ teaspoon salt
12 ounces tofu, well pressed (p. 121)
1 small sweet potato, steamed and cut into ½-inch cubes

Combine the first four ingredients with 2 tablespoons
sugar in a small saucepan. Simmer until most of the
liquid has been absorbed or evaporated. Cool to room
temperature, then drain. To the ground sesame seeds
in the *suribachi* add salt, tofu, and 1 tablespoon sugar.
Grind or mash together well. Mix in the potatoes and
vegetables.

Lotus Root Salad with Tofu Dressing

SERVES 2 OR 3

6 lettuce leaves
1 tomato, cut into thin wedges
Tofu-Garlic Dressing:
      6 ounces tofu, mashed
      ½ clove garlic, crushed
      1½ tablespoons lemon juice
      3 tablespoons oil
      ¼ teaspoon salt
      Dash of pepper
½ cup thin half-moons of lotus root, parboiled

Spread lettuce leaves in individual salad bowls and
arrange tomato wedges around the leaves. Combine
dressing ingredients in a small bowl and mix with a
whisk or chopsticks until smooth. Stir in the lotus root
and mound the mixture on the lettuce leaves.

TOFU WITH SANDWICHES AND TOAST

Tofu sandwiches may be used as the main course for a high-protein, low-calorie lunch. Thin slices of pressed tofu contribute to sandwiches much the same texture as a soft, mild cheese. The firm crunchiness of whole-grain toast and the softness of tofu make a particularly nice combination. The use of miso or shoyu is the key to seasoning. Due to protein complementarity (p. 23), serving tofu and wholewheat bread together can yield up to 42 percent more protein.

Clubhouse Sandwich with Fried Tofu

MAKES 3

One 7-ounce cake of firm tofu, cut horizontally into thirds
3 tablespoons oil
¼ cup whole-wheat flour
⅓ cup ketchup
½ teaspoon mustard
3 slices whole-wheat toast, each spread with butter and mayonnaise
3 small lettuce leaves, each cut into halves; or 1 cup alfalfa sprouts
6 tomato slices
6 dill pickle slices

Place tofu slices between double layers of dish toweling and allow to stand for 5 minutes while texture firms. Heat a skillet and coat with the oil. Dust tofu slices with flour, then fry for 2 to 3 minutes on each side, or until golden brown. Combine ketchup and mustard in a small bowl, mixing well, then spread on toast. Top each slice of toast first with lettuce (or sprouts), then with tomato and dill slices, and finally with fried tofu. Serve sandwiches open faced, cut into halves if desired.

VARIATIONS

• *Pan-fried Tofu Sandwich:* Omit whole-wheat flour.

Make tofu in Pan-fried Tofu (with garlic, p. 178). Spread 2 tablespoons mayonnaise or buttered toast, then assemble sandwich: first lettuce, then tomato (or sprouts) and tofu. Top with a second slice of toast.

● *Other Ideas:* Sprinkle slices of pressed, uncooked tofu with a little shoyu (or spread with a thin layer of miso). Serve on buttered bread or toast, topped with dill pickles or cucumbers, lettuce, tomatoes, sprouts, cheese, or sliced hard-boiled eggs. Season with a dash of pepper and, if desired, a few more drops of shoyu.

Breakfast Toast with Pan-fried Tofu

SERVES 1

1 slice of whole-wheat toast, buttered
1 serving of Pan-fried Tofu (p. 178) or Tofu Cutlet Sauté
  (p. 253)

Serve toast hot, topped with the tofu slices. A quick, easy, and delicious way to start the day with soy-and-grain protein complementarity.

Curried Tofu in Pita Bread

SERVES 3 OR 4

Also known as "pocket bread," pita is a round, hollow, Mid-eastern bread that can be cut crosswise into halves, each of which are opened to form a pouch. Stuffed with a variety of foods, it makes a novel and delicious sandwich.

2 tablespoons oil
2 cups sliced mushrooms
2 cups sliced onions
½ cup thinly sliced carrot (half moons)
2 cups shredded or sliced cabbage
14 ounces firm (Chinese-style) tofu, mashed (2 cups)
5½ to 6½ tablespoons margarine or butter
2 tablespoons whole-wheat flour
1 cup water
1 teaspoon curry powder
1 teaspoon salt
6 (whole-wheat) pita breads (7-inch diameter), each cut into
  halves

Heat a large skillet and coat with the oil. Add mushrooms and sauté for 2 minutes. Add onion and carrots, and sauté for 2 minutes. Add cabbage and sauté for 2 minutes more; remove from heat.

Melt 2½ tablespoons margarine in a small skillet. Add flour and sauté for 30 seconds, until lightly browned. Mix in curry powder and salt, then add water slowly, stirring constantly. Cook, stirring for 1 minute, then mix in tofu and cook for 1 minute more. Now combine tofu-curry mixture and fried vegetable mixture in a large bowl, mixing well.

Heat 1 tablespoon margarine in the large skillet. Add 3 pita bread halves and fry for 1 to 2 minutes on each side, or until golden brown, then remove from skillet and open into pouches with a spatula or knife. Repeat until all pita halves are fried and opened; allow to cool for 5 minutes. Stuff pita pouches with tofu-vegetable mixture. Serve hot or cold. For variety, use deep-fried tofu.

Tofu-Grilled Cheese Sandwich

SERVES 4

4 slices of whole-wheat bread, buttered
2 teaspoons mustard
¼ cup (tofu) mayonnaise (p. 145)
4 thin slices of tomato
12 ounces tofu, pressed (p. 121) and cut crosswise into eighths
Shoyu or 2 teaspoons red miso
4 slices of cheese

Spread each piece of bread with mustard and mayonnaise, and top with a slice of tomato and 2 slices of tofu. Season tofu with a few drops of shoyu or a thin layer of miso, then cover with the cheese. Broil until cheese melts.

Or place tofu on top of cheese and broil until tofu is lightly browned.

Sliced Tofu on Toast with Onion Sauce

SERVES 4

.4 slices of whole-grain toast, buttered
1 cup Onion Sauce (p. 46), cooled
1¾ teaspoons shoyu
2 ounces cheese, grated
12 ounces tofu, pressed (p. 121) and cut crosswise into
    eighths
Shoyu

Arrange the toast on individual serving plates. Combine onion sauce and shoyu in a bowl; mix well. Spoon the mixture over the toast, sprinkle on cheese, and top with 2 slices of tofu. Season with a few drops of shoyu.

TOFU IN SOUPS

Fresh tofu adds flavor, protein, and a delightful texture to almost any soup. Cut into small cubes, crumbled, thinly sliced, or made into dumplings, it should be added to the soup 1 or 2 minutes before you have finished cooking. (If cooked over high heat or for too long, tofu loses some of its softness and delicate texture.) Use about 2½ to 3 ounces of tofu per serving. In each of the following recipes, silken tofu, deep-fried tofu, grilled tofu, frozen tofu, or yuba may be substituted for the regular tofu.

Western-style Soups

Some of the Western-style soups we believe go best with tofu include onion, tomato, mushroom, cabbage, squash or pumpkin, bean, split pea, and lentil. The addition of a small amount of miso or shoyu, and perhaps an egg or some grated cheese, to a soup containing tofu often enhances its overall taste and texture.

Creamy Tomato & Tofu Soup

SERVES 4

1 tablespoon oil
1 onion, diced
1 tomato, diced
1 cup milk (soy or dairy)
1 teaspoon salt
Dash of pepper and/or Tabasco sauce
½ clove of crushed garlic; or ¼ teaspoon oregano, mar-
    joram, or garlic powder
12 ounces tofu
2 tablespoons minced parsley

Heat a pot and coat with the oil. Add onion and sauté over medium heat for 3 minutes, or until transparent. Add tomato and sauté for 2 or 3 minutes more. Add the next five ingredients and cook, stirring constantly, for 1 minute. Remove from heat and allow to cool briefly, then add tofu, transfer to a blender, and purée until smooth. Serve hot, as is or, for best flavor, chill and serve garnished with the parsley. Nice in summer.

Creamy Tomato-Rice Soup with Tofu

SERVES 5 OR 6

1 cup cooked Brown Rice (p. 51)
1¼ cups milk (soy or dairy)
¾ cup water
½ onion, diced
2 large tomatoes, diced
4 teaspoons shoyu or 1 teaspoon salt
Dash of pepper
½ teaspoon honey (optional)
Dash of basil or oregano
¾ cup grated cheese
12 ounces tofu or 6 ounces deep-fried tofu, diced

Combine the first nine ingredients in a blender and purée until smooth. Transfer to a heavy-bottomed pot and bring just to a boil. Cover and simmer for 15 minutes, stirring occasionally. Mix in the cheese and tofu, return just to the boil, and remove from heat. Serve hot or, for a richer, sweeter flavor, chill for 4 to 6 hours.

Tofu-Onion Soup

One of the most delicious of all Western-style soups with tofu. Simply substitute 12 ounces tofu for the deep-fried tofu in the recipe for Onion Soup with Tofu Cutlets (p. 230).

Japanese-style Soups

Savory miso soups and delicately flavored clear soups almost always feature tofu and are among the most popular of all home and restaurant preparations.

About Miso Soup

In Japan, more tofu is used in miso soup than in any other type of cookery. Of the three most popular ways of serving tofu—chilled, simmering, and in miso soup—only the latter is enjoyed throughout the year and at any of the day's three meals. And since miso soup is an indispensable part of the traditional Japanese breakfast—together with rice and *tsukemono* (salt-pickled vegetables)—tofu makers generally start work long before sunrise to be sure that fresh tofu is ready for early morning shoppers.

In Japan, entire cookbooks are devoted to the preparation of miso soup. By using fresh seasonal vegetables, sprigs and even flowers, the sensitive cook is able to reflect in a dark lacquerware soup bowl the great rhythms of the four seasons. And by combining various types of miso with the proper choice of seasonings and seasonal garnishes, it is quite easy to prepare a unique type of miso soup each day of the year. In fact some Japanese cookbooks contain detailed and elaborate charts suggesting different ways of preparing miso soup each day of the week at both breakfast and dinner throughout the year.

Yet of all the many ingredients used in miso soups, tofu is the most essential and widely used. The most popular forms are small cubes of regular tofu and thin slices of deep-fried tofu pouches, although each of the other types of tofu and yuba are also used on occasion.

For the Japanese, miso soup is much more than just a food; it is a cherished and traditional cultural possession which can inspire poetry and touch the heartstrings while warming the body and soul. For some, miso soup is one of the keystones of good health and family harmony, the hallmark of a good wife who expresses her love and judgment through cooking. A well-known Japanese proverb even goes so far as to say that only when a young woman has mastered the art of making fine miso soup is she ready to become a bride!

Miso Soup with Tofu and Onions

SERVES 2

2 cups dashi (p. 35), stock, or water
1 small onion, thinly sliced
2½ to 3 tablespoons red, barley, or Hatcho miso
4 to 6 ounces tofu, cut into ⅜-inch cubes
Dash of 7-spice chili powder

Combine dashi and onion in a small covered saucepan and bring to a boil. Reduce heat to medium and cook for 4 to 5 minutes. Place miso in a small cup, cream with about ½ cup cooking broth, and add to the soup. (Or, place miso in a small strainer or sieve, partially immerse strainer into broth in saucepan, and rub miso through strainer with the back of a wooden spoon. If desired, add to soup any kernels of grain or soybeans left in strainer.) Stir soup lightly, add tofu cubes and return just to the boil; remove from heat. Season with chili powder and serve immediately, Japanese-style if you wish, in covered lacquerware bowls.

Creamy Miso Soup

SERVES 4

1 tablespoon oil
1 onion, thinly sliced
1½ to 2 cups half-moons of eggplant or cauliflowerets
2 tablespoons butter
2 tablespoons (whole-wheat) flour
1 cup milk (soy or dairy)
½ cup water
2 ounces cheese, grated or minced
12 ounces tofu or 5 ounces deep-fried tofu, cut into small rectangles
2 tablespoons light-yellow or red miso
Dash of pepper

Heat the oil in a casserole. Add onions and sauté for 3 minutes, or until lightly browned. Add eggplants and sauté briefly or until all oil is absorbed; turn off heat.

Using the butter, flour, and milk, prepare a white sauce (p. 48). Add the sauce and ½ cup water to the casserole, cover, and simmer over low heat for 5 minutes. Add cheese and tofu, increase heat to medium, and cook for 3 minutes. Stir in miso thinned in a little of the cooking broth, and season with pepper. Stirring constantly, simmer for 1 minute more. Serve hot or cold.

Miso Soup with Tofu, Leeks, and Wakame

SERVES 2

2 cups dashi (p. 35), stock, or water
¼ large leek, or ½ onion, cut into thin rounds
3 to 4 ounces tofu, cut into ⅜-inch cubes
¼ to ⅓ cup fresh or reconstituted *wakame,* cut into 1-inch lengths
2 tablespoons red or light-yellow miso
Dash of 7-spice chili powder or 1 tablespoon thinly-sliced leeks

Bring dashi to a boil in a saucepan. Add leek or onion and return to the boil. Add tofu and *wakame,* and simmer for 1 minute. Stir in miso creamed with a little of the hot broth and return just to the boil. Serve immediately, garnished with the red pepper or leek slivers.

About Clear Soup (Suimono)

The dewlike freshness and utter simplicity of Japanese clear soups are a subtle delight to the senses. Within the dark hollow of a lacquerware bowl, the chef creates a miniature floating world in which textures, colors, and shapes are as mindfully balanced as flavors. For as the Japanese say, "A man eats with his eyes as well as his mouth." A tiny crescent of *yuzu* or lemon peel, a brilliant green sprig of *kinome,* or as few as two slender white mushrooms and a small cube of tofu can form a still life in the fragrant, steaming broth.

When used in clear soups, tofu may be cut into a variety of attractive shapes: chrysanthemum leaves, circles, half moons, cherry blossoms, triangles, tiny cubes called "hailstones" and larger cubes called "yakko," cylinders (which are then sometimes broiled), maple or ginkgo leaves, or little loops and bows. Some of these shapes are also used in miso soups.

Clear soups are usually served at the beginning of the meal. The ingredients are generally limited to about three, and each must be fresh and attractive. They are used either fresh or parboiled, then carefully arranged in the bottom of a lacquerware bowl. To avoid disturbing the decorative arrangement, the broth is then poured very gently down the sides of the bowl.

Clear Soup with Citrus Fragrance

SERVES 2

1½ cups Clear Broth (p. 36)
6 ounces tofu, drained (p. 120) and cut into 1½-inch cubes
½ leek or 2 scallions, cut into thin rounds
4 slivers of lemon or *yuzu* peel

Bring broth to a boil in a small sauce pan. Add tofu and simmer for 2 minutes, until heated through. Remove tofu carefully with a slotted spoon and divide

amóng two soup bowls. Garnish with sliced leeks and
lemon peel, then carefully pour in the simmering broth.
Serve immediately.

TOFU IN SAUCES

Friends or extra guests arriving just before mealtime? The spaghetti or curry sauce will only feed 6 but
there will be 12 for dinner? Mash 2 or 3 cakes of fresh
tofu, season with shoyu or miso, and stir into the sauce,
thereby adding body, flavor, and plenty of protein.
Seasoned this way, tofu also makes an excellent and
inexpensive réplacement for meat in many sauces. Most
sauces become even more delicious if reheated or
served cold after the flavors are given time to marry.
The various Creamy Tofu Dressings, Tofu Tartare
Sauce and Tofu Sour Cream (pp. 145 to 152) also
work well as sauces when served over cooked vegetables.

Quick Tofu-Sesame Sauce

MAKES 1¾ CUPS

12 ounces tofu
¼ cup sesame butter, *tahini,* or ground roasted sesame
    seeds
1 tablespoon shoyu
½ teaspoon salt
1 tablespoon honey

Combine all ingredients in a blender and purée until
smooth. (Or mash ingredients together with a fork.)
Serve over cooked vegetables or deep-fried tofu. If desired, substitute nut butters for the sesame.

Tofu Spaghetti Sauce

SERVES 4 TO 6

Regular or deep-fried tofu makes an excellent addition to any spaghetti sauce and may be used to replace

meat. Use it in your favorite recipes or try the following:

2 tablespoons oil
1 clove garlic, crushed
2 onions, diced
2 large tomatoes, diced
2 green peppers, diced
3 mushrooms, thinly sliced
½ carrot, grated or diced; or 2 leaves of Chinese cabbage, thinly sliced
6 green beans, thinly sliced (optional)
2 cups water
1 bay leaf
24 ounces tofu, crumbled (p. 125); or 10 ounces deep-fried tofu cutlets, diced
7 cakes of dried wheat gluten (optional)
½ cup ketchup
3 tablespoons butter
¾ teaspoon salt or 2½ tablespoons shoyu
Dash of pepper
⅓ cup grated or Parmesan cheese

Heat a large heavy pot and coat with the oil. Add garlic and onions and sauté for 3 to 4 minutes. Add the next five ingredients and sauté for 3 to 4 minutes more. Add water, drop in bay leaf, and bring to a boil; cover pot and simmer for 15 minutes. Add the next six ingredients and re-cover; simmer, stirring occasionally, for about 1 hour. Remove from heat and cool to room temperature. Remove bay leaf and serve, either reheated or cold, over spaghetti or buckwheat noodles. Top with cheese.

For variety, season with grated gingerroot, green beefsteak leaves, oregano, or basil.

Tofu-Apple-Onion Curry Sauce

SERVES 3 OR 4

Substitute 18 ounces tofu (pressed; p. 121) for the deep-fried tofu in the recipe for Apple and Onion Curry Sauce with Deep-fried Tofu (p. 236). Sauté the tofu in a little oil until tofu is firm and crumbly; add apples, potato, and water, and proceed as directed. For best flavor, allow sauce to stand for 6 to 8 hours before serving.

TOFU IN BREAKFAST EGG DISHES

One of the easiest and most delicious ways to incorporate tofu into your breakfast menu is by serving it in traditional Western-style egg preparations. Tofu goes well with cheese and all those vegetables which lend variety and zest to egg dishes. The Japanese often season their tofu-egg preparations with shoyu or Sesame Salt and a little sweetening.

Butter-fried Tofu with Fried Eggs

SERVES 2

6 ounces tofu, pressed (p. 121); or 4½ ounces firm tofu or
   deep-fried tofu cutlets
1 tablespoon butter or margarine
2 eggs
Salt and pepper, or shoyu

Cut tofu lengthwise into halves, then crosswise into ¾-inch-thick pieces. Place pieces between cloth towels for several minutes until pieces are firm.

Melt the butter in a large skillet. Add tofu and sauté over medium heat for about 1 minute until golden brown. Turn tofu pieces with a spatula and cook second side. Use spatula to clear a small space at center of pan between the tofu pieces. Break the eggs into this space, cover skillet, and cook until eggs are firm. Season with salt and pepper, or shoyu. Try in place of bacon-and-eggs.

VARIATIONS

• Break the tofu into small pieces and sauté together with your choice of vegetables. Top the eggs with cheese and minced parsley just before covering the skillet.

• *Poached Egg on Toast with Butter-fried Tofu:* Cut the tofu as above and fry in butter. Cover several pieces of buttered whole-grain toast with the tofu slices, sprinkle lightly with shoyu, and top with poached eggs.

Tofu Sautéed in Butter with Scrambled Eggs

SERVES 2

1 tablespoon butter
6 ounces tofu
2 eggs, lightly beaten
Salt and pepper

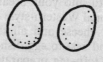

Melt the butter in a skillet. Add tofu and mash, then sauté over medium heat until lightly browned. Add eggs and scramble until firm. Season with salt and pepper.

If desired, sauté any of the following together with the tofu: chives, bean or alfalfa sprouts, crushed garlic, mushrooms, scallions or onions, green peppers or lotus root (each diced or thinly sliced). Season with ½ to 1 teaspoon shoyu.

Japanese-style Tofu, Eggs & Onions (Tamago-toji)

SERVES 2

1 tablespoon oil
1 small onion, thinly sliced
1 egg, lightly beaten
6 ounces tofu, thinly sliced
2 teaspoons shoyu
1 teaspoon honey

Heat the oil in a skillet. Add onion and sauté for 3 to 4 minutes, or until transparent. Stir in remaining ingredients, cover, and cook for 2 or 3 minutes until egg is firm.

If desired, serve seasoned with *sanshó* pepper or topped with grated cheese. Or serve as a topping for buckwheat noodles and garnish with crumbled, toasted *nori*.

Tofu-Egg Omelet with Mushrooms

SERVES 2 OR 3

6 ounces tofu, pressed (p. 121) and diced
3 eggs, lightely beaten
1 tablespoon shoyu
¼ teaspoon honey
2 tablespoons ground roasted sesame seeds, sesame butter, or *tahini*
1 tablespoon butter or oil
3 large fresh mushrooms, cut into thin strips
2 leeks or onions, cut into thin rounds

Combine the first five ingredients in a large bowl; mix well. Melt the butter in a skillet. Add leeks and mushrooms, and sauté for 2 or 3 minutes until fragrant and tender. Pour in tofu-egg mixture and cook over low heat. When omelet has an even consistency, fold and serve.

If desired, fill with grated cheese, cream cheese, or tomato wedges and minced parsley. Japanese chefs often cover omelets with several sheets of *nori* before rolling, then season the omelets with *sansho* pepper, green *nori* flakes, or Worcestershire sauce.

TOFU BAKED

Tofu may be used with excellent results in the baked dishes of countries throughout the world. It goes particularly well with all dairy products and with grains. The Japanese often sauté and season their vegetables with a little shoyu or miso (and sweetening) before adding them to tofu baked dishes in order to give a richer and more distinctive flavor. Always use firm or pressed tofu in casseroles where a firm or slightly dry consistency is desired. Experiment freely using tofu in your favorite recipes for oven cookery. Since baking—

which uses a relatively large amount of fuel or energy—has never been a traditional Japanese way of cooking foods, most of the following recipes are typically Western. For baked desserts, see page 210.

Tofu Italian Meatballs

SERVES 2 OR 3

A remarkably good facsimile of its namesake, this preparation is one of the many creative and delicious tofu recipes served as part of the vegetarian cuisine at Tokyo's Seventh-day Adventist Hospital.

12 ounces tofu, well pressed or squeezed
¼ cup chopped walnut meats
½ onion, minced
¼ to ⅓ cup bread crumbs
1 egg, lightly beaten
3 tablespoons minced parsley
Dash of pepper
4 teaspoons red miso or ½ teaspoon salt
Oil for deep-frying
¼ cup tomato juice or tomato soup
¼ cup ketchup
Dash of oregano
3 tablespoons Parmesan or grated cheese

Combine the first seven ingredients and 1 tablespoon miso. Mix well and shape into 1½-inch balls. Heat oil to 350°F in a wok, skillet, or deep-fryer. Drop in balls and deep-fry until cooked through and well browned (p. 185). Drain balls, then arrange in a loaf pan. Preheat oven to 350°F. Combine remaining 1 teaspoon miso with tomato juice and ketchup, mixing to form a sauce, and pour over tofu balls. Top with a sprinkling of cheese, and bake for 15 minutes, or until nicely browned. For best flavor, allow to stand for 6 to 8 hours. Serve hot or cold, as is or as a topping for spaghetti. Also delicious in Tofu Spaghetti Sauce (p. 169).

For variety, bake topped with Mushroom Sauce (p. 47) or Soymilk Cheese Sauce (p. 310).

Tofu-Cheese Soufflé

SERVES 4

3 slices of whole-wheat bread
2 tablespoons butter
6 ounces tofu, cut into ½-inch-thick slices
6 ounces (sharp cheddar) cheese, grated
1 tablespoon chopped onion or ¼ teaspoon onion powder
1¼ cups milk (soy or dairy)
2 eggs, lightly beaten
½ teaspoon salt or 2 tablespoons red miso
Dash of pepper

Butter the bread and tear each slice into 4 or 5 pieces. Coat a casserole lightly with butter, then layer bread, tofu, cheese, and onion, repeating the layers until all ingredients are used. Combine milk, eggs, salt or miso, and pepper, and pour into the casserole; allow to stand for 1 to 2 hours. Bake casserole in a pan of water for 45 minutes in a preheated 350°F oven.

Tofu & Brown Rice Casserole

SERVES 4

4½ teaspoons oil
1½ tablespoons butter
1½ onions, thinly sliced
1 cup cooked Brown Rice (p. 51)
12 ounces tofu, pressed (p. 121); or 9 ounces firm tofu
1 teaspoon salt
Dash of pepper
1 cup milk (soy or dairy)
¼ to ½ cup bread crumbs
2 ounces cheese, grated

Preheat oven to 350°F. Heat a large skillet or wok and coat with 2 teaspoons oil and the butter. Add onion and sauté until lightly browned. Add brown rice, then tofu, sautéing each for 2 minutes. Season with salt and pepper. Place tofu-onion mixture in a casserole or bread pan coated with remaining oil. Pour in the milk, then sprinkle with bread crumbs and cheese. Bake for about 15 to 20 minutes, or until cheese is nicely browned.

Mushroom & Onion Casserole with Tofu

SERVES 3

2 onions, diced
8 mushrooms, thinly sliced
1 tomato, cut into thin wedges
1 teaspoon oil
1 pint yogurt
2 ounces dried onion soup or mushroom soup
24 ounces tofu, cut into ½-inch cubes
2 tablespoons roasted sesame seeds

Preheat oven to 350°F. Combine the first three ingredients in a bowl; mix lightly. Layer one-half of mixture at the bottom of a lightly oiled casserole. Combine yogurt and dried onion soup in a bowl, mixing well. Pour one-fourth of yogurt-soup mixture over vegetables in casserole, and top with a layer of one-half of the tofu and 1 tablespoon sesame seeds. Then pour another one-fourth of the yogurt mixture over the tofu. Use the remaining ingredients to form an identical series of layers. Bake for 30 minutes.

Delectable Tofu & Onion Gratin

SERVES 4 OR 5

18 ounces tofu, diced
3½ cups Onion Sauce (p. 46)
2 cups dry bread pieces or croutons
2 teaspoons shoyu or 1 tablespoon red miso, dissolved in
    ½ cup water
¼ cup Parmesan or grated cheese

Combine the first four ingredients, mixing well, and pour into an oiled or buttered casserole or large bread pan; allow to stand for 1 to 2 hours. Preheat oven to 350°F. Sprinkle casserole with cheese and bake for 20 to 30 minutes, or until nicely browned. Serve hot or cold.

Buckwheat Noodle Gratin with Tofu

SERVES 5

2 tablespoons oil
1 onion, cut into thin wedges
½ carrot, cut into thin half moons
6 ounces tofu, pressed (p. 121) and mashed
1¼ teaspoons salt
2 tablespoons whole-wheat flour
½ cup milk (soy or dairy) or water
10 ounces (*soba*) buckwheat noodles, cooked (p. 50)
¼ cup minced parsley
5 slivers of *yuzu* or lemon peel

Preheat oven to 350°F. Heat a skillet and coat with 1 tablespoon oil. Add the onion and sauté until transparent. Add the carrot and tofu and sauté for 4 to 5 minutes more. Transfer to a large bowl and season with ½ teaspoon salt.

Reheat skillet and coat with 1 tablespoon oil. Add flour and sauté until fragrant and lightly browned. Gradually add the milk, stirring constantly, to form a smooth brown sauce. Simmer until sauce is thick, then season with ¾ teaspoon salt.

Place noodles in a lightly oiled gratin dish. Add sautéed vegetable-tofu mixture, then pour on the sauce. Sprinkle with 1½ teaspoons oil and bake for about 20 minutes, or until slightly crisp and nicely browned. Serve hot or cold, topped with parsley and garnished with slivered *yuzu*.

Tofu with Tahini Sauce

SERVES 6

36 ounces tofu, cut into nine 4-ounce cakes
13 tablespoons shoyu
2½ cups water, approximately
1 cup tahini
¼ teaspoon mace
1 tablespoon sesame oil
¼ cup chopped onion
¾ cup sliced green onions or scallions

Preheat oven to 350°F. Arrange tofu cakes in a shallow (9-by-13-inch) baking dish. Combine ¾ cup each shoyu and water, mix, and pour over tofu. Marinate for 20 minutes. Meanwhile, combine tahini, mace, and 1⅓ cups water in a bowl; whisk until smooth. Heat a heavy skillet and coat with the oil. Add chopped onion and the remaining 1 tablespoon shoyu, and sauté for 4 to 5 minutes, or until onions are soft and sweet. Add tahini sauce and cook over very low heat (this sauce burns very easily), stirring occasionally, for 12 to 15 minutes, or until mixture has the consistency of a chunky custard.

Turn over tofu pieces in marinade, cover baking dish, and bake in oven for 12 to 15 minutes, or until tofu is thoroughly heated but marinade has not begun to boil. Pour off most of the marinade and discard, then ladle tahini sauce over tofu and garnish with about ½ cup of sliced green onions. Serve hot, accompanied by a little shoyu and the remaining scallions.

TOFU FRIED, SAUTEED, STIR-FRIED, OR TOPPED WITH SAUCES

There are many ways of using tofu with cooked vegetables. Mastery of the Chinese technique for stir-frying will add a new dimension to your cooking repertoire. Sautéing with oil previously used for deep-frying (p. 185) will add flavor and savory aroma to even the simplest preparations.

Pan-fried Tofu
SERVES 2

Quick, easy, and delicious, this recipe may be served as an entree or used as the basis for tofu sandwiches.

1½ to 2 tablespoons oil or margarine
10 to 12 ounces firm tofu, cut crosswise into ⅜-inch-thick slices
2 teaspoons shoyu or ¼ teaspoon salt
Dash of garlic powder or nutritional yeast (optional)

Heat a skillet and coat with the oil. Add tofu slices and fry for 1 minute. Turn over slices, sprinkle with one half the shoyu and garlic powder, and fry for 15 to 30 seconds. Turn again, sprinkle on remaining shoyu and garlic, and fry for 15 to 30 seconds more, or until nicely browned. Serve immediately, while crisp and hot.

Crisp Pan-fried Tofu

SERVES 2

10 to 12 ounces firm (or pressed, p. 121) tofu, cut crosswise
    into ½-inch-thick slices
4 tablespoons whole wheat flour
2 to 3 tablespoons margarine or butter
Shoyu, Worcestershire sauce, or salt
Dash of pepper (optional)

Dust tofu slices in flour on a large plate. Melt butter in a large skillet. Add tofu slices and fry for 1 to 2 minutes, or until crisp and golden brown. Serve hot, topped with a sprinkling of shoyu and pepper. Also nice in tofu sandwiches.

Tofu with Onion Sauce and Cheese

SERVES 4

3 tablespoons oil
6 onions, thinly sliced
5 tablespoons shoyu
24 ounces tofu, pressed (p. 121) and cut into 1-inch cubes;
    or 18 ounces firm tofu
1¼ teaspoons honey (optional)
1 tablespoon sake or white wine
1 egg, lightly beaten
2 ounces cheese, thinly sliced
4 slices of whole-wheat toast (optional)

Using the oil, onions, and 3 tablespoons shoyu, prepare an Onion Sauce (p. 46). Add tofu cubes, honey, sake, and the remaining 2 tablespoons shoyu, and simmer over low heat for 10 to 15 minutes. Turn off heat, then pour egg over surface of sauce; top with a layer of cheese. Cover and allow to stand until cheese melts. Serve as is or over toast.

Butter-fried Tofu Teriyaki

SERVES 2

⅓ cup Teriyaki Sauce (p. 49)
12 ounces tofu, pressed (p. 121) and cut into 12 small rectangles about ½ inch thick; or 9 ounces firm tofu
1½ tablespoons butter

Place sauce and tofu in a shallow pan. Marinate for 1 hour, turning tofu rectangles over after 30 minutes. Melt the butter in a skillet. Add tofu and fry for 2 to 3 minutes on each side until golden brown. Serve any remaining marinade as a dipping sauce.

Chinese-style Bean Sauce with Tofu

SERVES 3

Although this popular type of preparation is called a "sauce," it is generally served as an entree in its own right.

2 tablespoons oil
1 teaspoon grated gingerroot
1 teaspoon crushed or minced garlic
2 small (togarashi) red chilies, minced
5 mushrooms, thinly sliced
3 green onions, whites thinly sliced and greens cut into 2-inch lengths
16 ounces tofu, pressed (p. 121) and cut into ½-inch cubes; or 12 ounces firm tofu
2 tablespoons red miso creamed with ½ cup water
1 tablespoon soy sauce
1 tablespoon honey
1 tablespoon cashew or sesame butter
½ teaspoon vinegar
1 teaspoon arrowroot or cornstarch, dissolved in 2 tablespoons water

Heat the oil in a wok or skillet. Add gingerroot, garlic, and red chilies, and sauté for 2 or 3 minutes. Add mushrooms and onion whites, and sauté for 2 or 3 minutes more. Add onion greens and tofu cubes and sauté for 1 minute. Combine miso, soy sauce, honey, cashew butter, and vinegar; mix well. Stir into tofu-mushroom mixture and simmer for 1 minute. Stir in dissolved arrowroot and simmer for about 30 seconds more, or until thick.

Fried Tofu Patties with Eggs and Vegetables

MAKES 8

24 ounces tofu, squeezed (p. 123)
Thin tips and leaves of 1 celery stalk, minced
1 small onion, minced
¼ cup green peas or thinly sliced green peppers or leeks (optional)
4 eggs, lightly beaten
2 tablespoons ground roasted sesame seeds, seame butter or *tahini*
½ teaspoon salt
1 tablespoon shoyu
4 teaspoons oil
½ cup ketchup or Ketchup-Worcestershire (p. 50); or 4 teaspoons shoyu

In a large mixing bowl, combine the first eight ingredients; mix well to form a batter. Heat a skillet and coat with ½ teaspoon oil. Spoon about one-eighth of the batter into the pan and press lightly with a spatula to form a patty about ⅜ inch thick. Fry until nicely browned, then flip with the spatula and press again until patty is about ¼ inch thick. Fry until second side is golden brown. Repeat with remaining oil and batter until all are used. Serve patties hot or cold, topped with ketchup.

Tofu Burgers with Mushroom Sauce

SERVES 3

3 tablespoons oil
1 small onion, minced
24 ounces tofu, crumbled (p. 125) and allowed to cool
3 eggs, lightly beaten
½ cup bread crumbs or bread crumb flakes
¾ teaspoon salt
Dash of pepper
Mushroom Sauce (p. 47) or ketchup

Heat a skillet and coat with 1 tablespoon oil. Add onion and sauté for 3 minutes, then allow to cool. Combine onion with tofu, eggs, bread crumbs, salt, and pepper in a large bowl, and use the mixture to make 8 patties. Heat the skillet and re-coat with 1 tablespoon oil. Add 4 patties, cover, and cook over low heat for about 5 minutes on each side. Repeat with remaining 4 patties. Serve hot or cold, topped with the sauce.

Iridofu (Crumbly Scrambled Tofu)

SERVES 3 OR 4

One of Japan's most popular tofu dishes, *Iridofu* has a light, dry texture and is remarkably similar to Western-style scrambled eggs in both flavor and appearance. This dish may be prepared with or without eggs, sweetened or unsweetened, and with or without the addition of any of the diced or slivered vegetables that are generally used in scrambled eggs.

1 tablespoon oil
1 small onion, diced
1 small carrot, diced
24 ounces tofu, crumbled into very small pieces (p. 125)
2 tablespoons ground roasted sesame seeds (optional)
½ teaspoon salt
2 teaspoons shoyu
Dash of pepper

Heat a skillet or wok and coat with the oil. Add onion and carrot and sauté for 3 to 4 minutes until onion is lightly browned. Add crumbled tofu and the remaining ingredients. Stirring constantly, sauté over medium-low heat for about 5 minutes, or until tofu is light, dry, and almost fluffy. Serve hot or cold.

Mabo-dofu *(Chinese-style Tofu with Red Chili Sauce)*

SERVES 2

The most popular Chinese-style tofu dish in Japan, *Mabo-dofu* usually contains a small amount of ground beef. It is representative of the many Chinese tofu dishes sautéed with pork, shrimp, chicken, or beef.

1 tablespoon corn or soy oil
1½ teaspoons sesame oil
1 clove garlic, crushed
¼ cup minced leeks, scallions, or onions
½ teaspoon minced red chilies
4 mushrooms, diced
½ cup water, stock, or dashi (p. 35)
1½ teaspoons sake
2½ teaspoons soy sauce
½ teaspoon salt
Dash of *sansho* or 7-spice chili powder
1½ teaspoons ketchup
24 ounces tofu or silken tofu, cut into pieces 1¼ inches square by ½ inch thick
2 teaspoons cornstarch, dissolved in 2 tablespoons water
1 tablespoon minced leek or scallion greens

Heat a wok or skillet and coat with both types of oil. Add the garlic, leeks, and red chilies, and stir-fry over high heat for 15 seconds. Reduce heat to medium, add mushrooms, and sauté for 1 minute. Add water and next five ingredients, bring to a boil, and cook for 30 seconds. Add tofu and return to the boil. Stir in dissolved cornstarch and simmer until thick. Serve hot, garnished with the greens.

Additional Suggestions for Serving Tofu
Sautéed or Stir-fried

● *Tofu in Fried Mexican Dishes:* Try tofu (pressed, then mashed or crumbled) in any of the following:

Fig. 32. Deep-frying Tofu Tempura

tostadas, enchiladas with cheese, *chili rellenos,* or re-fried beans. Fry tofu in oil and season with shoyu and chili powder.

● *Tofu with Fried Potatoes:* Combine well-pressed, mashed tofu with potatoes when preparing hashed browns, potato pancakes, or thinly-sliced browned potatoes.

● *Fried Tofu Topped with Sauces:* Fry thin slices of well-pressed tofu in butter or oil until golden brown. Serve topped with any of the following sauces: Mushroom (p. 47), Tomato & Cheese (p. 50), or Lemon-Miso White Sauce (p. 309).

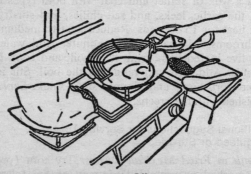

Fig. 33. Filling a Wok with Oil

TOFU DEEP-FRIED

Although three varieties of deep-fried tofu are available at most tofu shops (p. 215), tofu can also be deep-fried at home. One of the culinary arts raised to great heights by the Japanese, the technique of deep-frying comprises a world of its own, yielding light, crisp textures and delicate, delicious flavors. Learning to prepare fine, deep-fried foods is quite easy once you master the basic principles. This section contains recipes using nine different closely related methods for deep-frying tofu, listed here in order of ease of preparation: 1) without coating or batter; 2) rolled in kudzu powder (Japanese arrowroot) or cornstarch; 3) rolled in bread crumbs, bread crumb flakes, flour, or cornmeal; 4) dipped in lightly-beaten eggs and rolled in bread crumbs, kudzu powder, cornstarch, or flour; 5) rolled in flour or kudzu powder and dipped in eggs; 6) dipped into a thick batter of kudzu powder (or cornstarch) and egg whites; 7) dipped into a moderately thick batter of kudzu powder (or cornstarch) and water; 8) dusted with flour, dipped in lightly-beaten eggs, and rolled in bread crumbs to form a bound breading; and 9) coated with tempura batter.

About Deep-frying

Although deep-fat frying has long been a part of Western cookery, it has never attained the degree of popularity or artistry that it enjoys throughout the Orient, and particularly in Japan. Deep-frying is as common in the typical Japanese kitchen as baking is in the West, while it is faster and uses much less fuel. In only a few minutes, it transforms the simplest fresh vegetables, pieces of tofu, and even leftovers into prize creations. The art of deep-frying is a joy to practice and, fortunately, one of the easiest ways to begin learning is by making your own deep-fried tofu.

For the Japanese, whose diet is still very low in meats, deep-fried foods are an important source of both savory flavor and essential (unsaturated) oils. Some Westerners still have the image of deep-fried foods as being necessarily "greasy," while others believe that heating the oil to high temperatures impairs its nutritional value. Yet anyone who has lived in Japan or dined on tempura knows that deep-frying can yield foods that are remarkably crisp and light. And keeping the oil at its proper temperature, at 350°F or less, guarantees its health-giving benefits.

In Japanese, the verb *ageru* means "to deep-fry," and *agé-mono* or "deep-fried things" are the many foods that make up this vast world. The simplest form of deep-frying is called *kara-agé* or "deep-frying without a coating or batter." The three basic types of deep-fried tofu are each prepared in this way. After mastering this technique, you should find no difficulty in preparing fine, crisp tempura.

If you wish to make deep-frying a permanent part of your repertoire of cooking techniques, it is best to start with the proper tools. Most important is the deep-frying pot. While many Westerners use a heavy 3- to 4-quart kettle, or an electric deep-fryer, most Japanese use either a wok or a heavy-bottomed skillet 2½ to 3 inches deep and 10 to 12 inches in diameter.

For the best results use a simple vegetable oil. Japanese tofu masters prefer rapeseed oil, but many Western tofu shops also use soybean or cottonseed oil. Some chefs specializing in vegetable tempura prefer a combination of oils. If 10 to 30 percent sesame oil is added to any of the above basic oils, it will give the foods a delicious, nutty flavor. Other popular combinations are: peanut or corn (70%) and sesame (30%); peanut (75%), sesame (20%), and olive (5%); cottonseed (85%), olive (10%), and sesame (5%). For a light, crisp texture, avoid the use of animal fats in deep-frying.

Used deep-frying oil should be kept in a sealed jar and stored in a cool, dark place. When sautéing vegetables or frying eggs, you may use some of this oil to impart added flavor to the foods and help use up the oil. When deep-frying, try to use about one part fresh oil and one part used. Dark or thick used oil has a low smoking point and imparts a poor flavor. Foods deep-fried in used oil only are not as light and crisp as they could be. Pour oil from the storage jar into the deep-fryer carefully so that any sediment remains at the bottom of the jar. Then add fresh oil to fill the wok or skillet to a depth of 1½ to 2 inches (Fig. 33).

Maintaining the oil at the proper temperature (about 350°F) is the most important part of deep-frying. At first it may be easiest to measure the temperature with a deep-frying thermometer. More experienced chefs or tofu makers judge the oil's temperature by its appearance, aroma, and subtle crackling sound. If the oil begins to smoke, it is too hot. Overheating shortens the life of the oil. Japanese say it "tires" the oil—and imparts a bad flavor to the foods cooked in it. Tempura chefs drop a little batter into hot oil to test its temperature. If the batter submerges slightly, then rises quickly to the surface where it browns within about 45 seconds, the temperature is just right (Fig. 34). If the batter sinks to the bottom and rises only slowly to the surface, the oil is not hot enough; if it remains on the surface and dances furiously, the oil is too hot. Oil which is too hot will smoke—and burn the batter —whereas that which is too cold will not give the desired crispness.

Keeping the oil clean is another secret of successful deep-frying. This is especially important when using the batter or bound-breading methods. Use a mesh skimmer, or a perforated metal spatula or spoon, to remove all particles of food and batter from the oil's surface. Most cooks skim after every two or three batches of ingredients have been cooked. Place the small particles of deep-fried batter skimmed from the oil into a large colander or bowl lined with absorbent paper, and allow to drain thoroughly. These may be used later as tasty additions to soups, salads, sautéed vegetables, noodles-in-broth, or other grain dishes.

To ensure that tofu and other deep-fried foods are

Fig. 34. Testing Oil Temperature

too hot   just right   too cold

served at their peak of texture and flavor, do your deep-frying just before you are ready to serve the meal, preferably after your guests have been seated at the table. If you have a large quantity of ingredients to deep-fry and wish to serve them simultaneously, keep freshly cooked pieces warm in a 250°F oven.

After all foods have been deep-fried, allow the oil to cool in the wok or skillet, then pour it through a mesh skimmer or fine-weave strainer held over a funnel into your used-oil container. Seal the jar and discard any residue in the skimmer. Wipe all utensils with absorbent paper (washing is unnecessary) and store in a sealed plastic bag.

Crisp Tofu Slices *(Tofu no Kara-agé)*

SERVES 2

The following technique is the basis of all types of deep-frying; 12 ounces of tofu yield 5 ounces of Crisp Tofu Slices.

Oil for deep-frying
12 ounces (firm) tofu, pressed (p. 121; sliced tofu method)

Use the oil to fill a wok, heavy skillet, pot, or deep-fryer to a depth of 1½ to 2 inches. Heat over high heat until temperature registers 350°F on a deep-frying thermometer. Reduce heat to medium and slide half the tofu pieces down the side of wok into the oil. Deep-fry for 1½ to 2 minutes, or until tofu is light golden-brown and floating near surface of oil. Turn each piece with long chopsticks or tongs and continue deep-frying for 1 to 3 minutes more until each piece is golden brown. Using chopsticks, transfer freshly cooked pieces onto the draining rack and allow to drain for several minutes. Skim surface of oil, check oil temperature, and slide in remaining tofu. Transfer well-drained tofu onto pieces of absorbent paper placed on a large tray or platter and allow to drain for several minutes more. Arrange tofu on plates, or serve Japanese style in a basket, bamboo colander, or serving bowl lined with neatly folded white paper. Serve immediately as for Crisp Deep-Fried Tofu (p. 220), or use in any of the recipes in Chapter 9. For variety, marinate for 1 hour in Teriyaki Sauce (p. 49) before serving.

Tofu French Fries

SERVES 2

12 ounces (firm) tofu, pressed (p. 121; sliced tofu method)
Oil for deep-frying
½ teaspoon salt

Cut tofu crosswise into pieces about the size of French-fried potatoes. Heat oil in a wok, skillet, or deep-fryer. Drop in tofu and deep-fry until golden brown (p. 185). Drain, then sprinkle with salt. Serve hot and crisp. Delicious with Tofu Burgers (p. 267) and Tofu-Banana Milkshake (p. 308).

Sizzling Tofu with Gingerroot-Ankake Sauce

SERVES 4

Deep-frying with a kudzu powder & egg white batter gives each piece of tofu a crisp and billowy coating, light and delicate as spindrift.

¼ cup kudzu powder, arrowroot, or cornstarch
2 egg whites
24 ounces tofu, pressed (p. 121); or 18 ounces firm tofu
Oil for deep-frying
1 cup Rich Gingerroot-Ankake Sauce (p. 49)

Combine kudzu powder and egg whites in a small bowl; mix until smooth. Cut tofu into 12 equal cubes (or thin rectangles), dip into the batter, and deep-fry as for Crisp Tofu Slices (p. 189). Serve immediately, topped with the hot sauce.

Breaded Tofu Cutlets (Tofu Furai)

SERVES 2

12 ounces tofu, pressed (p. 121); or 9 ounces firm tofu
⅓ cup flour or cornstarch
1 egg, lightly beaten (with 2 or 3 teaspoons of water or milk, if desired)
¾ cup sifted bread crumbs or bread crumb flakes
Oil for deep-frying
Salt
Creamy Tofu Dressing (p. 143) or Tofu Tartare Sauce (p. 147)

Cut tofu lengthwise into halves then crosswise into ½-inch-thick pieces. Place between absorbent towels and allow to dry for several minutes Gently dust tofu, one piece at a time, with the flour, then dip in the egg and roll in the bread crumbs. Place on a rack and allow to dry for 10 to 15 minutes; tap off any excess crumbs.

Heat the oil to 350°F in a wok, skillet, or deep-fryer. Drop in the tofu and deep-fry until golden brown (p. 185). Add a piece of tofu to the oil about once every 15 seconds. No more than 6 pieces should be in the oil at one time. Drain briefly, then serve, inviting each guest to season the tofu with salt to taste, and top with the Dressing or Tartare Sauce.

Crispy Deep-fried Tofu

SERVES 2

The key to obtaining a crisp, delicately crunchy crust lies in using kudzu powder, although other coatings also work well.

12 ounces tofu, well pressed (p. 121); or 9 ounces firm tofu
3 to 5 tablespoons kudzu powder, cornstarch, arrowroot, or wholewheat (pastry) flour
Oil for deep-frying
Shoyu

Cut tofu into 6 rectangular pieces and roll each piece in the kudzu powder. Heat oil to 350°F in a wok, skillet, or deep-fryer. Drop in tofu and deep-fry until golden brown (p. 185); allow to drain. Invite each person to season his or her tofu to taste with shoyu and garnishes such as grated gingerroot, *daikon, wasabi,* or thinly sliced leeks. Also delicious served with lemon wedges and a little salt.

Thunderbolt Tofu *(Kaminari Agé)*

SERVES 2

This popular recipe derives its name from the crackling sound made when the soft tofu is dropped into the hot oil.

12 ounces tofu, cut crosswise into halves and drained (p. 120)
¼ cup kudzu powder, cornstarch, or arrowroot
Oil for deep-frying
¾ cup dashi (p. 35), stock, or water
3 tablespoons shoyu
3 tablespoons *mirin* or sake
2 tablespoons grated *daikon*
2 tablespoons thinly sliced leeks or scallions
1 sheet of *nori*, cut into ⅛-inch-wide strips

Pat the tofu pieces with a dry cloth to remove surface moisture and roll them in kudzu powder. Heat oil to 350°F in a wok, skillet, or deep-fryer. Drop in tofu and deep-fry until golden brown (p. 185); allow to drain, then place into deep serving bowls. Combine dashi, shoyu, and *mirin* in a small saucepan and bring almost to the boil. Pour this sauce over the tofu and top each portion with grated *daikon*, leek slices, and *nori*.

Agédashi-dofu (Deep-Fried Tofu in Dipping Sauce)

SERVES 4

Agédashi is one of Japan's favorite deep-fried tofu dishes. Its name is composed of two Chinese characters meaning "to deep-fry" and "to serve." What could be quicker or easier? The key to the texture lies in the use of kudzu powder and in serving the tofu immediately after it is deep-fried. The key to the flavor lies in the use of sesame oil and in cutting the tofu with chopsticks (rather than with a knife) after placing it in the dipping sauce. The roughly cut surface helps the sauce's flavor permeate the tofu. Agédashi is prepared with or without batter and is served in any number of different dipping sauces.

2 cakes of tofu (each 12 ounces), pressed (p. 121); or
    18 ounces firm tofu
Oil for deep-frying (3 parts vegetable and 1 part sesame, if
    available)
1 egg, lightly beaten
¼ to ½ cup kudzu powder, arrowroot, or cornstarch
Mirin-Shoyu (p. 38)
2 teaspoons grated gingerroot or a mixture of 1 teaspoon
    each grated *daikon* and grated carrot
2 tablespoons minced leeks

Cut each cake of tofu lengthwise into halves, then
crosswise into thirds. Pat each piece with a dry cloth.
Heat oil to 350°F in a wok, skillet, or deep-fryer. Dip
tofu into egg, then roll in kudzu powder. Deep-fry until
golden brown. Serve accompanied by a dipping sauce
and garnishes.

TOFU WITH GRAINS

Serving tofu with grains can increase the availability of their combined protein content by as much
as 30 to 40 percent. A number of the best combinations and proportions are given on page 25. Tofu
may be used in grain salads; fried, stir-fried or baked
grain and noodle dishes; or sauce toppings. Use tofu
with leftover grains in gruel.

Tofu with Fried Grains and Vegetables

SERVES 4

2 tablespoons oil
1 clove garlic, crushed
2 onions, thinly sliced
1 cup diced mushrooms, lotus root, celery, or eggplant
1 small carrot, grated or slivered
2 cups cooked (buckwheat) Noodles (p. 53) or Brown Rice
    (p. 51)
24 ounces tofu, crumbled (p. 125); or 12 ounces tofu,
    pressed (p. 121) and diced
1 to 1½ tablespoons shoyu
4 to 5 tablespoons ketchup
2 tablespoons Sesame Salt (p. 53) or ½ teaspoon salt
½ cup crumbled *nori* (optional)

Heat a skillet or wok and coat with the oil. Add consecutively: garlic, onions, mushrooms, carrot, and noodles (or rice), sautéing each for about 1 to 2 minutes. Add the next four ingredients and cook, stirring constantly, for about 3 minutes more. For best flavor, allow to cool for 4 to 6 hours. Serve topped with *nori*.

Italian-style Spaghetti with Tofu Meatballs

SERVES 4 OR 6

4½ to 5 ounces (whole-wheat) spaghetti or *(soba)* buckwheat
    noodles, cooked (p. 53)
Tofu Italian Meatballs (p. 174)
Tofu Spaghetti Sauce (p. 169)
Parmesan cheese and/or tabasco sauce

Divide the hot spaghetti among individual bowls and top with the meatballs and spaghetti sauce. Pass the cheese and tabasco.

Tofu With Tacos

MAKES 6

12 ounces tofu
⅔ cup brown rice or bulgur wheat, cooked (p. 51)
¼ cup peanuts
½ green pepper, diced
2 cloves of garlic, crushed
¼ teaspoon chili powder
¼ cup ketchup
½ teaspoon salt or 1 tablespoon red miso
2 to 3 tablespoons oil
6 *tortillas*
Garnishes:
   Chopped tomato
   Minced onion
   Shredded lettuce
   Grated cheese
Tabasco or taco sauce

Combine the first eight ingredients in a large bowl;
mash thoroughly. Heat the oil in a skillet and fry the
tortillas. Top each *tortilla* with your choice of garnishes, spoon on the tofu mixture, and season with
Tabasco sauce.

Tofu-filled Enchiladas

SERVES 2 OR 3

4 teaspoons oil
1 clove of garlic, minced or crushed
1 onion, minced
1 tablespoon whole-wheat flour
1½ tablespoons red miso or 1 tablespoon shoyu
1 cup water
Dash of 7-spice chili powder or Tabasco sauce
Dash of white or black pepper
¼ teaspoon oregano
2 tablespoons tomato ketchup
6 tablespoons Parmesan cheese
8 ounces tofu
1 green pepper, minced
5 tortillas, each 5 inches in diameter

Heat a skillet and coat with 1 tablespoon oil. Add
garlic and sauté for 30 seconds. Add one half the

onion and sauté for 3 to 4 minutes. Mix in flour and sauté for 30 seconds, then add 1 tablespoon miso and sauté for 15 seconds more. Add water a little at a time, stirring constantly until smooth. Mix in the next four ingredients and 2 tablespoons Parmesan, cover, and simmer for 15 minutes. Remove sauce from heat and allow to cool, then mix in 2 tablespoons minced raw onion.

While sauce is cooling, heat a wok or skillet and coat with 1 teaspoon oil. Add green pepper and the remaining onion, and sauté for 3 minutes. Stir in the remaining 1½ teaspoons miso, season with white pepper, and remove from heat. Combine with tofu and 2 tablespoons Parmesan; mash well.

Preheat oven to 350°F. Pour one half the sauce into a loaf pan or casserole. Dip one surface of a tortilla into remaining sauce, then holding this side upward, spread with one fifth of the tofu mixture. Roll tortilla loosely and place into loaf pan. Repeat with remaining tortillas and tofu until all are used. Pour remaining sauce over tortillas in pan and top with a sprinkling of 2 tablespoons Parmesan. Bake for 15 to 20 minutes, or until nicely browned. Serve hot or cold.

Tofu & Eggs Domburi

SERVES 4

1 tablespoon oil
1 cup minced leek, scallion, or onion
1 cup grated carrot
2 ounces deep-fried tofu pouches or burgers (or 4 mushrooms), diced
12 ounces tofu, pressed (p. 121) and mashed; or 5 ounces deep-fried tofu cutlets, minced
¼ cup cooked, chopped spinach (optional)
2 tablespoons shoyu
2¼ teaspoons honey
¼ teaspoon salt
2 eggs, lightly beaten
1½ cups brown rice, cooked (p. 51)

Heat a skillet or wok and coat with the oil. Add the next four ingredients and sauté for 4 minutes. Add tofu and sauté for 2 minutes more. Mix in spinach, shoyu, honey, and salt; cook for 1 minute. Stir in eggs, cover, and remove from heat.

Spoon hot rice into 3 large *(domburi)* bowls and top with tofu-and-eggs; serve immediately or allow to cool to room temperature. In Japan, the latter version is widely used in box lunches.

Brown Rice Porridge with Tofu and Vegetables

SERVES 3

½ cup brown rice
1 tablespoon (sesame) oil
½ small carrot, slivered or diced
2 onions, thinly sliced
½ cup diced celery, cabbage, or vegetable leftovers
12 ounces tofu
2½ tablespoons shoyu or 3½ tablespoons red miso
Dash of pepper

Use the rice to prepare Brown Rice Porridge (p. 51). About 15 minutes before porridge is ready, heat a wok or skillet and coat with the oil. Add carrot and sauté for 3 minutes. Mix in onion and celery and sauté for 5 minutes more. Add tofu, mash well, and sauté for 3 minutes. Stir in shoyu and pepper and remove from heat. Add sautéed tofu-vegetable mixture to the finished porridge, mix well, and allow to stand for 5 to 10 minutes before serving.

If desired, substitute 5 to 10 ounces diced deep-fried tofu for the regular tofu. Top with crumbled *nori* and diced leeks.

Bulgur Pilaf with Tofu

SERVES 4

3 tablespoons butter or oil
1 cup bulgur wheat
1 small onion, minced
2 cups stock or water
¼ teaspoon oregano
Dash of (freshly ground) pepper
9 ounces tofu
2 teaspoons shoyu or 1 tablespoon red miso
Sesame Salt (p. 53) or salt

Melt butter in a heavy skillet. Add bulgur and onion and sauté for 4 to 5 minutes. Add stock, oregano, and pepper, cover pan, and bring to a boil. Reduce heat and simmer for 15 minutes, or until all liquid is absorbed. Combine tofu and shoyu in a small bowl and mash together, then stir into the cooked grain. Serve hot seasoned with sesame salt.

For variety stir in 2 tablespoons minced parsley or ⅓ cup grated cheese just before serving.

TOFU BROILED

Since grilled tofu is one of the basic types of tofu prepared at tofu shops, regular tofu is not ordinarily grilled, broiled, or barbequed in the home. With one important exception: *Tofu Dengaku*. There are also many broiled dishes made from tofu that has already been deep-fried, since these acquire a particularly delicious flavor from direct contact with fire and lend themselves to basting and marinating.

Tofu Dengaku
SERVES 4

In *dengaku,* one of Japan's most popular treatments of tofu, firm pieces the size of small match boxes are pierced with bamboo skewers and lightly broiled. A topping of Sweet Simmered Miso is then spread on one of the tofu's surfaces, and the tofu is rebroiled until lightly speckled.

The two Chinese characters which form the word *dengaku* mean "rice paddy" and "music." It is said that the name originated about 600 years ago, when an ancient form of folk drama consisting of music and dance was popular in Japan's rural villages. In one famous play using a rice paddy as its stage setting, a Buddhist priest mounted a single stilt (resembling a pogo stick) called a "heron's leg." Precariously balanced, this character was called Dengaku Hoshi (Fig. 35), and he did a dance known as the *dengaku,* or "music in the rice paddy." The newly conceived broiled tofu dish, with its distinctive, individual bamboo skewers, apparently reminded many people of the dengaku dancer, and the tasty preparation soon became known as Dengaku.

About 400 years ago, Nakamura-ro in the Gion geisha section of Kyoto became the first restaurant to serve dengaku. Attractively dressed women kneeling at small tables in front of the restaurant near the famous Yasaka shrine cut the tofu in a swift staccato rhythm to the accompaniment of shamisen music, and the new dish soon became known locally as Gion-dofu. Today the dengaku at Nakamura-ro is famous throughout Japan, especially its springtime variety which is topped with fresh bright-green sprigs of *kinome* and served with thick sweet sake *(amazake).* It is prepared over a bed of live coals and served in lacquerware boxes (Fig. 36).

From the early 1600s until the late 1900s many tofu shops prepared and delivered dengaku to order, and by

Fig. 35.   Dangaku Hoshi (from the "Tofu Hyaku Chin")

田楽法師高足曲

about 1775 it had become very fashionable for Tokyo tea shops, way stations, and inns to serve this delicacy.

According to ancient chronicles, some of Japan's earliest types of dengaku were prepared in country farmhouses, especially during the winter. We have enjoyed sizzling-hot dengaku prepared from homemade tofu and homemade miso in several mountain villages. The well-pressed tofu is cut into pieces about 4 by 3 by 1 inch, or into ¾-inch-thick rounds. Each piece is pierced with a flat skewer 12 inches long made of green bamboo which has been soaked overnight in lightly salted water to prevent it from burning. The butt

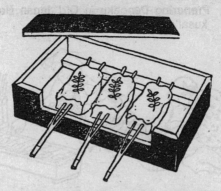

Fig. 36.   Skewered Tofu Dengaku

end of each skewer is poked into the sand or ashes around an open-hearth fireplace so that the tofu leans a few inches above and over a bed of live coals (p. 328). The savory broiled tofu is spread with plain miso on both sides, quickly rebroiled until the miso is fragrant, and served as a light wintertime snack with tea. This traditional method of broiling, which imparts a savory fragrance of woodsmoke to the tofu, is practiced at the Dengaku restaurant in Kamakura. Gifu Prefecture is especially famous for the dengaku served as a special treat during nighttime displays of fireworks. And in some villages, a special offering of dengaku— said to be the favorite food of the local gods—is made each year on November 14 at all *Ichi-fusha* shrines.

A unique type of dengaku called "quick dengaku" is prepared in some tofu shops after the master finishes making the day's supply of grilled tofu. He broils both sides of an entire 12-ounce cake of tofu, spreads one surface with sweet white miso, broils the miso until it is fragrant, then sits down to enjoy a hefty treat.

There are a great many varieties of dengaku in Japan. Although the most popular are generally prepared using regular tofu, others are made with grilled tofu or deep-fried tofu cutlets, burgers, or pouches.

Fig. 37. Preparing Dengaku in Old Japan (from Hokusai's Sketchbooks)

Occasionally, tofu is even replaced by skewered pieces of eggplant, *konnyaku, mochi, shiitake* mushrooms, green peppers, fresh or deep-fried wheat gluten, sweet or Irish potatoes, bamboo shoots, *daikon,* or boiled quail eggs.

Miso Topping: Use a total of ¼ to ½ cup of one or more of the following types of Sweet Simmered Miso
   Red or White Nerimiso
   Yuzu Miso
   Kinome Miso
   Walnut Miso
12 to 24 ounces tofu, pressed (p. 121); or 9 to 18 ounces firm tofu
Garnishes (optional):
   Kinome sprigs
   Slivered *yuzu* or lemon rind
   Poppy or roasted sesame seeds
   Hot mustard

Prepare the miso toppings in advance and allow to cool. In a large skillet or pan, heat water to about the temperature of a hot bath. Drop in the tofu, then cut into pieces as large as 2½ by 1 by ¾ inch or as small as 1¼ by ¾ by ½ inch. Pierce each of these under water using either 2 round bamboo skewers or 1 flat skewer as shown in Fig. 38. Cover a cutting board or flat tray with a dry dishtowel and raise one end of the

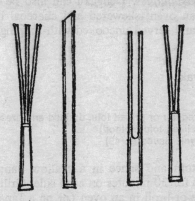

Fig. 38. A Variety of Skewers

board. Carefully place the pieces of skewered tofu on the cloth and allow to stand for about 15 minutes, or until tofu is firm.

Holding 3 to 4 pieces of skewered tofu at a time side by side over a gas burner, broil for about 30 seconds or until tofu is lightly speckled; or broil tofu on one side over a charcoal brazier or barbeque. Turn tofu over and coat broiled side with a ⅛-inch-thick layer of topping, then broil second side. Turn tofu again and broil miso topping until it too is speckled, then arrange garnishes, if used, atop miso. Repeat with remaining ingredients; if desired, use a different miso topping with each set of tofu pieces. Serve Dengaku hot with the meal or as an hors d'oeuvre.

VARIATIONS

● *Deep-fried Dengaku:* Cut well-pressed tofu into Dengaku-sized pieces and pierce each piece with 10-inch-long bamboo skewers. Deep-fry with or without batter until golden brown. Spread on the topping and serve hot. When deep-fried in a bound breading, this dish has an excellent crunchy texture.

• *Other Techniques:* Dengaku can also be broiled or baked in an oven; skewered and charcoal broiled; or skewered and served uncooked with topping.

Tofu Teriyaki

SERVES 4

24 ounces regular or grilled tofu, drained and pressed (p. 121; sliced tofu method)
⅔ cup Teriyaki Sauce (p. 49)

Combine tofu and sauce in a shallow pan; marinate tofu pieces for 30 minutes on each side. Grill tofu over a barbeque or broil in an oven (or on a Japanese-style broiling screen), basting with the sauce from time to time. Serve hot, accompanied by the remaining sauce for dipping.

TOFU SIMMERED IN ONE-POT COOKERY AND SEASONED BROTHS

In *nabe* (pronounced NAH-bay) "one-pot" cookery, the food is prepared right at the table in a large earthenware casserole or tureen placed on top of a charcoal brazier, tabletop burner, electric coil, or alcohol burner. An electric skillet can also be used, or the food may be prepared in the kitchen and brought steaming hot to the table. The *nabe* contains the entire meal, and each guest serves himself from the bounty of its many delicacies. Usually served during the cold months, *nabe* dishes almost always contain tofu together with a wide range of vegetables. The tofu is cooked for only a few minutes, since overcooking gives it an undesirably firm and porous structure.

Fig. 39. A Simmering Tofu Serving Container Heated by Coals from Within

Simmering Tofu *(Yudofu or Tofu no Mizutaki)*
SERVES 4 TO 6

One of Japan's three or four most popular tofu dishes, Simmering Tofu is the simplest of the many *nabe* dishes. The wintertime counterpart of Chilled Tofu, it brings out the delicate flavors of fine tofu and allows them to be enjoyed to their utmost.

Tosa-joyu Dipping Sauce (p. 38)
2 leeks or 4 scallions, sliced into very thin rounds
1 teaspoon 7-spice chili powder
1 tablespoon grated gingerroot
1 sheet of *nori*, toasted and cut ino thin strips (or crumbled)
A 5- to 6-inch square of *kombu*, wiped clean; or substitute
 ½ teaspoon salt
6 cups boiling water
3 pounds tofu, cut into 1¼-inch cubes or 2-inch squares
 ¾-inch thick

Bring the sauce to a boil and pour into a heat-resistant cup. Arrange the leeks, chili powder, gingerroot, and *nori* on a platter and place on the table. Set a charcoal brazier or gas burner at the center of the dining table. Atop heat source place a large casserole, tureen, chafing dish, or copper pot. Place *kombu* at the bottom of casserole and set the cup of dipping sauce atop the *kombu*. Now fill the casserole with boiling water, return to the boil, and drop in tofu.

Invite each guest to ladle some of the dipping sauce into a small dish provided for this purpose and add to it his choice of garnishes and seasonings. After 2 or 3 minutes, or as soon as the tofu begins to sway in the simmering water or float to the surface, each guest uses a slotted spoon or pair of chopsticks to lift out the tofu. Dip tofu into sauce-and-garnish mixture before eating.

Four Nabe Dishes Containing Tofu

Four popular *nabe* dishes are prepared in basically the same way as Simmering Tofu. After the broth is brought to a boil in the *nabe* pot, however, each guest adds to it his choice of ingredients which are arranged on large platters. After the foods have been cooked for 2 or 3 minutes or until tender, they are removed from the simmering broth one piece at a time and dipped into the garnished dipping sauce. *Nabeyaki Udon* features whole-wheat or buckwheat noodles, often freshly prepared by the head cook just before mealtime. *Yosenabe* means "a gathering of everything." In the countryside, Chinese cabbage and leeks are its basic ingredients, while in the cities and particularly along the seacoasts, this dish generally includes lobster, fish, clams, prawns, and sometimes chicken and pork. *Mizutaki* means "cooked in water." The main ingredient here is usually chicken and the broth is a chicken stock. *Chirinabe* is very similar to *Mizutaki* except that it usually contains chunks of white fish rather than chicken.

TOFU DESSERTS

Tofu can be adapted to fresh fruit purées, whipped cream toppings, puddings, dessert soufflés, Japanese-style confections—even cheese cake.

Uncooked Desserts

In each of these preparations, nigari tofu gives by far the best flavor and consistency. Most take only a few minutes to prepare and, containing little sweetening, can also be used as side dishes at any meal. See also Tofu Whipped Cream or Yogurt, Tofu Icing, Tofu Ice Cream, and Banana-Tofu Shake; all are listed under Dairylike Tofu Products.

Tofu-Fruit Whips or Puddings

SERVES 2 OR 3

These refreshing summertime desserts can be transformed into high-protein breakfast dishes by reducing or eliminating the sweetening.

½ pound fresh strawberries, peaches, or pineapple
12 ounces tofu, chilled
1 tablespoon honey
Chopped nutmeats or sunflower seeds (optional)

Combine all ingredients in a blender and purée until smooth. If desired, top with nutmeats. Serve immediately in small dessert dishes or use as a topping for pancakes, crêpes, or waffles.

VARIATIONS

● *Tofu-Strawberry Pudding:* Use 10½ ounces tofu, 1¼ cups chopped strawberries (or raspberries), ½ banana, 1 teaspoon vanilla, and 3 tablespoons honey. Purée as above. Serve chilled.
● *Tofu-Frozen Banana:* Use 6 ounces (silken) tofu, ¼ cup or more water, 1½ frozen bananas (chopped), and a dash of nutmeg. Serve immediately.
● *Other Combinations:* Each of the following combi-

nations is also tasty: banana-lemon, coconut-raisin, banana-raisin, and honey-lemon.

Chunky Tofu-Pineapple Purée

SERVES 3

1½ cups pineapple chunks, drained
12 ounces tofu, drained (p. 120)
1½ teaspoons honey (optional)

Combine 1 cup pineapple chunks with the tofu and honey in a blender and purée until smooth. Served topped with remaining pineapple chunks.

Tangy Tofu-Prune Purée

SERVES 2

1½ cups stewed prunes
8 ounces tofu
3 tablespoons lemon juice

Combine all ingredients in a blender and purée until smooth. For best flavor, chill for several hours before serving. Delicious also as a breakfast fruit dish or topping for buttered toast.

Tofu-Orange Juice Purée with Tangerines

SERVES 4

12 ounces tofu, pressed (p. 121)
1 cup orange juice
1 tablespoon honey
1 cup tangerine or orange sections, drained

Combine the first three ingredients in a blender and purée until smooth. Stir in the tangerine sections, spoon into dessert cups, and chill for several hours.

Fruit Cocktail Chilled Tofu

SERVES 2

6 to 8 ounces tofu or silken tofu, chilled and cut into ½-inch
    cubes
1 to 2 cups canned fruit cocktail or sections of fresh man-
    darin oranges, cherries, peaches and/or chunks of pine-
    apple

Combine all ingredients, mixing lightly, and chill for about 6 hours. Serve in small bowls or shrimp cocktail dishes.

Banana-Sesame Cream

SERVES 4

12 ounces tofu
2 tablespoons honey
2 bananas
¾ cup milk (soy or dairy)
1 to 1½ tablespoons sesame butter, *tahini,* or ground
    roasted sesame seeds

Combine all ingredients in a blender and purée until smooth. Serve chilled as a dessert, or use as a topping for pancakes, waffles, crêpes.

Tofu-Strawberry Dessert

SERVES 4 TO 6

24 ounces tofu, chilled and mashed
4½ tablespoons honey
2 teaspoons vanilla extract
12 to 15 strawberries, cut vertically into halves
¼ cup sliced hazel or almond nutmeats

Combine the tofu, honey, and vanilla in a large serving bowl; mix well with a fork. Dot the surface with strawberries, then sprinkle with sliced nutmeats.

Cooked and Baked Desserts

Tofu can be used like dairy products to add plenty of protein and a rich, creamy texture to your favorite desserts. Apples, raisins, and small amounts of honey make delicious natural sweeteners.

Tofu Cheesecake with Fruit Topping

MAKES ONE 8-INCH PIE

A close relative of this delectable recipe was developed by the Spruce Tree Baking Co. in Belair, Maryland, and is now a favorite throughout New England.

Shell: Use your favorite cheesecake crumb crust (whole-wheat flour and oil or graham crumbs and butter) or the following:
    ½ cup whole wheat flour
    1 cup whole wheat flour
    ½ cup margarine
Filling:
    17 ounces tofu
    1½ to 3 tablespoons sesame tahini
    ½ cup pure maple syrup
    2 tablespoons lemon juice
    ½ teaspoon sea salt
    1½ teaspoons pure vanilla extract
Strawberry Topping:
    1 cup whole strawberries
    10 tablespoons apple juice
    3 tablespoons pure maple syrup
    ⅛ teaspoon salt
    1½ tablespoons cornstarch

Sift together both flours. Cut in, then rub in margarine with fingertips until mixture resembles coarse sand (add no water). Wrap and chill for 1 hour or more, then using fingertips, press into an 9-inch pie tin to make crust of even thickness. Prick bottom with a fork and bake at 450°F for 10 minutes.

Purée tofu in two batches in a blender until smooth, then mix in a bowl with the remaining filling ingredients. Spoon into prebaked shell and bake at 350°F for 30 to 35 minutes, or until filling has set, maybe risen a little, and is golden yellow on top. Allow to cool to room temperature.

For topping, combine strawberries, ½ cup apple juice, maple syrup, and salt in a small saucepan; bring to a boil. Dissolve cornstarch in the remaining 2 tablespoons juice, stir quickly into fruit mixture until thick and clear, then pour topping over cooled pie. Allow topping to cool and set; serve cheesecake chilled.

VARIATIONS

• *Blueberry Topping:* Use 1 cup fresh or frozen (unsweetened) blueberries, ½ cup water, 2½ tablespoons maple syrup, a dash of salt, and 2 tablespoons cornstarch dissolved in 2½ tablespoons water.

● *Granola crust:* Whiz 2 cups of your favorite granola in a blender until it is fine crumbs. Mix in a large bowl with about 3 tablespoons apple juice then press into pie tin and prebake at 350°F for 10 minutes.

Tofu Mincemeat

MAKES 5¼ CUPS

4 (tart) apples, peeled, cored, and diced
½ cup apple juice
1½ cups raisins
Grated rind of 1 orange
Juice of 1 orange
24 ounces tofu, pressed (p. 121) and mashed; or 10 ounces deep-fried tofu cutlets or burgers, diced
½ to 1 cup nutmeats
½ teaspoon cinnamon
½ teaspoon cloves, allspice, or coriander (optional)
¼ cup Hatcho miso

Combine the first five ingredients in a heavy pot, bring to a boil, and simmer for 30 minutes. Add tofu, return to the boil, and simmer for 5 minutes more. Add the next three ingredients and miso creamed in a little of the cooking liquid; mix well and remove from heat. Allow to cool to room temperature, then cover and refrigerate for at least 8 hours. Use as a filling for mince pie or turnovers. Also delicious as a spread for buttered toast or served like chutney with curried dishes.

Tofu-Pineapple Sherbet

SERVES 3

¼ cup pineapple juice
1½ tablespoons lemon juice
2¼ teaspoons honey
1 egg, lightly beaten
½ cup crushed pineapple
1 cup finely-diced apple
¼ cup raisins
6 ounces tofu, rubbed through a sieve or puréed in a blender

Combine the first four ingredients in a saucepan. Simmer, stirring constantly, over very low heat for 4 to 5 minutes, or until thickened; allow to cool for 30 minutes. Stir in remaining ingredients, pour into a mold, and freeze for 1 hour, or until as firm as sherbet.

Tofu Custard Pudding

SERVES 3

12 ounces tofu
1 egg
2 to 2½ tablespoons honey
½ teaspoon salt
½ teaspoon vanilla extract
½ cup Tofu Whipped Cream (p. 151)

Combine first five ingredients in a blender and purée until smooth. Spoon the puréed mixture into 3 custard cups with tops. Cover cups, place in a heated steamer, and steam over low heat for 12 to 14 minutes, or until just firm. Or set the cups in a pan of hot water and bake at 325°F for about 20 minutes. Serve hot or cold topped with the whipped cream.

Tofu also gives a delicious creamy texture to chocolate puddings.

Tofu-Rice Pudding

SERVES 4

12 ounces tofu, mashed
1 cup cooked Brown Rice (p. 51)
1 cup milk (soy or dairy)
3 tablespoons honey
¼ teaspoon salt
¼ teaspoon cinnamon
¼ cup raisins
1 teaspoon oil
3 tablespoons crushed corn flakes or cracker crumbs
2 tablespoons butter

Preheat oven to 350°F. Combine the first seven ingredients in a large bowl; mix well. Coat a casserole or bread pan with the oil, spoon in the tofu-rice mixture, sprinkle with corn flakes, and dot with butter. Bake for 25 minutes, or until set. Or omit the corn flakes and simmer all ingredients in a large saucepan over low heat for 10 to 15 minutes, or until firm.

Gisei-dofu *(Tofu Cheesecake-Like Dessert)*

SERVES 8

Gisei means "fictitious or imitation." Traditionally, *Gisei-dofu* was any tofu preparation made to resemble a food prohibited by the precepts of Buddhism, like *ganmodoki* (p. 261) made to resemble the flavor of wild goose, and *yuba-no-kabayaki* designed to resemble the taste of broiled eels. In Zen Temple Cookery, regular Gisei-dofu was prepared in imitation of the flavor and texture of eggs, which the monks of most Japanese sects were forbidden to eat.

Gisei-dofu may also refer to any tofu preparation which contains—or rather conceals—a prohibited food. Whenever Buddhist monks drank sake, they referred to it as *hanya-to,* meaning "warm elixir of transcendental wisdom." When they dined on wild boar, they asked for some *yama kujira,* or "mountain whale." Likewise, they referred to eggs mixed with tofu as *Gisei-dofu,* or "mock tofu."

Gisei-dofu is one of the few representatives of tofu cuisine prepared in some traditional tofu shops. It usually contains no eggs and is broiled in sturdy copper pans over a charcoal brazier.

24 ounces tofu, parboiled (p. 119) and squeezed (p. 123)
1 egg
2 tablespoons natural honey
2 teaspoons shoyu
½ teaspoon (sesame) oil
3½ teaspoons *mirin,* sake, or white wine

Preheat oven to 350°F. combine the first four ingredients in a large bowl; mix well, stirring for about 5 minutes to develop cohesiveness. Press the mixture to a depth of 1 to 1½ inches into a small baking pan or pie tin coated with the oil. Place the bottom of a pan of equal size directly on top of the tofu mixture to serve as a pressing lid, then place an 8-ounce weight or 1 cup water in the upper pan. Bake for about 30 minutes, or until sides of tofu are a deep golden brown.

Remove from oven and immediately invert. Lift off upper pan so that tofu rests on top of the pressing pan. Brush and rub top and sides of tofu with *mirin,* then allow to cool. Cut into eighths to serve (Fig. 40).

Fig. 40. Gisei-dofu

VARIATIONS

• *Gisei-dofu Cookies:* After mixing the first four ingredients in the basic recipe, shape mixture into cookies and bake on a lightly oiled tin for about 15 minutes. Brush with the *mirin* and allow to cool before serving.

• To the basic recipe add 2½ tablespoons ground roasted sesame seeds, sesame butter, or *tahini.* Increase sweetening to 5 tablespoons honey or sugar, add ½ teaspoon salt, and omit *mirin.* Serve topped with a sprinkling of *sansho* pepper.

9
Deep-fried Tofu

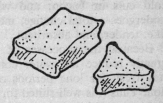

THREE TYPES OF deep-fried tofu are prepared in most Japanese (and many American) tofu shops: deep-fried tofu cutlets (*atsu-agé* or "thick agé") are whole cakes of tofu that have been pressed and deep-fried; deep-fried tofu burgers (*ganmodoki* or *ganmo*) are mashed, firmly pressed tofu mixed with sesame seeds plus land-and-sea vegetables; and deep-fried tofu pouches or puffs (*aburagé* or *agé*) are made by deep-frying thin, firmly pressed slices of tofu until they puff up, so they can later be served filled with salads, cooked grains, sushi rice, or minced vegetables. We will begin by discussing the properties common to all three types and giving recipes in which they can be used interchangeably. In the sections that follow, we will speak more of their unique individual qualities.

Of all the various types of tofu, we feel that deep-fried tofu is best suited to Western tastes and cooking. All three varieties have a distinct, hearty flavor, golden-brown color, and firm, meaty texture that remind some of fried chicken. In fact the word *ganmo* actually means "mock goose," and this tasty tofu was originally developed by chefs who longed for the flavor of wild goose meat, a delicacy once forbidden to all but the Japanese nobility.

Deep-fried tofu can be used as a delicious and inexpensive substitute for meat in a remarkably wide variety of recipes. Grilled or broiled, it has a savory barbequed aroma; added to casseroles, sautéed vegetable dishes, or curry and spaghetti sauces, it adds body, texture, and plenty of protein; served in sandwiches, egg dishes, or atop pizzas, it may be used like cold cuts or bacon; and when frozen, its structure undergoes a total change, making it even more meat-like, tender, and absorbent.

Because the processes of pressing and deep-frying greatly reduce the water content in this tofu, it will stay fresh for long periods of time without refrigeration. Thus it is well suited for use in lunch boxes or on picnics and hikes, even during the warm summer months. Perhaps more important, it can serve as a basic daily food in tropical regions such as India or Africa where facilities for cold storage are not widely available. And, in fact, deep-fried tofu comprises a relatively large proportion of the tofu prepared in semi-tropical Taiwan and the warmer, southernmost provinces of China and Japan.

In addition to imparting a rich flavor and aroma to tofu, the process of deep-frying also adds highly diges-

Fig. 41.   The Deep-frying Area in a Traditional Tofu Shop

tible polyunsaturated fats, usually from either rapeseed or soy oil. Thus when deep-fried tofu is used in place of meat, it serves as a source of the fatty acids necessary for a balanced diet and simultaneously helps to reduce the intake of saturated fats.

All varieties of deep-fried tofu are rich in protein:

tofu cutlets, burgers, and pouches contain respectively 10.1, 15.4, and 18.6 percent protein by weight. Thus both the burgers and pouches have a higher percentage of protein than either eggs or hamburger (which have 13 percent each). A typical 5-ounce serving of tofu cutlets, for example, provides about one-third of the daily adult requirements of usable protein.

Deep-fried tofu—like most deep-fried foods—is at its very best just after being prepared, while still crisp and sizzling. And each of the three basic types can easily be prepared at home from regular tofu using recipes given in the following three sections. Deep-fried tofu purchased commercially may be served as is, without reheating or further cooking, seasoned with any of the toppings or dipping sauces described in Getting Started. Or it may be lightly broiled to impart added flavor and aroma, then served in salads or other quick-and-easy preparations.

Deep-fried tofu is used in virtually every style of Japanese cuisine. Approximately one-third of all tofu served in Japan is deep-fried, and each day tofu makers prepare more than ten million tofu pouches alone!

In most Japanese tofu shops, the highly skilled work of preparing deep-fried tofu is entrusted entirely to the tofu maker's wife. She and her husband generally work side by side since, in most traditional shops, the cauldron in which the soymilk is prepared is located next to the deep-frying area (Fig. 41). Two containers of deep-frying oil are used in the preparation of the burgers and pouches; one is kept at a moderate temperature and used for the initial, slow cooking; the other is kept at a high temperature, which causes the tofu to expand and imparts a handsome, golden-brown coating to each piece. Only the simplest tools are necessary to prepare fine deep-fried tofu: long chopsticks, two small skimmers, and a draining basket set over an earthenware container (Fig. 42). The crisp, freshly-prepared tofu is transferred to attractive, handmade trays of woven bamboo where it is allowed to cool.

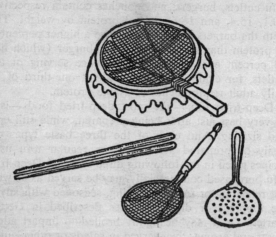

Fig. 42. Deep-frying Tools

In each of the following recipes, an equal weight of any of the three basic types of deep-fried tofu may be used interchangeably. However, since the texture and flavor of one type often seems to go best with each dish, that type will generally appear in the recipe title and be listed first in the ingredients, followed by the second and third choices. Because the size and weight of individual pieces of the basic types of deep-fried tofu differ widely from shop to shop and area to area, we have listed the total weight of tofu to be used in each recipe rather than the number of pieces. In our recipes we actually used pieces with the following weights and sizes:

Tofu cutlets: 5¼ ounces (150 grams), 4 by 2¾ by 1¼ inches.

Tofu burgers: 3½ ounces (100 grams), 4¾ inches in diameter by ⅜ inch thick.

Tofu pouches: 1 ounce (28 grams), 6 by 3¼ by ¼ inch.

PREPARATORY TECHNIQUES

Dousing

Dousing removes excess oil from the surface of deep-fried tofu, making the tofu lighter, easier to digest, and more absorptive of dressings and seasoned broths. In some dishes, dousing is also used to warm the tofu. Some cooks always douse deep-fried tofu, while others find the results are not worth the time and effort. Generally, we hold to the latter point of view. But if you are on a low-fat diet, douse!

Place uncut pieces of deep-fried tofu in a strainer or colander. Bring 2 or 3 cups of water to a boil in a saucepan. Douse first one, then the other side of the tofu. Allow to drain for about 1 minute before using.

Or, holding individual pieces of tofu with chopsticks or tongs, dip tofu quickly into boiling water, then drain in a strainer.

Broiling

This technique, too, rids the tofu of some of its excess surface oil, while imparting a crispier texture and savory aroma to it. If you broil, do not douse beforehand. Some cooks like the broiled texture and aroma so much that they use this technique as a prelude to most deep-fried tofu preparations.

● If using a *stove-top burner* or bed of *live coals,* skewer tofu with a long-tined fork and hold just above the flames until lightly browned on both sides and fragrant.
● If using a regular *bread toaster*, simply drop in the deep-fried tofu and toast. Fast and easy. Serve immediately.
● If using an *oven broiler,* place tofu on a sheet of aluminum foil and broil under a high flame until lightly browned on both sides.
● If using a grill over a *barbeque* or *brazier,* or a Japanese-style broiling screen over a stove-top burner,

broil tofu over high heat for 30 to 60 seconds on each side until speckled and fragrant. Turn with chopsticks or tongs. In our opinion, this method—used with a charcoal fire—gives the finest flavor and aroma.

• If using a *dry skillet,* preheat skillet over medium heat and drop in tofu. Pressing tofu down with chopsticks or fork, rub tofu over entire bottom of skillet until tofu is fragrant and lightly browned. Turn and brown second side.

DEEP-FRIED TOFU—QUICK AND EASY

The three basic types of deep-fried tofu are ready to serve in the form in which they are purchased or prepared at home. Thus, the following dishes require no cooking and can be prepared in less than 2 or 3 minutes.

Crisp Deep-fried Tofu

SERVES 1

This is our favorite recipe for serving deep-fried tofu. If you live near or visit a tofu shop, the master may invite you to sample his sizzling, freshly deep-fried tofu served in this simple way.

4 to 5 ounces homemade tofu pouches, burgers, or cutlets, freshly deep-fried; or storebought varieties lightly broiled (p. 219)

1 to 1½ teaspoons shoyu or Shoyu Dipping Sauces (p. 37)

½ teaspoon thinly sliced leeks or scallions, grated gingerroot, minced garlic, or any of the garnishes served with Chilled Tofu (p. 141)

Cut the hot tofu into bite-sized pieces and serve topped with the shoyu and garnish.

VARIATIONS:

• *Chilled Deep-fried Tofu:* Serve as above using deep-fried tofu which has been well chilled. In Japan, this is a popular summertime lunch or dinner preparation. If the tofu is cut with chopsticks at the table, it will absorb the flavors of seasonings and garnishes more readily.

● *Deep-fried Tofu with Miso Toppings:* Use either crispy hot or well-chilled tofu. If using burger balls, break them open and fill with a little of the miso. Cut tofu cutlets into thin slices. Spread one surface of the tofu with a thin topping of any of the following:

> Sweet white, red, barley, or Hatcho miso
> Yuzu Miso, Red Nerimiso, or any variety of Sweet Simmered Miso (p. 39)
> Any variety of Finger Lickin' Miso (p. 69)
> Any variety of Miso Sauté (p. 41)
> Mixed or Broiled Miso (p. 44)

● *Deep-fried Tofu Topped with Sauces:* Serve any of the following hot or cold over crisp or chilled deep-fried tofu:

> Ketchup-Worcestershire Sauce (p. 50), plain ketchup, or Worcestershire sauce
> All Basic Sauces (p. 46)
> Chili Sauce or Barbecue Sauces
> Mango or Apple Chutney

Grilled Tofu Cutlets with Shoyu or Barbecue Sauce

SERVES 1 OR 2

This is one of the simplest, easiest—and most satisfying—ways to serve deep-fried tofu.

5 ounces tofu cutlets, burgers, or pouches
2 teaspoons shoyu or Shoyu Dipping Sauce (p. 37); or
¼ cup Korean Barbecue Sauce (p. 50)

Broil tofu over a barbecue, or in an oven broiler, toaster, or hot unoiled skillet. Remove from heat and cut crosswise into 6 equal slices. Serve crisp and hot, topped with a sprinkling of the shoyu or shoyu sauce. Or dip briefly into the barbecue sauce, broil lightly once again, and serve in bowls topped with remaining sauce.

Tofu Cutlet Sauté with Shoyu or Dipping Sauce

SERVES 1 OR 2

Quick and satisfying: The various seasoning possibilities are only as limited as your imagination.

1½ tablespoons margarine, oil, or butter
5 ounces deep-fried tofu cutlets, burgers, or pouches, cut
    crosswise into ½-inch-thick slices
2 teaspoons shoyu or Shoyu Dipping Sauce (p. 37)

Melt the margarine in a skillet. Add tofu slices and sauté on both sides until brown and slightly crisp. Serve immediately, topped with a sprinkling of shoyu.

DEEP-FRIED TOFU HORS D'OEUVRES

Homemade deep-fried tofu served crisp and hot, or storebought tofu when lightly broiled, make hors d'oeuvre preparations with a wonderful flavor, aroma, and texture. During the summer the tofu can be served chilled.

Deep-fried Tofu with Curry Dip

SERVES 3

¼ cup cream cheese
2 teaspoons warm water
½ teaspoon shoyu
¼ teaspoon curry powder
10 ounces tofu cutlets, burgers, or pouches, cut into thin
    strips

Combine the first four ingredients in a small bowl, mixing until smooth. Spread on tofu strips or use as a dip.

Deep-fried Tofu Appetizers

MAKES 16

4 teaspoons Sweet Simmered Miso (p. 39), Miso Sauté
  (p. 41), or Finger Lickin' Miso (p. 69)
10 ounces tofu cutlets, burgers, or pouches, cut into 16 bite-
  sized pieces
Toppings: Cut to fit on top of each piece of tofu
  Cheese
  Cucumbers
  Tomatoes
  Fresh mushrooms
  Bananas

Spread miso on one surface of each piece of tofu, cover
with one or two slices of the toppings and, if desired,
secure with a foodpick. Combinations with cheese are
delicious if broiled until the cheese begins to melt.

Deep-fried Tofu Fondue

SERVES 2 TO 4

4 ounces Swiss or Gruyere cheese, grated or diced
2 teaspoons flour
1 teaspoon crushed garlic
5 to 7 tablespoons dry white wine or sake
2 teaspoons shoyu
1 teaspoon lemon juice
10 ounces tofu cutlets or burgers, cut into 1-inch cubes
Spices: your choice of grated gingerroot or powdered ginger,
  minced onion, pepper, paprika, nutmeg, or cloves

Mix cheese and flour in a small cup and set aside. Rub
a small, heavy enamel pot (or a fondue pot) with the
garlic, leaving garlic in pot. Add wine, shoyu, and
lemon juice and bring almost to a boil over medium
heat. Add floured cheese a little at a time, stirring constantly with a wooden spoon in a figure eight motion,
until cheese melts and fondue is smooth. When fondue
starts bubbling, stir in tofu and your choice of spices.

  To serve: if you have a fondue table set with a
warmer, place the pot on the warmer in the center of
your serving table accompanied by long (fondue)

forks. Invite each guest to spear the tofu while it's hot. Or serve the pot set in or over a container of hot water.

Tofu fondue may also be served cold or as a main dish.

DEEP-FRIED TOFU IN SALADS

Sliced, cubed, or diced, deep-fried tofu adds flavor, texture and protein to salads and harmonizes nicely with a wide range of popular dressings.

Western-style Salads

Deep-fried Tofu & Tomato Salad

SERVES 2

3½ ounces tofu cutlets, burgers, or pouches, lightly broiled (p. 219) and cut into ½-inch strips or squares
1 large tomato, diced fine
2 or 3 tablespoons Creamy Tofu Dressing (p. 143)
¼ teaspoon salt or 1 tablespoon sweet white miso
Dash of white pepper
½ to 1 teaspoon lemon juice (optional)
¼ cup diced cheese or pieces of torn lettuce (optional)

Combine all ingredients in a large bowl; toss lightly.

Deep-fried Tofu Salad with Tangy Tofu Cottage Cheese

SERVES 4

10 ounces tofu cutlets, burgers, or pouches
Shoyu
7-spice chili powder or paprika
Tangy Tofu Cottage Cheese (p. 150)
4 large lettuce leaves
1 tomato, cut into thin wedges
1 cucumber, sliced into thin diagonals
¼ to ½ cup raisins

Broil tofu lightly (p. 219) and cut crosswise into thin strips. While still hot, dip into shoyu and sprinkle with the chili powder, then combine with the tofu cottage cheese, mixing well. Arrange lettuce leaves in individual salad bowls, mound with the tofu cottage cheese, and serve topped with tomato and cucumber slices and a sprinkling of raisins.

Fresh Sea-vegetable Salad with Deep-fried Tofu and Miso-Mayonnaise

SERVES 4

7½ ounces tofu cutlets, burgers, or pouches, lightly broiled
    (p. 219) and cut crosswise into thin strips
1 cucumber, thinly sliced
1 green pepper, thinly sliced
1 cup fresh or reconstituted *wakame,* cut into 2-inch lengths
½ cup raisins
Miso-Mayonnaise Dressing:
    5 teaspoons red, barley, or Hatcho miso
    3 tablespoons mayonnaise
    3 tablespoons lemon juice
    Dash of pepper (optional)
1 tomato, cut into thin wedges
4 lettuce leaves

Combine the first five ingredients and the dressing; mix lightly. Arrange tomato wedges on lettuce leaves in a large salad bowl. Top with the salad mixture and chill for several hours before serving.

If *wakame* is unavailable, substitute 1 large diced apple or tomato.

Deep-fried Tofu & Brown Rice Salad with Mushrooms

SERVES 3 OR 4

1 teaspoon oil
⅓ cup minced onion
¾ cup minced mushrooms
1¼ cup cooked Brown Rice (p. 51)
1 tablespoon shoyu
Dressing:
    3 tablespoons mayonnaise
    2 tablespoons lemon juice
    ¼ teaspoon curry powder
5 ounces tofu cutlets, burgers, or pouches, diced
3 or 4 lettuce leaves

Heat a skillet or wok and coat with the oil. Add onion and one-half the mushrooms and sauté for 3 to 4 minutes. Remove from heat and stir in rice and shoyu; allow to cool to room temperature. Now add the remaining mushrooms, dressing, and deep-fried tofu, mix lightly and, for best flavor, allow to stand for several hours. Serve mounded on lettuce leaves.

Also delicious as a filling for tofu pouches.

Buckwheat Noodle Salad with Miso Mayonnaise

SERVES 4

3 ounces *(soba)* buckwheat noodles (or spaghetti), cooked (p. 53)
5 ounces tofu cutlets, burgers, or pouches, diced
1 large tomato, diced
1½ cucumbers, cut into thin rounds
⅔ cup diced celery
½ cup grated cheese or walnut meats; or 2 diced hard-boiled eggs (optional)
Dressing:
    ¼ cup mayonnaise
    1½ tablespoons red, barley, or Hatcho miso
    1 teaspoon lemon juice
    Dash of pepper
4 lettuce leaves
¼ cup parsley

Combine the first five (or six) ingredients with the dressing; mix lightly. Arrange lettuce leaves in individual bowls, mound with the salad, and top with a sprinkling of parsley.

Delicious served in tofu pouches.

Mock Tuna Salad with Deep-fried Tofu

SERVES 3 OR 4

1 tablespoon oil
1 small onion, thinly sliced
3 mushrooms, thinly sliced
2 green peppers or 12 green beans, slivered
3 eggs, lightly beaten
2 ounces of tofu cutlets, burgers, or pouches, thinly sliced
¼ cup (tofu) mayonnaise
2 teaspoons shoyu or 1 tablespoon red miso
Dash of pepper
1½ tablespoons minced parsley
2 or 3 lettuce leaves, torn into small pieces

Heat a skillet and coat with the oil. Add the next three ingredients and sauté for 4 to 5 minutes. Add eggs and tofu, and scramble until eggs are firm. Remove from heat and allow to cool to room temperature. Combine mayonnaise, shoyu, and pepper to make a dressing, then mix with the eggs. Just before serving, add parsley and lettuce; mix lightly.

Macaroni-Parsley Salad with Deep-fried Tofu

SERVES 4

4 lettuce leaves
¾ cup dry macaroni, cooked
⅔ cup chopped parsley
1 cup chopped celery
7½ ounces tofu cutlets, burgers, or pouches, cut into small
  cubes
Dressing:
  2 tablespoons mayonnaise
  2 tablespoons vinegar
  1½ tablespoons lemon juice
  1½ tablespoons red miso or 1 tablespoon shoyu
  1 tablespoon oil
  1 tablespoon minced onion

Line 4 individual salad bowls with the lettuce. Combine the next four ingredients and the dressing in a large bowl; mix well. Spoon onto the lettuce leaves.

Japanese-style Salads
(Aemono)

Deep-fried Tofu & Cucumber Salad with Miso Dressing

SERVES 2

3½ ounces tofu cutlets, burgers, or pouches, cut into 1-inch
   squares
1 cucumber or *uri* melon, sliced into thin rounds
½ cup Mustard-Vinegar Miso Dressing (p. 55)

Combine all ingredients, mixing lightly. Serve chilled.

Vinegared Cucumber-Wakame Salad with
Deep-fried Tofu

SERVES 4

2 cucumbers, sliced into thin rounds
1½ cups fresh or reconstituted *wakame* or slivered *kombu*
7 ounces tofu burgers, or 4 ounces tofu pouches, cut into
   thin strips, each 1½ inches long
Dressing:
   2 tablespoons shoyu
   6 tablespoons vinegar
   1 tablespoon honey
   3 tablespoons sesame butter

Combine the first four ingredients with the dressing,
mix lightly, and serve.

DEEP-FRIED TOFU WITH SANDWICHES
AND TOAST

These preparations are as delicious as they are easy
to prepare. Lightly broiled, deep-fried tofu serves as a
savory sandwich ingredient or may be used as a substitute for bacon or meat slices.

Deep-fried Tofu Sandwich with Lettuce & Tomato

MAKES 1

2 to 3 ounces tofu cutlets, pouches, or burgers, lightly broiled
    (p. 219) if desired, and cut lengthwise into 1-inch-wide
    strips
1½ teaspoons red miso or 1 teaspoon shoyu
2 slices buttered whole-grain bread or toast
1 tablespoon (tofu) mayonnaise and/or ketchup and mustard
1 lettuce leaf
1 large tomato slice

Spread tofu surface lightly with miso or shoyu, and buttered bread or toast with mayonnaise and/or ketchup and mustard. Top with lettuce, tofu, tomato, and a second slice of bread or toast. A tasty relative of the famous bacon, lettuce, and tomato sandwich.

Other nice additions include alfalfa sprouts, sesame butter, cucumbers or dill pickles, or cheese.

Pizza Toast with Deep-fried Tofu

MAKES 5

Use thin slices of deep-fried tofu in place of salami, sausage, or anchovies in your favorite pizza toppings. This variation on the traditional motif, now popular in many Japanese pizza parlors, can be prepared quickly and easily at home.

5 large, fairly thick slices of (whole-wheat or French) bread,
    buttered on one side
5 large, thin slices of (mozzarella) cheese
1¼ cups Tomato & Cheese Sauce (p. 50)
5 ounces tofu cutlets, burgers, or pouches, thinly sliced
3 to 4 mushrooms, thinly sliced
1 to 2 green peppers, thinly sliced
½ tomato, thinly sliced
Olive oil
¼ cup minced parsley (optional)
Oregano and/or thyme
1 cup grated cheese (optional)
Parmesan cheese
Tabasco sauce

Preheat oven to 350°F. Cover the buttered side of each piece of bread with a slice of cheese, and spread with the sauce. Arrange on top: slices of tofu, mushrooms, green peppers, and tomatoes, then sprinkle lightly with oil. If desired, top with grated parsley, herbs and cheese. Bake for 10 to 15 minutes, or until toast is nicely browned. Serve hot, topped with Parmesan cheese and Tabasco sauce.

DEEP-FRIED TOFU IN SOUPS

Thin strips or bite-sized cubes of deep-fried tofu can add a tender, meaty texture and savory aroma to your favorite soups. Seasoning the soup with a small amount of miso or shoyu will often give it a delicious, distinguishing accent. Try broiling the tofu lightly before adding it to split pea, lentil, or tomato soups.

Onion Soup with Tofu Cutlets

SERVES 4 OR 5

2 tablespoons oil
4 large or 6 medium onions, thinly sliced
10 ounces tofu cutlets, burgers, or pouches, thinly sliced
1 tablespoon butter
¼ cup red miso (or 3 tablespoons shoyu) thinned in 1 to 2 cups warm water
2 ounces cheese, grated or diced

Heat a large casserole and coat with the oil. Add onions, cover, and simmer over lowest possible heat for 3½ hours, stirring the bottom once every 20 minutes. Add the tofu, butter, and thinned miso; mix well. Allow to cool to room temperature, then refrigerate overnight. Add the cheese, bring just to a boil and, stirring constantly, simmer for 1 minute, or until cheese melts. Serve hot or, for a richer flavor, allow to cool to room temperature before serving. Or use as the basis for Baked Onion Soup (p. 234).

For variety, add 2 to 3 lightly beaten eggs and/or

½ cup thinly sliced lotus root 15 minutes before adding miso.

Tofu Cutlets in Rich Kabocha Soup

SERVES 6

30 ounces *(kabocha)* pumpkin or winter squash, cut into
   1-inch cubes
2½ cups water
10 ounces tofu cutlets, burgers, or pouches, thinly sliced
¼ cup red or barley miso (or 3 tablespoons shoyu) thinned
   in 1 cup hot water
2 tablespoons butter or margarine

Bring the *kabocha* and 1 cup water to a boil in a large casserole or heavy pot. Reduce heat to low, cover, and simmer for 1 hour. Add tofu and 1½ cups water, and simmer for 1 hour more. Stir in thinned miso and butter and simmer for 10 minutes. Serve hot, or for a richer, sweeter flavor, allow to cool for 6 to 8 hours.

For an even meatier texture, use tofu cutlets which have been frozen overnight and then thawed in warm water. Simmer ½ cup thinly sliced onions with the *kabocha,* and add 2 to 4 tablespoons sesame butter and a dash of pepper together with the butter.

Miso Soup with Deep-fried Tofu & Wakame

SERVES 2 OR 3

This is one of Japan's favorite traditional ways of serving miso soup. The *wakame* supplies an abundance of calcium and other minerals, while the tofu pouches and miso supply protein and unsaturated oils. Requiring less than 3 minutes to prepare, this soup is particularly popular at breakfast, and is renowned for its fine aroma and flavor.

1¾ cups dashi (p. 35) or stock
¼ to ⅓ cup fresh or reconstituted *wakame,* cut into 1-inch
    lengths
1 to 2 ounces tofu pouches or burgers, cut crosswise into
    thin strips
2 tablespoons red, barley, or Hatcho miso
1 tablespoon thinly sliced leeks or a dash of 7-spice chili
    powder

Bring dashi to a boil in a saucepan. Add *wakame* and
tofu and cook for 1 minute. Add miso creamed in a
little of the hot broth and return just to the boil. Serve
immediately, garnished with the leeks.

DEEP-FRIED TOFU IN BREAKFAST EGG DISHES

Use any variety of deep-fried tofu like bacon in your
favorite egg dishes. Most Japanese tofu-and-egg preparations are lightly seasoned with a mixture of shoyu (or
miso) and sweetening. Or substitute diced deep-fried
tofu for regular tofu in omelet recipes (p. 173).

Fried Eggs with Deep-fried Tofu

SERVES 2

2 tablespoons margarine or butter
5 ounces tofu cutlets, burgers, or pouches, cut crosswise
    into ¼-inch-thick slices
2 eggs
1 teaspoon shoyu or ¼ teaspoon salt
Dash of pepper

Melt the margarine in a skillet. Add tofu slices, cover,
and fry for 1 to 2 minutes, or until golden brown. Turn
tofu pieces with a spatula, then use spatula to clear a
space at center of pan between tofu pieces. Break 2
eggs into this space, cover, and fry for 1 to 2 minutes,
or until done to taste. Serve topped with a sprinkling
of shoyu (or salt) and pepper.

Scrambled Eggs with Tofu Cutlets and Onions

SERVES 3 OR 4

10 ounces tofu cutlets or burgers, cut into 1½-inch squares,
    each ½ inch thick
2 eggs, lightly beaten
½ onion, minced; or ½ cup chopped chives or wild onions
1 to 2 teaspoons shoyu
¼ teaspoon salt
1 tablespoon oil

Combine the first five ingredients, mixing lightly. Heat
the oil in a large skillet. Pour in the egg-and-tofu mixture and scramble gently for 2 or 3 minutes, pressing
tofu occasionally with back of spatula until each piece
is golden brown and fragrant. Serve hot or cold.

DEEP-FRIED TOFU BAKED

Diced or cut into thin strips, deep-fried tofu may be
substituted for regular tofu in most baked preparations
(p. 173).

Cheese-Onion Casserole with Tofu Cutlets

SERVES 3 OR 4

3 tablespoons butter
3 tablespoons whole-wheat flour
1½ cups milk (soy or dairy)
1 to 1½ tablespoons red miso or 1 tablespoon shoyu
1 clove garlic, crushed
Dash of pepper
10 ounces tofu cutlets or burgers, cut into bite-sized pieces
½ cup grated cheese
1 onion, thinly sliced
1 carrot, grated
½ cup cracker or bread crumbs

Preheat oven to 350°F. Melt butter in a skillet, stir in
flour, and brown for about 1 minute. Stir in milk, reduce heat to low, and simmer for several minutes to
form a thick sauce. Add miso, garlic, and pepper, mix-

ing until miso is well dissolved. Add tofu, cheese, onions and carrot; turn off heat and mix thoroughly. Pour into a bread pan or casserole, sprinkle surface with cracker crumbs, and bake for about 25 minutes.

Baked Onion Soup with Tofu Cutlets

Prepare Onion Soup with Tofu Cutlets (p. 230). Place in a casserole and cover surface with large pieces of whole-wheat bread. Sprinkle liberally with grated cheese and bake in a moderate oven until cheese just begins to brown.

Or pour 2 or 3 lightly beaten eggs over the bread before adding cheese.

DEEP-FRIED TOFU SAUTEED, STIR-FRIED, OR TOPPED WITH SAUCES

Deep-fried tofu makes an excellent substitute for regular tofu in most tofu sauces (especially Sesame, Spaghetti, Onion-Curry, and Onion & Raisin White Sauce). It is also delicious topped with any of the Soymilk Sauces (p. 309) or Basic Sauces such as Onion, Gingerroot, Teriyaki, Sweet & Sour, or Tomato & Cheese (pp. 46-50).

Onion Sauce with Deep-fried Tofu

SERVES 2 OR 3

1⅓ cups Onion Sauce (p. 46)
3 ounces tofu pouches, cutlets, or burgers, cut into small
    rectangles
1 tablespoon shoyu
¼ cup water
2½ ounces cheese, grated or finely diced
1 egg, lightly beaten

Combine Onion Sauce, tofu, shoyu, and water in a casserole or heavy pot and, stirring constantly, bring just to a boil over medium heat. Now cover pot and simmer for 3 minutes. Add cheese and simmer, covered, for 10 minutes more. Mix in egg, increase heat to high and cook, stirring constantly, for 1 minute, or until egg becomes firm. Allow to cool for 5 to 6 hours, then serve as is or as a topping for brown rice or *(soba)* buckwheat noodles.

Or combine all ingredients in a casserole, sprinkle surface with cheese (and bread crumbs), and bake at 350°F until nicely browned. Serve seasoned with *sansho* pepper.

Deep-fried Tofu with Barbecue Sauce

SERVES 4

10 ounces tofu cutlets
7 ounces tofu burgers or pouches, or substitute more tofu
    cutlets
Sauce:
    2 tablespoons ketchup
    2 tablespoons shoyu
    1 tablespoon sake or white wine
    1 tablespoon melted butter
    ¼ small onion, diced
    ¾ teaspoon honey
    Dash of chili pepper or 7-spice chili powder
    ½ clove garlic, crushed

Heat an unoiled skillet and broil the tofu cutlets and burgers lightly on both sides until fragrant. Remove from pan and cut tofu cutlets crosswise into 8 equal rectangles and tofu burgers into 12 equal wedges.

Combine all sauce ingredients in a small bowl; mix well. Mix sauce and tofu in the skillet and cook over medium heat for about 1 minute. Serve hot or cold.

Tofu Burgers Sautéed with Green Pepper, Garlic, and Miso

SERVES 2

7 ounces tofu burgers, cutlets, or pouches, cut into ½-inch
    strips
½ cup dashi (p. 35), stock, or water
3 tablespoons barley, red, or Hatcho miso
1 tablespoon honey
2 teaspoons sake
2 tablespoons oil
1½ teaspoons crushed or minced garlic
5 green peppers, cut lengthwise into sixths
⅔ teaspoon shoyu

Combine the first five ingredients in a saucepan and
bring to a boil. Cover and simmer for 5 minutes; set
aside.

Heat a skillet or wok and coat with the oil. Add
garlic and sauté for 1 minute. Increase heat to high,
add green peppers and sauté for 1 minute more. Add
tofu, any remaining cooking liquid, and the shoyu.
Stirring constantly, cook for 1 minute more. Serve hot
or cold.

Apple & Onion Curry Sauce with Deep-fried Tofu

SERVES 3 OR 4

Any type of tofu may be used with excellent results
in your favorite curry sauce. We like the tender yet
meaty texture of deep-fried tofu in this richly-flavored
preparation.

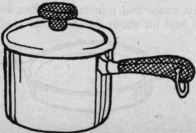

7½ ounces tofu cutlets, burgers, or pouches, diced
1 apple, diced
2 potatoes, diced (1¾ cups)
1 cup water or stock
3 tablespoons butter or margarine
1 clove of garlic, crushed
1 teaspoon grated or 1½ teaspoons powdered gingerroot
1½ onions, minced
5 to 6 mushrooms, thinly sliced
1½ to 2 teaspoons curry powder
2 tablespoons whole-wheat flour
3 to 3½ tablespoons red miso or 2 tablespoons shoyu
1 tablespoon honey
2 tablespoons ketchup
Toppings: Sliced bananas, grated coconut, raisins, diced apples, peanuts or almonds, chopped hard-boiled eggs, and chutney

Combine the first four ingredients in a heavy pot or casserole and bring to a boil. Cover and simmer over low heat. Meanwhile melt the butter in a skillet. Add garlic and gingerroot, and sauté for 30 seconds. Add onions and mushrooms, and sauté for 5 to 6 minutes more. Mix in curry powder and flour, and cook, stirring constantly, for 1 minute. Cream miso with about ⅓ cup broth removed from the pot, then stir into the curried mixture together with the honey and ketchup to form a smooth, thick sauce. Now mix sauce into contents of pot, cover, and simmer for 20 to 30 minutes, stirring occasionally. Serve over brown rice or buckwheat noodles, sprinkled with the toppings.

Tofu Cutlets with Pineapple-Sweet & Sour Sauce

SERVES 4 TO 5

2 tablespoons oil
1 clove garlic, crushed or minced
1 small onion, thinly sliced
1 green pepper, cut into 1-inch squares
2 small tomatoes, diced; or 1 cup cherry tomatoes, cut into
    halves
Pineapple-Sweet & Sour Sauce:
    1¼ cups pineapple chunks, drained
    1 tablespoon honey
    3 tablespoons vinegar
    ½ cup water
    2 tablespoons shoyu or 3 tablespoons red miso
    2 tablespoons ketchup
    ½ teaspoon grated gingerroot or 1 teaspoon powdered
        ginger
    1 tablespoon cornstarch or kudzu powder
7½ ounces tofu cutlets, burgers, or pouches, cut into 1-inch
    cubes

Heat the oil in a large skillet or wok. Add garlic and
onion and stir-fry over high heat, stirring constantly,
for 2 minutes. Add green pepper, tomatoes and sauce
ingredients, and cook, stirring constantly, for about 1
minute until thick. Mix in tofu and remove from heat.
Serve chilled. (To serve hot, increase amount of honey
and vinegar in sauce by 1 tablespoon each.)

Deep-fried Tofu with Hijiki & Carrots

SERVES 5 TO 6

1 tablespoon oil
⅓ cup dried *hijiki*, reconstituted
2 ounces tofu cutlets, burgers, or pouches, cut into thin strips
¼ small carrot, cut into matchsticks
4 teaspoons shoyu
2 teaspoons honey
¼ cup water
Dash of salt

Heat a skillet or wok and coat with the oil. Add all
ingredients and sauté over low heat for about 15 min-

utes. Allow to cool or, for best flavor, chill for several hours before serving.

For a spicier taste, add 1 teaspoon grated gingerroot, ¼ to ½ cup diced lotus root, and 1 to 2 tablespoons ground roasted sesame seeds or sesame butter to the *hijiki*-tofu mixture before sautéing. Or substitute ½ ounce dried-frozen tofu for 1 ounce deep-fried tofu.

DEEP-FRIED TOFU DEEP-FRIED

Tofu Cutlet Tempura with Miso Sauce

SERVES 2 OR 3

Orange-Sesame Miso Sauce:
    3 tablespoons barley, red, or Hatcho miso
    1 tablespoon sesame oil
    3 tablespoons boiling water
    ½ teaspoon grated orange rind
Oil for deep-frying
Tempura Batter (p. 54)
10 ounces tofu cutlets or burgers, cut into 1½-inch cubes

Combine all sauce ingredients in a small bowl; mix well. Heat oil to 360°F in a wok, skillet, or deep-fryer. Dip tofu cubes in tempura batter and deep-fry until crisp and golden-brown (p. 185); drain briefly. Serve hot, topped with the sauce.

Breaded Tofu Cutlets

SERVES 2 OR 3

10 ounces tofu cutlets, burgers, or pouches, frozen and
    thawed (p. 349) if desired
¼ cup flour
1 egg, lightly beaten
½ cup bread crumbs or bread crumb flakes
Oil for deep-frying
Worcestershire or Ketchup-Worcestershire Sauce (p. 50)

Dust uncut tofu with flour, dip in eggs, and roll in

bread crumbs. Place on a rack and allow to dry for 5 to 10 minutes.

Heat oil to 350°F in a wok, skillet, or deep-fryer. Drop in tofu and deep-fry until golden brown (p. 185); drain briefly. Serve topped with the sauce.

DEEP-FRIED TOFU WITH GRAINS

Combining soy and grain proteins gives a substantial increase in the total protein content of each of these preparations, as explained on page 22. Deep-fried tofu mixed with sauces (Sweet & Sour, Curry, Spaghetti, etc.) makes delicious toppings for brown rice, noodles, or other cooked grain dishes. Try also using deep-fried tofu in Chop Suey or Chow Mein, or in grain salads (pp. 153 and 224).

Fried Buckwheat Noodles with Deep-fried Tofu (Yaki-soba)

SERVES 3 OR 4

2 tablespoons oil (used tempura oil is excellent)
1 clove garlic, crushed or minced (optional)
½ cup slivered carrot
1 small onion, thinly sliced
1 green pepper, diced
2 thinly sliced mushrooms or ½ cup thin rounds of lotus root
¼ cup raisins
3½ ounces tofu burgers, pouches, or cutlets, thinly sliced
4½ to 5 ounces (soba) buckwheat noodles, cooked (p. 53)
1 tablespoon shoyu or ½ teaspoon salt
3 tablespoons ketchup (optional)
½ teaspoon salt
4 Paper-thin Omelets (p. 54), cut into thin strips; or substitute ¼ cup diced cheese
Crumbled toasted nori

Heat a wok or skillet and coat with the oil. Add the next six ingredients and sauté for about 4 minutes. Add tofu and sauté for 1 minute more. Add the next four ingredients and cook, stirring constantly, for 1 minute more. Divide among deep bowls and top with the omelet strips and *nori*. Serve hot or, for a richer flavor, allow to stand for 4 to 6 hours before serving.

Sizzling Rice with Deep-fried Tofu (*Chahan or Yaki-meshi*)

SERVES 3 OR 4

This recipe may also serve as a simple and delicious way of using leftover vegetables.

2 tablespoons oil
1 or 2 cloves of garlic, crushed or minced
1 small onion, diced; or ¼ cup minced chives
5 to 10 ounces tofu cutlets, burgers, or pouches, cut into
    bite-sized pieces
2 to 4 eggs, lightly beaten
2 cups cooked Brown Rice (p. 51)
2 to 3 tablespoons ketchup (optional)
2½ teaspoons shoyu
½ teaspoon salt
Dash of pepper

Heat 1 tablespoon oil in a wok or skillet. Add garlic and onion, and stir-fry for 3 minutes, then transfer to a separate container and reserve. Heat the remaining 1 tablespoon oil in the wok or skillet, add eggs, and scramble until firm and light. Add rice and stir-fry for 1 minute, then mix in tofu and pre-cooked garlic and onion, and stir-fry for 2 minutes more, using spatula to cut egg into small pieces. (If using a wok, hold the wok handles and flip the cooking foods into the air 3 or 4 times to create a drier texture.) Mix in the ketchup, shoyu, salt and pepper, and sauté for 2 to 3 minutes more. Serve hot or cold. In Japan this dish is often served topped with thin strips of toasted *nori* (a sea vegetable) and slivered omelets. Also delicious with toasted slivered almonds.

Curried Buckwheat Noodles with Deep-fried Tofu

SERVES 4 TO 6

2 tablespoons oil (used tempura oil is excellent)
1 carrot, sliced into thin rounds
1 onion, thinly sliced
⅓ cup raisins
½ apple, diced
¼ cup water
1½ teaspoons curry powder
1 teaspoon salt
2 teaspoons shoyu or 1 tablespoon red or barley miso
10 ounces tofu cutlets or burgers, cut into thin 1-inch squares
4½ to 5 ounces buckwheat noodles, cooked (p. 53)
Dash of pepper
¼ cup roasted soybeans or peanuts (optional)
¼ cup diced or grated cheese (optional)
¼ cup chutney (optional)

Heat the oil over high heat in a skillet or wok. Add carrots and stir-fry for 2 minutes. Add onions and stir-fry for 2 minutes more. Add raisins and apple and stir-fry for 3 minutes. Stir in water, curry powder, salt, shoyu, and tofu; reduce heat to medium and cook for 3 minutes. Stir in noodles, season with pepper, and remove from heat. Serve hot or cold. If desired, top with roasted soybeans, peanuts, cheese, and/or chutney.

Crisp Tortillas with Taco Sauce and Deep-fried Tofu

SERVES 5

Taco Sauce:
   ⅔ cup ketchup
   1¼ cups grated cheese
   2 tablespoons red miso
   2 tablespoons minced onion or leek
   1 teaspoon grated gingerroot
   1 teaspoon sake or white wine
   Dash of Tabasco sauce or pepper
   1 tablespoon water
2½ cups shredded lettuce or cabbage
15 ounces tofu culets, burgers, or pouches, thinly sliced
10 seven-inch *tortillas*
Butter

Place taco sauce, lettuce, and tofu in separate serving bowls. Heat *tortillas* in a medium oven for 5 to 7 minutes until lightly browned and crisp, then butter immediately and arrange on a large serving platter. Invite each guest to spread *tortillas* with sauce, sprinkle with lettuce, and top with sliced tofu.

Or, use Mushroom Sauce (p. 47) in place of the taco sauce.

Fox Domburi (*Kitsune Domburi*)

SERVES 4

This dish is named after foxes which, in Japan, are said to be very fond of tofu. A *domburi* is a deep serving bowl, usually heaped high with rice. Fox Domburi is one of the most popular dishes served in the many thousands of *soba* shops throughout Japan.

1 cup water, stock, or dashi (p. 35)
3 tablespoons shoyu
1½ tablespoons honey
1 tablespoon *mirin* (optional)
4 ounces tofu cutlets, burgers, or pouches, cut into ½-inch-wide strips
1 onion, thinly sliced
1 cup brown rice, cooked (p. 51)
Dash of *sansho* pepper (optional)

Combine the first four ingredients in a saucepan and bring to a boil. Add tofu and onion, then simmer for 7 minutes. Divide cooked rice among bowls and pour on hot broth, onions, and tofu. Serve seasoned with the pepper.

If desired, top with crumbled toasted *nori* or slivers of Sweet Vinegared Gingerroot (p. 53).

DEEP-FRIED TOFU BROILED

Try using your favorite barbecue sauces with deep-fried tofu. When cooked over a bed of live coals, the tofu develops a delicately crisp texture and savory barbecued aroma.

Savory Tofu Cutlets with Broiled Miso

SERVES 1 OR 2

5 ounces tofu cutlets, pouches, or burgers
1½ to 3 teaspoons red, barley, or Sweet Simmered Miso
  (p. 39)

Pierce tofu from one end with a large fork or 2 chop-sticks. Holding tofu just above a strong flame (or use an oven broiler), broil quickly on both sides until lightly browned. Spread both sides of the tofu with a thin layer of miso and re-broil for about 15 seconds per side, or until miso is fragrant and speckled. Cut tofu into bite-sized pieces and serve immediately.

Tofu Cutlets Shish Kebab

SERVES 4

Ingredients for skewering: (Use four or more)
    5 ounces tofu cutlets or burgers, cut into bite-sized
      cubes
    4 green peppers, cut into 2-inch triangles
    8 mushrooms
    1 apple, cut into bite-sized chunks or rounds
    8 chunks of firm pineapple
    4 firm small tomatoes
    4 small blanched onions
    1 celery stalk or cucumber, cut into bite-sized sections
    ⅔ cup Teriyaki Sauce (p. 49)

Place basic ingredients in a shallow pan and pour on sauce. Marinate for 1 hour, turning ingredients several times. Skewer pieces on 4 to 8 skewers and broil for 2 to 3 minutes, basting occasionally, until nicely speckled and fragrant.

DEEP-FRIED TOFU SIMMERED IN SEASONED BROTHS

Deep-fried tofu absorbs simmering liquids or broths best if first doused (p. 219). Avoid simmering for too long; lest a chewy, web-like structure and many small bubbles form in the tofu. Most of these dishes attain their peak of flavor if served 4, or as much as 48, hours after they have been prepared. During this time they should be allowed to stand in the remaining broth, covered and refrigerated. If tofu cutlets are frozen overnight, then thawed in warm water, they develop a very absorbent texture somewhat like tender meat (p. 349) and make an excellent replacement for regular tofu cutlets in most of the following recipes, or for regular tofu in Sukiyaki (p. 333) and other *nabe* preparations.

Grated Glutinous Yam with Deep-fried Tofu

SERVES 3

1⅔ cups dashi (p. 35), stock, or water
4 tablespoons shoyu
1 tablespoon honey
1 tablespoon *mirin*
4 ounces tofu cutlets, burgers, or pouches, doused (p. 219)
    and cut into thin strips
1 cup grated glutinous yam
3 eggs
¼ cup thinly sliced rounds of leek or scallion
Dash of 7-spice chili powder or *sansho* pepper
Crumbled toasted *nori*

In a saucepan combine the dashi, 2 tablespoons shoyu, honey and *mirin,* and bring to a boil. Add tofu and reduce heat to low. Cover pan and simmer for 10 minutes, then transfer tofu from pan and allow tofu to cool separately.

Stir 1½ tablespoons shoyu into cooled broth. Divide the grated yam among 3 deep bowls and break an egg into each. Top with the tofu and seasoned broth, and garnish with leeks, pepper, and *nori*. Invite each guest to beat the ingredients together with chopsticks or fork before eating.

This dish also makes a delicious topping for buckwheat noodles or brown rice.

Deep-fried Potatoes & Tofu Cutlets in Seasoned Broth
SERVES 6

Oil for deep-frying
7 small potatoes, quartered
2 cups water or dashi (p. 35)
5 tablespoons shoyu
2¾ tablespoons honey
10 ounces tofu cutlets, burgers, or pouches, cut into 1-inch
    cubes

Heat the oil to 350°F in a wok, skillet, or deep-fryer.
Drop in the potatoes and deep-fry until golden brown
(p. 185); drain well.

Combine water, shoyu, and sugar in a saucepan and
bring to a boil. Add potatoes, cover pan, and simmer
for 30 minutes. Add tofu, return to the boil, and remove from heat. Cover pan and allow to stand for 6
to 8 hours. Serve cold.

Oden (Japanese Stew)
SERVES 4 TO 8

When October nights grow chilly, Oden carts become a familiar and welcome sight along Tokyo's
streets. Each old-fashioned wooden stall, mounted on
two bicycle wheels, is equipped with a gaslight lantern
illuminating a compact, self-contained kitchen. Two
pans of foods simmering in a fragrant, dark broth are
heated by a small charcoal brazier. Large bottles of
shoyu, sake, and water stand ready to replenish the
steaming bubbling liquid, and a knife and pair of long
chopsticks are kept busy serving the many customers
who gather around this little oasis of warmth for a
quick night meal or snack. Here you can find tofu and
deep-fried tofu of all types simmering together with as
many as twenty other different foods. In nearby sub-
urban neighborhoods, the "Oden man" roams the night
streets at dinnertime, pulling his cart behind him and
ringing his familiar bell. Stopping at homes when some-
one hails him from the doorway, he provides one of

Japan's oldest ready-made meals and leaves a wake of savory aromas floating in the cold air behind him as he goes on his way (Fig. 43).

Fig. 43. The "Oden Man"

Throughout Japan, huge red paper lanterns hung outside the doorway of working class taverns and bars bear the name Oden in bold jet-black brushstroke letters. Each evening throughout the year—but especially during the cold months—steaming hot Oden is served inside as the favorite accompaniment to hot sake. And in fine Kyoto Oden shops such as *Takocho* or Kyoto-style shops in Tokyo such as *Otako*, Oden is served in an atmosphere of quiet refinement. Seated at high, square stools along a simple but elegant counter made of thick, unfinished wood, each customer orders his favorite items from the wide selection of ingredients cooking in a brightly polished one-by-three-foot copper tray located just behind the counter. As the guest refreshingly wipes hands and face with a hot, damp towel, the cheery, white-clad shopkeepers whisk his order onto a small plate, cut the tofu, *daikon*, or potatoes into smaller pieces with quick strokes of a razor-sharp knife, pour a little of the hot

broth over the food, add a dab of mustard, and place
the dish before the guest with no time lost.

Broth:

     5 cups dashi (p. 35), stock, or water
     7 to 8 tablespoons shoyu
     1 to 1½ tablespoons honey
     1½ tablespoons sake or white wine (optional)

Basic Ingredients: choose about 8

     10 inches of *kombu*, wiped clean with a damp cloth
       and cut crosswise into 2-inch-wide strips
     1 cake of *konnyaku*, cut into 4 triangles
     3 to 4 small potatoes, cut into quarters or halves
     5 to 10 ounces regular or frozen tofu cutlets, cubed; or
       tofu cutlet cubes
     4 to 8 small taro, cut into halves
     5 to 6 ounces lotus root, cut into half moons
     12 ounces *daikon*, peeled and cut into ½-inch-thick
       half moons
     2 large tofu burgers, quartered; 4 tofu treasure balls
       (p. 269); or 8 small burger balls
     4 hard-boiled eggs, peeled
     4 Tofu Treasure Pouches
     12 ounces tofu, grilled tofu, or silken tofu, quartered
     4 cabbage rolls (see below)
     4 *kombu* rolls (see below)
     4 tofu pouch rolls (see Shinoda Maki, p. 284)
     4 *konnyaku* noodle bundles (see below)
     4 prepared skewers (see below)
     1 carrot, cut into large irregular chunks
     4 rolls of *Oharagi* yuba (p. 373)
     10 ounces bamboo shoots, cut into large irregular
       pieces
     2 sweet potatoes, quartered
     2 turnips, quartered

Seasonings:

     2 teaspoons hot mustard
     4 tablespoons thinly sliced leek or scallion
     Dash of 7-spice chili powder

Pour dashi into a large pot or casserole. Tie 4 of the
kombu strips into simple overhand knots, and arrange
remaining *kombu* pieces over bottom of pot. Choose
about 7 more basic ingredients from the list. Arrange
those which require the longest cooking *(daikon, kon-*

nyaku) atop *kombu* and bring dashi to a boil over high heat. Reduce heat to low and simmer for 10 minutes. Add remaining uncooked vegtables (potatoes, taro, lotus root) and simmer for 10 minutes more. Stir in shoyu, honey, and sake, then add tofu ingredients. Return broth to the boil, then reduce heat to very low and cover pot. Simmer for at least 40 to 60 minutes, lifting pot and shaking it gently every 20 minutes to mix broth. Do not change the order of layering. For best flavor, allow Oden to stand for at least 6 to 8 hours, then serve reheated or as is. Divide the ingredients and broth among individual serving bowls and invite each guest to top his portion to taste with mustard and, if desired, other seasonings.

TO MAKE:

• *Cabbage Rolls:* Dip a large cabbage leaf into boiling water until pliable. On the concave surface place 2 to 4 tablespoons of any of the following: diced or slivered onions, carrots, lotus root, *shiitake* or cloud-ear mushrooms (fresh or sautéed); cooked transparent or rice flour noodles, or yuba. Roll the cabbage leaf

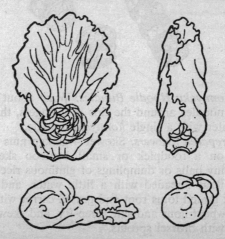

from one end, tucking in the sides, then tie with a piece of *kampyo* which has been soaked for a few minutes in water until pliable.

• *Kombu Rolls:* Reconstitute a large piece of *kombu* until pliable by soaking in water, then cut into a piece about 6 inches square. Cut eight 6-inch-long strips of carrot, burdock, lotus root, or butterbur and arrange in a bundle at the center of *kombu*. Roll up cut vegetables in the *kombu,* tie in 4 places with reconstituted *kampyo,* and cut crosswise to form 4 rolls about 1½ inches long.

• *Konnyaku Noodle Bundles:* Wrap about 10 *konnyaku* noodles around the tips of 2 fingers, then tie in the center with a single *konnyaku* noodle.

• *Prepared Skewers:* Skewer 4 ginkgo nuts or green beans on a foodpick or small bamboo skewer. Or make tiny balls or dumplings of glutinous rice flour or wheat flour kneaded with a little water, and skewer. Or mix grated lotus root and grated carrot with a little whole-wheat flour and salt; deep-fry, and skewer alternately with brussel sprouts.

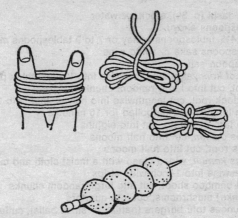

Nishime

SERVES 8

A popular dish at equinox rituals or ceremonial occasions and national holidays, *Nishime* is also frequently included in picnic box lunches as a special treat. At New Year's, grilled tofu is generally used in place of or together with the usual deep-fried tofu. Enough *Osechi* (New Year's) *Nishime* is made on the last day of the "old year" to last throughout the following week of festivities, and the flavor is said to improve with each passing day.

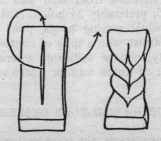

Fig. 44. Threading *Konnyaku*

3 cups dashi (p. 35), stock, or water
7 tablespoons shoyu
3½ to 4½ tablespoons honey or 7 to 9 tablespoons *mirin*
3 tablespoons sake or white wine
½ teaspoon salt
1 cake of *konnyaku,* cut crosswise into ¼-inch-thick pieces
1 carrot, cut into large random chunks
½ burdock root, cut lengthwise into halves, then into 1½-inch lengths and parboiled for 10 minutes
1 large taro or potato, cut into eighths
2 inches *daikon,* cut into half moons
½ lotus root, cut into half moons
8 inches *kombu,* wiped clean with a moist cloth and cut crosswise into 1-inch-wide strips
1 small bamboo shoot, cut into large random chunks
3 *(shiitake)* mushrooms, cut into quarters
10½ ounces tofu burgers (patties or small balls), cutlets, or pouches, doused (p. 219) and cut into bite-sized pieces
10 ounces grilled tofu, cut into large triangles (optional)
8 sprigs of *kinome*

Combine the first five ingredients in a large pot or casserole and bring to a boil. Meanwhile, cut a slit lengthwise down the center of each small piece of *konnyaku* and thread one end up through the slit and back again (Fig. 44). Add *konnyaku* and next 8 ingredients to the broth, and return to the boil. Reduce heat to low, cover pot, and simmer for about 40 minutes. Add tofu, stir vegetables so that uppermost ones are transferred to bottom of pot, re-cover, and continue simmering until all but about ¾ cup of broth has been absorbed or evaporated. Remove from heat and allow to cool for at least 5, preferably 24 hours. Divide ingredients among individual serving bowls, pour on remaining liquid, and garnish with a sprig of *kinome*.

For variety, add or substitute a small amount of frozen-, or dried-frozen tofu, or frozen tofu cutlets.

DEEP-FRIED TOFU DESSERTS

In these tasty treats, the combination of apples and tofu pouches makes healthful and satisfying desserts.

Cooked Apples with Deep-fried Tofu & Tofu Whipped Cream

SERVES 4

3 apples, cut into thin wedges
¼ cup raisins
1 cup water
2½ teaspoons honey
2 ounces tofu pouches, burgers, or cutlets, cut into small triangles
¼ teaspoon cinnamon
12 ounces tofu made into Tofu Whipped Cream (p. 151)

Combine 2 apples, raisins, water, and honey in a pressure cooker. Bring to full pressure, reduce heat to low, and cook for 15 minutes. Remove from heat and let stand under pressure for 10 minutes. Add tofu and remaining apple, and simmer uncovered over low heat for 15 minutes more. Sprinkle with cinnamon and allow to cool. Serve topped with Tofu Whipped Cream.

Cooked Apples with Deep-fried Tofu & Creamy Topping

SERVES 3 TO 4

2 apples, thinly sliced
2¼ teaspoons honey
2 ounces tofu pouches, cut crosswise into fourths
¼ cup water
¼ teaspoon cinnamon
Soymilk Whipped Cream (p. 305)

Combine the first four ingredients in a small saucepan and simmer until apples are just tender and most of the liquid has evaporated. Allow to cool, then sprinkle with cinnamon and serve topped with whipped cream.

For variety, add 1 to 2 teaspoons lemon juice before cooking.

DEEP-FRIED TOFU CUTLETS

In Japan tofu cutlets, whole deep-fried cakes of tofu, are referred to both as *nama-agé,* meaning "fresh or raw deep-fried tofu," and as *atsu-agé,* meaning "thick agé or deep-fried tofu." Both names are used interchangeably, and the former is used frequently in the United States.

Of the many and varied types of Japanese and Chinese tofu, we feel that tofu cutlets are perhaps the best suited to Western tastes and cuisine. We use more tofu cutlets in our daily cookery than any other type of tofu. They are unique in combining the softness and substantial quality of regular tofu with the crisp firmness and deep-bodied flavor and aroma acquired from deep-frying. Costing no more on a protein basis than regular tofu, they keep their form better during cooking and tossing in salads, and work better in casseroles and most other baked dishes due to their lower water content and tender, meaty texture. They are also easier to transport, maintain freshness longer and, due to lower water content, absorb seasoned broths and other flavors more readily than regular tofu. When frozen, they become more porous and tender than tofu burgers or pouches and are therefore particularly delicious in sauces, stews, and sautéed vegetable preparations.

In most parts of Japan, tofu cutlets are prepared from whole, 12-ounce cakes of regular tofu. (In some cases, day-old tofu is used.) The cakes are arranged on bamboo mats placed on top of large boards. Several layers of boards, mats, and tofu are combined to form a sort of "sandwich" that is placed (with one end raised) on a barrel and topped with two buckets filled with water (Fig. 45). The tofu is pressed for 20 to 40 minutes in order to reduce its water content and make it suitable for deep-frying. The firm, individual cakes are then dropped into high-temperature oil and deep-fried (without batter) for several minutes until crisp and golden brown (Fig. 46). The resulting tofu cutlets contain all of the protein from the original 12 ounces of tofu, but now weigh only 5¼ ounces (44% of their original weight) and are slightly reduced in size.

All of the tofu cutlets in Japan, like their Chinese

Fig. 45. Pressing Tofu for Tofu Cutlets

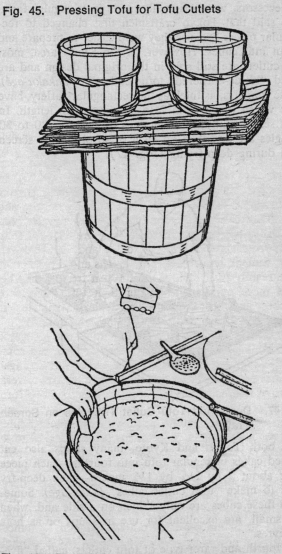

Fig. 46. Deep-frying Tofu for Tofu Cutlets

predecessors, were originally made in triangular form. It is said that Tokyo craftsmen first changed to rectangular pieces because they were easier to prepare and to cut into cubes. However, in the Kyoto area, most tofu cutlets are still sold in the original design and are called "three-cornered tofu cutlets" *(sankaku-agé)*. These triangles, as thick as the rectangular variety, have sides which range from 2 to 3½ inches in length. In most semi-traditional or modern tofu shops, 20 to 30 triangles are arranged on each of several large screen trays during deep-frying (Fig. 47).

Fig. 47. Deep-fried Tofu Cutlet Triangles on Screen Trays

In both Tokyo and Kyoto, many shops also cut pressed cakes of regular tofu into fourths—each piece being about 2 by 1½ by 1½ inches—then deep-fry these to make "tofu cutlet cubes" *(kaku-agé)*. Sometimes these cubes are only 1 inch on a side and, when that small, are excellent for use in soups or as hors d'oeuvres.

A fourth and rarer type of tofu cutlets, called "five-color agé" *(gomoku-agé)*, contain ingredients such as green peas, sesame seeds, minced carrots, burdock root, mushrooms, *kombu,* or *hijiki.* These are stirred gently into the soymilk curds just before the curds are ladled into the forming boxes. After this tofu is pressed and deep-fried, it has a unique flavor and texture somewhat resembling that of tofu burgers.

In Taiwan and China, where tofu burgers and pouches are rarely if ever seen, most of the deep-fried tofu is made from very firm Chinese-style Pressed Tofu and sold as triangles each 2 inches on a side and ⅜ inch thick. In some areas small tofu cutlet cubes are eaten as a snack served with maple syrup or honey.

In Western-style cookery, tofu cutlets are particularly delicious cooked whole, grilled, broiled, or barbecued like a steak. If you have a small charcoal brazier, try preparing the tofu indoors. Connoisseurs say it tastes best if the surface is lightly scored during cooking, then sprinkled with shoyu and served sizzling hot as an hors d'oeuvre.

In traditional Japanese cuisine, tofu cutlets are most commonly used in *nabe* dishes, where they are simmered with a variety of vegetables in a seasoned broth. Tofu cutlet triangles are always found in Oden, Japan's favorite wintertime potpourri, and are the most commonly used variety of tofu in the popular Nishime (p. 251). Tofu cutlets hold their shape well even after many hours of simmering, add their own fine flavor to the cooking broth, and absorb and retain the flavors of each of the many other ingredients with which they are cooked. They will absorb flavors even better if first doused with boiling water to remove excess surface oil.

In the United States at present, tofu cutlets are available at many stores that sell regular tofu. The Japanese-style cakes are golden-brown and about 3 by 2 by 1 inch in size. From 3 to 8 cakes are generally sold in a small polyethylene tub covered with an airtight seal of transparent film. Chinese-style hollow deep-friend tofu cubes are sold by the dozen in sealed plastic bags.

Most of the recipes in this book using tofu cutlets are included in the previous section. The few recipes that follow are those in which tofu cutlets are used in unique ways and cannot be replaced by tofu burgers or pouches.

Homemade Tofu Cutlets

SERVES 2 TO 4

Use fresh or day-old regular tofu. Tofu that is just beginning to spoil is rendered fresh and tasty by deep-frying. When short on time, pat the tofu with a dry dishtowel instead of pressing it to remove excess surface moisture. A 12-ounce cake of tofu usually weighs about 5¼ ounces after pressing and deep-frying. Consequently, the protein content by weight increases from 7.8 to about 15 percent.

2 cakes of tofu (12 ounces each); pressed (p. 121)
Oil for deep-frying

Heat the oil to 375°F in a wok, skillet, or deep-fryer (p. 187). Carefully slide in both cakes of tofu. Deep-fry for about 2½ to 3 minutes, or until tofu is floating on surface of oil. Stir occasionally to prevent tofu from sticking to pan. Turn tofu over and deep-fry for 30 seconds more, or until crisp and golden brown. Drain on a wire rack for several minutes, then pat dry with absorbent paper. For best flavor, serve immediately, topped with a few drops of shoyu and garnished with grated gingerroot (or *daikon*) and thinly sliced leek or scallion rounds. Or serve as for Crisp Deep-fried Tofu (p. 220).

To store, allow to cool, then refrigerate in an airtight cellophane bag.

VARIATIONS

• *Tofu Cutlet Triangles or Cubes:* After pressing, cut each cake of tofu diagonally into halves or into 4 equal cubes before deep-frying. Serve hot with shoyu, honey, or maple syrup. Or simmer with vegetables in *nabe* cookery or Sweetened Shoyu Broth (p. 36).

• *Five-Color Deep-fried Tofu:* Prepare any of the various types of Five-Color Tofu (p. 139). Cut into 12-ounce cakes, press, and deep-fry. Serve immediately with shoyu and desired garnish, or simmer with vegetables in Sweetened Shoyu Broth (p. 36).

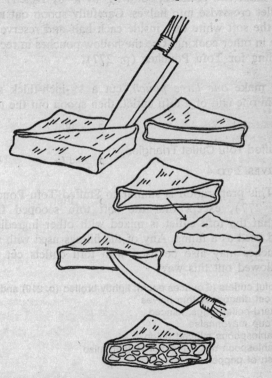

Fig. 48. Stuffing Tofu Cutlets

Tofu Cutlet Pouches

These pouches are an excellent substitute for regular tofu pouches which are difficult to prepare at home and are not yet widely available in the West. They can be filled with cooked grains, vegetables, eggs, or noodles and served like luncheon sandwiches. Or they may be coated with batter and deep-fried, or simmered in Sweetened Shoyu Broth (p. 36). Start with either homemade or storebought tofu cutlets.

To make *two pouches,* cut a (4- by 3- by 1-inch) tofu cutlet crosswise into halves. Carefully spoon out most of the soft white tofu inside each half and reserve for use in other cooking. Use the hollow pouches in recipes calling for Tofu Pouches (p. 277).

To make *one large pouch,* cut a ⅛-inch-thick slice from one end of a tofu cutlet, then spoon out the tofu.

Stuffed Tofu Cutlet Triangles

SERVES 2 TO 4

This preparation is similar to Stuffed Tofu Pouches (p. 277), except that the soft tofu scooped from within the tofu cutlet is mixed with other ingredients and used as a filling. Any of the fillings used with tofu pouches may also be used with tofu cutlets cut and hollowed out this way.

2 toful cutlets (5 ounces each), lightly broiled (p. 219) and
    cut diagonally into halves
2 hard-boiled eggs, minced
¼ cup mayonnaise
2 tablespoons minced onion
1 tablespoon red, barley, or Hatcho miso
Dash of pepper

Cut the tofu cutlets into halves as shown in Fig. 48; using a knife or two fingers, cut or scoop out the soft white tofu from the deep-fried covering. Combine this soft tofu with remaining ingredients and mash well, then use mashed mixture to stuff the 4 triangular pouches.

Homemade Frozen Tofu Cutlets

When we freeze tofu cutlets, we transform their internal structure. Like frozen tofu, they become highly absorbent and acquire a firm texture similar to that of tender meat or gluten meat. Reconstituted, frozen tofu cutlets may be cut into cubes or thin slices and then deep-fried like Frozen Tofu Cutlets (p. 351).

DEEP-FRIED TOFU BURGERS & TREASURE BALLS

In Japan, tofu burgers, deep-fried patties of pressed tofu mixed and kneaded with sesame seeds and vegetables, are called *ganmodoki* or *ganmo*. Treasure balls, their close relatives, containing more delicacies mixed with the tofu and shaped into small balls before deep-frying, are called *hiryozu*.

Tofu burgers have already started to become a hit in the West. Typical patties weigh 3½ ounces and are 3½ to 4½ inches in diameter, about the same size as a large hamburger. Their savory flavor and meatlike texture are also remarkably similar to those of hamburger, but tofu burgers, of course, contain no cholesterol and are low in saturated fats and calories. And the price is right: in 1975, good-sized tofu burgers sold in Japan for only 11 to 19 cents each! In 1976 the Gilman Street Gourmet, a natural food store in Berkeley, introduced tofu burgers at their deli and within a month they had become the best selling item. Who, we wonder, will be the first to start a chain of tofu-burger restaurants in America? Watch out, McDonald's!

The method of preparing deep-fried tofu is thought to have originated in Buddhist temples and monasteries about 500 years ago. At that time, the rarest, most expensive, and most sought-after food of the nobility was wild goose *(gan)*. The story is told that when these freshly deep-fried tofu creations were first served to the monks, they praised their flavor as surely being equal to that of the finest wild goose. As a result, these patties came to be known as *gan-modoki,* or simply *ganmo,* which means "mock goose."

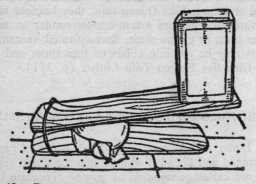

Fig. 49. Pressing Tofu for Tofu Burgers

Each morning in tofu shops throughout Japan, the tofu maker's wife places all tofu remaining from the previous day into a coarse-weave sack, twists the sack's mouth closed, and presses the tofu between two boards arranged like a kind of nutcracker (Fig. 49). After several hours, during which time all excess moisture has been expelled, she mixes sesame seeds and finely-slivered vegetables into the tofu, then kneads the mixture in a large basin or bowl as if she were kneading bread. Finally she kneads in a little grated glutinous yam and, sometimes, salt. After shaping the mixture into burger-sized patties (or tiny balls), she deep-fries them, first in moderate and then in hot oil, until they puff up slightly, turn golden brown, and develop a wonderful aroma that fills the shop. Like all types of deep-fried tofu, they are at their very best when served crisp and piping hot, topped with a sprinkling of shoyu. Most, however, are refrigerated before being sold.

At Daitoku-ji, one of the great, centuries-old temples in Kyoto, an entire ceiling is covered with the monochromatic writhing coils of a Chinese dragon. Portrayed with spiky whiskers and sharp horns, it races through a dark sky among swirling clouds. Two thick, whip-like whiskers stream back from flaring nostrils along its long snout. In one scaly claw, this fierce creature clutches the precious wish-fulfilling gem of Complete Perfect Enlightenment. Zen masters say that the awakening to one's true nature is like the shock of seeing the True Dragon.

The Zen dragon of enlightenment also appears in the world of tofu. For some reason, the process of deep-frying Tofu Treasure Balls causes the slivered vegetables to stick out helter-skelter from the surface of the tofu. Seeing this, the Japanese are reminded of the terrifying Chinese sky dragons with their bristling whiskers and spiky horns. Thus, in the Kyoto area, the unassuming little balls are given the awesome name "Flying Dragon's Heads" *(Hiryozu)*.

Probably the most famous Treasure Balls in Japan are those prepared at the Morika tofu shop and others in the Kyoto area. Each 2-inch-diameter ball contains seven different vegetable ingredients including ginkgo nuts and lily bulb sections. These delicacies are a popular ingredient in the *nabe* dishes served at many of Kyoto's finest restaurants.

Although most scholars believe that tofu burgers and treasure balls were first developed by the Japanese, there are several other interesting theories concerning their origin. The first suggests that they were an adaptation of the Portuguese skewered meatballs (called *hirosu*) which became popular in Japan during the 15th century. Since the Japanese word *gan* can mean "ball" as well as "goose," and since the names *hirosu* and *hiryozu* are very similar and are still used interchangeably to refer to Kyoto's round tofu burgers, this theory seems quite plausible. The second theory suggests that tofu burgers were first developed by the Chinese, who still prepare a similar type of homemade deep-fried tofu containing ground meat instead of minced vegetables. This tofu, however, is not available in most Chinese or Taiwanese tofu shops.

Most tofu shops presently use only two or three vegetable ingredients in tofu burgers, the favorites being grated carrots, slivered *kombu,* and burdock root. Many shops, in addition to patties or balls, also prepare Small Burger Balls which swell up to no larger than 1½ inches in diameter and are often served stuffed with minced vegetables and nuts. Some shops prepare firm tofu burger ovals containing a large proportion of varied ingredients; these are sometimes said to be Japan's earliest form of tofu burgers. To please children and for use in one-pot cookery and Dengaku, the tofu craftsman will occasionally use a cookie cutter to make tofu burgers in the shape of tiny gourds, flowers, or maple leaves.

Each year as the weather turns cold, tofu burgers and treasure balls make their appearance in various *nabe* dishes. Since earliest times, the Japanese have believed in heating the body, not the house. The methods they use for doing so, developed out of necessity in a country where fuel and other energy resources have always been scarce, could serve as practical models for ecological living in generations to come. Able to absorb and retain heat unusually well, tofu, and especially deep-fried tofu, is served in the winter as much for its ability to warm the body as to please the palate.

Beginning in about November, Japanese homemakers bring out their earthenware, casserole-shaped *nabe* (pronounced NAH-bay). A good *nabe* may be many generations old, and is usually rustically beautiful, simple, and rugged. Its heavy lid fits snugly down inside the pot's lips to prevent boiling over—a necessary precaution when cooking over wood fires. The earliest Japanese *nabe*—still found in many farmhouses—was a heavy iron pot that hung suspended from a large overhead hook above an open-hearth fireplace located at the center of the main room of the house (Fig. 50). During the long winter months, when the thick straw roofs of the farmhouses were heaped with snow, the small fire or bed of live coals and the bubbling *nabe* became a center of warmth and brightness. Since the rest of the house was dark and cold, the family gathered around the *nabe* while its steam danced and delicious aromas curled into the cold night air. Here one could feel that ancient and primitive magic of conviviality. We moderns, children of the electric lightbulb and central heating, easily forget that for most of man's several million years on this planet, he has cooked over wood fires and had no other source of light and heat at his table. This was not fire from slender white candles or a flame neatly contained in the glass chimney of a kerosene lamp. Rather, it crackled, spit sparks, and sent smoke up into the dark, arching roofbeams. The *nabe* and the many fine deep-fried tofu dishes associated with it were developed during this earlier age.

Today, the context has changed. The *nabe* has ac-

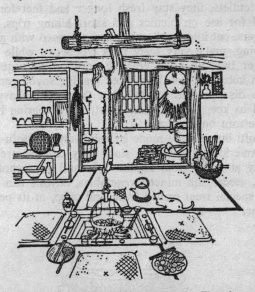

Fig. 50.   A Farmhouse Open-hearth Fireplace with Nabe Kettle

quired a sense of elegance that makes it the featured
dish in many of Japan's finest restaurants. Set over a
portable burner at the family dining table, it is associated with celebration: holding a large family reunion,
welcoming an old friend or an honored guest, or even
bringing home the monthly paycheck. Yet the *nabe*
and tofu—and especially tofu burgers and treasure
balls—have maintained their centuries-old association.
Because they serve as the focus of an atmosphere filled
with good cheer, they are always warmly welcomed.
Best known and most widely used in Oden (p. 246),
tofu burgers are indeed one of Japan's favorite wintertime foods.

Tofu burgers also make an excellent addition to
many Western-style dishes. They combine the substantial quality of tofu cutlets with the firm and meaty
texture of tofu pouches. Lower in water content than
tofu cutlets, they stay fresh longer and therefore are
ideal for use on picnics and short hiking trips. Tofu
burgers, cut into small cubes and seasoned with a miso
topping, make very tasty hors d'oeuvres, while small
burger balls make a creative addition to vegetarian
shish kebab. If you have tried making soyburgers and
were disappointed to find that they were heavy and
hard to keep from falling apart, try preparing homemade tofu burgers instead.

Tofu burgers are made by relatively few tofu shops
in America today. And, since they can be prepared
easily at home from regular tofu and your choice of
nuts, seeds, and minced vegetables, anyone can enjoy
this special treat served fresh and crisp, at its peak of
flavor.

Homemade Tofu Burgers

MAKES 8 PATTIES

You won't believe the wonderful flavor of these easy-to-make meatless entrees. We like to make a big batch and freeze the leftovers.

30 ounces tofu, pressed then squeezed (p. 121)
6 tablespoons grated carrots
4 tablespoons minced leeks, scallions, onions, or gingerroot
2 tablespoons (ground) roasted sesame seeds, sunflower seeds, peanuts, or chopped nutmeats
¾ teaspoon salt
Oil for deep-frying
Shoyu

Combine the first five ingredients in a large shallow bowl, mix well, then knead mixture for about 3 minutes as if kneading bread (Fig. 51a). When "dough" is smooth and holds together well, moisten your palms with a little oil or warm water and shape dough into 8 patties, each 3 to 3½ inches in diameter (Fig. 51b).

Fill a wok, skillet, or deep-fryer with 2 to 2½ inches of oil and heat to 375°F. Slide in patties and deep-fry for 4 to 6 minutes on each side, or until crisp and golden brown (Fig. 51c). Drain briefly on absorbent toweling, then serve hot, topped with a sprinkling of shoyu, as is or placed on a bun with your favorite burger trimmings. Or use as an ingredient in any of the recipes in Chapter 9.

VARIATIONS

• *Tofu Burger Balls:* Shape the basic dough into 12 balls, each 1½ inches in diameter, and deep-fry as for the patties.

• *Japanese-style Tofu Burgers (ganmo):* Combine 2 cups squeezed tofu, 1½ tablespoons grated carrots, 3 tablespoons reconstituted slivered kombu, 1½ tablespoons whole roasted sesame seeds, ¾ teaspoon salt, and 1 tablespoon grated glutinous yam. Prepare as for the basic recipe.

Fig. 51. Making Tofu Burgers

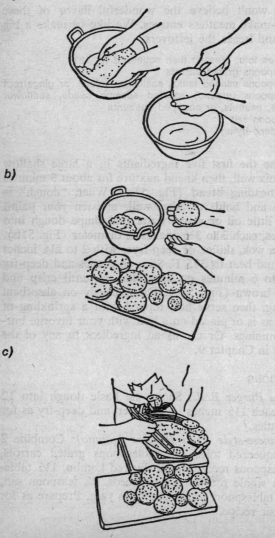

a)

b)

c)

Tofu Treasure Balls *(Hiryozu)*

MAKES 6

This popular traditional recipe comes from the Morika tofu shop located in the countryside town of Arashiyama west of Kyoto.

36 ounces tofu, squeezed (p. 123)
1 tablespoon matchsticks of carrot
1½ teaspoons whole roasted sesame seeds
1 refreshed cloud-ear mushroom, cut into ¼-inch-wide strips
1½ teaspoons paper-thin half moons of burdock root
1½ teaspoons flax or hemp seeds
2 tablespoons grated glutinous yam
6 shelled ginkgo nuts, boiled for 30 minutes
30 thin sections of lily bulbs
Oil for deep-frying

Combine the first six ingredients in a large bowl; mix well, then knead for 3 minutes. Add yam and knead for 2 minutes more. With moistened hands, shape dough into 6 balls. Press a ginkgo nut and 5 lily bulb sections into the center of each ball; seal hole. Deep-fry at 240°F for 10 minutes, or until balls float high in the oil, then increase heat to 350°F and deep-fry for 1 or 2 minutes more, or until balls are crisp and golden brown. Drain on a wire rack or absorbent paper. Serve as Crisp Deep-Fried Tofu (p. 220).

Stuffed Burger Ball Hors D'oeuvres

Cut a small slit in one side of regular or small burger balls and fill with any of the following: Applesauce or diced apples (fresh or cooked), cinnamon and raisins; sliced bananas, nutmeg, and raisins; Tofu Whipped Cream (p. 151), and fresh strawberries; a dab of Yuzu Miso (p. 40), Sweet Simmered Miso, or sweet white miso; peanut butter or peanuts, raisins, and honey; regular or Tofu Cream Cheese (p. 152), chopped dates and grated lemon rind; diced cheese and cucumbers with Creamy Tofu Dressing (p. 143).

Tofu Cheeseburger

MAKES 1

1 toasted hamburger bun or 2 slices of whole-wheat bread
1 tablespoon (tofu) mayonnaise (p. 145)
2 teaspoons butter
1 tablespoon ketchup
1 teaspoon mustard
1½ teaspoons miso or ½ teaspoon shoyu
1 tofu burger—4 to 4½ inches in diameter—lightly broiled
    (p. 219)
1 large, thin slice of onion and/or dill pickle
1 large slice of tomato and/or ¼ cup of alfalfa sprouts
1 large slice of cheese
1 lettuce leaf

Cut the bun horizontally into halves and spread with mayonnaise, butter, mustard, and ketchup. Spread the miso on one side of the burger patty, then place patty on the lower half of the bun. Stack onion, tomato, cheese, and lettuce on top of patty. Top with upper half of bun.

For variety, douse tofu burger in boiling water (p. 219), then simmer for 5 minutes in Sweetened Shoyu Broth (p. 36). Drain briefly before assembling burger. Substitute cucumber pickles or relish for the miso.

DEEP-FRIED TOFU POUCHES

The Morika tofu shop, located in the country-side west of Kyoto, is spacious and quiet, with the well-ordered look that comes from a long tradition of careful craftsmanship. Early one morning, we visited the shop to watch tofu pouches being prepared. Sunlight streamed in through the shop's tall windows falling on the large cooling tanks filled with cold, clear well water and on the glistening hand-cut granite blocks making up the shop's floor. By 4 o'clock in the morning, the first batch of tofu was ready and cooling in the tanks. Now the master's wife would use this specially-prepared tofu to make tofu pouches.

She carefully lifted one large block of tofu out of the water on a thick cutting board. Using a long, wide-bladed knife which she wielded with staccato swiftness, she sliced off thin pieces of the tofu, trimmed their tops to precisely the same thickness, then scooped them up with the knife and placed them carefully on a bamboo pressing mat (Fig. 52). The tofu seemed to come alive,

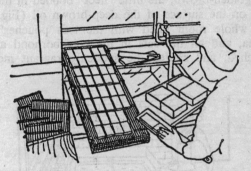

Fig. 52.   Cutting Tofu to Make Kiji for Tofu Pouches

each small piece dancing with the knife, leaping onto the shining blade.

After the sandwiched layers of thinly-sliced tofu—called *kiji*—had been pressed under heavy weights for several hours (as in the preparation of tofu cutlets; p. 253), they were taken to a deep-frying area. A grandmother, wearing a blue kerchief and traditional Japanese apron, worked with a pair of long chopsticks in front of two deep-fryers filled with bubbling, golden-brown oil. She carefully explained to us each step in the process of making tofu pouches, her gold teeth sparkling whenever she laughed.

Into the first container of moderate oil, she lowered a flat screen tray neatly spread with 16 thin tofu kiji, each about 5½ by 2½ by ½ inch thick. The oil hissed and steamed as the kiji sank out of sight. After several minutes, they began to reappear, slowly floating upward until their soft white edges were just above the surface of the oil. The woman carefully turned over each piece, and soon they were floating high and light. Lifting up the screen tray, she transferred it and all of the kiji into the second container of hot oil. The oil came alive, crackling and filling the air with steam. In an instant, as if by magic, each kiji had puffed up and swelled to almost twice its original size. Light, airy, and golden-brown, the little "fleet" bobbed in the sunlight on the surface of the deep-brown oil (Fig. 53). The whole room filled with the tofu pouches' deep aroma, and all the cats in the neighborhood awoke, stretched, and sniffed the suddenly-fragrant morning air.

Fig. 53. Deep-frying Tofu Pouches

After turning the tofu pouches twice more, lifting them out of the oil on the screen, and allowing them to drain briefly, our new friend said that we must try some right away while they were crisp, light, and steaming hot. That morning, sizzling-crisp tofu pouches, served topped with a few drops of shoyu, became one of our favorite ways of enjoying tofu.

Tofu makers say that it is only when a young apprentice is able to prepare fine tofu pouches that he may call himself a full-fledged craftsman and receive permission to leave his master in order to start his own shop. Making tofu pouches takes more time and skill than making any other type of tofu. The tofu from which the pouches are prepared is treated somewhat differently from regular tofu: the soymilk is cooked for only a short time and then cooled quickly by adding a large amount of cold water to it; the curds, coagulated with nigari, are broken up very fine and a relatively large amount of whey is removed; the curds are then pressed with heavy weights for a long time in the forming boxes. This complex procedure is designed to make the tofu swell during deep-frying so that, when cooled, the pouches can be cut crosswise into halves and the centers opened to form small pouches.

A typical tofu shop prepares about 300 tofu pouches each morning. These come in three different sizes; in general, most pieces are about 6 by 3¼ by ⅜ inch thick; some shops make 2½-inch-square pieces which are specially used as Inari-zushi; and Kyoto shops make pieces up to 9 inches long and 3½ inches wide.

All tofu pouches have a tender, slightly chewy texture and much less body than either of the other types of deep-fried tofu. Since they have a high oil content (31%) and are the most expensive type of deep-fried tofu on a weight basis, they are generally used in fairly small quantities. Yet their remarkable versatility makes them popular in almost the entire panorama of Japanese cuisine, where they are used in three basic forms: as pouches, flat sheets, and thinly-sliced strips.

Tofu pouches may be filled with almost any fresh or cooked ingredients and served as light hors d'oeuvres or hearty main dishes. Leftovers placed in tofu pouches are transformed instantly into new and tasty dishes which may be used in box lunches in much the same way as a sandwich. In Japan, pouches are often filled with grains, noodles, or vegetables and simmered in stews or *nabe* dishes. Stuffed pouches are also very delicious when deep-fried with batter. The most popular way of using tofu pouches in Japanese cookery is with Inari-zushi; the pouches are simmered in a sweetened shoyu broth, filled with vinegared rice, and served as a favorite lunch-box ingredient at picnics and special occasions.

If a tofu pouch is used as is, or is cut along three sides and opened to form a flat sheet, foods such as cucumbers and strips of cheese seasoned lightly with miso or shoyu may be rolled up inside. The roll can be pierced with food picks, cut crosswise, and served as an hors d'oeuvre.

Sliced into thin strips, tofu pouches may be used interchangeably with tofu cutlets and burgers. They are particularly popular in miso soups, especially in combination with *wakame,* and may also be used like bacon or ham in breakfast egg dishes, or sautéed like thinly-sliced beef with a wide variety of vegetables.

It seems likely that the Japanese invented tofu pouches since they are not presently found in Taiwan or China. While most of the tofu pouches in Japan are still made in neighborhood tofu shops, an increasingly large proportion are prepared in huge, mechanized factories (the largest of which produces 200,000 pieces daily!) and sold at supermarkets for about two-thirds the price of traditional tofu pouches.

Traditional masters say that there are four requirements for making the most delicious tofu pouches: the tofu must be coagulated with nigari from soymilk cooked in a cauldron; the pouches must be made to expand without the addition of chemical agents; each slice of tofu used must be sufficiently thick so that the pouches have body and can be opened easily; and they must be deep-fried (by hand) in rapeseed oil. Unfortunately, the tofu used to prepare tofu pouches in most factories is solidified with calcium sulfate, and the tofu pouches are made to expand with a chemical agent consisting primarily of calcium carbonate (a white powder found in limestone, chalk, and bones) and phosphate salts. The tofu is cut into very thin slices (which sometimes tear upon opening) and is deep-fried in inexpensive soy oil using an automatic conveyorized machine. The difference in quality is readily apparent.

Japan's most unique relative of tofu pouches is Deep-fried Tofu Crisps *(Kanso Aburagé)*, which come in light crisp sheets that are mild in flavor, golden-brown in color, and about 6 by 8 by ¼ inch in size. Rich in protein (24%) and natural oils (64%), they have a very low water content (4½%) which allows them to be stored for more than 3 months at room temperature without spoiling. Like their two long-lasting relatives (dried-frozen tofu and dried yuba), tofu crisps are very well suited for areas such as Africa and India where spoilage is a major problem. A traditional, natural food, they have been prepared for several hundred years in the city of Matsuyama on the large island of Shikoku, as well as on Okinawa. (They are often sold as Tofu Milk Crisps, since 1 part of dairy milk curds [resembling cottage cheese] is mixed with 5 parts of soymilk curds to give the tofu additional calcium and amino acids). The curds are ladled into shallow, cloth-lined trays which are then stacked and pressed under a hydraulic press until the tofu is very thin. These tofu sheets are then deep-fried in 5 temperatures of oil ranging from 250 to 392°F until they are almost as crisp as a light biscuit. Tofu crisps are generally served in miso soups or sautéed and simmered with vegetables. In Western-style preparations they may be topped with various spreads and fresh vegetables like canapés, used like croutons in salads and soups, or mounded with lettuce and cheese like *tacos* or *tortillas*.

At present, two unique varieties of tofu pouches are made and sold in the United States. The first—which we call Deep-fried Tofu Puffs—is prepared at most Japanese tofu shops. Made from pressed tofu shaped like a small square rod, this variety puffs up during deep-frying until it looks like a golden-brown sausage 4½ inches long and 2 inches in diameter. Unlike tofu pouches, they stay puffed up even after they cool. Some varieties also puff up to form triangular shapes.

Three Tofu Puffs (weighing a total of 1½ ounces) are often sold in plastic bags under such names as Fried Soybean Cakes, Fried Tofu, or simply Tofu Pouches. Each puff is meant to be slit open at one end. Unlike tofu pouches, these puffs are not easily opened into flat sheets.

The second variety—which we call Hollow Deep-fried Tofu Cubes—is made in many Chinese tofu shops. Like tofu puffs, these 1-inch cubes stay puffed up after deep-frying and can therefore be stuffed with other foods and cooked or served as hors d'oeuvres. One or two dozen cubes are generally sold at Chinese markets in plastic bags under such names as Nama-agé or Raw-fried Bean Curd.

Imported, canned tofu pouches are now sold in Japanese markets as Shinoda-maki and Inari-zushi no Moto, or Prepared Fried Bean Curd. Filled with vinegared rice, the latter may be served without further preparation as Inari-zushi.

Opening Tofu Pouches, Puffs, and Large Sheets

In the recipes that follow, the word tofu pouch refers to pieces 6 by 3¼ by ⅜ inches. Tofu Puffs sold in the U.S. may be slightly smaller, so when using them, decrease the filling proportionally.

• *Tofu pouches:* Cut tofu pouch crosswise into halves. To open the center, carefully work your thumbs between the two deep-fried surfaces (Fig. 54).

• *Large tofu pouches:* Cut a thin slice from one end of each tofu pouch, then open the center by working your thumbs between the deep-fried surfaces.

• *Tofu puffs:* One Western-style tofu puff is about 4½ inches long and 2 inches in diameter. With the point of a sharp knife, cut a slit across one end of each puff. If desired, pull or scoop out any tofu which may remain inside.

• *Large sheets:* Using a knife or pair of scissors, open each tofu pouch into a sheet 6 inches square by cutting into 1 long and 2 short sides.

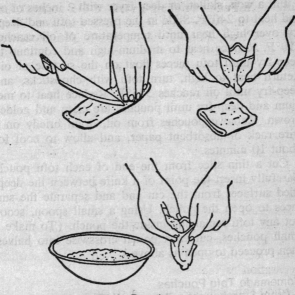

Fig. 54. Opening Tofu Pouches

Homemade Tofu Pouches
(from Storebought or Homemade Tofu)

MAKES 4 TO 6

This is the quick and easy way to prepare homemade tofu pouches although they will not expand quite as much as when you use the lengthier process starting with whole soybeans described below. Twelve ounces of unpressed tofu will yield 5 ounces of tofu pouches.

12 to 20 ounces tofu
Oil for deep-frying

Cut tofu horizontally into ½-inch-thick slices, 4 to 6 inches long and 3 to 3½ inches wide. Press slices using the sliced tofu method (p. 122), except place a cutting board and a 5- to 10-pound weight on the tofu and press for about 40 minutes.

Fill a wok, skillet, or deep-fryer with 2 inches of oil and heat to 240°F. Slide in the pressed tofu and deep-fry over high heat until temperature of oil reaches 310°F. Reduce heat to medium-high and continue to deep-fry until tofu pieces float on the surface of oil. Return heat to high, turn tofu with chopsticks, and deep-fry until oil reaches 385°F. Reduce heat to medium and deep-fry until pouches are crisp and golden brown. Remove pouches from oil, drain briefly on a wire rack or absorbent paper, and allow to cool for about 10 minutes.

Cut a thin slice from the end of each tofu pouch. Carefully insert the point of a knife between the deep-fried surfaces from the cut end and separate the surfaces to open the pouch. Using a small spoon, scoop out any tofu remaining inside the pouch. (To make 2 small pouches, cut each pouch crosswise into halves, then proceed to open as above.)

Homemade Tofu Pouches
(from Storebought or Homemade Tofu Cutlets)

If tofu cutlets are available at your local market, they can easily be transformed into tofu pouches by following the method for Homemade Tofu Cutlet Pouches (p. 259).

Homemade Tofu Pouches *(from Whole Soybeans)*

This recipe should be attempted only after you have mastered the process for Homemade Tofu (p. 127). Although quite time consuming, it yields excellent pouches which expand nicely and are light and crisp.

1½ cups whole dry soybeans
18 cups water
¾ teaspoon baking powder or calcium carbonate
Coagulant as for Homemade Tofu
Oil for deep-frying

Prepare the tofu for homemade tofu pouches as for Homemade Tofu but with the following modifications:

1) Begin by heating 5¼ cups water in cooking pot.
2) Rinse pressed okara with 1½ cups warm water.
3) Bring soymilk to a boil and simmer only 3 minutes; turn off heat and immediately stir 6 cups (unheated) water into soymilk. 4) Add baking powder to coagulant solution before stirring solution into soymilk. 5) After removing whey, stir curds slowly, then set colander or strainer back on curds, place ½-pound weight into colander, and ladle off any remaining curds which settle in colander. 6) Ladle curds quickly and rather roughly into forming container. 7) Press curds in the container with a 3- to 4-pound weight for about 30 minutes.

Remove tofu from container and proceed to cut and deep-fry it as for Homemade Tofu Pouches (from storebought or homemade tofu; p. 277).

Homemade Deep-fried Tofu Slices
(from Storebought or Homemade Tofu)

Many of the recipes in Chapter 9, Deep-fried Tofu, call for "tofu pouches" which do not need to be opened into pouches or large sheets. This type can be quickly and easily prepared at home as described in the recipe for Crisp Tofu Slices (p. 189).

Tofu Pouches, Puffs, and Hollow Deep-fried Cubes

Tofu pouches, puffs, or hollow cubes may be stuffed with fresh vegetables, salads, fruits, or a wide variety of cooked foods and served instead of sandwiches or as finger foods. The pouches may first be simmered in a sweetened shoyu broth, then filled with sushi rice or other cooked grains. Once filled, pouches can be simmered (in seasoned broths), deep-fried, baked, steamed, or even smoked to create a rich variety of flavors and textures. To create a dappled, felt-like exterior, turn pouches inside-out before filling. Leftovers

Fig. 55. Tofu Treasure Pouches

can be rejuvenated and transformed when used as fillings.

In most of the following recipes 4 to 6 hollow tofu cubes may be substituted for 1 pouch or puff.

Fresh Vegetable Salads in Tofu Pouches
SERVES 2

½ tomato, diced
¼ cucumber, diced
¼ onion, diced
¼ cup diced cheese
3½ ounces tofu burgers or cutlets, diced (optional)
1½ tablespoons (tofu) mayonnaise (p. 145)
1½ tablespoons ketchup
Dash of pepper
4 tofu pouches or puffs (p. 277), broiled (p. 219) if desired

Combine the first eight ingredients in a small bowl; toss lightly. Spoon the mixture into tofu pouches until each is one-half to two-thirds full. Fold over mouth of each pouch and fasten with a foodpick (Fig. 56).

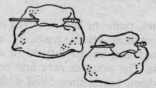

Fig. 56. Tofu Pouches Sealed with Foodpicks

Cooked Grains and Noodles in Tofu Pouches
SERVES 3

In the following recipe for Sizzling Rice, the use of green peppers, carrots, mushrooms, bean sprouts, or lotus root sautéed with the onions will give a variety of flavors. Or mix into the cooked rice: ground roasted sesame seeds, sunflower seeds, nutmeats, or diced cheese.

2 tablespoons oil
1 small onion, diced
2 eggs, lightly beaten
2 cups cooked Brown Rice (p. 51)
3 tablespoons ketchup
½ teaspoon salt
Dash of pepper
9 tofu pouches or puffs (p. 272), lightly broiled (p. 219) if
    desired

Heat a wok or skillet and coat with the oil. Add the onion and sauté over high heat for 2 minutes, or until lightly browned. Add beaten eggs and stir briefly until light and dry, then immediately add rice. Reduce heat to medium-high and fry rice for 3 to 4 minutes, stirring constantly. Add ketchup, salt, and pepper and fry for 2 minutes more; turn off heat. Spoon 3 to 4 tablespoons of the rice mixture into each pouch. Fold over mouth of pouch to form a flap and fasten with a foodpick (Fig. 56). Serve hot or cold.

Inari-zushi *(Vinegared Sushi Rice in Sweetened Tofu Pouches)*

SERVES 5

In Japan, the most popular way of serving tofu pouches is in the form of *Inari-zushi*. Packed into lightweight wooden boxes and topped with thin slices of vinegared gingerroot, Inari-zushi are often found at picnics and outings of all kinds where they play much the same role as do sandwiches in the West. Served at most sushi shops, they are very inexpensive and are prepared in a different way by each chef.

Inari-zushi is said to have originated in Tokyo about 1848, the creation of one Jiro Kichi, chef at the *Jukkenten* restaurant. Kichi peddled his new culinary treats at night through the streets of Tokyo carrying a four-sided paper lantern called an *andon*. On this he painted a red Shinto *torii* gateway, the hallmark of the Inari shrine where the goddess of rice is said to abide. Since foxes are said to be very fond of deep-fried tofu pouches, and since the fox is the patron animal of Inari shrines, this pictorial symbolism and its curious logic seemed natural and appropriate; Inari-zushi soon spread throughout Japan.

20 tofu pouches or puffs, doused with boiling water (p. 219)
1⅔ cups water
3¾ tablespoons honey
5 tablespoons shoyu
2 teaspoons *mirin* (optional)
3¾ cups Sushi Rice (p. 52)
20 slices Sweet Vinegared Gingerroot (p. 53)

Combine the first five ingredients in a large saucepan, cover, and bring to a boil. Reduce heat to low and simmer for 20 minutes. Set aside and allow to cool overnight. (Meanwhile begin soaking the rice for Sushi Rice.)

The next morning while cooking the rice, simmer the pouches until just heated through. Drain pouches thoroughly in a strainer set over a bowl and allow to cool to room temperature. Reserve the remaining broth for use as a cooking liquid for potatoes or other vegetables.

Using your fingertips, gently form 2½ to 3 table-spoons of the rice into egg-shaped ovals. Place one oval into each tofu pouch so that the pouch is ⅓ to ½ full. Fold over the mouth of each pouch, and arrange pouches on a serving tray or place in Japanese-style wooden lunch boxes. Top each sushi pouch with a slice of the gingerroot.

Tofu Treasure Pouches with Crunchy Vegetables (Fuku-bukuro)

SERVES 4

Small tofu pouches loaded with vegetables and tied with *kampyo* are known as "bags of wealth and good fortune" *(fuku-bukuro)* or "treasure sacks" *(takara-zutsumi)*.

½ cake of *konnyaku*, cut into small rectangles
1 small carrot, cut into matchsticks
4 inches of lotus root, cut into thin quarter moons
4 *(shiitake)* mushrooms, cut into thin strips
¼ cup reconstituted, diced cloud-ear mushroom (optional)
2 tablespoons green peas
8 tofu pouches or puffs (p. 277), turned inside-out
8 strips of *kampyo*, each 13 inches long, reconstituted
3 cups dashi (p. 35), stock, or water
4 tablespoons shoyu
1 tablespoon honey
2 tablespoons sake

Heat an unoiled skillet. Put in *konnyaku* and cook over medium heat for several minutes, or until surface of *konnyaku* is dry. Transfer to a large bowl and combine with the next five ingredients. Spoon *konnyaku*-and-vegetable mixture into each of the tofu pouches. Fold over the mouth of each pouch, then tie with *kampyo* (Fig. 57).

Combine the last four ingredients in a small saucepan and bring to a boil. Add tofu pouches, cover, and simmer for 20 to 25 minutes; allow to cool. Now divide pouches among individual serving bowls, top with any remaining broth, and serve hot or cold.

Fig. 57. Kampyo-tied Pouches

Deep-fried Apple Turnovers in Tofu Pouches

SERVES 2

1½ small apples, cut into thin wedges
¼ cup raisins
1½ teaspoons honey
3 tablespoons water
¼ teaspoon cinnamon
4 tofu pouches or puffs (p. 277)
1 tablespoon whole-wheat flour
Oil for deep-frying

In a small saucepan simmer apples, raisins, honey, and water for 6 to 8 minutes until apples just begin to soften. Sprinkle with cinnamon, then spoon mixture into tofu pouches. Fold over the mouth of each pouch and fasten with a foodpick. Combine flour with just enough water to make a thick paste and use to seal the mouth of each pouch.

Heat the oil to 350°F in a wok, skillet, or deep-fryer. Slide in the pouches and deep-fry until crisp and golden brown (p. 185). Remove foodpick, drain, and serve piping hot.

Or dip each pouch into tempura batter (p. 54) and roll in bread crumbs (or dust with flour, dip in lightly beaten eggs, and roll in bread crumbs) before deep-frying.

Foods Rolled in Tofu Pouches and Large Tofu Pouch Sheets

Fresh crisp vegetables or cheeses may be rolled up in a single tofu pouch and served as hors d'oeuvres. Or the pouches may be opened into large sheets and used to wrap various ingredients into a compact roll which may then be simmered in seasoned liquids, steamed, or deep-fried.

Shinoda-maki *(Tofu Pouches & Cabbage Rolls)*

SERVES 4

The name *Shinoda* is given to numerous dishes in which a large tofu pouch sheet is used as a wrapper for a cylindrical core of other ingredients. This name—like the name *Inari*—is connected with foxes, an animal whose favorite food is said to be these deep-fried pouches. In a well-known *kabuki* play, a fox turns into a lovely woman—as foxes often do in Japan to deceive gullible men—marries, and has a child. Eventually the time comes when she must turn back into a fox. At the difficult moment of parting from her child she says: "If you miss me and long to be together, come to the forest of Shinoda in Izumi." Thus Shinoda became known as a favorite hangout for foxes, and the name soon came to be used with tofu pouch rolls. Shinoda-maki are often used as an ingredient in Oden (p. 246) or other *nabe* dishes. Fasten the rolls with foodpicks if *kampyo* is not available.

4 large leaves of Chinese or regular cabbage
4 tofu pouches, opened into large sheets (p. 276)
6 carrot strips, ⅜ inch square and 6 inches long
8 strips of *kampyo*, each 12 inches long, reconstituted
1½ cups water
2 tablespoons shoyu
2¼ teaspoons honey
½ teaspoon salt
4 slivers of *yuzu* or lemon rind

Trim the stems of cabbage leaves smooth, then dip leaves in boiling water until pliable. Place 1 opened tofu pouch with its deep-fried surface facing downward on a cutting board or *sudare*. Cover tofu sheet with 2 cabbage leaves. Lay 3 carrot strips crosswise near one end of the leaves, and top with a second sheet with its deep-fried surface facing downward. With the carrot strips as the core, roll up the layered preparation and tie with *kampyo* in 4 places (see p. 250). Repeat with remaining ingredients to form a second roll.

Combine the water, 1 tablespoon shoyu, and 1¼ teaspoons honey in a 2-quart saucepan and bring to a boil. Add the rolls (*kampyo* bow facing down) and simmer for 15 minutes. Add remaining shoyu and honey, and the salt, and simmer for 10 minutes more; allow to cool. Cut each roll crosswise into fourths and divide among 4 deep bowls. Serve topped with the remaining broth, garnished with a sliver of *yuzu*.

Rolled Tofu Pouch Hors D'oeuvres

SERVES 2

2 tofu pouches, lightly broiled (p. 219) if desired
Vinegar-Miso Spread:
    2 teaspoons vinegar
    1 teaspoon red, barley, or Hatcho miso
    1½ teaspoons honey
    Dash of *sansho* green pepper (optional)
½ cucumber, cut into 3-inch-long matchsticks

Coat one surface of each tofu pouch with the spread. Lay cucumber matchsticks at one end of the coated surface, then roll up pouch (Fig. 58). Secure each roll with 3 foodpicks. Cut rolls crosswise into thirds to serve.

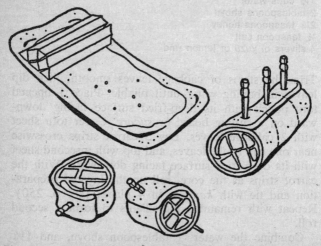

Fig. 58. Making Rolled Tofu Pouch Hors D'oeuvre

Or use 4 strips of cheese, 6 parboiled green beans, and 6 strips of cucumber for the core of each roll. Substitute red, harley, or Sweet Simmered Miso (p. 39) for the miso spread used above. Sauté the rolls briefly in butter before cutting them into thirds.

10

Soymilk

ON A CLEAR cold morning in late October, Akiko and I paid our first exploratory visit to a Japanese tofu shop. Above the shop's steam-matted windows was written its name, Sangen-ya, in bold, black characters. The shop's master, Mr. Toshio Arai, greeted us cheerfully, accepted our gift of crisp autumn apples, then quickly returned to the bubbling cauldron behind him. Into it he ladled some 25 gallons of freshly-ground soy purée (Fig. 59) and on top of it he placed a 3-foot

Fig. 59   Ladling Soy Purée into the Cauldron

cedar lid, all the time explaining that he was preparing soymilk later to be made into silken tofu. After about 10 minutes, steam billowed up from beneath the lid, filling the shop with a delightful aroma. The master uncovered the cauldron and with a specially-made split bamboo rod, stirred down its swelling contents just before they were about to overflow (Fig. 60). Lowering

Fig. 60. Stirring Down the Purée

the flame, he continued to simmer the bubbling purée
for about 10 minutes more, stirring it down from time
to time. As he worked, he explained that there were
four basic requirements for preparing the very finest
soymilk: first, the soybeans used had to be best-grade
whole beans, and the water well water; second, a relatively small amount of water had to be used to give the
resulting soymilk a thick, rich consistency; third, the
purée had to be cooked in a cauldron and, ideally,
over a wood fire to evoke its full flavor; and finally,
the purée had to be simmered long enough to ensure
lasting freshness and make best use of its potential
nutrients (see p. 76).

When the purée had finished cooking, he ladled it
into a large, coarsely woven sack set into a cedar barrel
next to the cauldron. He raised the sack with a hand-
turned hoist and allowed the soymilk to drain into the
barrel through a layer of finely-woven silk cloth. Lowering the sack onto a sturdy rack placed across the
mouth of the barrel, he then pressed it thoroughly
(Fig. 61) until the okara had yielded its last drop of
precious soymilk.

Now, from the deep wooden barrel, he scooped out
a large ladleful of this steaming soymilk and used it to
fill seven earthenware mugs (Fig. 62): one for each
of his three children, his wife, his visitors and, of

Fig. 61. Pressing Soymilk from Okara

course, for himself. Into each mug he spooned a little wildflower honey—chunks of the honeycomb still suspended in it. A tiny pinch of salt and *kampai*—"bottoms up."

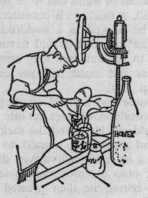

Fig. 62. Serving Fresh Soymilk

Within the space of less than 40 minutes, we had witnessed a truly remarkable process: the transformation of soybeans into milk. Its consistency and appearance resembling that of creamy, fresh dairy milk, this delicious drink had a natural full-bodied flavor, a mellow aroma, and a subtle, mild sweetness. Highly nutritious and low in cost, it soon became a regular part of our daily meals; we picked up a bottle each morning together with our day's supply of tofu.

Nutritionally, soymilk compares very favorably with dairy milk, as will be seen by comparing the following figures showing the composition of a 100 gram portion of soy, dairy, and mother's milk:

	Soymilk	Dairy Milk	Mother's Milk
Water (grams)	88.6	88.6	88.6
Protein	4.4	2.9	1.4
Calories	52	59	62
Fat	2.5	3.3	3.1
Carbohydrates	3.8	4.5	7.2
Ash	0.62	0.7	0.20
Calcium (mg.)	18.5	100	35
Sodium	2.5	36	15
Phosphorus	60.3	90	25
Iron	1.5	0.1	0.2
Thiamine (B_1)	0.04	0.04	0.02
Riboflavin (B_2)	0.02	0.15	0.03
Niacin	0.62	0.20	0.2

(Source: *Standard Tables of Food Composition [Japan]*)

When prepared with the same percentage of water as that found in dairy milk (it is usually made with less), soymilk contains 51 percent more protein, 16 percent less carbohydrate, 12 percent fewer calories (18 percent fewer calories per gram of protein), and 24 percent less fat (48 percent less saturated fat). At the same time, it contains 15 times as much iron, many of the essential B vitamins, and no cholesterol. Finally it contains one-tenth the amount of dangerous agricultural chemicals (DDT among them).

(Unlike some varieties of commercial soymilk or that described above for the sake of comparison, the rich soymilk used to make silken tofu sold in most tofu shops contains an average of 5.5 percent protein and, in some cases, as much as 6.3 percent; its complement of minerals and vitamins is also, of course, about 25 percent higher.)

Because it contains only 52 percent as much calcium as mother's milk (18 percent as much as found in dairy milk), soymilk is often enriched with calcium or calcium lactate when used in baby formulae. But whereas 7 to 10 percent of all American babies—as well as many adults—are allergic or otherwise sensitive to dairy milk (an even larger percentage find that it creates digestive difficulties), there is no evidence of similar reactions to regular or enriched soymilk.

Although various types of "vegetable milks" can be prepared from nuts (almonds, peanuts, walnuts, coconut) and seeds (sunflower and sesame), the soybean is, perhaps, the only plant known to man capable of yielding milk in large quantities at reasonable cost. And it strikes us as a deeply mysterious coincidence that the substance of a simple seed, ground and cooked with water, should be so similar to the life-giving milk produced in the bodies of mammals and used to suckle their young.

Soymilk has been used for centuries throughout East Asia in much the same way that dairy milk is now used in the West. Today many people who could not possibly afford cow's milk find that soymilk s greatest appeal lies in its remarkably low cost. Whether prepared at home or in tofu shops, specialty shops, or factories, it can be produced for about one-half to one-third the cost of cow's milk. Thus, in many parts of the world where dairy milk is not generally consumed and does not give promise of ever being able to meet the needs of growing populations, soymilk could serve as a practical source of high-quality, essential nutrients both for infants and growing children in their crucial formative years, and for adults of all ages. Moreover, it is already finding popular appeal in the affluent West, especially among the many people interested in natural, health, and diet foods, and in a growing number of communities that find they can produce their own soymilk fresh each morning for a fraction of the price they would have to pay for dairy milk. *The Farm,* a community of one thousand people, for example, has recently started its own soy dairy capable of producing 80 gallons of rich soymilk every day at a cost of only 7½ cents per quart. *Farm* spokesmen report that the community's "babies love soymilk" and that most of its 250 children have been weaned onto it directly. And many tofu shops in America now sell bottled soymilk (available plain, or sweetened with honey or honey-carob) to a growing number of patrons.

As we studied the tofu-making process in Taiwan, we noticed a continuous stream of people, each bringing a teapot or kettle to the local tofu shop to purchase several quarts of fresh soymilk. We learned that this is commonly served as part of the family breakfast and is considered an essential source of protein for babies and young children. Here, as well as on the mainland, soymilk is also bottled on a large scale by shops and factories and is delivered each morning to regular customers: workmen are said to consider it an excellent source of energy and stamina. We found that most tofu makers took special pride in the flavor of their own preparation; in every shop we visited, we were unfailingly offered a large cup of hot soymilk, generally sweetened with a little brown sugar. And almost every block in the city of Taipei seemed to have at least one shop or cafe specializing in spicy hot soymilk soups and sweetened soymilk drinks available from early morning until well after midnight.

In the 1950s, soymilk appeared in a new form, as a bottled, non-carbonated soft drink produced on a large scale by industrial methods. Aimed at replacing the empty calories of conventional soft drinks with protein and other essential nutrients, this product has been given an up-dated image by means of modern advertising techniques and slogans emphasizing health and nutrition. *Vitasoy,* the first beverage of its kind, was developed by Mr. K. S. Lo, and idealistic Hong Kong businessman, whose primary motivation was to provide nourishment for the masses at a price they could afford. Each 6½-ounce bottle contains 3 percent protein (6.8 grams) and retails for less than 3½ U.S. cents, or about two-thirds the cost of the same sized bottle of Coca Cola. Sold from sampans, sidewalk stands, and grocery stores, it is enjoyed ice cold in summer and piping hot in winter. By 1974, *Vitasoy's* sales had skyrocketed to more than 150 million bottles per year, making it Hong Kong's best selling soft drink.

Soon after *Vitasoy* caught on in Hong Kong, *Vitabean,* a similar beverage marketed by the Yeo Hiap Seng Company, came on the scene in Singapore and Kuala Lumpur (Malaysia). Pasteurized and packaged in decorative, aseptic, tetrapak cartons containing 10 fluid ounces (284 cc), *Vitabean* can stay fresh for weeks without refrigeration. By the late 1960s, America's Monsanto Corporation had formed a joint venture with the Vitabean Company to market a variety of soymilk beverages (among them, *Puma*) in South America. Not long thereafter, the Coca Cola Corporation, apparently deciding to join rather than fight, opened its own soymilk soft drink plant in Rio de Janeiro, where it is producing *Saci*. And in India, Africa, and a growing number of other areas, protein-rich soymilk drinks flavored to suit local tastes (malt, orange, coffee, cinnamon, and vanilla) are now being sold for about one-fourth the price of cow's milk.

Recognizing the nutritive value of these soymilk beverages, prestigious international organizations such as UNICEF and the Food and Agricultural Organization (FAO) have recently given them their endorsement. The World Health Organization (WHO) has gone so far as to build a one-million-dollar soymilk factory in Indonesia and smaller plants in the Philippines (Manila) and other areas where soymilk has long been a traditional breakfast drink. Perhaps the world's most modern soymilk plant, privately owned by a Mr. Cheng, is located in Bangkok, Thailand; it is fully automated from the time the beans are de-hulled until the finished product is bottled and packed for distribution. A product comprised of a mixture of soymilk and ordinary skim milk is also being marketed here.

In the West, the growing recognition of the value of soymilk has been greatly stimulated by the work of Dr. Harry W. Miller. In 1936, while working as a medical missionary in Shanghai, Dr. Miller started the first soy dairy where soymilk was prepared on a large scale, sterilized in bottles, and distributed daily. Largely through Dr. Miller's efforts, soymilk fortified with vitamins and minerals has finally come to be used in the United States, too, primarily for feeding infants. His life's dream was to see soymilk made available to people throughout the world, especially to the increasing number of children suffering from malnutrition.

The research work of Dr. Miller and other nutritionists around the world, based on experiments with large numbers of infants and young children, shows clearly and conclusively that soymilk can be used as a complete and effective substitute for dairy or human milk. When fortified with sulphur-containing amino acids, calcium, and vitamins A,B,C, and D, the nutritional balance of the product approaches its ideal as a baby food. In 1937, when Dr. Miller patented the first such formulated drink, he was advised that if he called it by its common and obvious name, soymilk, he would be fought by the dairy industry; so he latinized the name to *Soyalac*. The actual cost of preparing this milk in the United States is about one-half the cost of obtaining dairy milk (before bottling and distribution). Reports in various publications suggest that, for this reason, the American dairy industry may be growing increasingly concerned about the use of soymilk and other soy products to extend, or even replace, dairy products.

In Japan, soymilk is prepared by a number of large

companies and sold in tetrapak cartons, or in condensed form, in cans. Now available in a variety of flavors (plain, honey, vanilla, coffee, orange, barley-malt, strawberry, or chocolate) at virtually all natural and health food stores and at most supermarkets, some types are even dispensed from vending machines or delivered door to door. (Many Japanese tofu makers used to deliver a bottle of soymilk each morning to a large number of their regular customers, but the tradition has gradually declined with the increasing availability of commercial soymilk and the post-war trend toward drinking dairy milk.) A formulated, canned soymilk for infants (and those allergic or sensitive to dairy milk) and at least four varieties of powdered, spray-dried soymilk packaged in cartons are available at most pharmacies or natural food stores. Plain powdered soymilk contains 44 to 52 percent protein, 28 percent fat (mostly polyunsaturated), and 12 percent carbohydrates; stored at room temperature, it will keep its flavor indefinitely and is an excellent lightweight ingredient for use on camping trips or picnics. One type of powdered soymilk, called *Bonlact,* is especially formulated for infants and growing children. Another, used primarily as a health food by adults on low-fat or reducing diets, is fortified with lecithin and linoleic acid, methionine, fruit sugar, plus vitamins and minerals. The most popular spray-dried soymilk is packaged together with a small envelope of lactone coagulant and sold at most food markets as instant homemade tofu.

Soymilk is well thought of by medical practitioners as well as laymen. Many Japanese doctors view it as an effective natural medicine and prescribe it as a regular part of the diet for diabetes (because it is low in starch); heart disease, high blood pressure, and hardening of the arteries (because it is free of cholesterol, low in saturated fats, and rich in lecithin and linoleic acid); and anemia (because it is rich in iron and is thought to stimulate the production of hemo-

globin). It is also used to strengthen the digestive system (since health-giving lactic acid bacteria thrive and multiply in its presence) and alkalize—hence fortify—the bloodstream (since it is among the most alkaline sources of protein).

In his full-length book, *The Wonders of Soymilk,* Mr. Teisuke Yabuki carefully documents case after case where doctors or patients attribute the cure of various diseases to soymilk. Some prescribe it as an effective remedy for chronic nosebleed or bruises that won't heal; others find that it alleviates arthritis, softens corns, or restores healthy black hair. Some doctors assert that since soymilk contains an abundance of water-soluble vitamins (some of which dissolve in the whey during the tofu-making process), they actually prefer soymilk to tofu for use in diets related to vitamin-deficiency diseases.

Tofu makers have frequently told us that a number of their customers order soymilk daily for use as a medicine as well as a tasty beverage. Many Japanese claim that soymilk helps bring out the natural luster of the skin, and, in fact, people who work in tofu and yuba shops are well known for their fine complexions. Many a tofu maker has told us how, when his nursing wife's milk supply decreased or failed, she fed the baby soymilk, often using it as a basic food until weaning time. And even today, many pregnant and nursing women drink soymilk to increase the quality and flow of their milk. Soymilk is also thought to be effective in curing constipation and intestinal disturbances in children.

In Japanese tofu shops, soymilk is the source of each of the six types of tofu. The rich soymilk served as a drink is generally used to make silken tofu, while regular tofu is made from soymilk with a much thinner consistency. The secret of delicious soymilk lies above all in its thickness, which varies widely from shop to shop.

The point can well be made that soymilk is a better and more convenient way of using soybeans as a food than tofu: it is considerably easier to make, takes less than one-half the time, requires less fuel and equipment, and therefore costs less; it contains 83 percent of the protein originally present in the soybeans (tofu contains only 73½ percent due to losses in the whey and soaking water); it is a simpler food since no coagulant need be added in its manufacture; it contains the full, subtle sweetness of the soybeans, which gradually diminishes in proportion to the length of time the resultant silken or regular tofu is soaked in water; and it can be fed even to babies who are too young to eat tofu.

In recent years, a number of large commercial manufacturers of soymilk have developed methods for producing soymilk with a flavor quite similar to that of dairy milk. The characteristic soy flavor, which is found in water-soluble soybean enzymes rather than in the protein or oil, is removed by dehulling the beans, washing and draining them thoroughly several times before and after soaking, grinding them together with boiling water, and cooking the purée for a fairly long time at a high temperature, about 8 minutes at 238°F). Some makers then pasteurize the soymilk at 293°F for a few seconds and package it in foil-lined tetrapak cartons in which it will keep for up to 1 month without refrigeration. Although this mild-flavored, modern product is said to have a wider appeal than its traditional counterpart, we—like almost all people in China and most Japanese tofu makers—definitely prefer the flavor of the natural product.

Used for centuries to make fermented tofu, a soft Chinese cheese-like product fermented in brining liquor, soymilk can also be used to make Western-style cheeses. Furthermore, it can be fermented with the same starters as dairy milk to make delicious and inexpensive homemade yogurt (p. 302). In Western-style cookery, soymilk may be used in any recipe calling for dairy milk.

The soymilk used in the recipes that follow may be the type freshly prepared at home (you can prepare excellent soymilk in a blender in less than 20 minutes) or any one of the varieties of fresh, powdered, or canned soymilk now available throughout the United States at most natural- and health-food stores, many Japanese and Chinese markets, and a growing number of supermarkets.

Homemade Soymilk (from Whole Soybeans)

MAKES 7½ TO 8 CUPS

This delicious soymilk contains about 3.7 percent protein (vs. 3.3 for dairy milk) and takes only 20 minutes to prepare. Using storebought soybeans (29 cents/lb.), it will cost roughly 11 cents a quart, or less than one third the price of dairy milk. This "boiling water-grind" technique, developed at Cornell University, is quicker and easier than traditional methods, and it inactivates the soy enzyme lipoxygenase yielding soymilk with a flavor more like that of dairy milk. The necessary utensils (described at Homemade Tofu) are found in any typical kitchen. A stainless steel or glass blender is ideal. If using a plastic blender bowl that will not stand boiling water, or a food mill or juicer, see the first Variation below. To make silken tofu or yuba, use the rich soymilk described in the second Variation. Note: do *not* use soybeans that are more than one year old: they yield a starchy thick milk that clogs the pressing sack.

1½ cups dry soybeans, washed and drained 3 times, soaked in 4 to 6 cups water at room temperature for about 10 hours, then drained and rinsed well
12 cups (hot) water, approximately

1) Run 12 cups water (preferably hot) into a large teapot or kettle and bring to a boil. Place a deep, 6-to-8-quart pot in sink, set a large colander in mouth of pot, and line colander with a moistened pressing sack 15 inches wide and 15 inches deep made of *coarse-weave* linen (with the mesh big enough to poke a pin through), or a coarse-weave 2-foot-square dishcloth. Divide soaked beans into three equal portions (about 1⅓ cups each).

2) Preheat a glass, stainless steel, or heatproof plastic blender bowl by slowly pouring in 2 to 3 cups boiling water. Allow water to stand for 1 minute, then discard. In the blender combine one portion of beans with 2 cups *boiling* water (from teapot) and purée at high speed for 1 minute, or until very smooth. Pour purée into sack in colander. Purée remaining portions of beans with 2 cups water each and pour into sack. Rinse out blender with ¼ cup boiling water to retrieve any purée, and pour into sack.

3) Twist mouth of sack closed. Using a glass jar or potato masher, press sack repeatedly against bottom of colander to extract as much soymilk as possible. Shake solids (okara) into one corner of sack, twist further closed, and press again. Open mouth of sack wide in colander, stir okara briefly, then pour 2½ cups boiling water over okara. Stir again. Twist sack closed and press repeatedly with jar. Transfer pot containing soymilk to stove. Reserve okara for use in cooking. (Or, to get ½ cup more soymilk, open sack wide, allow okara to cool for 5 minutes, then twist closed sack and use your hands to squeeze out remaining soymilk.)

4) Bring soymilk to a boil over medium-high heat,

stirring bottom of cooking pot constantly with a wooden spatula or spoon to prevent sticking. When foam suddenly rises in pot (or milk comes to a boil) reduce heat to medium and simmer for about 7 minutes. Remove pot from burner. Or heat for 30 minutes in a covered double boiler or in a covered saucepan set in a pot of boiling water.) If desired, add to the 7½ cups soymilk one of the following popular flavoring combinations (listed with our favorites first):

● *Honey-Vanilla Soymilk:* Add 2½ to 4 tablespoons honey, ¼ teaspoon or less vanilla extract, and a pinch of salt; mix or purée well.
● *Rich & Creamy Soymilk:* To any of the flavoring combinations above or below, add 2 to 3 tablespoons vegetable oil; purée at high speed until well dispersed. For extra thickness, add ¼ teaspoon granular lecithin.
● *Carob-Honey Soymilk:* Add 4 tablespoons honey or natural sugar, a pinch of salt and, if desired, ¼ teaspoon vanilla extract. *After* milk has cooled, whip in 2½ to 4 teaspoons carob (or cocoa) powder, which has first been creamed in a little of the cold soymilk.
● *Malt, Mocha, or Coffee Soymilk:* Add 2 to 3 tablespoons granular malt, mocha, or coffee to the Honey-Vanilla Soymilk, above.
● *Sesame or Calcium-rich Soymilk:* To Honey-Vanilla or Rich & Creamy Soymilk, add 5 to 8 tablespoons sesame butter, a rich calcium source. Or cool milk and add 1 teaspoon calcium lactate.
● *Orange Soymilk:* Stir 1¼ cups orange juice into cold soymilk.
● *Other flavorings:* Try strawberry, grated gingerroot, cinnamon & anise, nut butters, egg yolk or whole egg, butter, or coconut.

6) Soymilk may now be served hot. Or for a richer, creamier consistency, a deeper sweetness, and a flavor more like that of dairy milk, chill by covering and setting pot in circulating cold water for 10 to 15 minutes.

This quick cooling increases shelf life. Pour soymilk into clean (or sterilized) bottles and cover tightly. Refrigerated, it will keep for 3 to 6 days; if frozen, it will keep indefinitely.

VARIATIONS

• *Non-boiling Water Grind:* If using a plastic blender that will not stand boiling water, substitute hottest tap water when puréeing, but mix okara with boiling water. If using a food mill or juicer, grind beans without water, mix ground beans with 6 cups boiling water, and allow to stand for 2 to 3 minutes. Rinse out mill or juicer with ¼ cup boiling water, then transfer purée to pressing sack and proceed from Step 3.

• *Rich Homemade Soymilk* (makes 3¼ cups): Soak only 1 cup dry soybeans. Drain, divide into 2 equal portions, and purée each portion with 1¾ cups boiling water. Rinse blender with ¼ cup boiling water, cook milk for 7 minutes, extract milk in pressing sack, then sprinkle okara with ½ cup boiling water and re-press. Use to make silken tofu, soft tofu, or yuba. Or, use in cooking like cream.

• *High-yielding Soymilk:* In Step 3, rinse okara with 3½ to 4½ cups boiling water. Yields 8½ to 9½ cups thinner (but still good) soymilk.

Dairylike Soymilk Products

You will be seeing more of these tasty, low-cost, healthful products sold commercially throughout the world in years to come. All are easily made at home. For related dairylike products made from tofu, see Chapter 8.

Soymilk Yogurt or Soygurt

MAKES 1 PINT

Soygurt can be prepared more quickly and easily than dairy yogurt and requires less starter. Unlike dairy yogurt, it can be made at room temperature without an incubator, although the use of an incubator gives faster results, a slightly smoother consistency, and a better flavor. When prepared from homemade soymilk, the cost is about one-sixth that of commercial dairy yogurt, while the protein content may be considerably higher. During the fermentation, the lactic acid bacteria *(Lactobacillus)* in the starter produce lactic acid, which acts as a protein coagulant; some cultures also contain *Streptococcus thermophilus* bacteria. If you prefer not to use a standard dairy yogurt as a starter, obtain a pure culture *Lactobacillus acidophilus* or *Lactobacillus bulgaricus* which is sold at some natural or health food stores or by mail order from Chr. Hansen's Lab, Inc., 9015 West Maple St., Milwaukee, WI 52314. Dr. H. L. Wang and her colleagues at the U.S.D.A. Northern Regional Research Center (1815 N. University St., Peoria, IL 61604) have isolated strains of *Lactobacillus* especially suited for making soymilk yogurt. Since soymilk yogurt tends to have a slightly more acidic flavor than dairy yogurt, some people like to add a sweetener. If incubated for too short a time, the subtle tartness of fine yogurt will not develop; if cultured too long, the yogurt will sour and separate into curds and whey. The best time is 4 to 5 hours at 105°F. A gas oven with a pilot light makes a good incubator.

2 cups Homemade Soymilk (preferably rich, p. 299)
1 tablespoon honey or pure maple syrup (optional)
1½ teaspoons yogurt; or pure-culture *Lactobacillus* starter
  as directed

Mix hot soymilk and honey, and allow to cool to 112°F. (Or heat cold soymilk to 112°F.) Remove thin yuba film from soymilk surface and reserve. Stir starter into soymilk, then pour inoculated milk into one or more clean (preferably sterilized) jars, and cover. Incubate at 105°F for 4 to 8 hours (check after 4 hours; some starters not well adapted to soymilk may take as long as 25 hours), at 98.6°F for 12 to 14 hours, or allow to stand at room temperature (70°F or above) for 14 to 18 hours. Yogurt is ready when it separates cleanly and easily from the sides if you tilt the jar slightly. Set aside several tablespoons of the new yogurt for use as starter with your next batch. Serve yogurt as is, or sweetened. Serve yuba topped with a few drops of shoyu.

VARIATIONS

• *Fruit Yogurts:* Together with the honey, add pure fruit preserves; strawberry and peach work especially well.

• *Creamier Soymilk Yogurt:* A little free whey may appear atop yogurt; to prevent this, heat 2¼ teaspoons agar flakes in a little water until flakes dissolve, then stir into the hot soymilk as a stabilizer. (Note: most commercial yogurts contain a gelatin stabilizer.)

• *Refreshing Yogurt Drink:* Combine equal parts soymilk yogurt and ice water in a blender; purée until smooth.

• *Soymilk Smoothie:* Purée soymilk yogurt and a little ice in a blender with raspberries, blackberries, strawberries, peaches, melon, or bananas.

Soymilk Kefir

MAKES 1 QUART

Kefir is a Russian and Near Eastern fermented milk drink with a rich, thick consistency, a delicious balance of sweetness and tartness, and in some cases a slight effervesence. The starter, generally called "kefir grains," is a symbiotic association of various lactic acid bacteria *(Lactobacillus)* and lactose-fermenting yeasts; it is now widely available at natural and health food stores. Follow the directions on the package, substituting 1 quart of rich soymilk for dairy milk and decreasing the incubation time by 20 percent.

Soymilk Mayonnaise *(Soyanaise)*
MAKES 1½ CUPS

Now sold commercially in the United States and Japan, this product has a delicious, rich flavor. However we prefer its close counterpart, Tofu Mayonnaise, since the latter requires the use of much less oil and is therefore lighter, more digestible, and less costly. Soymilk Mayonnaise may separate after storage.

¾ cup (rich) soymilk
¾ cup oil
1 to 1½ tablespoons vinegar or lemon juice
¾ teaspoon salt
½ to 1 teaspoon honey (optional)
¼ teaspoon wet mustard (optional)

Combine soymilk and one half the oil in a blender, and purée at high speed for 1 minute. Slowly add remaining oil in a thin stream. Gradually pour in vinegar or lemon juice, then add the remaining ingredients; purée for 30 seconds more, or until fairly thick. Chill briefly to further thicken.

To make Soymilk Mayonnaise Dressings, add any of the combinations of seasonings used for Creamy Tofu Dressings (p. 143).

Soymilk Whipped Cream
MAKES 1¾ CUPS

1 cup (rich) soymilk
½ cup oil
2 tablespoons honey or pure maple syrup
½ teaspoon vanilla
Pinch of salt
¾ teaspoon lemon juice

Combine soymilk and one half the oil in a blender and purée at high speed for 1 minute. Slowly add remaining oil in a thin stream. Add honey, vanilla, and salt, then slowly add lemon juice; purée for 30 seconds more, or until nicely thickened. Chill briefly. Serve immediately to prevent separation.

VARIATION

• *Soymilk & Tofu Whipped Cream:* Combine in a blender 1 cup soymilk, 12 ounces tofu, and 2 tablespoons honey or pure maple syrup; purée until smooth. Delicious served over desserts. Makes 2½ cups.

Banana-Honey Soymilk Ice Cream
(Ice Creme or Ice Bean)

MAKES 3 QUARTS

8 cups (warm) soymilk, the thicker the better
2 pounds bananas
1 to 1¼ cups honey
8 to 10 tablespoons (cold-pressed) safflower or soy oil
1 tablespoon pure vanilla extract (optional)
1 tablespoon lecithin (liquid or granules), slippery elm, or
    locust bean gum (optional; for creamy smoothness)
½ teaspoon salt (optional)

Combine all ingredients in several batches in a blender and purée until smooth. Pour into a large pot and cool in cold water (or refrigerate). Blend once again when cool. Have ready a hand-churned rock-salt ice cream freezer. To pack the freezer, use 1 cup of coarse rock salt for every 3 to 6 quarts of cracked ice. Pack about one-third of freezer with ice, then add layers of salt and ice around the central container until freezer is full. Allow to stand for 3 minutes while you fill container three-fourths full of soymilk mixture. Turn slowly at first (40 rpm) until a slight pull is felt, then triple speed for 5 or 6 minutes. Repack ice and finish by turning at 80 rpm for a few minutes more. The ice cream should be ready in 10 to 20 minutes. (If it proves granular, you used too much salt in the packing mixture, overfilled the central container with the ice cream mixture, or turned too rapidly.) Soymilk ice cream is smoothest, creamiest, and tastiest just after it is churned; during frozen storage, crystals may begin to form.

VARIATIONS

• *Banana-Honey-Walnut:* Add 1 cup chopped walnut meats just before churning.
• *Maple-Walnut:* Substitute 1⅓ cups pure maple syrup for the honey and 1 cup chopped walnut meats for the bananas. Add nuts to mixture after 5 to 6 minutes of triple speed churning.
• *Carob:* Substitute ½ cup roasted carob powder for the bananas.
• *Vanilla:* Substitute 2 vanilla beans or ¾ teaspoon pure vanilla extract for the bananas.
• *Almond crunch:* Substitute 1 cup chopped almonds for the bananas; add nuts as for maple-walnut above.

Soymilk Popsicles

MAKES 6

½ cup (homemade) soymilk
¾ cup pineapple, banana, peach, or strawberry chunks
1 tablespoon honey

Combine all ingredients in a blender and purée for 30 seconds, or until smooth. Pour into popsicle molds, insert popsicle sticks, and freeze for 6 to 12 hours.

VARIATIONS

• *Coffee:* Use 1 cup soymilk, 1 teaspoon instant coffee powder, and 2 tablespoons honey.
• *Carob or chocolate:* Use 1 cup soymilk, 1 tablespoon carob or cocoa powder, and 2 tablespoons honey.
• *Ice cream:* Use only one-fourth of each ingredient for Soymilk Ice Cream, above.

Soy Buttermilk

SERVES 3

The lemon juice partially coagulates the soy protein which, when puréed, gives this beverage a thick, rich

texture; the lemon adds a tasty tang. If a blender is
not available, use an egg beater or whisk.

3¼ Cups fairly hot soymilk, preferably homemade (p. 299)
1½ tablespoons honey (optional)
1½ teaspoons lemon juice and/or 2 tablespoons oil

Combine soymilk and honey in a blender and purée
for 15 seconds. Slowly add lemon juice while continuing to purée for 30 seconds more. Allow mixture to
stand for at least 1 minute, then purée again briefly,
just before serving.

Banana Soymilk Shake *(Soy Shake)*

MAKES 2 CUPS

1 cup chilled soymilk
¼ cup toasted wheat germ or Okara Granola (p. 99)
1 raw egg (optional)
1 or 2 chilled or frozen bananas
1 to 2 teaspoons honey or pure maple syrup
Dash of nutmeg

Combine all ingredients in a blender and purée until
smooth. Other flavors include vanilla, carob, strawberry, pineapple, or peach. The addition of nut butters
or barley malt syrup also works well.

Soymilk Cheese

No one has yet developed a method of making
quality soymilk cheese using conventional or traditional cheese- or yogurt-making processes. Although
a number of soy protein isolate cheeses are now
on the market, their production involves the use
of cheese-making microorganisms and, sometimes,
processes (such as homogenization with oil) that
are not readily accessible to the average person.
Nevertheless, we feel there must be a way to prepare
good homemade soymilk cheese; the person who develops a practical method will have made a major

breakthrough of great potential benefit to people everywhere. Please experiment and let us know of your
successes so we can share them with others.

SOYMILK FRUIT WHIPS AND SAUCES

Soymilk Fruit Whip

MAKES 2½ CUPS

2 cups chilled soymilk
½ to 1 cup fresh or frozen fruits or berries

Combine all ingredients in a blender and purée until
smooth.

Banana-Raisin Whip

MAKES 2 CUPS

½ cup chilled soymilk
2 chilled or frozen bananas
⅓ cup raisins
1 teaspoon lemon juice

Combine all ingredients in a blender and puree until
smooth.

Lemon-Miso White Sauce

SERVES 2

2 tablespoons butter or oil
2 tablespoons (whole-wheat) flour
1 cup soymilk
4 teaspoons red or barley miso; 2½ teaspoons shoyu; or
    ⅔ teaspoon salt
2 teaspoons lemon juice
¼ teaspoon grated lemon rind (optional)
12 ounces tofu or 7½ ounces deep-fried tofu cutlets, cut into
    bite-sized cubes
Dash of pepper, paprika, or cayenne
1 tablespoon minced parsley (optional)

Use the first four ingredients to prepare a White Sauce (p. 48). When sauce is partially thickened, add lemon juice (and rind) together with tofu. Continue to cook, stirring gently, for about 2 minutes more, or until sauce is well thickened. Stir in pepper and, if used, the parsley, and remove from heat.

VARIATIONS

• *Soymilk-Mushroom Sauce:* After adding milk, add ¼ diced onion and 6 thinly-sliced mushrooms. Simmer over low heat, stirring constantly, for 4 to 5 minutes, then add 1 teaspoon lemon juice, a dash of pepper, and 1 tablespoon white wine or sake. Add tofu or substitute 5 ounces deep-fried tofu cutlets, burgers, or pouches. Finish cooking as above.

• *Soymilk-Cheese Sauce:* Sauté 1 clove of crushed garlic in the butter for 15 seconds, then add flour, soymilk, and miso as above. Omit lemon juice. Stir in pepper and ½ teaspoon powdered hot mustard. Simmer, stirring constantly, for 2 minutes, or until sauce has thickened. Stir in ½ to 1 cup (1½ to 3 ounces) grated cheese and 5 ounces deep-fried tofu (or 12 ounces regular tofu) cut into cubes. Serve hot or cold.

• *Herb Sauce:* Use 2 teaspoons each minced chives and parsley, and ⅛ teaspoon marjoram. Sauté chives and parsley for 3 minutes, then add marjoram with flour and proceed as for basic recipe.

11

Silken Tofu

IN JAPAN, silken tofu is called *kinugoshi*. *Kinu* means "silk"; *kosu* means "to strain": well-named, *kinugoshi* tofu has a texture so smooth that it seems to have been strained through silk. Soft and white, it melts in the mouth like custard or firm yogurt. Made from thick soymilk, silken tofu has a subtle bouquet (especially when prepared with nigari) and natural sweetness resembling that of rich, fresh cream.

The Japanese language contains an abundance of words used to describe nuances of feeling, texture, and taste. *Shita-zawari,* for example, refers to the particular feeling that a food makes as it touches the tongue, and *nodo-goshi* to the gentleness with which it goes down the throat: silken tofu is the epitome of exquisite *shita-zawari* and *nodo-goshi*. Free of even the fine-grained structure and internal cohesiveness of regular tofu, silken is so delicate that a chopstick slices—almost glides—evenly and effortlessly through it, leaving behind a nearly smooth surface.

At the tofu shop or market, a cake of silken tofu is almost indistinguishable from one of regular tofu. Their shape and proportions appear the same, but the silken tofu is usually slightly smaller, its color is a bit whiter, and its surface is smoother and less porous. The two types are made from the same basic ingredients and sell for about the same price.

Nevertheless, silken tofu is prepared by a fundamentally different process, one characterized above all by its use of relatively thick soymilk. The boxes used to give form to the silken tofu have neither draining holes nor lining cloths. While still hot, silken

Fig. 63. Pouring the Soymilk

tofu soymilk is simply poured in (Fig. 63) and, in most neighborhood shops, coagulated with calcium sulfate placed at the bottom of the boxes just before the soymilk is added. (Traditionally, silken tofu was prepared by carefully stirring a solution of nigari and water into the soymilk just after it had been poured into the box [Fig. 64]). The tofu is allowed to stand in

Fig. 64. Adding Coagulant

the boxes for 20 to 30 minutes until it becomes firm. *The curds and whey never separate and the tofu is never pressed*. Finally, the tofu is trimmed away from the sides of each box with a long knife (Fig. 65), the

Fig. 65. Trimming Silken Tofu from Sides of Box

box and tofu are immersed in cold water, and the tofu is carefully removed and cut into 12-ounce cakes.

When making regular tofu, some of the protein, vitamin B, natural oils, and sugars dissolve in the whey and are removed with it. Since whey is never removed from silken tofu, the latter contains more of the nutrients originally in the soybeans. At the same time, it has a slightly higher water content, hence a somewhat lower percentage of protein than that contained in regular tofu (5.5% vs. 7.8%). It is this higher water content that gives silken tofu its softer consistency. Its homogenous, fine-grained structure prevents the loss of natural sugars (as well as coagulant) when the tofu is soaked in water, so that silken tofu generally retains more of the soymilk's sweetness. However, because of its delicate, fine grain, silken tofu must be pressed and firmed very gently, and when simmered with sauces or in seasoned broths, it does not readily absorb other flavors. Although its versatility in cooking is, therefore, limited, its sensuous texture and creamy sweetness make it a much favored delicacy.

In Japan, silken tofu, like cool silk, is associated with summer. When served chilled, it can be as luscious as a succulent melon. Refreshingly light, it quenches thirst and cools both body and spirit while providing the energy to carry one through a hot day's work. During the hottest months, most silken tofu in Japan is served as Iceberg Chilled Tofu, a simple refreshing dish designed to bring to life and celebrate the tofu's flavor.

With the first autumn colors on the maple leaves, silken tofu begins to appear in the second of its most popular roles, Simmering Tofu, the cold-weather equivalent of Chilled Tofu and one of Japan's most popular *nabe*, or one-pot cookery, dishes. At many fine restaurants, the *nabe* is heated over a charcoal brazier and served outdoors, with no sources of light or heat other than the glowing coals, perhaps a paper lantern, and the piping-hot tofu.

Other main uses of silken tofu are in miso soups, clear soups, and dishes served with various shoyu dipping sauces or miso toppings. Regular tofu can always be substituted for silken tofu, but keep in mind that the texture of the dish may not be quite as soft and smooth. Silken tofu, however, *cannot* always be substituted for regular tofu, particularly if the recipe calls for the tofu to be pressed, skewered, broiled, or sautéed in cube form. Silken tofu is also not generally used in dishes such as scrambled eggs, omelets, or casseroles since it may contribute more water than is desirable. Silken tofu yields good results when steamed or puréed to make cream sauces, spreads, dips, dressings, or foods for babies or elderly adults.

In many Japanese shops, silken tofu is prepared only during the warm months from about May until October and, during this time, the demand is often greater than that for regular tofu. In some shops, a little freshly-grated *yuzu* (or lime) rind or gingerroot is mixed into the soymilk before adding the coagulant to impart a light fragrance.

At present, there are six different types of silken tofu sold in Japan. The primary factors determining the quality of each are the thickness of the soymilk and the type of coagulant used. The most traditional varieties, those solidified with nigari, were probably first developed in Japan. However, since the preparation of this tofu required a great deal of skill, and since nigari silken tofu was too fragile to be easily transported, it was made at only a small number of Japan's finest tofu shops. Hence it was considered a rare delicacy—which most Japanese never had an opportunity to taste.

The earliest form of nigari silken tofu, *shikishi-dofu,* was prepared in about 30 to 50 tiny wooden kegs, each about 4 inches deep, 4 inches in diameter, and coated inside with lacquer. Hot soymilk was poured into each container, nigari stirred in, and the silken tofu allowed to form. The individual kegs were then immersed in water and the tofu removed, to be sold in its cylindrical form.

Beginning in the year 1703, a second form of nigari silken tofu came to be prepared in Japan at Tokyo's Sasa-no-yuki tofu shop and restaurant. Today, as far as we know, no other shop in Japan makes nigari silken tofu, primarily for lack of a sufficiently talented master. (The present master asserts that it took him six years to learn the process.) Sasa-no-yuki's delicious silken tofu, with its unmatched nigari-evoked sweetness, is the delight of tofu connoisseurs throughout Japan. The words *sasa-no-yuki* mean "the snow on small bamboo leaves," a precise description of the delicate softness of this tofu from which the shop took its name. For three centuries, the terms "nigari kinugoshi" and "Sasa-no-yuki" have been almost synonymous, and today, too, the restaurant offers 12 separate dishes, each featuring its silken tofu.

The transformation of silken tofu from a rare and somewhat aristocratic food into one that was truly democratic came about through a quirk of history. At the beginning of World War II, the Japanese government seized all of the nigari from the country's salt fields to use as a source of magnesium to build light-weight aircraft. Tofu makers were suddenly forced to switch to calcium sulfate coagulant. Although considered at the time to make less delicious tofu, it required less skill and less time to use and produced firmer tofu that was easier to transport. This made it possible for virtually every craftsman in the country to begin making silken tofu. Thus most Japanese first tasted silken tofu in the 1950s. And although it is now as common as regular tofu, and takes less time and effort to make, even calcium sulfate silken tofu retains a sense of its aristocratic origins, being sold in equally priced but slightly smaller cakes than regular tofu. This second type of silken tofu, which is still the most popular variety in Japan, has been prepared in China using gypsum (natural calcium sulfate) since ancient times.

Each of the four modern types of silken tofu is made with lactone (glucono delta-lactone) which, except for calcium sulfate, is the most widely used coagulant in Japan today. When mixed with soymilk and heated, it produces gluconic acid, which coagulates the milk to form silken tofu in much the same way lactic acid, produced by a starter, is used to make yogurt. Developed in the late 1800s, it is a fine, white, basically odorless, crystalline powder, prepared from corn starch by a fermentation process. Widely used by the food industry as an acidulant in baking powders, and as a coagulant and pH-lowering agent in dairy puddings and cottage cheeses, it is also found in nature, for example, in bee's honey and in the human body. Its great importance for use in tofu production lies in the fact that small amounts can be mixed with cold soymilk and the soymilk then run into containers, which are sealed and immersed in hot water for about 50 minutes. The heat activates the lactone which causes the tofu to form right in the package with no separation

of curds and whey, and protected from spoilage microorganisms. In Japan, all such types of tofu coagulated
in containers with lactone are called *juten-dofu* ("filled
tofu"). Together they constitute an estimated 30 percent of all tofu produced in Japan, and their share of
the market is rapidly growing. Because the tofu is
neither soaked nor packed in water, it is easy to use
and retains the full natural sweetness of fresh soymilk.
Although it is well adapted to large-scale, mechanized
tofu production, lactone can also be used by uncon-
scientious manufacturers to make silken tofu from very
thin soymilk.

The third type of silken tofu, then, is simply called
lactone silken tofu. It is made in both small tofu shops
and large factories, and is generally packed in water in
heat-sealed (or unsealed) plactic containers. In most
cases, the lactone is used together with calcium sulfate
in ratios of 7:3 or 5:5 to give a better flavor and
texture. Lactone is also included with the powdered
soymilk in packages of instant homemade tofu now
sold at many Japanese food markets in the West.

The fourth type of silken tofu (and the most popular) is Packaged Lactone Silken Tofu. The mixture of
chilled soymilk and a little lactone is run automatically
into open-top, rectangular polyethylene containers,
which are then covered with a sheet of plastic film,
heat-sealed, and immersed in hot water while the tofu
forms. In some cases the tofu is solidified in sausage-
shaped polyethylene bags and sold as Bagged Lactone
Silken Tofu *(fukuro-dofu)*. These methods allow the
tofu to be mass-produced in highly automated factories, the largest of which have a daily output of
100,000 cakes (Fig. 66). Japan's least expensive tofu,
the 10½-ounce packaged cakes are distributed over
an area of several hundred miles and sold at supermarkets at about 68 percent the cost (on a usable
protein basis) of regular tofu and 60 percent the cost
(on an equal weight basis) of the silken tofu sold in
neighborhood tofu shops. Furthermore, since the tofu

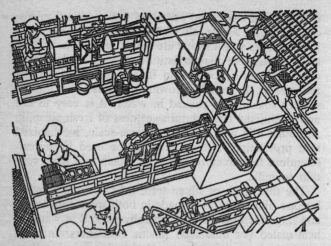

Fig. 66. A Modern Silken Tofu Factory

is sterilized and sealed in the container, it stays fresh for up to 1 week if refrigerated. In some cases, however, the low price of the tofu only too faithfully reflects the thinness of the soymilk from which it is made. Although its flavor is often rather weak and the use of lactone gives it a texture somewhat like that of jello, however, it presently retails for as low as 15 cents per pound and consequently has found a very large market. Recently a number of higher quality (and slightly higher priced) varieties of Packaged Lactone Silken Tofu have become available. Made with richer soymilk (containing 5.0 rather than the typical 4.4 percent protein), they are solidified with a combination of lactone and calcium sulfate.

The fifth type is called Sealed Lactone Silken Tofu (buro-dofu). The soymilk-lactone mixture is funneled into thick-walled polyethylene containers through a very small opening. The opening is then pinched closed and thermally sealed so that (unlike the previous type of silken tofu) absolutely no air can enter. After being heated and solidified as above, this tofu (which contains no preservatives) stays fresh for 2 to 3 months. Moreover, the sturdy container makes it possible to carry the tofu (in box lunches, for example) without fear of leakage or crushing the delicate curd structure. Although the cost of the container makes the retail price of this tofu about 85 to 90 percent higher than the previous variety, it is still relatively inexpensive and its convenience is winning it wide acceptance. Sealed Lactone Silken Tofu is now sold in three different flavors: regular, peanut, and egg. In the peanut type, nuts are ground together with the soybeans and made into soymilk; in the egg type, eggs are stirred into the chilled soymilk and the mixture reheated slightly before it is funneled into the containers. These two varieties contain up to 26 percent more protein than regular silken tofu and are popular items at many natural- and health food stores.

The sixth type of silken tofu is called Ever-fresh Lactone Silken Tofu. Developed in 1977 by Morinaga, Ltd. in Tokyo, it is sold in aseptic Tetra-Pak containers, which completely lock out spoilage microorganisms and air. Free of preservatives, it will stay fresh *without refrigeration for six months!* Thus it obviously has revolutionary potential throughout the world. Ideal for summertime, picnics and camping, for sale and distribution by companies without (or with overcrowded) refrigeration, and for use in tropical countries, it is made from rich soymilk (10.5% solids and 4.7% protein) and also contains nigari coagulant. Thus it has a delicious rich flavor and is firm enough to deep-fry or purée. Now available in America at reasonable prices, it is a type of tofu we will surely be hearing more about.

Another type of modern tofu, closely resembling but nevertheless different from silken tofu, is *pressed silken tofu*. Like silken tofu, it is solidified using calcium sulfate without the separation of curds and whey. But the coagulation takes place in the curding barrel rather than in the silken tofu box, and the solidified curds, ladled into the forming boxes used for regular tofu, are pressed with heavy weights until the tofu is firm. Pressed silken tofu has almost the same smooth, homogeneous texture as silken tofu, plus some of the internal strength and cohesiveness of regular tofu. Very fine-grained and difficult to press, it is generally used in recipes calling for silken tofu.

It has been estimated that during the summertime in Japan, the total consumption of regular tofu is only about one-fourth that of the five types of silken tofu including pressed silken tofu.

Silken tofu is now prepared by many Japanese and Chinese tofu shops in the United States. Sold in 12-ounce cakes in the same type of containers as regular tofu, it is commonly called Kinugoshi Soft Tofu or, in some Chinese shops, *Sui-toufu*. It is usually coagulated with either lactone (GDL) or calcium sulfate. Some Japanese markets and co-op stores now also sell an instant homemade silken tofu, consisting of powdered soymilk and a small envelope of lactone coagulant. One package makes about 21 ounces and takes 15 to 20 minutes to prepare; directions are given on the package. A high-priced, canned silken tofu is available in some Japanese markets but, in our opinion, its flavor does not meet up to expectation. Fortunately, fresh silken tofu is very easy to prepare at home, even using nigari.

HOMEMADE SILKEN TOFU

Homemade Silken Tofu *(from Whole Soybeans)*

MAKES 27 OUNCES

Silken tofu is easier and faster to prepare than regular tofu and requires no special settling container. The yield is also considerably greater—1 pound of beans makes about 4½ pounds of tofu—and only half as much coagulant is required. We feel that silken tofu

made with natural nigari or magnesium chloride nigari
is the most delicate and delicious. However, silken
tofu made with calcium sulfate is the firmest and
easiest to prepare. Silken tofu is usually ready to serve
about 50 minutes after you start to prepare soymilk.
In the following method, the silken tofu is served like
a custard or molded salad. For information about coagulants, see p. 110.

3¼ cups Homemade Rich Soymilk (p. 302)
Coagulant:

1) For delicate, subtly-sweet nigari silken tofu: ½ teaspoon magnesium chloride or calcium chloride; ⅜
teaspoon granular or powdered natural nigari; ⅓ to
1 teaspoon liquid natural nigari from (home-
processed) sea salt; or ½ to 1½ teaspoons liquid
natural nigari from a salt refinery

2) for firm, mild silken tofu: ½ teaspoon Epsom salts
(magnesium sulfate) or calcium sulfate; or 1 teaspoon lactone (GDL)

3) For firm, subtly tart silken tofu: 4 teaspoons lemon
or lime juice, or 1 tablespoon (apple cider) vinegar

2 tablespoons water

Prepare Homemade Soymilk (p. 299). Place a 1½-
to 3-quart serving bowl or a casserole on a firm surface
(where it will not be jiggled or disturbed for 20 minutes) and pour in the freshly made hot soymilk; cover.
In a small cup quickly mix the coagulant with 2 tablespoons water and stir until dissolved. Stir soymilk back
and forth briskly for 3 to 5 seconds, then quickly pour
in all of the coagulant solution. Continue stirring soymilk for 3 to 5 seconds more, making sure to stir to
bottom of container. Now stop spoon upright in center of soymilk and wait until turbulence ceases; lift
out spoon. Let soymilk stand uncovered and undisturbed for 20 to 30 minutes while it cools and solidi-
fies. Now cover with plastic wrap and refrigerate, or
float bowl in cold water until chilled. To serve, bring
the bowl to the table or ladle the silken tofu into individual serving dishes. Serve as for Chilled Tofu (p.
141).

VARIATIONS

• *Fragrant Silken Tofu:* Just before adding the coagulant, stir any of the following into the hot soymilk: ¼ teaspoon grated rind of *yuzu,* lemon, or lime; ¼ to ½ teaspoon grated gingerroot; 10 to 15 minced mint leaves; 10 green beefsteak leaves which have been soaked in water for 10 minutes, drained, squeezed gently in a dry towel, and minced. Serve the latter garnished with 2 teaspoons *benitade.*

• *Peanut Silken Tofu:* Cream 2 or 3 tablespoons smooth peanut butter with a little of the hot soymilk, then stir into the soymilk just before adding coagulant. Or purée 3 to 4 tablespoons whole peanuts with the soybeans when preparing soymilk, and increase the amount of coagulant used by about 25 percent.

• *Silken Tofu with Eggs:* Whisk 2 lightly beaten eggs into the hot soymilk just before stirring in coagulant.

Silken Tofu Custard *(Shikishi-dofu)*

SERVES 3 OR 4

The earliest silken tofu made in Japan was prepared in this simple but attractive way. If possible, use calcium sulfate coagulant: it curdles the soymilk slowly, and the curds and whey do not separate while the soymilk-coagulant mixture is being poured into the serving cups.

Prepare 3½ cups Rich Homemade Soymilk (p. 302). Place 3 or 4 custard or coffee cups where they will be undisturbed. Mix the coagulant with 2 tablespoons water as for Homemade Silken Tofu (p. 320), then stir quickly into hot soymilk in the cooking pot. Immediately pour this soymilk-coagulant mixture into the cups. Cool and chill as for Homemade Silken Tofu. Serve in the cups seasoned with shoyu, or top with Ankake Sauce (p. 49), or any of the dipping sauces or toppings used with Chilled Tofu (p. 141).

VARIATIONS

● *Silken Tofu Custard with Crisp Vegetables:* Dice or sliver any or all of the following: lotus root, carrot, mushroom, ginkgo nuts, green peas, trefoil, burdock root. Simmer in Sweetened Shoyu Broth (p. 36) until just tender. Place 3 tablespoons of the vegetables in the bottom of each custard cup before pouring in the soymilk-coagulant mixture; wait several minutes. Poke a few vegetable pieces into the surface of the solidifying curds and sprinkle a few pieces on top.

● *Sweetened Silken Tofu with Fruits:* Fill each of 5 custard cups about two-thirds full with fresh strawberries, thinly-sliced peaches, bananas, or apples. Prepare one-half of the regular recipe for Rich Homemade Soymilk (p. 302). Stir quickly into the hot soymilk: 1 to 2 tablespoons honey, ¼ teaspoon vanilla extract, and ⅜ teaspoon calcium sulfate coagulant. Pour the mixture immediately into the cups to cover the fruits. Allow to cool, then cover with plastic wrap and chill before serving.

● *Rich Silken Tofu Custard Dessert:* Add ½ cup powdered milk (soy or dairy) to 3¼ cups hot rich soymilk just before stirring in ¾ teaspoon calcium sulfate coagulant. Pour mixture immediately into cups. Serve chilled as is, or top with a small amount of honey, dark brown sugar, maple syrup, or crunchy granola. Or serve accompanied by any of the shoyu dipping sauces and garnishes used with Chilled Tofu (p. 141).

Homemade Pressed Silken Tofu

MAKES 23 TO 25 OUNCES

Pressed silken tofu is made by pressing silken tofu in a cloth-lined forming container. The result is firmer, more cohesive, and less delicate than silken tofu, but softer, smoother, and higher-yielding than regular tofu. Always use calcium sulfate coagulant.

Prepare Rich Homemade Soymilk (p. 299), but rinse the okara with 2½ cups (rather than ½ cup) water. Coagulate as for Homemade Silken Tofu (p. 320), using ½ teaspoon calcium sulfate. After stirring in coagulant, allow tofu to stand for about 8 minutes, then carefully ladle the soft curds in large, unbroken scoops into the cloth-lined forming container (as for regular Homemade Tofu, p. 127). Avoid leaving gaps between adjacent scoops of curds. Put on the lid and press with a ½-pound weight for about 5 minutes, then add 1½ pounds more and press for an additional 20 minutes, or until whey no longer drips from the settling container. Cool under water for 10 to 15 minutes before removing cloths from tofu. Serve as for Chilled Tofu (p. 141).

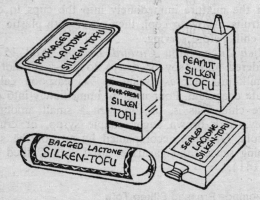

12

Grilled Tofu

As MORNING and evening cool and late summer turns into early fall, many tofu shops gradually stop making silken tofu and shift their attention to grilled tofu *(yaki-dofu)*. Easily recognized by its speckled brown surface and distinctive barbecue-broiled flavor and aroma, a cake of grilled tofu is a little longer and thinner than one of regular tofu. And unlike regular tofu, which is so soft and yielding, grilled tofu is firm and compact, its texture resembling that of Chinese-style tofu. Simmered in Sukiyaki and other types of *nabe* cookery, or skewered and broiled to make Dengaku, it always keeps its shape. And because it contains relatively little water, it readily absorbs the flavors of seasoned broths, soups, or casseroles.

Grilled tofu is prepared from the same curds used to make regular tofu. However, to create a strong, cohesive structure, the tofu maker stirs these curds in the curding barrel until they break into fine particles. Then, after ladling off more whey than usual, he places the curds quickly (and rather roughly) into the forming box and presses them with a heavy weight (10 to 12 pounds) for a relatively long time (40 to 50 minutes). Finally, he cuts the finished tofu into cakes about 5 inches long, 3 inches wide, and 2 inches thick and these he presses for about one hour between alternate layers of bamboo mats sandwiched between large wooden boards (as when pressing tofu to make deep-fried tofu cutlets; Fig. 45). At each step in the process, the tofu becomes firmer and more compact so that it will hold together when skewered and grilled over a charcoal fire.

A traditional master grills tofu with the effortless precision of a circus juggler and the speed of a chuck-wagon flapjack cook. Sitting squarely in front of a small, round charcoal brazier, he places two iron bars on opposite sides of its glowing mouth. Using a sturdy, metal skewer about 12 inches long, he then pierces a cake of well-pressed tofu to the hilt and sets it over the hot coals (Fig 67). Quickly skewering a second

Fig. 67.   Traditional Master Making Grilled Tofu

cake, he flips over the first and slides it to the opposite side of the brazier, while setting the second in its place and skewering a third. At just the right instant—a second too long and the tofu will burn, too short and it will lack the proper color and aroma—the master snatches the first cake from the fire, checks to see that its surfaces are nicely browned, and plunges it into a tub of cold water, withdrawing the skewer. He then flips over the second cake, sets a third in its place, and skewers the next piece. With a small paper fan, he sends several quick strokes of air down into the live embers. The charcoal-broiled fragrance of the sizzling tofu fills the shop and a thin curl of white smoke rises through a shaft of morning sunlight.

(In the spirit of traditional craftsmanship, nothing

is wasted. When the work is done, the coals—which were originally scooped from the dying fire under the cauldron—will be placed in a charcoal brazier and used to warm the living room and boil the morning tea.)

Grilled tofu may have been one of the earliest ways of preparing tofu in Japan. Since it is not found at all in present-day Taiwan or mentioned in writings on Chinese tofu, this variety may be another Japanese invention. In many Japanese farmhouses, regular tofu was generally broiled around a bed of coals in the open-hearth fireplace. Country-style tofu, made very firm, lent itself well to skewering without the need for additional pressing. And broiling the tofu—especially during long winter evenings—gave the family a chance to come together near the warmth and light of the fire. Skewered on specially-cut pieces of bamboo (below), the freshly-grilled tofu was either served sizzling

hot, seasoned with a little miso or shoyu, or used as a basic ingredient in miso soups, Nishime, Oden, or Simmering Tofu.

Even today, many of Japan's rural festivals are not considered complete unless they end with a fireside feast featuring grilled tofu. We've witnessed one such feast in a small village in Japan's snowy northeast provinces. At its conclusion, a large bonfire was built and all the members of the village gathered round. After each person had prepared a 2-foot-long bamboo skewer, the village tofu makers passed around cakes of freshly prepared tofu. With flames leaping and everyone singing and clapping in time to the rhythmic beating of huge drums, the skewered tofu was stuck upright in the ground as near to the fire as possible, then snatched back when done. The grilled tofu, together with hot sake, was served late into the night.

Grilled tofu's ancient ancestor may have been pre-

Fig. 68. Open-hearth Grilling

pared without skewers on a lightly oiled, hot iron
griddle—a method still used in a few rural tofu shops
and farmhouses.. Apparently, the predecessor of the
present round charcoal brazier used in tofu shops was
an oblong brazier about 2 feet long. We have watched
one highly-skilled tofu maker prepare five cakes of
grilled tofu at once on such a brazier using an elaborate
version of the method described earlier (Fig. 69). On
the whole, the use of live coals and the traditional
skewers is rapidly disappearing. Most Japanese shops
now arrange cakes of well-pressed tofu on metal trays
or thick wooden boards and broil them under the
flame of a hand-held, propane blow torch. In more
modern shops, the tofu-containing metal tray is placed
on rollers and passed slowly under several rows of
propane burners. This modern variety of grilled tofu—
recognizable by the absence of skewer holes—is similar in appearance to traditional grilled tofu, but lacks

Fig. 69.   An Early Method of Elaborate Grilling

the latter's charcoal aroma and some of its ability to absorb flavors during cooking.

Grilled tofu is one of the featured ingredients in Japan's New Year's cuisine. In accordance with an ancient custom, no fresh food is cooked during the first three—and sometimes the first seven—days of the new year. Thus, during the last two days in December, most housewives are busy from morning until night preparing the New Year's food and setting it aside in special layered, lacquerware boxes reserved for the occasion. Since the basic New Year's dishes were standardized in the centuries before refrigeration, the only foods used traditionally were those which could be kept fresh for a fairly long time. Since grilled tofu stayed fresh longer than regular tofu (due in part to its low water content and in part to the effects of broiling) it was chosen as the ideal variety for use in the holiday menu. Moreover, since it was very firm, grilled tofu could be simmered in sweetened shoyu broths—which acted as a natural preservative—without losing its form so that it looked attractive when served. Today used most widely in a dish called New Year's Nishime (p. 251), grilled tofu is said to reach its peak of goodness several days after it has been cooked, when the flavors of the broth and fresh vegetables have mellowed and permeated it.

The tofu maker spends the last few days of the old year working from morning until night trying to fill all his orders for grilled tofu. At the end of the year's work, as the great temple bells throughout Japan sound the midnight hour, the master may use his freshly made grilled tofu to prepare a special type of Dengaku. He spreads one entire surface of the cake with a thin layer of miso, then broils the miso quickly until it is fragrant and flecked with brown. This steaming hot Dengaku, a small feast in itself, is meant to welcome in the new year.

Many of our fellow Westerners have been surprised to learn that tofu is one of the indispensable ingredients in Japan's most famous overseas dish: Sukiyaki. If you have ever tasted real Sukiyaki, you have also tasted grilled tofu. Indeed, in Japan, more grilled tofu is used in Sukiyaki than in any other type of cuisine.

In Western cookery, grilled tofu is particularly suited to the barbeque and broiler. You can prepare your own over the live coals of an outdoor barbeque, a small indoor Japanese-style brazier, or in an oven broiler. Or try cooking pre-grilled tofu in these various ways, treating it almost as if it were a large steak and basting it with a favorite sauce. Grilled tofu can also be substituted in most recipes calling for regular tofu and is especially delicious in Western-style egg dishes.

Grilled tofu is usually about 10 percent more expensive than regular tofu since each cake is larger, contains less water, and requires additional time, effort, and fuel to prepare. In Japan, its season usually comes to an end in March or April, when the tofu maker packs away his charcoal brazier and begins to prepare silken tofu.

At present in the United States, fresh grilled tofu is available in only a few areas. An imported, canned variety called *yaki-dofu* or Baked Bean Curd is sold at some Japanese markets, but the tofu loses much of its flavor and fine texture in canning and after lengthy storage. For best results, make your own.

Homemade Grilled Tofu

Grilled tofu can be prepared quickly and easily at home.

Preparing the Tofu: Firm tofu may be grilled without additional preparation. Regular tofu should be thoroughly pressed between layers of toweling or bamboo mats before skewering, but may be broiled in an oven broiler without pressing if you are in a hurry or want a softer texture. When preparing Homemade Tofu (p. 127) to be made into grilled tofu, use a nigari-type coagulant if possible, ladle the curds into the settling container rather quickly and roughly, and press the curds with a fairly heavy weight for a longer time than usual. Cut the finished tofu into 2-inch-thick pieces and press again in toweling or between bamboo mats.

Grilling or Broiling: The appropriateness of the cooking method depends first on whether or not the tofu is to be skewered, and second on the nature of your heat source. A charcoal or wood fire gives the best flavor.

SKEWERED TOFU

1. *Charcoal Brazier:* Skewer 12-ounce cakes of pressed tofu from one end using a pronged metal skewer, two metal shish kebab-type skewers, two sturdy bamboo skewers which have been soaked in (salted) water, or a large fork with tines longer than the tofu.

Place 2 parallel bars across the brazier to support both ends of the skewers. Grill each piece of tofu for about 15 to 30 seconds on each side, or until nicely browned.

2. *Open-Hearth Fireplace or Campfire* (planted skewer style): Prepare skewers 12 to 18 inches long by sharpening both ends of a flat, 1-inch-wide piece of bamboo or wood; skewer tofu from one end. Plant the base of the skewer upright in the ashes or ground near the bed of coals so that the tofu leans slightly over the coals and each side of the tofu browns in 1 to 2 minutes.

3. *Open Fire or Stove-Top Burner* (marshmallow style): Skewer the tofu with a long metal fork or forked stick. Hold just above the flames or coals and brown on both sides.

UNSKEWERED TOFU

1. *Oven Broiler:* Place 12-ounce cakes of tofu (pressed or unpressed) on a lightly-oiled baking sheet or sheet of aluminum foil and broil for 3 to 5 minutes on both sides until nicely browned.

2. *Barbecue or Brazier:* Place well-pressed tofu on the grill or grating like a steak. When one side is nicely browned, turn over with a large spatula or fork.

3. *Griddle:* Heat a heavy griddle and coat lightly with oil. Fry each cake of tofu on both sides until golden brown. Turn with a wide-blade knife or spatula. Country-style grilled tofu is still prepared in this way.

Serving or Storing Grilled Tofu: Grilled tofu is most delicious when served still hot and fragrant, as in the following recipe. However if you wish to save some homemade grilled tofu for later use, plunge the hot tofu into a large container of (circulating) cold water as soon as the tofu is removed from the fire. Allow tofu to cool thoroughly, then place in a covered container and refrigerate. If tofu is to be stored for more than 24 hours, refrigerate in cold water to cover.

Sizzling Grilled Tofu *(Quick and Easy)*

These simple serving suggestions are for connoisseurs who prepare their own grilled tofu at home and want to enjoy it "fresh from the fire" when its flavor and aroma are at their peak.

- *Grilled Tofu with Miso:* Cut the cake of freshly grilled tofu horizontally into halves. Place each half on a plate with the grilled side up. Coat with your favorite variety of Sweet Simmered Miso (p. 39) or Finger Lickin' Miso (p. 69). Serve immediately.
- *Country-style Tofu Dengaku:* Prepare grilled tofu skewered and grilled over a bed of coals. When tofu is golden brown, spread both large surfaces with a thin coating of red, barley, or Hatcho miso; broil for about 1 minute more on each side until miso is fragrant. Invite each guest to hold the tofu "popsicle-style" while eating.
- *Grilled Tofu Steak:* Marinate tofu for 30 to 60 minutes before grilling, using Teriyaki (p. 49) or your favorite steak sauce. Grill slowly, basting lightly with the marinade. Serve topped with marinade or Ketchup-Worcestershire Sauce (p. 50).
- Serve the hot tofu with any of the dipping sauces and garnishes used with Chilled Tofu (p. 141). Cut tofu as for Grilled Tofu with Miso, above.
- Serve cubes of freshly grilled tofu topped with Ankake Sauce (p. 49) and a little slivered gingerroot; or with grated *daikon* and a little shoyu.

Sukiyaki

SERVES 4

A Japanese cookbook written over 350 years ago contains the following recipe for *Sukiyaki:* "Obtain either wild goose, wild duck, or antelope, and soak the meat in *tamari* shoyu. Heat a well-used Chinese plow *(kara-suki)* over an open fire. Place the meat on the plow, garnish with thin rounds of *yuzu,* and broil on both sides until the color changes. Serve and be happy."

The word *sukiyaki*—pronounced skee-YA-kee— means "broiled on the blade of a plow." Although the modern preparation generally features beef as the basic ingredient, sukiyaki was traditionally prepared with wild game, fowl, fish, or shellfish. Wild boar was also a favored ingredient, and seafoods such as tuna, yellowtail, wreath shells, and scallops were and, in areas such as Kyoto, still are widely used in the dish.

Before reaching its present form, sukiyaki passed through a number of unusual historical transformations. The earliest preparation was undoubtedly developed by farmers, hunters, and fishermen who broiled their catch over an open fire using a plow or whatever other utensil was available. Since the earliest plow, the predecessor of the present *nabe*, was nothing but a flat iron plate, it was unable to hold cooking liquids. It was probably for this reason that the meat came to be marinated or basted with tamari shoyu, a technique that is still practiced in some Japanese restaurants. Gradually, sake or *mirin* came to be used in the marinade, various vegetables and grilled tofu were broiled with the meat, and the traditional flat plow or griddle became inadequate to hold the juices of this cornucopia of new ingredients. A new container was needed, and at this point, the ancient tradition of broiling wild meat on a plow merged with the newly-imported tradition of *shippoku*, a type of beef-*nabe* cookery which originated about 300 years ago, just after the first contact with Western traders and missionaries.

Developed in the international port town of Nagasaki, *shippoku* was said to have its historical culinary roots in Holland, Portugal, China, and Korea. As a result of the merger, the original sukiyaki ingredients eventually came to be cooked in heavy iron or Korean-style stone pots, and the dish was served as a one-pot meal prepared at the table. Consequently "sukiyaki" became a misnomer, for the new dish was neither broiled nor prepared on a griddle-like plow. But neither was the new sukiyaki a true *nabe* dish, since its ingredients were not simmered in a seasoned broth. Rather, this unique Japanese creation straddled three categories: it was a broiled dish insofar as the meat was first cooked in a sizzling-hot pan; it was a *nabe* dish since it was a one-pot dish prepared at the dining table; and it was a *nimono,* or simmered dish, insofar as the meat and vegetables were simmered together in a rich mixture of shoyu, sake, and dashi.

Up until this time, the Japanese had never apparently considered using beef or other livestock in sukiyaki. According to a popular legend, *kamado-gami,* the god of the kitchen hearth, is said to have instructed the Japanese people in ancient times to refrain from eating the meat of all four-legged animals, especially of livestock. This admonition was reinforced by the nation's emperors and the vegetarian teachings of Buddhism, so that for about 1200 years—from the 8th until the 19th century—most Japanese did not eat meat. However with the arrival of Christianity in the 16th century, and the public knowledge that missionaries considered meat important in the diet, some Japanese—and particularly Christian converts—came to know its taste. But with the expulsion of Christianity from Japan in the late 16th century, the eating of beef was also forbidden, and sukiyaki was once again prepared exclusively with seafood, wild game, or poultry. Those who developed a longing for broiled meat, but who were not allowed to prepare it in the family's common pot or in the presence of those who kept the faith, were compelled as a last resort to prepare their sukiyaki in the traditional way, substituting a plow or mattock for the kettle and enjoying the forbidden delicacy alone and in secret in the barn, field, or forest. This tradition of "underground sukiyaki" is said to have continued until about 1900.

With the opening of Japan to the West in the mid 19th century and the relaxation of traditional prohibitions, meat eating gradually became fashionable in the cities. Yet most Japanese tasted their first beef with considerable trepidation, having been warned by priests and traditionalists that their action was an affront to their ancestors and that dire consequences would befall them. Little by little, however, beef sukiyaki came to be accepted.

The first Japanese who worked up the courage to actually eat beef did not prepare it Western-style as steak or roast beef. Rather, they cut the meat into paper-thin slices, employing the same method they had used for centuries to prepare *sashimi,* or raw fish. And they seasoned this meat with shoyu in much the same way they would season simmered vegetable or tofu dishes. Many Japanese probably ate their first beef in the form of sukiyaki, and different parts of the country soon developed unique styles of serving it. To this day in the Kyoto area, restaurants place dispensers of shoyu, *mirin,* and sugar on the table and allow each guest to season his food to taste, whereas restaurants in Tokyo have developed their own unique mixtures of these ingredients to form standard cooking liquids.

Throughout the world people now associate sukiyaki with fine Japanese cookery. In a sense, this is ironic because Japanese cuisine still makes relatively little use of meat, and much of sukiyaki's historical influence came from abroad. The ancient delicacy of Japanese hunters and the imported *nabe* preparation have now been totally transformed to become Japan's most famous international dish. And although tofu plays a relatively inconspicuous role in creating the flavor of the dish, sukiyaki has nevertheless been the vehicle whereby thousands of Westerners have had their first taste of "soybean curd."

Although most present-day sukiyaki uses beef as the featured ingredient, our recipe uses deep-fried tofu burgers or ganmodoki—mock goose—in deference to the earliest traditions of using wild fowl. Homemade frozen tofu and frozen tofu cutlets, the textures of which resemble that of tender beef, make excellent substitutes. Although regular tofu is occasionally used in sukiyaki, grilled tofu is generally preferred for its ability to absorb the flavors in the rich broth; its substantial, almost meaty texture; its ability to keep its form during the frequent stirring; and its barbeque flavor. In Japan, more grilled tofu is used in sukiyaki than in any other type of cuisine.

3 tablespoons oil
12 ounces tofu burgers; or 4 pieces of frozen or dried-frozen
   tofu (p. 349); or 12 ounces (frozen) tofu or gluten cutlets,
   cut crosswise into ¾-inch-thick strips
12 ounces grilled tofu, cut into ¾-inch cubes
4 leeks, including green portions, cut diagonally into 2-inch
   lengths; or 10 green (or 4 regular) onions, thinly sliced
4 ounces trefoil or spinach leaves
8 ounces *konnyaku* noodles, parboiled and cut into thirds
8 small cakes of dried wheat gluten, reconstituted (optional)
8 *(shiitake)* mushrooms, thinly sliced
4 ounces chrysanthemum leaves, watercress, or Chinese cabbage, cut into 2-inch-wide strips
2 small bamboo shoots, thinly sliced and parboiled
Sukiyaki-Shoyu Mixture:
   ¼ cup dashi (p. 35), stock, or water
   ½ cup shoyu
   ¼ cup sake
   ¼ cup *mirin* or 3 tablespoons natural sugar
4 eggs

Arrange tofu and vegetables on a large platter. Preheat a 10- to 12-inch skillet set on a tabletop burner, or set an electric skillet to 350°F. Coat skillet with the oil, add about one-third of each of the tofu and vegetable ingredients, and sprinkle with one-third of the shoyu mixture. Cook over medium heat for 5 to 6 minutes, turning ingredients gently from time to time. Using chopsticks or long-handled forks, serve from the skillet as ingredients become done. Replenish the sauce and each ingredient, and continue cooking while the guests eat.

To serve, each person breaks a raw egg into his serving bowl and beats it lightly with chopsticks. The tofu and vegetables are dipped into the egg, then eaten. The usual accompaniment for sukiyaki is plain rice. Reserve any leftover sauce to use when sautéing other vegetable dishes, or as a broth for noodles.

Alternate ingredients and seasonings include celery stalks, bean sprouts, green peppers, thinly sliced carrots or *daikon,* and slender white *enokidake* mushrooms. Season with pepper and hot mustard, and garnish with a little parsley.

Other Ways of Serving Grilled Tofu

Grilled tofu may be used in place of regular tofu with excellent results on sandwiches and toast, in egg dishes and soups, and in sautéed vegetable and grain dishes. In Japan it is particularly popular in Tofu Dengaku (p. 199), Simmering Tofu (p. 205) and most other *nabe* cookery, Oden (p. 246), New Year's *Osechi* Nishime (p 251), and Miso Soup (p. 165).

In country farmhouses grilled tofu is used in a Nishime stew in which it is combined in a large iron pot with *daikon,* potatoes, *konnyaku,* seasonal vegetables, and an unsweetened miso broth which may include dried fish. The stew is simmered for at least 30 minutes and served steaming hot on winter evenings.

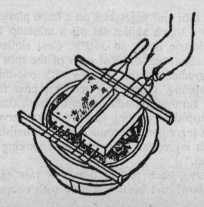

13

Frozen and Dried-frozen Tofu

THE METHOD for preparing frozen tofu was first discovered in the cold mountainous regions of northern China about 1,000 to 1,500 years ago. It was found that if regular tofu was cut into ½-inch-thick slabs, arranged on boards or bamboo mats, and then set out in the snow overnight until frozen solid, the structure and basic character of the tofu underwent a radical transformation. All the water in the tofu—about 86 percent of the tofu's total weight—turned to ice, and the protein and other solids congealed into a lacy but firm network. When the frozen tofu was later placed in warm water, the ice thawed, leaving only the network of protein and solids; this network looked like a beige, fine-grained natural sponge or a zwieback biscuit. With the loss of water, the tofu became a highly concentrated source of protein and energy. Like a delicate sponge, it was resilient, highly absorbent, and cohesive enough to hold together when pressed or cooked. Its soft texture was appealing and, in some types of cooking, seemed remarkably similar to that of very tender meat. This tofu had its own special flavor, which was enhanced by the flavors it so readily absorbed when simmered or sautéed.

As well as showing a way to transform regular tofu into a completely new food with unique uses in cooking, the discovery of frozen tofu also made it possible to preserve tofu—otherwise highly perishable—for long periods of time. After the arrival of frozen tofu in Japan over 1,000 years ago, it became possible for families in country farmhouses or monks in snowbound temples to make a large quantity of tofu, freeze what wasn't eaten, and then enjoy tofu daily for as long as the supply lasted, or until the snows melted. In rural areas, where there were no tofu shops, this saved the time and fuel required to make a small batch of fresh tofu every few days. Since it was almost impossible to obtain fish or other seafoods during the winter in the snowy mountain provinces, frozen tofu became a popular element in the daily diet and was soon known throughout much of Japan as "one-night frozen tofu."

Made almost exclusively in rural farmhouses and temples, frozen tofu has never been sold at neighborhood tofu shops. At present, some people make it at home by placing fresh tofu into the freezing compartment of their refrigerator. And it is sold on a limited scale in the frozen foods section of some department stores as six ½-inch-thick slices sealed in a cellophane bag. However, it is no longer a common commercial food in Japan, because modern, lightweight, dried-frozen tofu is now available at low prices in the dry goods section of most markets.

For us in the West, though, the process of freezing tofu can be an easy way to ensure a ready supply, either after making a large batch of homemade tofu or after purchasing a large quantity from a store. Homemade frozen tofu will generally have a better flavor than, but will not be quite as light, fine-grained and expensive as, the commercial dried-frozen variety. Since storebought dried-frozen tofu is generally permeated with baking soda or other agents which cause the tofu to expand and soften during cooking, homemade frozen tofu will be more natural. The less water the tofu contains and the faster it freezes, the finer will be the grain structure and the more delicate the texture of the finished product. Good quality frozen tofu can be prepared with less than 12 hours of freezing, and may be used immediately or stored under refrigeration indefinitely. It makes an excellent, low-cost replacement for gluten meat or cutlets in vegetarian menus.

Deep-fried tofu cutlets and silken tofu can also be used to make frozen tofu: the first develops a firm, meaty texture; the second, a fine, delicate consistency.

Dried-frozen Tofu

But preserving tofu by freezing it outdoors had two basic limitations: first, the tofu could only be stored in its frozen form for as long as the air temperature remained below freezing; and, second, the tofu was very heavy and susceptible to thawing when transported from place to place. The Japanese, therefore, began to experiment with drying frozen tofu to create a lightweight, staple food that could be preserved well into springtime. Since this idea seems never to have occurred to the Chinese, dried-frozen tofu is thought to have originated in Japan. Two different traditional methods of freezing and drying arose independently in the snowy, mountainous regions of the nation.

The home of the first experiment, Mount Koya, stands high and solitary in a vast forest of cedars south of Kyoto, Japan's ancient capital. Kobo Daishi, one of Japan's great Buddhist saints, founded a monastery there in 816, and it continues to serve as the headquarters of the Shingon sect of esoteric Buddhism. Tradition has it that the method for making dried-frozen tofu was first discovered there in about 1225 by a Shingon priest.

The priests and monks living in Mount Koya's snow-bound temples chose a day for making tofu when the night temperatures were expected to be bitterly cold and there were winds to help hasten the freezing process in order to give the tofu the desired fine-grained texture. Beginning work in the late afternoon, they prepared a large quantity of firm tofu, cut the cakes into ½-inch-thick slabs, and pressed these in layers between bamboo mats or boards to expel excess water. Waking at about 3 a.m., the coldest hour, they set the tofu out in the snow on the mats or boards in a place that received no direct sunlight during the day.

The next morning, after the tofu slabs had been out in the cold for about 8 hours and were frozen solid, the monks took them into a specially built shed, arranged them on shelves, and allowed them to stand undisturbed (out of direct sunlight) at temperatures below freezing for about one to three weeks. During this second freezing, the tofu slabs developed an even finer grain and firmer structure and became more resilient. They were then thawed in warm water and pressed lightly to expel the melted ice. The entire shed was then heated in much the same way as a sauna (using large charcoal braziers) and each slab was dried until it turned light beige and was as hard and crisp as a zwieback biscuit. It was found that if this dried tofu was stored in a cool, dry place, it could be preserved for about 4 months after the last snows had melted.

Farm villages in the area learned the technique from the monks, and many large freezing and drying sheds were built in the mountain valleys. "Koya-dofu" soon came to be made on a fairly large scale as a communal wintertime occupation and source of income during the lean months. In some areas, an entire village would turn out on cold days and work together, freezing and drying the tofu. By the Edo period (1600–1868) Koya-dofu was known throughout Japan. In 1911, it started to be made on an even larger scale throughout the year using artificial refrigeration.

The second traditional experiment with dried-frozen tofu began around the year 1575 in the cold mountains of Nagano north of Tokyo. A famous samurai warrior, Takeda Shingen, thought of drying frozen tofu to make a lightweight, nutritious food that his soldiers could carry in their backpacks. The soldiers apparently learned how to prepare the tofu, then taught the method to local farmers. After the pieces of well-pressed tofu had been placed overnight in the snow

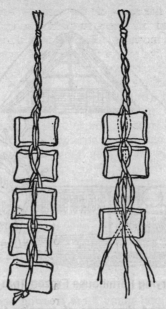

Fig. 70.   Tying Frozen Tofu with Rice Straw

and frozen solid, they were wrapped in straw mats, placed in the shade in a barn or tool shed, and left at below-freezing temperatures for about one week. Then five pieces of tofu at a time were tied together with several pieces of rice straw (Fig. 70), and these strands were hung from poles under the eaves of farmhouses (where they received no direct sunlight). After several weeks of thawing during the day and freezing again at night, the tofu became completely dry and crisp.

This technique, which obviated the special drying shed and equipment used on Mount Koya, was simple and inexpensive, so that most tofu of this type came to be made on a small scale by individual farmers. Carrying the light tofu in backpacks, these farmers often walked from village to village selling it as a source of wintertime income. To this day, strands of drying tofu can be seen hanging under the verandas of

Fig. 71. Drying Farmhouse Frozen Tofu

farmhouses and the eaves of temples throughout the Nagano area (Fig. 71).

Today, dried-frozen tofu is produced year round in huge automated factories (most of which are still located in the Nagano area). Since the tofu is neither perishable nor fragile, it is well suited to centralized, large-scale production and nationwide (or worldwide) distribution. Each package is stamped with the date of manufacture; its average shelf life is 8 months. If kept longer than this before use, dried-frozen tofu, upon being reconstituted, loses some of its softness, freshness, and ability to expand and absorb cooking liquids.

In 1928, it was found that if thawed tofu was steeped in a solution of baking soda before being dried, it swelled during cooking and became softer and more absorbent than the traditional dried-frozen variety. From 1929 until 1971, each cake of tofu was permeated with ammonia gas, which served the same function as the baking soda. However in 1972 baking soda again came to be used in a new, improved form as the main active ingredient (together with small quantities of various salts) in *kansui*, the agent intended to make the reconstituted tofu soft and absorbent. Not only is the new tofu free of the ammonia smell, it has better stability, a longer shelf life, and is relatively unaffected by changes in temperature. In 1975 Asahimatsu, by far the largest maker, accounting for about 55 percent of total dried-frozen tofu production, began to sell its product accompanied by a packet of instant powdered dashi soup stock. An immediate hit in Japan, it is now widely available in America and Europe as well—ready to serve in 10 minutes.

At present Asahimatsu's three large and modern factories employ over 300 people; each day they use 45 tons of soybeans and turn out 1.2 million cakes of dried-frozen tofu. The only ingredients used are whole soybeans, well water, calcium chloride nigari coagulant, and the baking soda expanding agent. The tofu is made in a continuous production line that takes about 25 days from start to finish. The basic techniques are essentially the same as those developed for making Koya-dofu 750 years ago. The first freezing is carried out in a very cold refrigerated room with strong winds provided by huge electric fans. The frozen tofu is then stored in a refrigerated warehouse for 20 days. It is then placed on a wide conveyor belt, thawed under a spray of warm water, pressed between heavy rollers, sprinkled with a 0.1 to 0.3 percent solution of *kansui* (baking soda), re-pressed, and dried in a 300-foot-long tunnel dryer. Sealed 5 to 10 pieces at a time in airtight cellophane bags, packaged in small paper boxes, and dated, it is shipped throughout Japan and the rest of the world.

Dried-frozen tofu is now also sold in four other forms. *Traditional dried-frozen tofu* is made from tofu containing no expanding agent, tied into strands with rice straw, and sold mostly as a tourist item or in natural food stores. *Tofu meal* is coarsely ground dried-frozen tofu resembling cornmeal, and *tofu flour* is its more finely ground counterpart. Both can be used to add protein to breads, pancakes, waffles, casseroles, or sautéed vegetable preparations. The meal makes an interesting cholesterol-free extender or substitute for scrambled eggs. Although they are more expensive, both are preferable to soy flour in that they have a milder flavor, are more digestible, and require no additional cooking to deactivate trypsin inhibitors. *Tofu croutons* are made by cutting dried-frozen tofu into ½-inch cubes.

Present-day dried-frozen tofu differs from both its traditional counterpart and from homemade frozen tofu in that it has a very fine, firm grain structure, and is much softer and more absorbent. When reconstituted, it swells by about 26 percent, as compared with 7 percent in the case of tofu containing no baking soda. Dried-frozen tofu has relatively little flavor of its own: it is used mostly for its texture and ability to acquire flavor from seasoned broths and sauces.

Dried-frozen tofu is also highly valued as a concentrated source of nutrients. It contains 53.4 percent protein and 26.4 percent natural oils, and is only 7 percent carbohydrate and 10 percent water. An excellent energy source, it provides 436 calories per 100 grams, and contains more than 7 times the amount of protein and energy as an equal weight of regular tofu. In Japan, it is advertised as providing both the highest percentage of protein and the least expensive energy of any known food. The economies of large-scale production make it possible to produce dried-frozen tofu at about 96 percent the cost (on a usable protein basis) of regular tofu made in small shops. Its relatively low cost has been a major factor in its growing popularity and, combined with its durability even when not refrigerated, would make it an excellent food for use in developing areas such as India, Africa, and South America.

In Japan, a carton containing ten pieces of dried-frozen tofu (each 2½ by 2 by ⅝ inch thick) weighs only 5.8 ounces (165 grams). The same amount of protein in the form of fresh tofu would weigh about 6 times as much. Thus, its light weight and ease of preservation obviously make dried-frozen tofu an ideal back-packing food, now available in the West at prices far below those of most freeze-dried camping foods.

Highly versatile and requiring only a few minutes of cooking, dried-frozen tofu is well suited to a wide variety of Western-style dishes. We have found it preferable to regular tofu in a number of sautéed vegetable preparations, egg dishes, and casseroles. Preliminary experiments in Japan indicate that it can be flavored to resemble meat and can therefore be used in many of the same ways as textured soy protein.

In Japanese cookery, it is commonly used in *nabe* cookery, Sukiyaki, simmered and sautéed dishes, and sushi rice preparations. Properly seasoned, dipped in tempura batter or eggs, then rolled in bread crumbs and deep-fried, it makes an excellent cutlet. While still dry, it can be grated, and the gratings added to almost any dish. It is also, of course, a popular ingredient in Zen Temple Cookery.

At present in the United States, dried-frozen tofu is available at most Japanese markets and some co-op stores at very reasonable prices. It can also be prepared quite easily at home.

Reconstituting Frozen and Dried-frozen Tofu

IMPORTANT: In the following recipes, "1 piece of frozen tofu" refers either to 5 or 6 ounces of tofu made into Homemade Frozen Tofu (p. 349), or an equivalent weight of regular tofu which has been frozen and sold commercially. The phrase "1 piece of dried-frozen tofu" refers to a standard ½ ounce (16.5 gram) piece of the commercial variety, measuring about 2½ by 2 by ½ inches. In many recipes the two types can be used interchangeably.

Frozen Tofu (or natural dried-frozen tofu): Remove tofu from freezer and place in a large pan or bowl. Add several quarts boiling water, cover, and allow to stand for 5 to 10 minutes until completely thawed. (If a large cake of tofu was frozen initially, cut crosswise into ½-inch-thick slices after cake is partially thawed to hasten the process.) Pour off hot water and add lukewarm or cold water. Gently but firmly press tofu several times between the palms of both hands to expel all hot water. Lift tofu out of water and press firmly before using (Fig. 72). This last

Fig. 72. Pressing Frozen Tofu

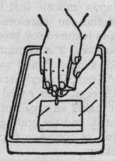

pressing makes the tofu light and dry so that it will readily absorb liquids during cooking.

Dried-frozen Tofu (containing baking soda): Remove dried tofu from airtight package, float in a pan or bowl partially filled with hot (120°F) water, and allow to stand for 3 to 5 minutes while tofu swells. Do not allow to stand for too long, lest the tofu eventually begin to fall apart. Lift tofu out of water and press firmly between palms of hands to expel excess water, then use in the recipe of your choice.

Grated Dried-frozen Tofu: Grate dried-frozen tofu on a metal grater to give a fine, granular texture. Place gratings in a bowl, cover with hot water (175°F), and soak for 2 minutes. Pour into a dishcloth set over a strainer, allow to drain, then squeeze or press to expel excess water.

Storing and Cooking Dried-frozen Tofu

Use commercial dried-frozen tofu within 8 months of the production date printed on the package. Store in a cool place, out of contact with direct sunlight.

If dried-frozen tofu is simmered for too long or over very high heat, or if the broth in which it is cooked contains no salt (or shoyu), it may begin to fall apart. However if too much salt or shoyu are used in the cooking broth, it may shrink somewhat and become firmer than desirable.

Homemade Frozen Tofu

MAKES 2 "PIECES"

Although regular tofu is generally used as the basis for frozen tofu, both silken tofu and tofu cutlets may also be used. Due to freezing, the latter develops a texture remarkably similar to tender meat. If using homemade tofu (p. 127), make it as firm as possible by pressing with a heavy weight for a long time in the settling container.

10 to 12 ounces tofu, cut crosswise into halves

Arrange tofu pieces on a plate, leaving at least ½ inch between pieces, then place in the freezer with the temperature turned down as cold as possible. (Or place outdoors on a very cold winter night.) Its color turned from white to dark amber, the tofu will be completely transformed and ready to use after 48 hours; the most porous and resilient texture, however, is attained after 1 week of freezing. If you do not wish to use the tofu immediately, seal it in a polyethylene bag and store in the freezer. Lengthy storage actually improves the texture.

Homemade Dried-frozen Tofu

MAKES 10 TO 20 PIECES

The traditional methods of preparing *Kori-dofu* and *Koya-dofu* are described earlier. During winter, we have had good results using the former method, which requires no special equipment. Our 20-ounce batch of tofu was ready and well-dried after about 1 week.

To prepare homemade dried-frozen tofu in any season for use in camping or traveling, try the following:

10 to 20 pieces of (homemade) frozen tofu, reconstituted
(p. 347) and cut crosswise into ¼-inch-thick slices

Preheat oven to 170°F. Arrange the thin, slightly moist tofu slices on large baking sheets, leaving at least ½ inch between slices. Place in oven for about 2 hours, or until tofu color has turned from amber to light beige and slices are crisp and dry. Remove and allow to cool. Seal in polyethylene bags and store in a cool dry place. Use within 2 to 3 months.

Frozen Tofu with Eggs and Onions *(Tamago-toji)*

SERVES 2 OR 3

1 piece of frozen or dried-frozen tofu, reconstituted (p. 347)
and cut into ½-inch cubes; or 7 ounces (frozen or regular) deep-fried tofu, cut into strips
½ cup dashi (p. 35), stock, or water
1 tablespoon honey
1½ tablespoons shoyu
1 tablespoon oil
1 onion or leek, thinly sliced
1 egg, lightly beaten

Combine tofu, dashi, honey, and shoyu in a bowl; beat lightly. Heat a skillet and coat with the oil. Sauté onion for about 1 minute, then add tofu-dashi mixture and simmer, stirring occasionally, for 7 to 10 minutes. Turn heat to high, mix in egg, and cook, stirring constantly, for about 1 minute more, or until egg is just firm.

Frozen Tofu & Onion Sauce with Eggs and Cheese

SERVES 4

Frozen tofu makes a good addition to most sautéed or stir-fried dishes, especially when seasoned with shoyu or miso. Try substituting it for regular tofu in recipes beginning on page 178. It is also delicious used in (or topped with) sauces such as Mushroom (p. 47), Spaghetti (p. 169), Onion-White (p. 46), or Curry (p. 236). Or try the following:

2 tablespoons oil
6 onions, thinly sliced
3 pieces of frozen or dried-frozen tofu, reconstituted (p. 347) and torn into ½-inch pieces
3 tablespoons red or barley miso; or 2 tablespoons shoyu
2 or 3 eggs
2 ounces cheese, cut into small cubes
⅔ cup water

Using the oil and onions, prepare an Onion Sauce (p. 46); simmer for 1½ hours. Stir in tofu and remaining ingredients and simmer for about 15 minutes more, or until sauce is well thickened. For best flavor, allow to cool to room temperature. Serve either cold or reheated.

Frozen Tofu Cutlets

SERVES 2

One of our favorite tofu recipes, these cutlets often bear a remarkable resemblance to fish or veal cutlets, depending on the type of sauce with which they are served.

2 tablespoons grated gingerroot
4 tablespoons shoyu
1½ cups water
4 pieces of frozen or dried-frozen tofu, reconstituted (p. 347) and cut into large ⅜-inch-thick slices
½ cup flour
1 egg, lightly beaten
½ cup bread crumbs or bread crumb flakes
Oil for deep-frying
1 lemon, cut into 4 wedges

Combine gingerroot, shoyu, and water in a large saucepan and bring to a boil. Reduce heat to low, add tofu,
and simmer for 15 to 20 minutes. Lift out tofu, allow
to cool slightly, then press each piece lightly with your
fingertips to expel about one-fourth of the liquid. Dust
well with flour, dip in egg, and roll in bread crumbs.
Heat the oil to 375°F in a wok, skillet, or deep-fryer.
Drop in tofu and deep-fry until golden brown (p.
185). Serve hot or cold with lemon wedges.

To lend more of a seafood flavor, serve with Tofu
Tartare Sauce (p. 147). To give the feeling of breaded
veal, serve with Worcestershire or Ketchup-Worcestershire Sauce (p. 50).

Deep-fried Frozen Tofu with Chinese Sauce

SERVES 2

1½ pieces of frozen or dried-frozen tofu, reconstituted
    (p. 347) and torn into 12 pieces
6 tablespoons kudzu powder, arrowroot, or cornstarch
Oil for deep-frying
Chinese Sauce:
    1 teaspoon grated gingerroot
    2 tablespoons water or stock
    1½ tablespoons honey
    2 tablespoons soy sauce or shoyu
    1 tablespoon ground roasted sesame seeds
    1 tablespoon vinegar
15 snow peas, parboiled and cut crosswise into halves

Roll tofu in 4 tablespoons kudzu powder or arrowroot,
then set aside briefly to dry. Heat oil to 350°F in a
wok, skillet, or deep-fryer. Drop in tofu and deep-fry
until golden brown (p. 185); drain briefly.

Combine all sauce ingredients and bring just to a
boil. Stir in 2 tablespoons kudzu powder or arrowroot
dissolved in 3 tablespoons water. Add snow peas, then
simmer for 30 seconds more. Divide tofu pieces among
two serving bowls and serve topped with the hot sauce.

You can also serve this dish as a topping for deep-
fried noodles or fried rice.

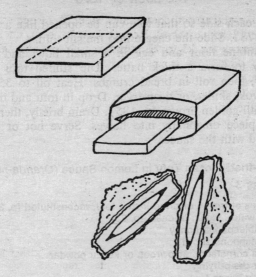

Fig. 73. Deep-fried Frozen Tofu with Cheese

Deep-fried Frozen Tofu Stuffed with Cheese

SERVES 2

2 pieces of frozen or dried-frozen tofu, reconstituted (p. 347)
1 tablespoon shoyu
½ cup water
2 slices of cheese, each 3 by 2 by ¼ inch
2 tablespoons flour
1 egg, lightly beaten
¼ cup bread crumbs or bread crumb flakes
Oil for deep-frying
Tofu Tartare Sauce (p. 147), Ketchup-Worcestershire (p. 50),
    or ketchup

Combine tofu, shoyu, and water in a small saucepan
and bring to a boil. Reduce heat and simmer for 5
minutes, pressing tofu occasionally to aid absorption
of the liquid. Remove tofu and allow to cool briefly.

Make a horizontal slit from one end of each piece of
tofu to the other, leaving about ¼ inch of uncut tofu

along each side so that tofu can be opened like a tube (Fig. 73). Slide the cheese into the slit tofu.

Combine flour and egg in a small bowl and mix lightly to form a thick batter. Dip stuffed tofu into batter, then roll in bread crumbs. Heat oil to 350°F in a wok, skillet, or deep-fryer. Drop in tofu and deep-fry until golden brown (p. 185). Drain briefly, then cut each piece diagonally into halves. Serve hot or cold topped with the sauce.

Deep-fried Frozen Tofu in Lemon Sauce *(Oranda-ni)*

SERVES 3

3 pieces of frozen or dried-frozen tofu, reconstituted (p. 347)
1 cup water, stock, or dashi (p. 35)
1½ tablespoons honey
2 tablespoons shoyu
½ cup cornstarch, arrowroot, or kudzu powder
Oil for deep-frying
3 lemon slices
3 sprigs of parsley

Combine the first four ingredients in a small saucepan and bring to a boil. Reduce heat to low, cover pan, and simmer for 10 minutes, pressing the tofu once or twice with a spatula to aid absorption of the cooking liquid. Remove tofu and allow to cool, then dust liberally with cornstarch.

Heat oil to 350°F in a wok, skillet, or deep-fryer. Drop in tofu and deep-fry until golden brown (p. 185). Return initial cooking liquid to a boil, drop in the hot deep-fried tofu, and simmer for 1 minute more. Cut tofu pieces diagonally into halves, then divide among 3 serving bowls. Top with remaining cooking liquid and serve garnished with lemon and parsley.

Onion-Sauce Flavored Frozen Tofu Cutlets

MAKES 18

We like to prepare a large batch of these cutlets and freeze the leftovers for use on hiking trips.

2 tablespoons oil
7 onions, thinly sliced
¼ cup red, barley, or Hatcho miso
2 tablespoons shoyu
2½ cups water
Dash of pepper
9 pieces of Homemade Frozen Tofu (p. 349), reconstituted
   (p. 347) and cut into ½-inch-thick slices
½ cup flour
2 eggs, lightly beaten
½ cup bread crumbs or bread crumb flakes
Oil for deep-frying
Ketchup-Worcestershire Sauce (p. 50) or lemon wedges

Heat the oil in a casserole or heavy pot. Add onions, cover, and simmer over very low heat for 2 hours, stirring occasionally, to form an Onion Sauce (p. 46). Mix in miso, shoyu, water, and pepper, and return to the boil. Add tofu, cover, and simmer for 40 to 60 minutes more. Now remove tofu and allow to cool briefly. Press tofu lightly between your fingers to expel about one-fourth of the liquid it contains.

Dust cutlets with flour, dip in egg, and roll in bread crumbs; set aside briefly to dry. Heat oil to 350°F in a wok, skillet, or deep-fryer. Drop in tofu and deep-fry until golden brown (p. 185). Serve topped with Ketchup-Worcestershire Sauce or garnished with lemon wedges; or top with remaining Onion Sauce.

Frozen Tofu Simmered in Sweetened Broth
(Fukuyose-ni)

SERVES 2

Probably the most popular way Japanese restaurants serve frozen tofu, the following recipe is that provided us by Tokyo's Sasa-no-Yuki. There the tofu is served with young butterbur, tiny "maiden" bamboo shoots, and a roll of deep-fried, fresh yuba which has been simmered in a lightly seasoned broth.

2 pieces of frozen or dried-frozen tofu, reconstituted (p. 347)
1 cup water
1½ tablespoons honey
1 tablespoon shoyu
Vegetables: butterbur *(fuki)*, carrot slivers, tiny bamboo
   shoots, *(shiitake)* mushrooms, green beans, snow peas,
   konnyaku rectangles, wheat gluten cakes, or deep-fried
   fresh yuba rolls

Combine tofu, water, honey, and shoyu in a saucepan
and bring to a boil. Reduce heat to low, cover pan,
and simmer for 15 to 20 minutes. Remove tofu and
allow to cool, then cut into bite-sized cubes.

Add your choice of vegetables to the remaining
cooking liquid and simmer until tender. Arrange tofu
and vegetables in individual bowls, pour any remaining
cooking liquid over the top of each portion, and serve
cold or chilled.

For variety, garnish each serving with a sprig of
kinome.

VARIATIONS

• Try the following cooking liquid: 1 cup dashi (p.
35), 1½ teaspoons shoyu, 1 tablespoon honey, 1½
teaspoons each sake and *mirin*, and a dash of salt. For
added richness, mix in 2 to 3 tablespoons sesame
butter.

• *Simmered Frozen Tofu Wrapped in Tofu Pouches
and Kampyo (Shinoda-maki):* Cut each piece of reconstituted tofu lengthwise into thirds. Using 6 tofu
pouches, cut each along 3 sides, then open to form
flat sheets. Roll up one piece of tofu in each of the
sheets and tie in two places with pieces of reconstituted *kampyo.* Simmer rolls for 15 minutes in the
dashi described in the recipe above. Cut rolls crosswise into halves and serve with the simmered vegetables.

Deep-fried Frozen Tofu Dessert with Apples

SERVES 2

1 apple, cut into thin wedges
3 tablespoons raisins
½ teaspoon honey
½ cup water
1 piece frozen or dried-frozen tofu, reconstituted (p. 347)
¼ cup flour mixed with 2 tablespoons water
½ cup bread crumbs or bread crumb flakes
Oil for deep-frying
¼ teaspoon cinnamon
½ to 1 cup milk (soy or dairy)

Combine the first four ingredients in a small saucepan and simmer for about 5 minutes. Cut tofu into 6 or 8 equal pieces, add to the cooking apples, and continue to simmer until apples are tender and most of the liquid is absorbed or evaporated. Set aside and allow to cool briefly.

Mix the flour and water to form a thick batter. Remove tofu pieces from the cooked apples, dip into the batter, and roll in bread crumbs. Heat the oil to 350°F in a wok, skillet, or deep-fryer. Drop in the tofu and deep-fry until golden brown (p. 185). Divide drained tofu between 2 serving bowls and top with the apples, a sprinkling of cinnamon, and the milk.

14
Fermented Tofu

THIS DISTINCTIVE TYPE of tofu, which comes in various forms, originated in China and is sometimes known in the West as "Chinese cheese." But unlike typical cheeses, this variety is ripened immersed in a brining liquor. Different from any tofu prepared in Japan or, for that matter, any food familiar to most Westerners, it has a soft—almost creamy—consistency and a pronounced flavor and aroma reminiscent of a Camembert cheese. We use small amounts as a key ingredient in dips, spreads, dressings, and casseroles that invariably have guests hurrying back for more while asking "How did you make *that*?" For pure vegetarians, or vegans who eat no dairy products, it is the answer to the occasional longing for some of the cheese's rich goodness. In China, it is served as a seasoning or accompaniment for *congee* (hot breakfast rice porridge) or rice, as an appetizer or hors d'oeuvre with alcoholic drinks, or as an ingredient in stir fried dishes or simmered sauces used to add zest and flavor. Moreover, the spicy brining liquor *(toufu-ru chih)*, is a popular seasoning ingredient, often used in dipping sauces. Fortunately at least several types of fermented tofu are now available in the West, at most Chinese food markets and a growing number of natural food stores and supermarkets. Wine-fermented tofu is produced by Quong Hop and Wo Hop in San Francisco.

Fermented tofu is known by a bewildering array of Chinese names. In Mandarin (the official language of modern China) it is generally known as *toufu-ru,* but may also be referred to as *toufu-ju, furu, rufu,* or *tou-ru.* In Cantonese (and in many Western tofu shops run by Cantonese masters) it is called *fuyu* or *funan*. In Shanghai it is generally known as *sufu* or *tou-sufu*. In most Western scientific literature it has come to be referred to as *sufu* (which means "molded milk"), an unfortunate choice of term since it is not at all familiar to most Chinese.

Each of the various types of fermented tofu develops its unique flavor, texture, color, and aroma from both the fermentation process and the brining liquor, brine, mash, or other medium in which it is immersed. For example, to make wine-fermented tofu, the most popular type, ¾- to 1¼-inch cubes of firm tofu are inoculated with spores of an *Actinomucor elegans, Mucor racemosus,* or *Rhizopus* mold. The first two microorganisms were traditionally obtained from the rice straw which covered the tofu during the farmhouse incubation process; the latter is the same used to make Indonesian tempeh. Placed on woven bamboo trays or skewered and arranged in racks, the inoculated cubes are incubated at about 68°F for 3 days, or until each cube is covered with a fragrant cottony-white mycelium. The freshly molded cubes are then placed in pint bottles, which are filled with a brining liquor generally containing rice wine, salt, and red chilies or other spices and seasonings. The main function of the mold is to produce enzymes, especially protease, which break down protein molecules into simpler, more digestible amino acids. Placing the tofu in the brining liquor serves several purposes: it extracts enzymes from the mycelium so that they can permeate the tofu to do their work of developing its prized soft consistency and mellow flavor; it halts the growth of the mold and any contaminating microorganisms; and it imparts a richly seasoned flavor. After ripening for one to two months in the brining liquor, the bottled tofu is shipped to markets where it may be allowed to age for another two to four months before being placed on sale. Like cheeses, wines, miso, shoyu, and many other fermented foods, fermented tofu improves in texture, flavor, and aroma as it ages. After 6 to 8 months, it virtually melts in the mouth. Its color turns from yellowish white to a soft light brown; the brining liquor grows richer and mellower. It is said that if the fermented tofu remains motionless when the jar is spun quickly on its axis, it has been properly aged and is ready to use. It will keep for as long as one to two years, even in semi-tropical climates.

Documents show that fermented tofu was being produced in China prior to 1600, and it may have originated much earlier. The standard Mandarin term *toufu-ru* has an unusual and probably ancient etymology; the ideographic character *fu* (also used in the Chinese word for tofu, *toufu*) means "spoiled," and the character *ru* means "milk." Although the Chinese had a highly developed civilization long before the beginning of the Christian era, they never developed the art of dairy farming or, consequently, of making cheese. But their northerly neighbors, the Mongols, whom the Chinese regarded as uncivilized barbarians, were quite skilled in the preparation of fine goat's cheese. The Chinese called this cheese *furu,* or "spoiled milk." Centuries later, the Chinese learned how to prepare their own variety of fermented cheese, but from soy rather than dairy milk, probably with some help (or at least inspiration) from the Mongols. And the name which they had used derogatorily for the Mongolian cheese gradually came to be used for their own tofu cheese: their insult boomeranged and remains with them to this day. Consequently some modern Chinese and Japanese—especially those operating expensive restaurants—write the character *fu* in the words tofu, toufu, and toufu-ru with a different character which, although pronounced "fu" means "affluent, ample, or abundant."

Although over the centuries, tofu spread from China to most other parts of East Asia, fermented tofu was not as well received. Throughout Southeast Asia today it is still produced in relatively small quantities. In the

Philippines it is known as *tahuri,* in Vietnam as *chao,* and in Indonesia as *taokoan* or *takoa.* In the United States, however, its popularity is growing. The five basic types of Chinese fermented tofu, listed in order of popularity, and one variety recently developed in the U.S., are described below:

Wine-fermented Tofu (pai toufu-ru): Literally "white fermented tofu," this variety is also called simply "fermented tofu" *(toufu-ru).* The proportions of alcohol and salt in its brining liquor vary from maker to maker. The most common liquor contains 10 percent alcohol and 12 to 25 percent salt, although some may contain twice as much alcohol as salt.

At least five varieties of wine-fermented tofu are sold in markets and marketplaces throughout Taiwan and China, and each derives its name from the most prominent seasoning. Wine-fermented Tofu with Chilies *(la toufu-ru, la-chiao furu,* or *la furu)* is spicy hot; the minced chilies also serve as a natural preservative. Wine-fermented Tofu with Chilies and Sesame *(mayu-la toufu-ru)* contains added sesame oil. A milder and particularly delicious type is the same as the former, minus the chilies. Other seasonings include anise, cinnamon, lemon juice, slivered lemon rind, bonito flakes, tiny dried shrimp, and diced ham. Wine-fermented Tofu with Spices *(wu-hsiang toufu-ru)* contains five-spice powder (cinnamon, ginger, cloves, nutmeg, anise) in the liquor, while a Dried Wine-fermented Tofu *(hsia-tsu)* is dried after brine fermentation, then sold in paper cartons.

Brine-fermented Tofu (pai-toufu-ru): This type is similar to wine-fermented tofu except that the brining solution contains no alcohol. In Chinese the two products are known by the same name.

Red Fermented Tofu (hung toufu-ru, nanru, or nanyu): This variety is prepared like brine-fermented tofu except that "red rice" is added to the brining liquor (to give it a deep red color, thick consistency, and distinctive flavor and aroma), less brining solution is used, and the solution may contain soy sauce with, or in place of, salt. Red rice (called *ang-kak* in China and *beni-koji* in Japan) is made by fermenting white rice with the mold *Monascus purpureus,* then grinding the mixture before adding it to the brine. The liquor may or may not contain minced chilies. Red fermented tofu is now available in the West at Chinese markets sold as Red Bean Curd in small (4-to-6-ounce) cans. One popular variety is Red Fermented Tofu with Rose Essence *(mei-kui toufu-ru, mei-kui hung nanru,* or *nanyu)* containing rose essence, ketchup, caramel, and natural sugar in the thick brine; the fragrance of any dish in which it is served is distinctive. Red Fermented Tofu is especially popular in hot sauces served with one-pot cookery, meats, and fresh or live "dancing" shrimp.

Redolent Fermented Tofu (ch'ou toufu): Prepared by aging either fresh or molded tofu in rice wine and its lees *(chu-tsao),* this product has a heady alcoholic flavor and aroma. The Chinese character *ch'ou* actually means "foul smelling." While many Chinese themselves dislike its strong aroma and flavor, slippery texture, unusual color, and aftermath of bad breath, its devotees claim that once a taste is acquired for this unique food, it is forever regarded as a delicacy. Its deep-fried preparations are said to be positively addicting. In Taiwan, a popular variety with a green color is prepared in homes and marketplace stalls by placing pressed tofu squares into a crock containing rice wine lees, crushed leaves, a green *Mucor* mold, cloves, and orange peels. After the tofu has fermented 12 hours or more and is ripe and redolent, vendors peddle it in the streets. A type called *tsui-fang* ("drunken cheese") is fermented in a mixture of rice wine lees and a large proportion of the wine itself.

Savory Fermented Tofu (chiang-toufu): A close relative of Japan's popular Tofu Pickled in Miso *(tofu no misozuké),* this variety has a reddish-brown color, a rich and somewhat salty flavor, and a firm texture. It is prepared by pickling firm cubes of tofu (which are sometimes dried briefly or fermented with mold before pickling) in either Chinese-style miso *(chiang)* or soy sauce *(chiang-yu)*. Rice wine lees are occasionally mixed with the *chiang*, giving the finished product much the same rich sweetness as Japanese finger lickin' miso (see Chapter 4). Savory Fermented Tofu Sauce *(chiang-toufu chih)* is prepared by mixing the pickled tofu with its pickling medium, then grinding the mixture until it is smooth; it is used as a condiment for Chinese lamb or beef dishes.

Tofu Tempeh: Developed recently in the United States, this food consists of firm tofu slices that are inoculated with spores of a *Rhizopus* mold (as used for Indonesian tempeh). Incubated at 88°F for 20 to 26 hours until covered with a fragrant white mycelium, they are dipped quickly into a light brine (2 teaspoons salt in ½ cup water), then shallow- or deep-fried until crisp and golden brown. Served with a sprinkling of shoyu, the fried slices taste like tender fried chicken. The plain fermented tofu looks and tastes quite like a soft or creamy Camembert cheese.

Homemade Wine-fermented Tofu

MAKES 1 PINT

12 ounces tofu, firmly pressed and cut into pieces ¾ inch square by ½ inch thick
½ teaspoon tempeh starter (*Rhizopus oligosporus* mold spores, available from The Farm, 156 Drakes Ln., Summertown, TN 38483), or *Actinomucor elegans* mold spores
1 cup rice wine (sake) or Kaoling wine
6 teaspoons salt, dissolved in ¼ cup hot water

Sterilize a flat cookie sheet, baking tin, or large plate (at least 12 inches square) with boiling water; invert and drain dry. Wash hands. Sprinkle starter over bottom of cookie sheet, then distribute it evenly with a cotton swab or sterilized knife. Arrange tofu cubes atop one half of starter, rubbing gently to inoculate bottom of each cube, then turn cubes over onto remaining starter to inoculate the second side. Now use swab (or one tofu cube) to apply started to the un-inoculated sides of each tofu cube. Obtain a tupper-ware, plastic, wood, or sturdy paper box about 6 by 8 by 2½ inches deep. Cut 4 to 5 sets of vertical slits opposite each other in the two long sides, as shown. Skewer tofu cubes on bamboo or metal skewers, leaving ¼ inch space between adjacent cubes, then set skewers in slits in box. Cover box with perforated aluminum foil and incubate at about 86°F(30°C) for 22 hours (or 68°F for 3 days), or until all cubes are covered with a ¼-inch-thick mycelium of fragrant white mold. (If the mycelium smells of ammonia or is gray, the fermentation has gone for too long.) Lift tofu on skewers out of box and stand skewers upright in a sterilized 1 pint jar; withdraw skewers leaving tofu neatly stacked in jar. Combine wine and salt solution, mixing until salt dissolves, and fill jar containing tofu with this brining liquor. Screw lid on tightly and allow to stand, untouched, for 1 month. Open jar and examine tofu; aroma should be pleasantly heady and molds should be pure white. If a foul odor or reddish molds are found, discard and try again. For best flavor, re-cover and wait for 1 to 5 more months before serving.

For tofu tempeh, cut pressed tofu into ½-inch-thick slices, inoculate as above, and incubate on a slatted metal rack inside a box as for the tofu. Do not immerse in brining liquor. Fry tempeh in oil or margarine. Serve topped with a sprinkling of shoyu.

Wine-fermented Tofu Salad Dressing

MAKES ¾ CUP

3 small cubes of wine-fermented tofu or 2 large cubes of red
    fermented tofu (about 2 ounces)
1 teaspoon brining liquor
6 ounces tofu
3 tablespoons lemon juice
¼ cup oil
¼ teaspoon salt

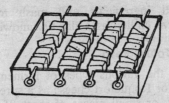

Combine all ingredients in a blender and purée until smooth. Tasty over fresh vegetable salads. Or simply blend or mash the fermented tofu and brining liquor with ¾ cup mayonnaise.

Wine-fermented Tofu Dip with Curry

MAKES ¾ CUP

6 cubes of wine-fermented tofu, well drained (about 4 ounces)
4 ounces cream cheese
1 tablespoon lemon juice
¼ onion, grated or minced
½ teaspoon curry powder or 1½ teaspoons Worcestershire sauce
2 teaspoons sake, white wine, or the brining liquor

Combine all ingredients and mash together until smooth. For best flavor, cover and refrigerate for at least 1 hour (preferably 2 to 7 days). Serve with crackers, potato chips, toast rounds, cucumber, jicama or carrot slices, or celery stalks.

To make a spread, omit the lemon juice, use Worcestershire sauce instead of curry powder, and add 1 tablespoon softened butter.

Wine-fermented Tofu & Sour Cream Dip

MAKES 1¼ CUPS

1 cup sour cream (dairy or tofu)
2 or 3 cubes of wine-fermented tofu
1 tablespoon minced chives
1 tablespoon minced parsley
¼ teaspoon salt
Dash of curry powder
Dash of paprika or 7-spice chili powder

Combine all ingredients and mash together until smooth. Serve chilled as a dip or sandwich spread.

Fermented Tofu Spread

Use any of the various types of fermented tofu like Camembert or Roquefort cheese as a spread for crackers, canapés, or small pieces of toast. If desired, garnish with a small slice of cheese, hard-boiled egg, tomato, cucumber, or a sprig of parsley.

Fermented Tofu with Hot Rice

This is the most popular way of serving fermented tofu among the Chinese. Place hot (brown) rice or rice porridge in an individual serving bowl, and top with 1 or 2 cubes of fermented tofu and, if desired, 1 tablespoon thinly sliced leeks or scallions. Some people prefer to use the tips of their chopsticks to take a tiny piece of the tofu with each bite of rice; others like to mix the fermented tofu together with the grain.

15
Yuba

IF YOU HAVE ever simmered a pot of milk over very low heat or set a bowl of hot milk aside to cool, you have no doubt noticed the thin, delicate film that soon forms on the milk's surface. The longer it is allowed to set, the firmer and thicker it becomes. And if you have ever tried lifting this film off and tasting it, you may well have found it to be soft, warm, and delicious. In the same way, if fairly thick soymilk is gently heated, a thin film soon covers its surface. In Japan this film is called *yuba,* and since ancient times it has been considered a true delicacy. It is easily prepared at home, and since it is best when fresh and warm, yuba made in your own kitchen and served as an hors d'oeuvre or as part of a meal will have a tenderness and fragrant richness that can far surpass that of the yuba ordered from even the finest traditional shops.

. Yuba in its commonly-sold dried form is a nutritional treasure-trove containing a remarkable 52.3 percent high-quality protein. This makes it one of the richest natural sources of protein known to man. Easy to digest, yuba also contains 24.1 percent natural oils (mostly polyunsaturated), 11.9 percent natural sugars and, in its dried form, 8.7 percent water. Thus it is extremely lightweight and easy to carry. Furthermore, a 100-gram portion contains some 432 calories, making it a highly concentrated energy source that is ideal for camping. Finally, yuba is rich in minerals, as shown in Figure 5 on page 20. Because of its nutritional excellence, yuba is a popular item at Japanese natural food and health food stores. Recommended to mothers before and after childbirth, it has been said for centuries to stimulate the flow of milk. Widely used in Japanese hospitals as a concentrated source of protein, doctors also recommend it to patients suffering from high blood pressure (it is believed to aid in the removal of cholesterol) and diabetes.

In spite of its nutritional excellence, yuba is appreciated primarily for its unique flavor and texture. The Japanese say that the natural sweetness and the subtle richness of yuba remind them of the flavor of fresh cream. Like cream, yuba rises to the surface of the soymilk from which it is made and embodies the condensed essence or elixir of the soymilk's flavor and nutrients. The most popular way of enjoying yuba's fine flavor is also the simplest: a delicate half-done sheet is lifted with the fingertips from the surface of steaming soymilk and placed in a small bowl; sprinkled with a few drops of shoyu, it is served immediately. Soft and warm, it melts on the tongue—and is gone.

Fresh yuba looks like a diaphanous veil of creamy silk and is usually sold in single sheets about 15 by 17 inches. When dried, it turns beige and has a crisp, brittle texture, yet it softens as soon as it is reconstituted or added to soups, stocks, egg dishes, or the like. In Japan, the dried form is also popular as a deep-fried hors d'oeuvre; it turns as crisp and crunchy as a potato chip.

The art of making yuba was transmitted from China to Japan about 1,000 years ago. During the following centuries, yuba developed a well-established role as one of the indispensable delicacies in both Zen Temple and Tea Ceremony Cookery. Today, in restaurants serving these two varieties of haute cuisine, yuba will often appear in more than half the dishes in a typical six-course meal. Kyoto's beautiful *Sorin-an* restaurant, which specializes in yuba cuisine, features homemade fresh yuba in a selection of more than 15 delectable dishes. Likewise, many Chinese restaurants—including those in the United States—generally have a special section on the menu devoted solely to yuba or "bean curd skin" preparations.

In Japan, yuba is (and has traditionally been) served largely as a gourmet food. A special product of the ancient capital, Kyoto, where most of the country's yuba shops are still located, it gradually acquired an aura of aristocracy, refinement, and elegance through its close association with the Imperial Court. And because it is made by slow traditional methods on a small scale, most of Japan's yuba is quite expensive. In Taiwan, China, and Hong Kong, on the other hand, yuba is a very popular food sold at prices anyone can afford. Although much of the yuba there, too, is still made in tiny cottage shops, modern methods have also been developed for preparing good-quality yuba on a large scale. This yuba, in its dried form, is now sold throughout the world.

Although, strictly speaking, yuba is not a type of tofu and is not made or sold at neighborhood tofu shops, it is nevertheless grouped together with tofu in most books on Japanese foods and cooking. This is partially because yuba, like all tofu, is made from soymilk; partially because its history parallels that of tofu; and partially because the two foods have closely related flavors and are therefore used in many of the same types of cookery.

Yuba and tofu shops have a great deal in common. And although yuba is made commercially only in special shops, a small amount is produced inadvertently each day at neighborhood tofu shops when soymilk cools in the curding barrel just before it is solidified into curds. This yuba is picked off to prevent it from entering the tofu, where it could form an interface and cause a large block of tofu to split apart. It is either eaten fresh at the tofu shop by the tofu maker and his family, served to guests or visitors as a special treat, or set aside and dried to be used later in cooking.

Like tofu shops, virtually all of Japan's yuba shops are run by a single family whose home adjoins the shop. Many of Kyoto's 23 shops have been in the family for centuries. Yuba Han, for example, is a beautiful example of classical Kyoto architecture; the building itself is 120 years old with massive rafters arching below a 20-foot-high ceiling. Here one can find a unique collection of all the ancient tofu-making tools still in daily use: large granite grinding stones, an iron cauldron heated by a wood fire, and a lever press weighted by heavy granite pendants. This historic shop and its tools were used as the basis for the drawing on the cover of this book. The Yuba-cho shop is run by a master (now assisted by his two sons) who has been making yuba in the same shop for fifty years. This cheerful old man, now a Living National Treasure, prepares his yuba for the Imperial Household.

In most shops, yuba is prepared in large copper or stainless steel steaming trays supported by a sturdy brick dais. One steaming table may be 8 to 10 feet

Fig. 74. Steaming Table in a Yuba Shop

long and 3 feet wide (Fig. 74); most shops will have
at least two such tables. Thick soymilk, prepared with
the same tools and in the same way as in tofu shops,
is poured into the trays to a depth of about 1½ inches.
Each tray is divided into rectangular compartments by
removable wooden frames. The soymilk is heated from
below by steam or low flames until it is steaming but
not bubbling (about 175°F). After 5 to 7 minutes,
when a firm film has formed in each compartment, the
master makes his or her rounds, lifting off each sheet
with a 2-foot-long bamboo skewer, then hanging the
yuba-draped skewer in a rack over the steaming table.
Here the yuba drains and begins to dry.

To visit Kyoto's yuba shops early in the morning
and watch the craftsmen at work is àn unforgettable
experience. Sunlight shines from the high windows
down through the steam rising from heating soymilk
and makes pinpoint rainbows in the air. Falling on the
sheets of translucent yuba, the light renders them
shimmering white. The delicious fragrances of fresh
soymilk and wood-smoke are everywhere. At times, the
entire shop can suddenly take on a surrealistic, almost
unreal appearance as through this hushed world, half-
visible figures move slowly along the steaming white
pools. Hundreds of sheets of pale yuba teem and hover
in the thick mist like the frail ghosts of a vision and
flutter in the magical netherworld light like silken banners on the lances of dream knights. As the day warms
or the sun's position shifts, the visual reverie can vanish as quickly as it came, leaving us in a world only
slightly less enchanted.

In Japan, yuba is sold in three different states: fresh,
half-dried, and dried. These are rolled, cut, trimmed,
or otherwise fashioned into a variety of unique and
delicate forms. Among these, our favorite is sweet
yuba; the last sheet lifted (or partially scraped) from
the bottom of the steaming tray. Sweet yuba has a rich
flavor and slightly reddish color and is considerably
thicker than other types. Eaten fresh and warm at the

yuba shop, its flavor is ambrosial; deep-fried and lightly salted, it is more addicting than potato chips. In Japan, it is the least expensive of all varieties.

In China yuba is called *toufu-p'i* ("tofu skin") or *toufu-i* ("tofu robes"). Local craftsmen, cooks, and food sculptors use it to do some of the most outrageously delightful and ingenious things we have ever seen done to any food. Imagine walking by the display case of an attractive restaurant or marketplace yuba shop and seeing perfect replicas of plucked hens, roosters and ducks, light-brown fish (complete with fins, gills, eyes, and mouth), juicy hams, tripe, liver and rolled meats—all made from yuba! Rich red sausage links hang in rows and deep-fried drumsticks are handsomely arranged on a large platter—together with a lifesized pig's head. Most of these imitation meat dishes are prepared by pressing fresh yuba into a hinged (wooden or aluminum) mold, then placing the well-packed mold in a steamer until the yuba's shape is fixed. In some cases the finished products are deep-fried or simmered in a sweetened or seasoned soy broth (in the same way the Chinese "whole-cook" many fish and other animals). Served at *su-tsai* restaurants which specialize in Buddhist vegetarian cookery, each has its own well-known name.

At present in the United States, Chinese-style dried yuba is available at most Chinese dried-goods markets in two forms: dried yuba sheets (called Dried Bean Curd, Bean Curd Sheets, or Bean Curd Skin) and u-shaped rolls (called Bamboo Yuba or Bean Curd Sticks). Five varieties of Japanese dried yuba (flat sheets, long rolls, small rolls, large spirals, and *Oharagi*) are available at some Japanese markets and natural food stores. We know of no yuba shops in the United States nor of any commercial sources of fresh yuba. The latter, however, is easy to make at home. And its fine flavor can always be enjoyed when preparing homemade soymilk, for then yuba inevitably appears of its own accord.

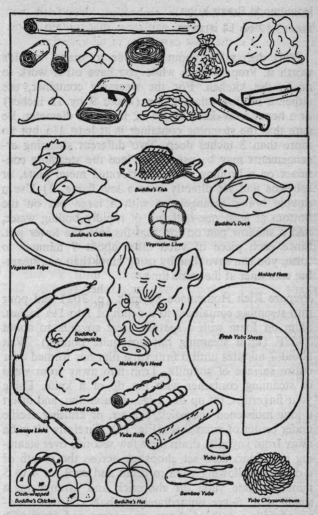

Varieties of Yuba

Homemade Fresh Yuba
MAKES 12 TO 14 SHEETS

This dish takes about an hour to make, but it's worth it. Prepare yuba while you have other work to do in the kitchen. For the steaming container, use either a shallow enamel pan (about 9 by 12 inches) or a heavy iron skillet about 12 inches in diameter. Be sure that the steaming container is at least 1½ but no more than 3 inches deep. Two different steaming arrangements may be used: 1) Place the steaming container on a broiling screen, perforated metal plate, or asbestos pad set directly over a low flame. 2) Use a double boiler arrangement with a large pot on the bottom at least one-half full of rapidly boiling water, and a shallow pan on top that fits into the lower pot. Since each piece of yuba takes about 7 minutes to form, you can save time by using more than one steaming container at the same time.

Prepare Rich Homemade Soymilk (p. 302) and pour into steaming containers to a depth of 1 to 1½ inches. Skim off foam with a spatula. Heat soymilk to about 175°F (until steaming but not quite boiling). Wait about 7 minutes until a firm yuba film has formed over entire surface of soymilk. Trim film away from walls of steaming container with the tip of a knife. Using your fingertips, lift up one edge of yuba film, and insert a long moistened chopstick, skewer, or knitting needle under center of yuba sheet (Fig. 75). Carefully lift yuba away from soymilk, drain for a few seconds over steaming container, then set chopstick across the mouth of a deep pot allowing yuba to drain and cool for 4 to 5 minutes. Slide yuba off chopstick and arrange on a small plate. Serve immediately as hors d'oeuvres seasoned with a dash of shoyu, or reserve and serve with other yuba during the meal.

Continue lifting off yuba sheets at 7-minute intervals until all soymilk has evaporated from steaming containers and only a thick reddish film remains on bottom of pan. This is "sweet yuba" *(amayuba),* a true

Fig. 75. Lifting Yuba Away from Soymilk

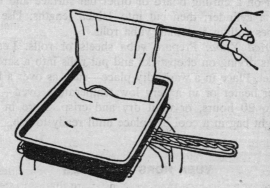

delicacy. Carefully scrape it off with a spatula and arrange with the other yuba. Place any crisp scraps or soft scrapings into a small bowl and serve together with the yuba as Warm Fresh Yuba (p. 376).

VARIATIONS

• *Half-formed Yuba (Tsumami-agé):* Using your fingertips, lift the delicate yuba sheets off the surface of the steaming soymilk at about 4 to 5 minute intervals, just before the yuba has had a chance to become attached to the sides of the container. Place yuba directly into a small cup and serve immediately.

• *Large Sheets of Fresh Yuba:* Prepare homemade fresh yuba, however when lifting yuba off surface of soymilk, insert moistened chopstick or skewer along one edge of sheet (rather than under the center) so that sheet hangs like a flag from chopstick. Allow yuba to drain as above for 15 to 20 minutes until it is no longer moist; carefully remove chopstick and lay flat sheet on a dry cutting board. Use as called for in the following recipes. For larger sheets use a 12- by 15-inch pan.

• *Fresh Yuba Rolls (Maki-yuba):* After yuba has dried on the chopstick for 4 to 5 minutes, place the flat yuba sheet on a cutting board or other flat surface and roll into a cylinder; then cut into 1-inch lengths. Use in recipes calling for small yuba rolls.

• *Dried Yuba:* Prepare yuba sheets or rolls. Leave sheets drying on chopsticks and put rolls into a screen basket. Place in a warm dry place—such as over a hot water heater or in a very low temperature oven—for 10 to 20 hours, or until dry and crisp. Store in an airtight bag in a cool dry place until ready to use.

YUBA HORS D'OEUVRES

In Japan, yuba is prized for its use in delicate and ambrosial hors d'oeuvres. The variety of shapes, textures, and flavors which you can offer your guests is almost unlimited.

Warm Fresh Yuba

SERVES 3

If you prepare your own yuba at home, this is the only recipe you need to know. Here is how most yuba masters offer fine yuba to their guests. The simpler, fresher, and warmer the yuba, the more completely your guests will enjoy it.

12 sheets of homemade fresh yuba, half-formed yuba, or
    fresh yuba rolls
3 tablespoons shoyu, Wasabi-Shoyu, or Yuzu-Shoyu (p. 37)

Serve the yuba warm and fresh in small bowls or arranged on a serving platter accompanied by tiny dishes containing the dipping sauce. Or serve with any of the following mixtures:

- Honey-Vinegar Dipping Sauce
  - 3 teaspoons honey
  - 2 teaspoons (rice) vinegar
  - 1 teaspoon *mirin*, sake, or white wine
- Honey-Lemon Dipping Sauce
  - 3 teaspoons honey
  - 4 teaspoons lemon or lime juice
- White Miso Dipping Sauce
  - 1½ teaspoons sweet white miso
  - ½ teaspoon honey
  - 1 teaspoon vinegar

Yuba-Cucumber Rolls

MAKES 8 TO 10

1 small cucumber, cut lengthwise into quarters and crosswise into 4-inch lengths
2 or 3 sheets of fresh yuba
Wasabi-Shoyu, Yuzu-Shoyu (p. 37), or shoyu

Arrange cucumber pieces in groups of 3 and wrap with a sheet of fresh yuba. Cut crosswise into 1-inch rounds and serve with the dipping sauce.

Butter-fried Yuba

SERVES 1

1 tablespoon butter or margarine
2 or 3 sheets of fresh yuba

Melt the butter or margarine in a skillet. Add yuba and fry lightly on both sides, until lightly browned. Tastes somewhat like chicken.

Crunchy Sweet-Yuba Chips

This is one of our very favorite yuba preparations.

The crisp texture resembles that of potato chips, but the flavor and aroma are truly unique.

Oil for deep-frying
10 to 15 sheets of dried sweet yuba (p. 347)
Salt

Heat the oil to only 275°F in a wok or skillet. Drop in yuba and deep-fry for about 3 to 5 seconds, until yuba turns reddish golden brown and is covered with tiny bubbles. Drain thoroughly, salt lightly and serve immediately. Also delicious served with a dip of Tofu Mayonnaise (p. 145) seasoned with a little extra lemon juice and sweetened with honey.

Kaori Yuba *(Sweet Miso Deep-fried in Fresh Yuba)*

MAKES 6

1 large sheet of fresh yuba, cut into six 4½-inch squares
9 tablespoons fresh yuba trimmings
3 tablespoons Yuzu Miso or Red Nerimiso (p. 39)
Oil for deep-frying
Shoyu or Wasabi-Shoyu (p. 37)

In the center of each yuba square layer 1 tablespoon fresh yuba trimmings, 1½ teaspoons Yuzu Miso, and ½ teaspoon yuba trimmings, in that order. Fold over the four corners of the yuba to form an envelope (Fig. 76). Deep-fry at 350°F for about 40 seconds, turning from time to time with chopsticks. Drain briefly, place on absorbent paper, and serve with dipping sauce.

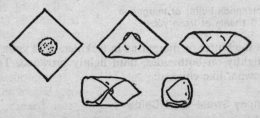

Fig. 76.   Yuba Envelopes

Appendix A

Tofu Restaurants in Japan

THIS SECTION has been included first, to give Western readers a sense of the key role tofu plays and the excellent reputation it enjoys in the most distinguished traditions of East Asian cuisine; second, to provide creative suggestions for Westerners who might like to start tofu restaurants or include tofu on the menu of restaurants now in operation; and finally, to serve as a guide for those living or traveling in Japan who wish to enjoy tofu restaurant cookery.

Some of Japan's oldest and finest restaurants have built their reputation around tofu cuisine. If you ask a Japanese to recommend one restaurant where you can enjoy tofu cookery at its best, though, he will probably suggest Sasa-no-yuki. Founded in 1703, Sasa-no-yuki has been managed by one family for twelve generations and has long been known throughout Japan for its unequalled nigari silken tofu, its delicious variety of tofu dishes at democratic prices, and its warm and friendly atmosphere. The name of the restaurant is proudly displayed in flowing characters written on two cloth *noren* that hang in front of the doorway. As you duck under these into the traditional Japanese entrance room, two doormen greet you with a hearty welcome. They check your shoes as you step onto long, thick beams of smoothly polished wood. Their loosely fitting blue coats—resembling *Happi* coats—give an added taste of old Japan. Perhaps the true genius of Sasa-no-yuki is that everyone feels welcome and at home here: aristocrat or working man, country grandmother or schoolboy. As in the Japanese tea house, where all are asked to come together as equals and friends, the charm here is found in refined simplicity. This book began, quite unexpectedly, with the first evening we enjoyed tofu at Sasa-no-yuki. We ended up trying one dish of every type on the menu!

The Nakamura-ro restaurant, too, has a long and distinguished history. Said to be the oldest of all existing Japanese restaurants, it began about 400 years ago as a simple teashop serving travelers, pilgrims, and townspeople who came to pay homage at the revered Yasaka Shrine in Kyoto's Gion Quarter. Over the centuries, the shop grew into a restaurant and became famous for its "Gion-dofu." In front of the shop, kneeling behind small wooden tables and wearing distinctive kimonos and elaborate hairdos (Fig. 77), women cut cakes of tofu into thin slices with a speed and syncopated rhythm that have become legendary.

Fig. 77. Cutting Tofu for Dengaku (from the "Tofu Hyaku Chin")

Visitors were entertained by a *shamisen* player who took her rhythms from the beat of the knives. Each small piece of tofu was pierced with bamboo skewers, spread with miso, broiled over a charcoal fire, and served piping hot as Dengaku (Fig. 78). Gradually the shop's spirited atmosphere and its savory tofu became the subject of poem and song, and its spacious interior gardens attracted writers, poets, and other distinguished figures throughout the four seasons. The present master and head chef, Mr. Shigemitsu Tsuji,

Fig. 78. Busy Making Dengaku (from the "Tofu Hyaku Chin")

is famous throughout Japan as a cook, lecturer, and author. He has recently published an entire volume devoted solely to tofu cuisine, his specialty. In the seven rooms adjoining the famous old gardens, he and his staff offer both a moderately-priced luncheon of tofu dishes and an expensive but exquisite meal of Tea Ceremony Cuisine, served in the banquet style and featuring tofu in many of the dishes. The original tea shop at Nakamura-ro retains the charm and familial warmth of old Japan. In one corner of the room is the original stone grill where Dengaku used to be broiled (Fig. 79). Two gracefully-curved tea

Fig. 79. Nakamura-ro

kettles with elegant wooden lids fit down into the raised stone hearth at the center of the room; here hot *amazake* (thick sweet sake) is kept simmering. In one corner of the room, an old, hand-carved bucket and pulley hang from the ceiling above an indoor well. This is a delightful setting for enjoying Dengaku considered by many to be the best in Japan.

Another of Japan's oldest and most well-known tofu restaurants is Okutan, founded over 300 years ago and now in its twelfth generation. Started originally as a tea house inside the spacious grounds of Nanzenji temple in Kyoto, Okutan soon began serving Zen Temple Cookery and Simmering Tofu to the many pilgrims, worshippers, and visitors who came to the famous temple from throughout Japan. The restaurant continues to preserve an atmosphere of quiet serenity which reflects the spirit of Zen. While strolling along Kyoto's historic tree-lined "Philosopher's Path," hungry students, statesmen, poets, and gourmets have for centuries entered Okutan's rustic front gate and stopped to enjoy a light meal. Today, for many Japanese, the name Nanzenji is associated just as much with Simmering Tofu as it is with Zen. At Okutan, lunch and early dinner are served both indoors in teahouse-style rooms or outdoors on raised *tatami* mats set among the trees and greenery around a large, meandering pond. In summer the shaded garden is cool and filled with the rock-splitting sound of a thousand cicadas. In winter the trees are bare and the only sound to be heard is the bubbling of Simmering Tofu in the earthenware *nabe* set over a tabletop charcoal brazier (Fig. 80).

Fig. 80. The Garden at Okutan

Like Sasa-no-yuki with its silken tofu, Nakamura-ro with its Dengaku, and Okutan with its Simmering Tofu, many of Japan's oldest and finest tofu restaurants have a single specialty, the preparation of which is a carefully guarded secret. Takocho, perhaps the most famous place in Kyoto to enjoy Oden, is no exception to this rule. Founded in 1888, Takocho is known for the savory broth that makes this Oden a true delicacy. A generations-old secret of the shop, it has a fragrance that fills the shop's single cozy room and makes passers-by want to step inside and see "what's cooking." More than 15 separate Oden ingredients (including five types of tofu) simmer in a shiny brass pot behind the thick, natural-wood counter. The elegant, dark beams and white plaster walls create something of the same convivial atmosphere found in the inns of Old England.

Tofu is one of the key ingredients used in both of Japan's main schools of haute cuisine: Tea Ceremony Cuisine *(Kaiseki Ryori)* and Zen Temple Cookery *(Shojin Ryori).* Often called Buddhist Vegetarian Cookery, the *Shojin* school began to flourish in Japan in the thirteenth century and served as one of the first vehicles for introducing laymen to the many tofu dishes prepared by monks in monasteries and temples. Restaurants soon opened in the major temples of Japan's larger cities and led the way in developing much of the tofu cookery now famous throughout the country. Today, many of Japan's best known centers of tofu cuisine are located in or near major temples. At one of Kyoto's largest temples, Daitokuji, the *Shojin* restaurant Izusen is known for its attractive garden atmosphere, its selection of more than eight different tofu dishes, and its reasonable prices. Tenryuji, an active Zen temple in Arashiyama near Kyoto, is surrounded by about eight restaurants specializing in tofu cookery, and Nanzenji temple in eastern Kyoto by at least this many tofu restaurants. *Shojin* Cookery is said to be the art of simplicity raised to perfection. From it have originated almost all of the basic principles which characterize the best in Japanese cuisine. Rich in protein, inexpensive, and highly-versatile, tofu serves as the backbone of the *Shojin* meatless diet.

Tea Ceremony Cuisine, an offshoot of Zen Temple Cookery, was taken to the level of a fine art during the sixteenth century by the great tea master Sen-no-Rikyu. Though originally the school of gourmets who cherished the life of tasteful frugality, *Kaiseki* is now among the most elegant and expensive types of cookery served in Japan. And tofu will often appear in over half the dishes on the menu. The Nishiki restaurant in Kyoto offers a type of modified *Kaiseki* cuisine at prices available to everyone. Yet a full *Kaiseki* banquet can serve as an unforgettable introduction to the finest in Japanese culture and tofu cookery, an aesthetic experience that will refresh the senses, delight the intellect, and nourish the soul.

Closely related to *Kaiseki* and *Shojin* cookery are *Fucha Ryori,* the tea ceremony cookery developed in Chinese temples, and *Sansai Ryori,* the tradition which features edible wild plants gathered fresh from the mountains throughout the four seasons. When the great Chinese priest Ingen came to Japan in 1661 to found Manpukuji temple and transmit the Zen teachings of the master Huang Po, he also introduced the Japanese to *Fucha* cuisine and to Chinese-style Pressed Tofu *(toufu-kan)*. The headquarters of this school is at the attractive Hakuun-an restaurant located next to Ingen's temple; and here they still serve Pressed Tofu and a wide variety of other tofu dishes. *Sansai* restaurants, usually located in rural areas, offer more than 30 different varieties of tasty mountain vegetables and numerous tofu preparations. Many of these restaurants are located in temples and reflect the finest of the spirit of Zen Temple Cookery.

In Japanese tofu restaurants, the beauty of the setting is generally considered as important as the food itself. In most cases, the setting is one of natural beauty permeated by a sense of the season, which is also reflected in the ingredients appearing on the menu. The Rengetsu tofu restaurant, set snugly at the foot of

Kyoto's eastern mountains, is composed of a number of private dining rooms opening onto a lovely courtyard beneath the spreading branches of an 800-year-old tree. Rengetsu means "lotus moon," and these two Chinese characters are written in weather-worn brush strokes on a plank of wood that hangs before the restaurant's welcoming gate. In the evening, each room seems filled with the same warm and golden light that glows in the paper-covered windows of the large stone lantern near the entranceway, while on balmy summer nights, Rengetsu becomes a harbor of coolness. A cedar dipper, set across the mouth of a stone basin overflowing with water, invites guests to drink and rinse their hands. The young bamboos in the garden and the flat, natural stones underfoot are kept moist and glistening with an occasional sprinkling of water. Along one side of the courtyard, a tiny stream emerges from a grotto of rushes and ferns, and flows around both sides of a large granite grinding stone (once used in a tofu shop) which now serves as a stepping stone. Crossing the brook, guests step onto a large, flat rock at the entranceway to their room, where they remove their shoes before entering.

In restaurants such as the Dengaku in Kamakura, the atmosphere is contained entirely within the walls of a single room no larger than 12 feet square. In the center of a floor made of jet-black river pebbles is a large open-hearth fireplace similar to that found in country farmhouses but raised several feet above floor level. Four massive timbers form the edges of the hearth and serve simultaneously as the dining table for guests seated around the perimeter on low stools with seats of woven rice straw. In the rectangular hearth, partially filled with black sand, glows a small charcoal fire. Several wooden platters are piled with neatly-arranged pieces of grilled tofu, three varieties of deep-fried tofu, and numerous fresh vegetables. Antique pottery bowls are filled with three varieties of Sweet ered Miso. The hostess pierces each guest's choice of foods with a foot-long bamboo skewer, daubs on his or her choice of miso with a wooden spatula, and plants the base of the skewer firmly into the sand at a slant so that the tofu or vegetables are close to the live coals. Now and then she pours out water for tea from an iron pot suspended near the fire on a rustic hook hanging from the ceiling. The sizzling hot Dengaku is as delicious as the mood is warm.

In temple restaurants the atmosphere is one of utter simplicity: the uncluttered *tatami* room with its single scroll and flower; the garden of raked sand broken by a single outcropping of rocks; the fragrance of incense and perhaps the sound of a bamboo flute that helps us, in its pauses, to hear the silence. The simplicity of tofu seems to harmonize perfectly with this atmosphere.

In most tofu restaurants, the menu changes continually with the seasons, creating both a challenge for the chef and a delightful sense of variety for the regular customer. During the peak of winter, a piece of dried-frozen tofu in white miso soup may bring to mind the image of a snowbound temple. In the spring, Chilled Tofu may be garnished with a sprig of *kinome* from the tree in the garden. It has been rightly said that, in the finest Japanese cuisine, the right food is honored at the right season in the right setting. In fact, many Japanese tofu cookbooks arrange their recipes according to the four seasons rather than by types of food. It is precisely tofu's adaptability and versatility that allows it to be used throughout the year as host to an unending parade of seasonal delicacies.

In most of the restaurants mentioned above, great attention is given to the way in which the food is served and the care with which each guest is treated. The Japanese believe that a dish must please the eye as well as the palate. Thus chefs have made an art of cutting and slicing so that each ingredient is given added character. Generally, a meal is composed of a large number of small courses, each served in a distinctive container, each a work of art in itself, carefully arranged and meticulously prepared. The colors, shapes, and textures are as carefully balanced as the flavors. Each ingredient is honored in and of itself; the chef works to enhance and bring to life its innate natural flavors. Thus Japanese cookery is an excercise in nuance and subtlety, the use of restraint and reserve in the highest sense to do full honor to every food.

At the Sagano restaurant in western Kyoto, for example, guests are ushered into private rooms facing a large and carefully manicured garden of emerald moss, inlaid with several clusters of large rocks and set against a background of towering bamboos. The rooms are decorated with original woodblock prints, earthenware sake jugs, and antique Japanese lutes. The waitress serving each room is dressed in a kimono of hand-dyed indigo *kasuri* cloth. A *tasuki,* or band of bright red cloth, passes over both shoulders and crosses in front to tie up the kimono's sleeves as she works. An *obi,* or wide brocade sash, is wrapped firmly around her waist, and white *tabi,* or Japanese socks, make her feet look light and cool. First she brings in a large cup of tea, then chopsticks which she rests upon a small coral support, then a moist towel for refreshing each guest's hands and face. In summer, Chilled Tofu is served floating with chunks of ice in a handsome wooden container, and a variety of fresh and colorful garnishes are served in tiny dishes. The tofu dessert, Gisei-dofu, is presented on handmade square ceramic plates and decorated with a sprig of maple.

At the tofu restaurant Goemon, located in the center of a busy section of Tokyo, the guests enter down a long path lined on both sides with stone lanterns lit with candles. An unexpected oasis of beauty and quiet amid the cacophony of modern Tokyo, the restaurant garden surrounds a small stream. A large cauldron— the type used in tofu shops—is filled with water from a bamboo pipe and overflows to form the stream's headwaters. The sound of a windbell fills the spacious rooms. In the winter, guests are seated at low tables, each containing a charcoal brazier filled with live coals. The hostess places an earthenware *nabe* over the brazier and invites guests to add their choice of several types of tofu and other carefully cut ingredients arranged on a large platter. Tofu and yuba are served in various forms in many of the delicate portions accompanying the main dish. In summer, Chilled Tofu is served in handsome lacquerware boxes accompanied by a thin crescent of watermelon and surrounded by chunks of ice. In a half section of fresh bamboo, a single red cherry is surrounded by strips of Takigawa-dofu soymilk jelled with agar arranged to swirl like a meandering river.

Most tofu restaurants bear living witness to tofu's remarkable versatility. At Hisago in Tokyo, over 200 tofu dishes are served throughout the four seasons and more than 85 are available at any one time. The inspirational source of many of these recipes is a two-volume book of tofu cuisine written about 200 years ago. The *Tofu Hyaku Chin,* which combines the virtues of a travel and restaurant guidebook and a cookbook, was written to introduce the Japanese people to about 230 different varieties of tofu cuisine served in the different provinces. The famous novelist Tanizaki Junichiro is said to have personally prepared each of the 100 tofu recipes described in the first volume. Ms. Fukuzawa, the founder of Hisago, worked with these traditional vegetarian recipes to develop much of her present repertoire.

At Sorin-an, located in a temple surrounded by rice fields in the countryside west of Kyoto, homemade yuba is the featured ingredient in each of the restaurant's 15 dishes. Likewise, at Sasa-no-yuki, each of the twelve dishes on the menu, several of which are also available on a "take out" basis, has silken tofu as its main ingredient. In many Zen temple restaurants, tofu will be used in more than half of all dishes made throughout the four seasons. And in Japan's most famous book on *Shojin* Cookery, more than one-quarter of the recipes use tofu and many more use yuba.

One might well expect that at most of the restaurants described here, the cost of a meal would be relatively high. Yet because tofu itself is so inexpensive, most restaurants featuring tofu can offer very reasonable prices—especially considering the beautiful setting, gracious hospitality, and elegant service that invariably accompany the fine food. At Sasano-yuki, for example, the average price in 1975 for any of the 12 dishes on the menu was only 41 cents. In many Zen temple restaurants, a full 7-course meal costs between $2.50 and $3.50.

Most of these restaurants purchase their tofu wholesale from a nearby tofu shop, often going out of their way to obtain tofu made with nigari and prepared in the traditional way. The many excellent tofu restaurants of Arashiyama, west of Kyoto, have grown up around the famous Morika tofu shop and built their reputations on Morika tofu's fine flavor. Sasa-no-yuki is the only tofu restaurant we know of that prepares its own tofu. The restaurant's owner, Mr. Takichi Okumura, is himself a master of the tofu-making process; he learned it when he was a boy from the former master, his father. A distinguished restauranteur and tofu connoisseur, he feels strongly that the flavor of the tofu itself is the indispensable foundation for fine tofu cuisine: "Unless the tofu exhibits its own natural sweetness and bouquet, it can never become a dish worthy of the Japanese cuilinary tradition, not even in the hands of the most talented chef." Thus he insists on serving tofu made with nigari and the best-grade Japanese soybeans, prepared fresh each day in the shop located in the basement of the restaurant.

In addition to restaurants specializing in tofu cookery, there are many more which serve tofu regularly in dishes such as Sukiyaki, Miso Soup, Nishime, Chilled Tofu, or Simmering Tofu. Each of Japan's Chinese restaurants has a special section on the menu devoted to tofu cookery, and most of the thousands of *soba* shops use deep-fried tofu in a variety of noodle dishes. In the large number of restaurants specializing in Inari-zushi and in most sushi shops, deep-fried tofu pouches are one of the main ingredients. And in the shops, bars, and wintertime street stalls featuring Oden, tofu is found in its many forms.

Japan's most bizarre—indeed barbaric—restaurant tofu dish is called Yanagawa-dofu. Several small, live loaches (fresh-water eels) are placed in a large tureen containing cold water and a cake of tofu. The pot is placed over a tabletop burner in front of the diners and the water is slowly brought to a boil. The loaches frantically burrow into the soft, cool tofu, trying to escape the heat. Once inside, they are cooked.

Tofu is also one of the main items on the menu at the many natural food restaurants which have opened throughout Japan in recent years. Most of these restaurants make a special point of advertising the tofu as nigari-based and using it in both traditional Japanese and Western-style preparations. Surely, tofu salads, soups, egg dishes, sauces, sandwiches, and burgers would make excellent additions to the menus of many natural food and other restaurants in the West, as well.

(A listing of the addresses of each of the restaurants mentioned above is given in the unabridged edition of *The Book of Tofu*.)

Appendix B

Tofu Shops and Soy Dairies in the West

ALASKA

Anchorage 99502—Northland Soy Products, 5650 Old Seward Hwy Unit J. Ph. 907-349-4235. Bernie Soupanauong.

ARKANSAS

Fayetteville 72701—Summercorn Tofu Shop, 401 Watson St. Ph. 501-521-9338. Steve Kectner & David Druding.

ARIZONA

Tucson 85705—Unicorn Village Soyfoods, 332 7th St. Ph. 602-622-4963. Les Snyder.

CALIFORNIA

Alhambra 91803—American Food Co, 800 S Palm Ave. Ph. 213-570-1620. Jackson Wu.

Arcata 95521—The Tofu Shop, 768 18th St. Ph. 707-822-7409. Matthew Schmit.

Carmel Valley 93924—Jack and the Beanstalk, 65 W Carmel Valley Pob 525. Ph. 408-659-4366. Paul & Nobukatsu Terui.

Chico 95926—California Kitchen, 903 Cherry St. Ph. 916-893-0986. Al Parrott.

Duarte 91010—Soyfoods of America, 1091 E Hamilton Rd. Ph. 213-358-4526. Ken Lee.

Escondido 92025—Palomar Mountain Soyfood, 31405 N Highway 395. Ph. 714-749-2476. Alex Press.

Fairfax 94930—Wildwood Natural Foods, 135 Bolinas Rd. Ph. 415-459-3919. Paul Orbuch & Bill Bramblett.

Fresno 93706—Goto Tofu Co/ Star Tofu, 943 E Street. Ph. 209-268-1717.

Gardena 90247—Meiji-Ya, 1569-F Redondo Beach Blvd. Ph. 213-770-4677. Charles Iwana.

Los Angeles 90066—Aloha Grocery Store, 4515 Centinela Ave. Ph. 213-822-2288. Mr Uehara.

Los Angeles 90021—C.R. Food, 1701 E 7th St. Ph. 213-622-0556. Munung Peter Kang.

Los Angeles 90013—Hinode Tofu Co, 526 S Stanford Ave. Ph. 213-624-3615. Shoan Yamauchi. Largest Plant In Western World Mdrn Fac.

Los Angeles 90023—Might Soy, 2805 E Washington Blvd. Ph. 213-266-6969. Mr Maung Ming.

Los Angeles 90037—Sam Woong Foods Corp, 4607 S Main St. Ph. 213-232-5197. Mr Aoki.

Los Angeles 90031—Wy Ky, 237 San Fernando Rd. Ph. 213-222-0779. William Lee.

Mt Shasta 96067—Many Happiness Tofu, 305 Smith St. Ph. 916-926-3939. Susan Ergas.

Nevada City 95959—Ananda Tofu Shop, 14618 Tyler Foote Rd. Ph. 916-292-3505. Michael Moody.

Ojai 93023—Ojai Tofu Co, 602 E Ojai Ave. Ph. 805-646-3285. Carl G Tolbert.

Petaluma 94953—Sonoma Natural Foods, 100A Poultry PO Box 603. Ph. 707-778-8638. Dik & Sharon Rose.

S San Francisco 94080—Quong Hop & Co, 161 Beacon St. Ph. 415-873-4444. Stanley Lee & Jim Miller.

Sacramento 95814 — Sacramento Tofu Mfg. Co, 1915 6th St. Ph. 916-447-2682. Mr Kunishi.

San Diego 92103—San Diego Soy Dairy, 2965 Fifth Ave. Ph. 714-296-8029. Gary Stein.

San Francisco 94124 — Azumaya Inc, 1575 Burke Ave. Ph. 415-285-8500. Jack & Bill Mizono, #2 Largest Us Tofu Plant.

San Francisco 94133—Silver Sprout Co, 124 Russ St. Ph. 415-431-5031. Paul Louie.

San Francisco 94107—Wo Chong Co, 1001 16th St. Ph. 415-431-5666. Walter W Louie.

San Francisco 94108—Wo Hop Co, 759 Clay St. Ph. 415-982-7176.

San Jose 95112—Fuji Tofu Co, 248 Jackson St. Ph. 408-297-1666. Reiso And Steve Kake.

San Jose 95112—San Jose Tofu Co, 175 E Jackson St. Ph. 408-292-7026. Kenny Takeshi Nozaki.

Santa Cruz 95062—Clearway Soyfoods, 1037 17th Ave. Ph. 408-476-6390. Buddy Hamel.

Watsonville 95076—Murata's Market, 226 Riverside Dr. Ph. 408-724-5118. Mr Murata.

Whitethorn 95489 — Yerba Santa Tofu Shop, Whitethorn Star Route. Ph. 707NL.

COLORADO

Boulder 80301—White Wave, 1990 N 57th Ct. Ph. 303-443-3470. Steve Demos.

Denver 80221—Denver Tofu Co, 6150 N Federal Blvd. Ph. 303-426-0122. Mr Maruhisa Yamamoto.

Ft Collins 80526—Nupro Foods, 1819 W Prospect Rd. Ph. 303-493-0138. Carol & John Hargadine.

CONNECTICUT

Middletown 06457 — The Bridge, 598 Washington St. Ph. 203-346-3663. Roberto Marrocchesi & Bill Spear, Trad Fds For Modern Times.

DISTRICT OF COLUMBIA

Washington 20002—Sam Sung Food Inc, 409 Morse St. Ph. 202-544-6660. Henry & Kim Salazar.

FLORIDA

Coral Gables 33146—Sunshine Soy Co, 4015 Laguna. Ph. 305-447-1277. Danny Paolucci.

Lake City 32055—Lecanto Tofu, Rte 3 Box 150. Ph. 904-746-5374. Jean Huffman.

Longwood 32750—Aqua Agra, 100 Highline Dr. Ph. 305-339-8157. Don Wilson.

Miami 33127—Bob & Toni's Tofu Works, 764 NW 29th St. Ph. 305-635-6052. Bob & Toni Heartsong.

Miami 33127—Swan Gardens, 1111 NW 22nd. Ph. 305-324-8910. Dick Mcintyre.

Miami 33142—Tropi-Pak, 3664 NW 48th St. Ph. 305-635-1968. Dennis Murasaki.

Plant City 33566—Marjon Foods, 3508 Sydney Rd. Ph. 813-752-3482. John Miller.

Pompano Beach 33060—Aberdeen Foods Inc, 631 S Dixie Hwy E. Ph. 305-782-2685. Tony.

GEORGIA

Atlanta 30317 — The Soy Shop, 1863 Memorial Dr SE. Ph. 404-377-8433. Sara & Steve Yurfan.

HAWAII

Hilo/Hawaii 96720—Kreston's Enterprise, 265-D Kekuanaoa St. Ph. 808-935-6973.

Hilo/Hawaii 96720—Natural Pacific Tofu, 153 Makaala St PO Box 4352. Ph. 808-935-3220. David Gantz.

Hilo/Hawaii 96720 — Puueo Poi Factory, 265-D Kekuanaoa St. Ph. 808-935-8435. Leslie Ahana Chang.

Honolulu/Oahu 96817—Aala Tofu Co, 513 Kaaahi St. Ph. 808-845-0221. Mr Shojin Yamauchi.

Honolulu/Oahu 96817—Aloha Tofu Factory, 961 Akepo Ln. Ph. 808-845-2669. Jack & Kazu Uehara, Largest Plant In Hawaii.

Honolulu/Oahu 96819—Better Food Tofu Factory, 727 Bannister St. Ph. 808-841-8616. Richard Higa.

Honolulu/Oahu 96814—Green Mill Food Mftrs, 914 Coolidge St. Ph. 808-949-2370. Tom Uehara.

Honolulu/Oahu 96814—Kanai Tofu Factory, 515 Ward Ave. Ph. 808-538-1305. Richard & Mark Kaneda, 2nd Largest Plant In Hawaii.

Honolulu/Oahu 96822—Manoa Soy Works, 2561 Manoa Rd. Ph. 808-949-1815. Bev Lum.

Honolulu/Oahu 96816 — Mrs Cheng's China Bean, 1829 E Palolo Ave. Ph. 808-737-2571.

Kapaa/Kauai 96746 — Kapaa Poi Factory, RR 1 Box 366. Ph. 808-822-5426. Kenneth Lai.

Lihue/Kauai 96766 — Matsumoto Tofu Shop, 3469 Maono St. Ph. 808-245-6141. Mr Matsumoto.

Wahiawa/Oahu 96786 — Hawaii

Tofu, PO Box 26. Ph. 808-621-6941. Mrs Nemoro.

Wahiawa/Oahu 96786—Rural Food Products, 117 Mango St. Ph. 808-621-5603. Mr Haruo Honda.

Wailuku/Maui 96793 — Tamashiro Tofu Shop, 326 Alahee Dr. Ph. 808-244-5215. Mr Tokusaburo Tamashiro.

Wailuku/Maui 96793—Teruya Tofu Factory, 1830 Mill St. Ph. 808-244- 5313. Mr Takeshi Teruya.

IOWA

Fairfield 52556—American Pride, 208 N 2nd St. Ph. 515-472-9244. Earl Kaplan.

IDAHO

Boise 83702—Boise Co-Op, 1515 N 13th St. Ph. 208-342-6652.

ILLINOIS

Champaign 61820—Midwest Soy Products Inc, 608 S Belmont Ave. Ph. 217-398-5756. Anthony & Patricia Kao.

Chicago 60657—Chicago Tofu Co, 3255 N Holstead. Ph. 312-525-3823. Mr Minoru Kanki.

Chicago 60613—Korea Farm, 3456 N Clark. Ph. 312-348-1625. Mr Young Sun Yo.

Chicago 60614—Nomura Tofu Co, 2119 N Clark St. Ph. 312-935-9766. Mr Willer Woo.

Chicago 60640 — Phoenix Bean Products, 5438 N Broadway. Ph. 312-784-2503.

Chicago 60660—Sam Hwa Bean-sprout Co, 5642 N Broadway. Ph. 312-271-0330. Sam Hwa.

Morton Grove 60053—Tofu Inc, 6216 Madison Ct. Ph. 312-967-0090. Eileen Friedman.

INDIANA

Bloomington 47401 — Love Life Foods, 901 S Rogers St. Ph. 812-332-9662. Jay Mckinney.

Ft Wayne 46804—Zakhi Soyfoods, 124 S Hadley Rd. Ph. 219-432-1291. Victor Zakhi.

Greenwood 46142—Tris Inc, 340 Greenhills Ct. Ph. 317-881-1299. David Yang.

Indianapolis 46239 — Jomar Inc, 8404 E Brookville Rd. Ph. 317-353-1008. Fred Mark.

Mishawaka 46544—Michiana Soyfoods, 2027 N Merrifield Ave. Ph. 219-259-1729. Kris Klawitter.

KANSAS

Lawrence 66044—Central Soyfoods, 832 Louisiana. Ph. 913-843-0653. Jim Cooley.

Wichita 67202—Rose Kitchen Tofu, 515 E Central. Ph. 316-267-8024. John Guffey.

MASSACHUSETTS

Boston 02111—Cheng Yah Wong, 83 Tyler St. Ph. 617-426-7588. Mr Wong.

Boston 02111—Tun Hing Lung Co, 9 Hudson St. Ph. 617-426-4827.

Greenfield 01301 — New England Soy Dairy, 305 Wells St. Ph. 413-772-0746. Tom Timmins, Largest New-Age And Caucasian Tofu Plant.

Leominster 01453—Nasoya Foods, Mechanic St Exit Box 841. Ph. 617-537-0713. John Paino & Bob Bergwall.

Webster 01570—Soy Magic Coop Inc, 39 Tower St. Ph. 617-943-3049. Lucy Morrison.

MARYLAND

Baltimore 21218—American Soyfood Indus, 2222 Aisquith St. Ph. 301-235-5554. Larry Betzler.

Baltimore 21230—Bud Inc Soyfoods, Raleigh Industry Ct, 1100 Wicomico St. Ph. 301-837-4034. Aaron Liu & Wang Chen.

Chevy Chase 20015—Swan Tofu, 4812 Leland St. Ph. 301NL. Terrence Billotte.

Laurel 20810—Eastern Food Products Co, 9157-3 Whiskey Bottom Rd. Ph. 301-792-0440. Mr Kim.

MAINE

Anson 04911—Mainley Tofu, PO Box 209. Ph. 207-696-5845. Peter Beane.

Bar Harbor 04609—Island Tofu Works, %Golbitz-Kingma 318 Main. Ph. 207-288-4969. Peter Golbitz.

Waterville 04901. — Soy Beings, 13-C Railroad Sq. Ph. 207-872-8790. Richard Tory.

MICHIGAN

Ann Arbor 48104—Soy Plant, 771 Airport Blvd. #1. Ph. 313-663-8638. A Collective.

Detroit 48208—Abbey Hearth Inc, 6327 14th St. Ph. 313-895-9366. Brother David.

Detroit 48205 — Wah Hing Co, 12347 Gratoit. Ph. 313-527-2210.

Traverse City 49684—Oryana Food Cooperative, 601 Randolph. Ph. 616-947-0191.

MINNESOTA

Duluth 55804 — Greatwater Soyfoods, 1039 E Pioneer Rd. Ph. 218-525-3913. Doug Hamdorf And Demetria Nanos.

Minneapolis 55414 — Continental Soyfoods, 510 Kasota Ave. Ph. 612-378-0464. Pat Aylward.

Minneapolis 55413—Eastern Foods Corp, 3225 E Hennepin Ave. Ph. 612-331-3353. Mr. Lee R Lee & Calvin Lutzke.

MISSOURI

Drury 65638—Brush Creek Tofu. PO Box 129. Ph. 417-261-2553. Marie Steinwachs.

Jamestown 65046—Imagine Foods Inc, RR 1 Box 11. Ph. 816-849-2583. David Carlson.

Kansas City 64141—Chunco Foods Inc, PO Box 883. Ph. 913-362-8097. Peter Chun.

Springfield 65802 — Muckfoot Farms, 300 N Waverly. Ph. 417-866-1337. Paul Day.

Springfield 65802 — Springfield Comm Tofu, 300 N Waverly. Ph. 417-866-1337.

St Louis 63133—Light Foods, 6144 Bartmer. Ph. 314-721-3960. Bob Davis.

MONTANA

Helena 59601—South Fork Tofu Cafe, 322 Fuller Ave. Ph. 406-443-5586.

St Ignatius 59865—The Tofu Factory, Rte 1 Box 216. Ph. 406-745—4538. Gerald Minsk & Brenda Adley.

NORTH CAROLINA

Asheville 28801—White Clouds of Tofu, 300 Hillside St. Ph. 704-252-0854. Joelen Bell.

Boone 28607—Bean Mountain Soy Dairy, 121 W Howard St. Ph. 704-264-0890. Jerry Mckinnon.

Fletcher 28732—Blue Ridge Soyfoods, PO Box 5321. Ph. 704-684-8501. Bob Hunt.

Hillsborough 27578—Fertile Hills, Rte 1 Box 171-E. Ph. 919-732-6626. Ken Dawson.

Hillsborough 27278—Libby Outlaw Tofu Shop, Box 34. Ph. 919-732-3359.

NEBRASKA

Lincoln 68504—Prairie Soyl, 4029 Progressive Ave #4. Ph. 402-466-8638. Julie Diegel & Marla Lowell.

Omaha 68124—Midwest Oriental Foods, 8243 Hascall. Ph. 402-391-7730. Mr Kim.

Omaha 68103 — Omaha Oriental Foods, 2763 Farnam St. Ph. 402-345-1736. Mr Iksu Shin.

NEW HAMPSHIRE

Ashland 03217—Sugar Ridge Soyfoods, Box 726. Ph. 603NL. Mary Bates.

Bethlehem 03574—North Country Soyfoods, Box 572 Jefferson St. Ph. 603-869-2677. Jay & Pat Gibbons.

Gilsum 03448—Willowbrook Soyfoods, Vessel Rock Rd. Ph. 603-357-3762. Viney Loveland Robert Clark.

NEW JERSEY

Paterson 07505—Cnk Corp, 165 Main St. Ph. 201-742-3830. L H Cho.

NEW MEXICO

Dixon 87527—Tofu Shop, Box 94. Ph. 505NL. Mr Toufic Haddad.

Espanola 87532—Golden Temple Foods, PO Box 747. Ph. 505-753-3270. Hargobind S Khalsa.

Jemez Springs 87025—Bodhi Mandala Tofu Shop, Box 8. Ph. 505-829-3854. Bob Mammoser & Michael Arnold.

Santa Fe 87501—Southwest Soyfoods, 2889 Trades West. Ph. 505-471-8979. Richard Jennings.

NEW YORK

Albion 14411—Sopro Products Inc, 111 West Ave. Ph. 716-589-7074. Stephen Hwa.

Brooklyn 11237 — Tokyo Food Processing, %Japan Food 40 Varick Ave. Ph. 212-456-8805. Mr Shirata & Mr Terry Terahira.

Buffalo 14223 — Sung's Oriental Grocery, 471 Englewood Ave. Ph. 716-836-3611.

Haverstraw 10927—Local Tofu, 26 Main St. Ph. 914-429-2292. Sam Weinreb.

Ithaca 14850—Ithaca Soy, 403 N Plain St. Ph. 607-272-4903. David Scovronick + Robt Shapiro.

Long Island City 11101— Hashizume Food Products, 2-01 50th St. Ph. 212-392-2860. Koyuu Yokoyama.

New York 10014—Caldron Tofu Shop, 308 E 6th St. Ph. 212-473-9543. Gloria Bremmer.

New York 10013—Chia Sheung, 376 Broome St. Ph. 212-226-3838. Mr Wu.

New York 10013—Fong-Inn, 46 Mott St. Ph. 212-962-5196. Kevin Chan, Started In 1935.

New York 10023—K Tanaka & C, 326 Amsterdam Ave. Ph. 212-874-6600. Mr Eisuke Murakami.

New York 10013—Mandalay Food Products, 450 Broome St. Ph. 212-966-0338. Mr U Han Kyu & John Tun.

New York 10013—Sun Hop Hing, 4 Bowery St. Ph. 212-227-4812.

Ogdensburg 13669—Soyanara, 711 Montgomery St. Ph. 315-393-3836. Pat Duprey.

Rochester 14607 — Northern Soy, 30 Somerton St. Ph. 716-442-1213. Andy Schecter & Norman Holland.

Woodhaven 11421 — Panda Food Products, 79-20 Jamaica Ave. Ph. 212-271-4669. Hal Siegel.

OHIO

Cincinnati 45214 — Soya Food Products Co, 2356 Wyoming Ave. Ph. 513-661-2250. Ben & Nina Yamaguchi Edw Willwerth.

Cleveland Hts 44118 — Cleveland Tofu Co, PO Box 18153. Ph. 216-791-5100. Bob Carr & Brooks Jones.

Columbus 43227—Rising Sun Soy Farms, 2810 Banwick Rd. Ph. 614-231-4073. Tim Nusser & C H Burnett.

OREGON

Ashland 97520 — Ashland Soy Works, 280 Helman. Ph. 503-482-1865. James Muhs.

Corvallis 97330 — Sunbow Farm Products, Rte 2 Box 46. Ph. 503-929-5782. Mia Posner & Harry Mccormack.

Durham 97223 — Dae Han and Company, 18300 SW Boones Ferry Rd. Ph. 503-620-8983. Yeun Mo Koo.

Eugene 97405—Devis Country Soy Sausg, 2240 Lorane Hwy. Ph. 503-344-7454. Virginia Ruffulo.

Eugene 97402 — Surata Soyfoods, 302 Blair Blvd. Ph. 503-485-6990. Cal Miller & Lisa Rein.

Jacksonville 97530—Ruch Co-Op Soy Dairy, 6091 Hwy 238. Ph. 503NL.

Ontario 97914—Kanetomis Soybean Produs, 336 SW 5th St PO Box 568. Ph. 503-889-6584. Jim Kanetomi.

Portland 97214—Ota Tofu Factory, 812 SE Stark. Ph. 503-232-8947. Mr Ota.

PENNSYLVANIA

Allentown 18103—Real Foods, 1501 Lehigh St. Ph. 215-791-4100. Jim Saunders.

Avondale 19311 — Green Valley Farms Tofu, PO Box 506. Ph. 215-268-2456. Warren Reynolds.

Honesdale 18431 — Liberty Soyfoods, 111 W 11th St. Ph. 717-253-0245. Jamie & Nancy Stunkard.

Mertztown 19539 — Cricklewood Soyfoods, Rd #1 Box 161. Ph. 215-682-4109. Karl & Renate Krummenoehl.

Philadelphia 19120—Formo Foods, 5146 N Fifth. Ph. 215-457-6724. Steve Sieh.

Summit Station 17979 — Kirpalu Yoga Retreat, Box 120. Ph. 717-754-3051. Chris Yorsten.

TENNESSEE

Greenbriar 37073—Millers Soy Inc. Rt 2 Box 2088. Ph. 615-643-7506. Harry Miller Jr & Mike Bishop.

Memphis 38117—Mid South Soyfoods, PO Box 17254. Ph. 901-365-7003. G Barzizza.

Summertown 38483—The Farm Soy Dairy, 156 Drakes Ln. Ph. 615-964-3584.

TEXAS

Austin 78721 — Purist Foods, 4100-A Ed Bluestein St 105. Ph. 512-928-0191. Reed Murray.

Dallas 73204 — Jung's Oriental Foods, 2519 N Fitzhugh. Ph. 214-827-7653.

Dallas 75204—Yong Ho Pak Food Inc, 3201 Ross Ave. Ph. 214-821-0542. Yong Ho Pak.

Elgin 78621 — Yaupon Soyfoods, 404 S Main. Ph. 512-285-3810. Chico Wagner & Doug Cox.

Houston 77081—Banyan Enterprise Usa, 7332 Rampart St #113. Ph. 713-995-6885. David Chiu.

UTAH
Hurricane 84737—Knitty Gritty City Inc, PO Box 736. Ph. 801-635-4369. Joanne Michaels.

VIRGINIA
Crozet 22932—Virginia Soyworks, Rte 2 Box 505. Ph. 804-823-2364. Shag Kiefer.
Floyd 24091—Annelies Breads & Tofu, Rte 2 Box 72. Ph. 703-789-7080. Annelies Brady.
Norfolk 23508—Luck Bean Cake, 3925 Hampton Blvd. Ph. 804-489-1493. Dan Nguyen.
Stanley 22851—New Ark Foods, Rte 1 Box 252B. Ph. 703-778-3890—Melinda Siska.

VIRGIN ISLANDS
St Croix 00840—Tofu in-Sted, Box 805 Frederickstead. Ph. 809NL. Monty Thomson.
St Thomas 00801—Veggie Table, PO Box 8029 31 Altona. Ph. 809-774-1810. P A Callwood.

WASHINGTON
Seattle 98104—Hoven Foods Co, 502 6th Ave S. Ph. 206-623-6764. Yung-Ching Lui.
Seattle 98112—M.K. Tofu Co, 1800 Yessler Way. Ph. 206-622-1365.
Seattle 98104—Star Tofu Mfg Co, 608 S Weller St. Ph. 206-622-6217.
Seattle 98104—Uwajimaya Inc, 519 Sixth Ave S. Ph. 206-624-6248. Tommie Oiye.
Twisp 98856 — Methow Valley Foods, General Delivery. Ph. 509-996-2372. Bernie Bigelow & Joyce Campbell.
Vashon 98070—Island Spring, PO Box 747. Ph. 206-622-6448. Luke Lukoskie.

WISCONSIN
Chilton 53014—Beantime Soyfoods, N4469 Highway 55. Ph. 414-439-1746. Glenny Whitcomb.
Madison 53703 — Bountiful Bean Plant, 903 Williamson St. Ph. 608-251-0595. Chris Burant.
Milwaukee 53212—Magic Bean, 2310 N Richards St. Ph. 414-263-1297.
River Falls 54022—Creative Soyfoods Inc, 526 N Clark St. Ph. 715-425-0467. David Nackerud.

WEST VIRGINIA
Charleston 25414—Happy Dragon Tofu, Box 112. Ph. 304-725-4437. Elizabeth Martin.
Spencer 25276—Spring Creek Soy Dairy, 136 Main St. Ph. 304-927-1815. Stan Kenner.

TOFU: FOREIGN

AUSTRALIA. Colac 3250—Kims Bean Curd, 1/53 Calvert St. Kim West.
AUSTRALIA. Gembrook 3783— Blue Lotus Foods, PO Box 44. Ph. NL. Eng Eu.
AUSTRALIA. Leichhardt 2040— Soyfoods Australia, 355 Parramatta Rd. Ph. 025600792. Marcea Newman & John Fenwick.
AUSTRALIA. Marrakville NSW— Sin Ma Trading Co, 9 Meeks Rd.
AUSTRALIA. Melbourne — Tofu Shop, 78 Bridge Rd Richmond. Ph. 034296204. Malcolm Green.
AUSTRALIA. Melbourne VIC— Chung Hing Bean Curd Mfg, 268 Victoria St. Ph. 03328496.
AUSTRALIA. Melbourne VIC— Hong Oriental Food, 189 Lt. Bourke St. Ph. 036632811.
AUSTRALIA. Melbourne VIC— Jon Weekes Tofu 6/405 Alma Rd Caulfield.
AUSTRALIA. Mt Waverly 3149— Earth Angel Soyfoods, 53 Stanley Ave. Ph. 035448020. Debbie Schmetzer.
AUSTRALIA. Mullumbimby 2482 —Chinese Farmhouse Tofu, Motts Rd Main Arm. Ph. NL. Ian Mott & Yuen Har Louie.
AUSTRALIA. N Adelaide 5006— Protein City, 28 Lombard St. Ph. 082673635. Terrell & Laryssa Neuage.
AUSTRALIA. NSW 2492—Homeland Tofu Shop, Homeland Foundation, Upper Thora Bellingen. Ph. 066558514. David Wilson.
AUSTRALIA. Randwick NSW— Castle Trading Pty Ltd, 93 Belmore Rd.
AUSTRIA. Merzg 34—Weg Der Natur, A2380 Perchtoldsdorf. Lawrence Dreyer.
BELGIUM. B-2070 Ekeren—Jonathan Pvba, Kapelsesteenweg 693.

Ph. 031644173. Jos Von De Ponseele, Near Antwerp.

BELGIUM. Hallaar — Alternatur, Korte Spekstraat. Makes Soymilk And Yogurt.

BELGIUM 9830. St Martens-Latem—Lima Foods, Edgar Gevaertdreef 10. Ph. 09824176.

BELGIUM. 1000 Brussels—Establissents Takanami, Rue Antoine Dansaert 107. Ph. 02-511-6635. Mr Takanami, Also Makes Miso.

BELGIUM. 1070 Bruxelles—Establissements Takanami, Rue Des Trefles 128. Ph. 025228192. Mr Takanami.

BELGIUM. 2000 Antwerp—De Brandnetel, Consciencestreat 48. Ph. 0313961. Jan Lansloot.

BELGIUM. 3000 Leuven—Seven Arrows Tofu, Hoogaardenstr 83.

BRAZIL. Sao Paulo—Agro Nippo Productos. Vila Clarice 210-350 Pir, Ave 15 De Novembro. Ph. 2612348. A Large Tofu And Soymilk Factory.

BRAZIL. Sao Paulo—Agro-Nippo Produtos Alim. Piribuba, Av Jose Alves De Mira 185.

BRAZIL. Sao Paulo—Proteija Ind & Comercio, Estrada D No 1300 Itaquera.

CANADA M1V1N9. Agincourt ONT—Nutri Soy Foods, 20 Big Red Ln. Ph. 416-291-6823. Harry Kwok.

CANADA G0C1E0. Bonaventure PQ—La Maison Du Tofu Carmel, Cp 567. Ph. 418-752-5869. Dennis Connolly.

CANADA. Calgary ALTA—Norman Leong Tofu, 2031 53rd Ave SW. Ph. 403-243-6531. Norman Leong.

CANADA G1H2M7. Charlesbourg/PQ—Tofu Quebec Inc, 451 47th St E. Ph. 418-622-0471. Pierre Lafianne.

CANADA B0E1J0. Cleveland NS—Rubenstein Tofu Shop, Rr 1. Mark Rubenstein.

CANADA V0R1T0. Denman Island BC—Metta Tofu Products, Wren Road. Ph. 604-335-0108. Ray Lipovsky.

CANADA V9L4T6. Duncan BC—Thisledown Soyfoods, Rr 5 Church Rd (5855). Ph. 604-748-9514. Jean & Jan Norris.

CANADA V0G1J0. Edgewood BC—Winnie Imrie Tofu, Rte 1

Comp 9 Site 1. Ph. 604-269-7275. Winnie Imrie.

CANADA J8X1H5. Hull PQ—La Soyarie, 25 Rue St Etienne. Ph. 613-235-5356. Koichi & Francine Watanabe.

CANADA. Montreal PQ—Soy-Can Dairy Ltd, 59 St James St W #601. Ph. 514NL.

CANADA H2W1V3. Montreal QUE—Nanda-Line Soy Products, 4058 Rue St Urbain. Ph. 514NL. Nantha Kumar.

CANADA H1Z2J9. Montreal/QUE—Tofuco Foods Inc, 3637 Cremazie E #1215. Ph. 514-376-5010.

CANADA J0R1T0. Prevost QUE—Unisoya Inc. Cp Box 278. Ph. 514-224-2628. Norbert Argiles.

CANADA G1K6S2. Quebec QUE—Tofu Quebec, 344 Rue St Roch. Ph. 418-525-7207. Guy De Valter & Pierre La Flamme.

CANADA E0A2L0. Rexton NB—Robert Richard Tofu, Box 225.

CANADA V6X1T3. Richmond BC—Mandarin Enterprises, 11031 Bridgeport Rd #1107. Ph. 604-270-1815. Mr Eng Lim.

CANADA S7H4K1. Saskatoon SASK—Flying Dragon Foods, 3311 8th St E. Ph. 306-373-9040. Tak K Sue.

CANADA S7M1N4. Saskatoon SK—Oriental Trading Co, 340 Ave C South. Ph. 306-652-3697. Art Mark.

CANADA M1L2C9. Scarbourough ONT—Victor Food Products, 102 Hymus Rd. Ph. 416-752-0161. Stephen Yu.

CANADA V0S1N0. Sooke BC—Sooke Soyfoods, 2625 Otter Pt Rd Rr 2. Ph. 604-642-3263. Wayne Jolley.

CANADA J0N1L0. St Janvier PQ—Soybios, Cp 929. Ph. 514-430-0305. Norbert Argiles & Ron Bazar.

CANADA P7E2P6. Thunder Bay ONT—Cantai Tofu Corp, 700 S Leland Ave. Ph. 807NL.

CANADA M6R1X1. Toronto ONT—Pyung Hwa Food Co, 2139 Dundas St W. Ph. 416-534-0237. Mr Jhasun Koo.

CANADA M4L1Z9. Toronto ONT—Shaw Grocery, 1447 Gerard St E. Ph. 416-466-8058. Mr Yen Yung Shaw.

CANADA M6P1Y6. Toronto ONT —Soy City Foods, 2847 Dundas St W. Ph. 416-762-1257. Pat Guardino & Paul Whitehead.

CANADA M5T2R4. Toronto ONT —Wah Chong Co, 80 Ossington Ave. Ph. 416-532-0841. Anthony Kim.

CANADA. Toronto ONT—Yet Sing Co, 11 Baldwin St. Ph. 416-977-3981.

CANADA V6A1C5. Vancouver BC—Shinbo Tofu Co, 450 Alexander St. Ph. 604-255-8141. Philip Saburo.

CANADA V6A1G4. Vancouver BC—Sunrise Co, 300 Powell St. Ph. 604-685-8019. Mr Leslie Joe.

CANADA V6A1G4. Vancouver BC—Yet Chong Co, 348 Powell St. Ph. 604-681-2712. Mr. Chong Kok.

CANADA V9B4Z3. Victoria BC— Dayspring Soyacraft Corp, Po Box 7285 Station D. Ph. 604-382-2144. Michael & Paul Hsieh.

CANADA. Winnepeg MAN—Yees Grocery, 209 Pacific Ave. Ph. 204-942-7668. Philip Yee.

DENMARK. 2500 Valby—Tofu Denmark, Valbylanjady 231, Per Freurgaard.

ECUADOR. QUITO—Fundacion Tofu, Casilla 252-a. Ph. 540288. Richard Jennings.

ENGLAND. Bristol 16—Cauldron Foods, Sunny Bank Chapel Lane, Fishponds. Ph. 658881. Philip Marshall & Peter Fagan.

ENGLAND. E Sussex BN71XH— Full of Beans Wholefoods, 97 High St Lewes. Ph. 079162627. John & Sara Gosling.

ENGLAND. Leicester LE21BU— the Regular Tofu Company, 75 Chandos St. Ph. 053-354-9839. John Holt.

ENGLAND. London—Hong Kong Supermarket, Shaftsbury Ave.

ENGLAND. London N1—Dragon & Phoenix Co. Kings Cross, 172 Pentonville Rd. Ph. 018370146.

ENGLAND. London N64NA— Paul's Tofu, 155 Archway Rd. Highgate. Ph. 013481192. Paul Jones.

ENGLAND. Newport/Pemb—Bean Machine, 45 Maes Ingli. Ph. 820896. Zorah Groom.

ENGLAND. Surrey KT66QN—

Yu's Tofu Shop, 21 Langley Ave Surbiton. Joseph Yu.

FRANCE. Castelnau Montmr— Presb St Paul De Marmiac, Penne Du Tarn. Olivier Hattier.

FRANCE. Paris—Sojatour Tofu Shop.

FRANCE. 13007 Marseille—Ets Co-Lu, 38 Rue Chateaubriand. Ph. 91314414. Andrew Mooney.

FRANCE. 74330 Poisy—Les Sept Marches. Les Cruesettes, Chemin Des Mouille.

FRANCE. 75011 Paris—Institut Tenryu, 2 Rue Rochebrune. Ph. 8059135. Tsuyoshi Ito.

FRANCE. 75013 Paris—Le Bol En Bois, 35 Rue Pascal. Ph. 7072724. Noboru Sakaguchi, Combination Nat Foods Restaurant/Tofu.

FRANCE 81140 Penne Tarn— Olivier Attie Tofu. Par Castelnau, Presb De St Paul D'mammiac.

FRANCE. 81140 Penne Tarn— Olivier Attie Tofu. Par Castelnau, Presb De St. Paul D'mammiac.

FRANCE. 91580 Cerny—Soy Sarl, Plateau De L'ardenay. Ph. 64575201. Bernard Storup & Jean De Preneuf.

GUATEMALA. Solala—Solala Soy Dairy, %C Figallo Molina Belen. Run Jointly With Members Of The Farm Tennessee.

GUYANA. Ecd—Sarvodaya Dev Educ Org, 423 Golden Grove. Peter Kempadoo.

INDIA. Dalhousie Hp—Himalayan Tofu, Jeet Villa. Ph. 15. Susan Jootla.

INDIA. 605104. Kottakuppam— Pour Tous Food Process, Aspiration Auroville. Alain Bernard.

INIDIA. Tamil Nadu—Hannes Bakery. Kottakarai, 605101 Auroville.

INDONESIA. Jakarta—Duta Proteina Indonesia, Po Box 3137. Lusiani T Saputro.

ISRAEL. Doar Na Hamercaz— Pillar of Dawn Tofu, Moshav Me'or Modi'im. Ben Zion Solomon.

ISRAEL. Jerusalem 91061—Golden Jerusalem Tofu, Zichron Tuvia 19 Pob 6212. Ph. 02249569. Zvi Weisberg.

ISRAEL. Ramat Gan — Little Prince, Rehov Mac-Donald 16. Joseph Fresco.

ITALY. Rome—Ohnichi Intl Foods Co. Lottizzazione Indus, V Salaria Km 25.

ITALY. Rome—Sfall Tofu Shop.

ITALY. Torino—Aldo Fortis Tofu. Ph. 017263503.

ITALY. 46100 Mantova—Circolo L'aratro, V Cavour 35. Ph. 037-636-8760. Sergio Mambrini.

ITALY. 47037 Rimini—Centro Macrobiotico Tofu, Via Cuoco 9. Gilberto Bianchini.

ITALY. 50123 Firenze—Fondazione Est-Quest, Via De Serragli #4. Ferro Ledvinka.

JAPAN 039-01 — Aamori-Ken — Taishi Shokuhin Kogyo. Oaza-Gawa Mito-Cho, Okinaka 68 Morita-Aza. Ph. 017-923-5111. Large Tofu Factory.

JAPAN. Fujisawa-Shi 251—Maruka Shokuhin. Kanagawa-Ken, Fujigaoka 2-10-2. Ph. 046-626-3261. Large Factory.

JAPAN. 822-01. Fukuoka-Ken—Taiyo Shokuhin. Wakamiya-Cho, Shimofujiwara 400-1 Oazu. Ph. 094-952-3141. Large Factory.

JAPAN. Fukuoka-Ken 838—Okay Shokuhin, Miwa-Cho. Ph. 094-622-7131. Large Factory.

JAPAN. Ina-Shi 396 — Tokiwa Reito Shokuhin, Nagano-Ken Ina 5057. Ph. 026-572-7277. Tsuru Habutae Frozen Tofu.

JAPAN. Isezaki-Shi 372—Nihon Beans. Gunma-Ken, Kita Senmoku-Cho 1435. Ph. 027-024-8111. Large Factory.

JAPAN. Ishikawa-Shi 272—Takatsuka Marugo, Chiba-Ken Soya-Cho 7-30-12. Ph. 047-372-2581. Japan's Largest Mfgr Of Reg Tofu.

JAPAN. Kamakura-Shi — Masuda Tofu-Ten, Ogigandani 119. Ph. 046-722-3503. Hiroshi Matsuda. Traditional.

JAPAN. Kanagawa-Ken 252—Home Shokuhin, Ayase-Cho 1090 Takaza-Gun. Ph. 046778617. Nigari Tofu Factory.

JAPAN. Kanazawa-Shi 921—Habutae-Dofu. Ishikawa-Ken, Nishi Kanazawa 2-162. Ph. 076-249-1171. Frozen Tofu.

JAPAN. Kobe Hyogo-Ken—Nada Kobe Seikyo. Higashi 5-1-9.

Higashinada-Ku Sumiyoshi. Ph. 078-811-0001. Large Factory.

JAPAN. 616. Kyoto Arashiyama—Morika Tofu-Ten. Saga Ukyoku, Fujinoki-Cho 42 Shakado. Ph. 075-872-3955. Shinji Morii. Traditional.

JAPAN 399-25. Nagano-Ken—Asahi-Matsu Kori-Dofu, Dahsina 1008 Iida-Shi. Ph. 026-526-9031. Largest Mfgr Of Dried Frozen Tofu.

JAPAN 399-46. Nagano-Ken—Daiya-Dofu. Kamiina-Gun, Minowa-Machi 9945-2. Ph. 026-579-2572. Dried-Frozen Tofu, Asahimatsu Subsidiary.

JAPAN. Nagano-Shi 380—Misuzu-Dofu. Nagano-Ken, Wakazato-Cho 1606. Ph. 026-226-1671. Dried-Frozen Tofu.

JAPAN 663. Nishinomiya-Shi—Nagai Sogo Shokuhin. Hyogo-Ken, Takamatsu-Cho 15-26. Ph. 079-866-2001. Large Tofu Factory.

JAPAN. Saitama-Ken 361—Asahi Shokuhin. Ooza-Mochida Gyoda-Shi, Aza-Nagamachi 1991. Ph. 048-555-2351. Silken Tofu.

JAPAN 062. Sapporo-Shi—Nichiryo Daily Shokuhin. Hokkaido, Higashi X 148 Toyohira-Ku. Ph. 011-851-1364.

JAPAN 166. Tokyo—Yamato Tofu. Suginami-Ku, Horinouchi 3-16-45. Ph. 033121101. Large Factory.

JAPAN. Tokyo 100-91—Mitoku Co Ltd, Cpo Box 780. Ph. 032016706. Akiyoshi Kazama.

JAPAN. Tokyo 130—Tengu Tofu. Kotobashi 4-29-16, Sumida-Ku. Ph. 036534411. Large Factory.

JAPAN 440. Toyobash-Shi—Yamaguchi-Ya. Shimoji, Aichi-Ken Higashiguchi. Ph. 053-254-4105. Large Tofu Factory.

MEXICO. Col De Valle—Sr Natural, Vasconcelos 143 Ole NI. Mr Hugo Victoria.

MEXICO. Guadalajara/Jal — Jamie Valencia Tofu, Ave Ninos Heroes 1633-307. Jaime Valencia.

MEXICO. Mexico 13 DF—Eng D Figuieroa Tagle, Proquide Sa 5 Febrero 743.

MEXICO. Mexico 22 DF—Americo Larralde, Timantitla 15 Tlalpan.

NEPAL. Kathmandu—Kathmandu Tofu Shop.

NETHERLANDS. Amsterdam 1054—Michel Horemaus, Le Helmerstraat 67-1.

NETHERLANDS. Arnheim—Hwergelmir Foundation. For A Natural Life, Eiland 2.

NETHERLANDS. Heerewaarden —Jakso, Voorne 13 6624 Kl. Ph. 088772189. Tomas Nelissen & Peter Dekker.

NETHERLANDS. 1017 Amsterdam —Stichting Oost W Centrum, Achtergracht 17-19. Ph. 020240-203. Adelbert Nelissen.

NETHERLANDS. 1021JK Amsterdam—Manna, Meeuwenlaan 70. Ph. 020323977. Sjon Welters & Robt Hendriks.

NETHERLANDS. 2518 Ck Den Haag—Witte Wonder Prod, Piet Heinstrat 80. Ph. 070-464-5225. Cees Van Rest & Niko Van Hagen.

NETHERLANDS. 3615 Westbroek —Soy-Lin, Burgemeester Huydecoper 18. Mr F M Lin.

NETHERLANDS. 9243WC Bakkeveen—De Morgenstond, Kreilen 3. Ph. 05169651. Wout Gerritsma.

NEW ZEALAND. Auckland I— Harvest Wholefoods, 403 Richmond Rd Grey Linn. Greg-Ricky-Eliz Chalmers.

NEW ZEALAND. Christchurch 1 —Soysource Tofu, Flat 3 39 Fendalton Rd. Ph. 558691. Jon Judson.

NEW ZEALAND. Wanganui— John Francis, Brunswick Rd 1.

PHILIPPINES. Manila—Feliciano Laiz Tofu. 1518 Sande St Tondo. Ph. 269761.

PHILIPPINES. Metro Manila — Chinese Tofu, 25 Mauban St Caloocan.

PHILIPPINES. Quezon City — Cherry Food Industry, 74 Speaker Perez. Ph. 613424.

PORTUGAL. Setubal—Jose Parracho Tofu. Quinta Da Portugesa, Fieguesia Da Annuciada. Jose Parracho.

PORTUGAL. 1200 Lisboa—Unimave Tofu, R Mouzinho Da Silveira 25.

PORTUGAL. 1300 Lisboa—Shogun Produtos Alimen. 44-Rc-Dto, R Gen Joao De Almeida. Ph. 644868. Joaquim Reis & Francisco Varatojo.

S AFRICA. 7925 Capetown—Cedric Lindholm Tofu, 203 Lwr Main · R Observatory. Cedric Lindholm.

SRI LANKA. Colombo—Boncheese, 128 Kitulwatte Rd. Ph. 596992. Mr U N Gunasekera.

SWEDEN. 19063 Orsundsbro—Aros Sojaprodukter, Bergsvagen 1. Ph. 017160456. Ted Nordquist.

SWITZERLAND. Bern—Restaurant Sesam, Byouxstr. Ph. 032257077.

SWITZERLAND. CH-8002 Zurich —Soyana, Friedensgasse 3. Ph. 012028997. Walter Daenzer.

SWITZERLAND. CH-8810 Horgen —Gauthier Loeffler Tofu, Zugerstr 1401. Ph. NL. Gauthier Loeffler.

SWITZERLAND. CH8913 Ottenbach—Sojalade, Dorfplatz. Ph. 017690349. Verena Krieger.

SWITZERLAND. Geneva CH-1201 —Le Grain D'or, Rue Voltair 29.

SWITZERLAND. 1227 Geneva—Natural Products Promo. Carouge, 11 Ch Faubourg-Cruseilles. Ph. 022432416. Eric W Dougoud.

SWITZERLAND. 1260 Nyon—Soy Joy, Ch De La Prelaz 1. Martin Halsey.

SWITZERLAND. 1345 Vaud—Joya, Le Lieu. Joanna White.

SWITZERLAND. 6330 Cham-Opplinger Tofu, Weinbergsstrasse 13. Hans R Opplinger.

W GERMANY. D-5000 Koln 1—Bittersuss, Handelstr 35. Thomas Kasas.

W GERMANY. Prien-Chiemsee—Auenland Tofu/Sojaprod, Hub 4. Peter Wiegand.

W GERMANY. 8000 Munchen 19 —Alexanders Tofu Shop, Leonrodstr 19. Ph. 089160474. Alexander Nabben.

W GERMANY. 8492 Furth Wald —Svadesha Pflan-Feinkost, Aussere Kotzingerstr 52a. Ph. 099-73-1066. Ruediger Urban.

Appendix C

Varieties of Tofu in East Asia

In addition to the various types of Japanese tofu and soymilk products we have discussed in this book, a number of other interesting varieties are found in other parts of East Asia.

China and Taiwan

Taiwan, with a population of 15 million people, has about 2,500 tofu shops. There are no statistics yet available on the number of shops in mainland China, but if the proportion of shops to people is the same as in Taiwan, we can expect there to be 158,000 shops serving China's 950 million people. Unless otherwise stated, all Chinese terms are standard Mandarin. The "t" in toufu is pronounced like the "d" in "doe."

Chinese-style Firm Tofu (*toufu; dowfu* or *daufu* in Cantonese). The most popular type. Coagulated with calcium sulfate (gypsum) and sold in 3-inch squares weighing about 4½ ounces each. Contains 10 percent protein. One special type made in Shantung province is called *t'aian toufu;* another made in Anhui province, Chunnan, is called *pa-kung-shan toufu.*

Pressed Tofu (*tofu-kan*): Similar to firm tofu but pressed until as firm as ham. Contains 22 percent protein. Often simmered in mixtures of water and burnt millet sugar, molasses, tumeric, or tea to create a variety of colors and flavors and increase shelf life.

Five-Spice Pressed Tofu (*wu-hsiang toufukan* or *hsiang toufukan*): Made by simmering pressed tofu squares in a mixture of soy sauce, oil, and "five spice powder" (ground anise, cinnamon, cloves, plus fennel and Szechuan chili powder or ginger and nutmeg). Now prepared in San Francisco, it has a flavor and texture resembling smoked ham.

Soy-sauce Pressed Tofu (*chiang-yu toufu-kan*): Made by simmering small squares of pressed tofu in a mixture of soy sauce and water.

Pressed Tofu Sheets (*pai-yeh* or *ch'ien-chang*): Tofu pressed into very thin sheets that look like a 6-to-12-inch-square of canvas.

Pressed Tofu Noodles (*toufu-ssu* or *kan-ssu*): Made by cutting pressed tofu sheets into noodlelike strips.

Pressed Tofu Loops (*pai-yeh chieh*). Made by cutting pressed tofu sheets into ½-inch-wide strips. Each is then tied into a simple overhand knot.

Salt-dried Tofu (*toufu-kan*): Made from squares of pressed tofu that are rubbed with salt, tied together with strands of rice straw, and hung in the sunlight to dry.

Hard Tofu (*lao-toufu*): A general term for all tofu that is not soft.

Chinese Silken Tofu (*shui-toufu, nan-toufu, nen-toufu,* or *shih-kao toufu*): One popular type is like a soft Japanese silken tofu; another is so soft it cannot be cut into cakes.

Smooth Soymilk Curds (*toufu-nao*): Literally "tofu brains." Sold in the West as Tofu Pudding. Sold by street vendors in China topped with a brown sugar & peanut sauce.

Curds-in-Whey (*toufu-hua* or *tou-hua*): Literally "tofu flowers." Available at some Chinese restaurants in the West.

Deep-fried Tofu (*yu-toufu* or *cha-toufu*): A general term for deep-fried tofu cutlets, cubes, triangles, or netlike cutlets.

Hollow Deep-fried Tofu Cubes (*toufu-kuo* or *cha-toufu*): Made by deep-frying 1-inch cubes of firm tofu.

Sautéed Tofu (*kuo-lao toufu*): Made by thinly slicing firm tofu and frying it over low heat in a skillet until it turns a rich brownish yellow.

Frozen Tofu (*tung-toufu* or *ping-toufu*): Made by setting firm tofu out overnight in the snow.

Fermented Tofu (*toufu-ru*): See Chapter 14. Varieties include *nan-ru, nan-chiang toufu, ru-fu, mei-kui ru-fu,* and *chiang-toufu*.

Soymilk (*toufu-chiang tou-chiang*, or *tou-ru*): See Chapter 10.

Chinese-style Yuba (*toufu-p'i, tou-yu p'i*, or *yu-p'i*): See Chapter 14.

Bamboo Yuba (*fu-chu*): U-shaped, dried rolls.

Okara (*tou-cha*): See Chapter 6.

Indonesia

Over 11,000 tofu shops make tofu for this country's 130 million people.

Indonesian tofu (*tahu*): Similar to Chinese firm tofu (*toufu*). In many shops, the whey, allowed to stand overnight until it ferments, is used as the coagulant. Pressed tofu simmered in turmeric (also called simply *tahu*) is popular.

Deep-fried Tofu Cubes (*tahu goreng*): 1¼-inch cubes deep-fried fresh by market vendors. Served crisp and hot, often with a fiery chili perched on top.

Tofu Chips (*krupuk tahu*): Salted tofu sliced into long, thin strips and sun-dried. Broiled until crisp, then eaten as a snack or topping for Gado-gado (cooked vegetables with peanut sauce).

Fermented Tofu (*taokoan* or *takoa*): Steamed and pressed into thin slices before being fermented.

Okara (*ampas tahu*): Usually made into delicious okara tempeh or okara onchom.

South Korea

There are more than 1,000 tofu shops scattered throughout this country of 32 million population. If there were a proportional number in North Korea, there would be 470 shops for 15 million people.

Korean Tofu (*tubu*): Slightly firmer than its Japanese counterpart; not as firm as Chinese *toufu*.

Deep-fried Tofu Strips (*yubu*): Each strip is about 7 by 1 by ¾ inch. Unique.

Soymilk Curds (*sun tubu*): Widely used.

Okara (*piji*): Also popular.

Philippines

Philippine Tofu (*tokwa*): Identical to Chinese firm tofu (*toufu*).

Soymilk curds (*tajo*): Pronounced ta-HO; made by Chinese. Sold topped with a little brown sugar.

Brine-fermented Tofu (*tahuri*): Made like Chinese brine-fermented tofu but with an *Aspergillus elegans* mold and a little soy sauce in the brining liquor.

Thailand

Thai Tofu (*tao-hu*): Identical to Chinese firm tofu (*toufu*). Made mostly by Chinese.

Deep-fried Tofu (*tao-hu tod*): Small (1¼-inch) cubes of deep-fried tofu. Often sold strung on split bamboo and tied in a loop.

Soymilk (*nom tua-liung*): Sold hot each morning by Chinese. A thin soymilk is called *nam tao-hu*.

Soymilk Curds (*tao-huey*): Sold by street vendors, topped with grated gingerroot and brown sugar syrup.

Red Fermented Tofu (*tao-hu yee*): A Chinese product. Sold in 2-inch squares wrapped in either banana leaves or paper.

Lactone Silken Tofu (*tau-hu lord* or *lawd*): A modern product.

Vietnam

Vietnamese Tofu (*dau hu* or *dau phu;* these and all of the following terms are spelled with many diacritical marks): Similar to Chinese firm tofu.

Smooth Soymilk Curds (*dau hu*): Similar to the Chinese product of the same name. Served warm in a sauce of brown sugar and ginger.

Fermented Tofu (*chao*): Similar to Chinese fermented Tofu.

Soymilk (*sua dau nanh*): Identical to Chinese soymilk.

Pressed Tofu Sheets (*mi cang*): Identical to the Chinese product.

Yuba (*dau phu truc*): Identical to Chinese yuba.

Appendix D

Table of Equivalents

Temperature

C = 5/9 (F-32)
F = 9/5C + 32
350°F = 177°C
375°F = 191°C

Volume

1 tablespoon = 3 teaspoons = 14.75 cc.
1 cup = 236 cc = 16 tablespoons
1 quart = 4 cups = 0.946 liters
1 U.S. gallon = 4 quarts = 3.785 liters = 231 in^3 =
   5/6 Imperial gallon.
1 bushel = 8 gallons = 4 pecks
1 *sho* = 10 *go* = 1800 cc = 7.63 cups

Weight

1 ounce = 28.38 grams
1 pound = 16 ounces = 454 grams
1 ton (U.S.) = 2,000 pounds = 0.907 metric tons

Natural Equivalents

1 gallon of water weighs 8.33 pounds
1 quart of soybeans weighs 1.69 pounds
1 bushel of 1st grade soybeans weighs 56 pounds

Bibliography

English Works

Aihara, Cornellia, *The Chico-san Cookbook,* Chico, Calif.: Chico-san Inc., 1972. Contains a number of good macrobiotic tofu recipes.

Aihara, Herman and Cornellia, *Soybean Diet,* G.O.M.F., 1544 Oak St., Oroville, Calif. 95965, 1975. Contains numerous macrobiotic tofu recipes and instructions for preparing homemade tofu, miso, shoyu, and *natto.*

Altschul, A.M., *Proteins, their Chemistry and Politics,* New York: Basic Books, 1965. Good basic information on soy protein.

Bauer, Cathy, and Anderson, Juel, *The Tofu Cookbook,* Emmaus, Penn.: Rodale Press, 1979. Quite creative. Meat is used in a number of the recipes.

Brandemuhl, M., *Soybean History: Aspects of Buddhist Influence,* Anthropology Dept., Univ. of Wisconsin, 1963. An inquiry into the obscure, legendary origins of the soybean and of tofu, and the role of Buddhism in this history.

Chang, W.W., *An Encyclopedia of Chinese Food and Cooking,* New York: Crown Publishers Inc., 1970. Contains a large number of tofu recipes.

Chao, Buwei Yang, *How to Cook and Eat in Chinese,* New York: Random House, 1945. A delightful book containing numerous tofu recipes.

Chen, Philip S., *Soybeans for Health and a Longer Life,* New Canaan, Conn.: Keats Publishing Co., 1956. Contains basic information and numerous recipes using tofu, soymilk, soy sprouts, and other soybean foods.

Chiang, Cecelia S., *The Mandarin Way,* Boston: Little, Brown and Co., 1974. Contains information on the role of tofu and soymilk in Chinese cookery and a number of tofu recipes.

Farr, Barbara, *Super Soy,* New Canaan, Conn.: Keats Publishing, 1976. Tofu and other soyfood recipes.

Hagler, Louise, ed., *The Farm Vegetarian Cookbook,* revised ed., Summertown, Tenn.: The Book Publishing Co., 1978. Probably the best and most creative soyfoods cookbook available. Fantastic graphics. Recipes avoid the use of eggs and dairy products.

Heartsong, Bob and Toni, *The Heartsong Tofu Cookbook*, Miami, Fla.: Banyan Books, 1978. Handwritten text full of many new tofu ideas.

Horvath, A.A., *The Soybean as Human Food*, Peking: Government Bureau of Economic Information, 1927. Interesting information on the early history of tofu in China.

Japan Dietetic Association Corp., *Standard Tables of Food Composition*, Tokyo: Daiichi Shuppan K.K., 1964. The basic source of information on the nutritional composition of all Japanese foods; bilingual.

Jones, Dorthea, *The Soybean Cookbook*, New York: ARC Books, 1968. One of the first and best-known soybean cookbooks. Contains 72 tofu recipes, plus many others using soymilk, soy sprouts, and other soy foods.

Joya, Mock, *Things Japanese*, Tokyo: Tokyo News Service, 1958. Contains a lengthy, highly informative section on all of the basic Japanese foods.

Kellner, O.J., *Tofu Cakes*, Tokyo: Bulletin of the College of Agric., Vol. 1, No. 4, 1889. Some of the earliest research done on Japanese tofu.

Kikkoman Shoyu Co., *The Kikkoman Way of Fine Eating*, Tokyo: Kikkoman, 1973. Contains many fine recipes using shoyu in Western- and Eastern-style recipes.

Kikuchi, Grace, *Tofu Recipes*, 1974: A 47-page pamphlet containing 30 tofu recipes—many with meat—available from the author: 260 Sumac Ln., Ann Arbor, Mich. 48105.

Landgrebe, Gary, *Tofu Goes West*, Palo Alto, Cal.: Fresh Press, 1978. A nice selection of tasty, American-style tofu recipes. Creative uses of frozen tofu.

McGruter, Patricia G., *The Great American Tofu Cookbook*, Brookline, Mass.: Autumn Press, 1979. A variety of American-style recipes.

Miller, Harry W., *Nutritional Value of Soymilk*, Riverside, Calif.: International Nutrition Research Foundation, 1970. Basic factual and historical information on soymilk.

————, *Meeting the World's Nutritional Needs with Soybean Milk*, Soybean Digest, 25 (8 i.e. 7) 19-21, 1965.

Newman, Marcea, *Sweet Life*, Boston: Houghton Mifflin, 1975. Recipes for tasty tofu desserts made with limited sweeteners and no dairy products.

Ohsawa, Lima, *The Art of Just Cooking*, Tokyo: Autumn Press, 1974. Contains a large number of macrobiotic tofu recipes.

Olszewski, Nancy, *Tofu Madness*, Island Spring, P.O. Box 747, Vashon, Wash., 98070, 1978. One of our favorite tofu cookbooks.

Piper, C.V. and Morse, W.J., *The Soybean*, New York: Peter Smith, 1923. A classic. The first comprehensive work on the soybean published in the West. Good material on tofu and other soybean foods in China and Japan.

Rudzinsky, Russ, *Japanese Country Cookbook*, San Francisco: Nitty Gritty Publications, 1969. A well-illustrated Japanese cookbook with some good tofu recipes.

Shurtleff, W.R. and Aoyagi, A., *The Book of Kudzu*, Lafayette, CA.: The Soyfoods Center. An introduction to this fine Japanese natural food and medicine.

———, *The Book of Miso*, Berkeley, CA.: Ten Speed Press, 2d ed., 1983. A companion volume to the present work describing another of East Asia's great soybean foods.

———, *The Book of Tempeh: Super Soyfood from Indonesia*, New York: Harper & Row. Everything you wanted to know about this protein powerhouse with a flavor and texture like Southern fried chicken.

———, *Tofu & Soymilk Production: The Book of Tofu, Vol. II*, Lafayette, Cal.: The Soyfoods Center, 1979. How to start and run your own tofu shop and soy dairy.

Smith, Allan K., and Circle, Sidney J., *Soybeans: Chemistry and Technology*, Westport, Conn.: Avi Pub. Co., 1972. The definitive, modern work on soybeans. Contains detailed information on large-scale tofu manufacturing based on the research of Dr. Smith and Dr. Watanabe.

Steinberg, Raphael, *The Cooking of Japan*, New York: Time-Life Books, 1969. Captures the full scope and feeling, sublety and beauty of Japanese cookery. Excellent treatment of Tea Ceremony Cuisine. Includes many famous Japanese recipes containing tofu. Superb color photography.

Tsuji, Kaichi, *Zen Tastes in Japanese Cooking*, Tokyo:

Kodansha, 1971. The finest work available on Tea Ceremony Cuisine by a great Japanese *Kaiseki* chef. Many
striking color plates; a beautiful and inspiring volume
containing numerous tofu recipes.

U.S. Dept. of Agriculture, *Oriental Methods of Using
Soybeans as a Food*, ARS-71-17. Wash., D.C.: U.S.-
D.A., 1961. Contains good information on tofu and
soymilk in China, Korea, and Japan.

————, *Soybeans in Family Meals*, Home and Garden
Bulletin No. 208. Supt. of Documents, U.S. Govt.
Printing Office, Wash., D.C., 20402, 1974. Contains
recipes for tofu, okara, soymilk, sprouts, and other
basic soybean foods.

————, *Composition of Foods*, U.S.D.A. Agricultural
Handbook No. 8, U.S. Govt. Printing Office, Wash.,
D.C. 20402. Contains detailed statistics on tofu, soy-
milk, and many other soybean foods.

U.S. Dept. of Health, Education and Welfare, *Food
Composition Table for Use in East Asia*, Available from:
Nutrition Program, Center for Disease Control, H.E.W.,
Atlanta, Georgia 30333, 1972. Nutritional statistics on
all of the basic types of tofu in East Asia.

Watanabe, T., *New Protein Food Technologies in Japan*,
Chap. IX in A.M. Altschul, New Protein Foods, Vol.
1-a, Technology, New York, N.Y.: Academic Press,
1974. A description of modern tofu manufacturing
processes in Japan.

Woods, John, *The Protein for Pennies Cookbook*, New
York: Peter W. Wyden, 1974. Contains a number of
good tofu recipes.

Yamaguchi, H.S.K., *We Japanese*, Yokohama, Japan:
Yamagata Press, 1934-1950. Almost 600 pages of en-
tertaining information on Japanese culture and foods,
including tofu.

Japanese Works

Although most of our Western readers cannot read
Japanese, we include the following list of books, which
we have used extensively in our research, as an indica-
tion of the nature and extent of the literature on tofu
published in Japanese. For easy reference, and since most
of these works do not have individual authors, we have

listed them in order of the English translation of their titles.

Book of Tofu, The (Tofu no Hon), Abe, Koryu and Tsuji, Shigemitsu, Tokyo: Shibata Shoten, 1974. The most recent and definitive work on tofu with hundreds of fine recipes and the best available history of tofu in China and Japan.

Chinese Cuisine: Famous Recipes (Chugoku Meisaifu), Tokyo: Shibata Shoten, 1973, 4 volumes. A treasure-trove of information on Chinese tofu including many good recipes.

Chinese Tofu (Chugoku-dofu), Lin Hai—Yin Taiwan, 1972. Written (in Chinese) by numerous Chinese authors, primarily from a literary point of view. Contains sections on tofu in Chinese proverbs, classics, and festivals.

Encyclopedia of Japanese Cookery (Ryori Hyakka), Tokyo: Shufu-no-tomo, 1972. Contains a large number of tofu recipes.

Encyclopedia of Food and Drink (Inshoku Jiten), Tokyo: Heibonsha, 1972. Contains detailed historical information on tofu and most of Japan's famous traditional tofu dishes.

Food Composition Tables (Nihon Shokuhin Hyojun Seibunhyo), Tokyo: Norinsho, 1964. A complete and detailed set of tables giving the composition of nutrients in all Japanese foods.

History of Dried-Frozen Tofu (Koya-dofu no Rekishi), Miyashita, Tokyo: Kori-dofu Association, 1962. A large and complete work with many fine old photographs. Interesting information on the early history of tofu.

Macrobiotic Cookery (Makurobiotiku Ryori), Ohsawa, Lima, Tokyo: 1971. Contains many simple but delicious tofu recipes prepared the macrobiotic way.

Making Tofu in the Traditional Way (Tofu Shusetsu), Tokyo: National Tofu Association, 1972. A well-illustrated pamphlet of traditional tofu-making tools and techniques.

One Hundred Unique Tofu Recipes (Tofu Hyaku Chin and Zoku Hen), Tokyo Shinshu Shorin, 1972. The famous classic written over 250 years ago describing tofu cookery throughout Japan's provinces. A modern edition by Koryu Abe, nicely illustrated.

Research Into the Standardization of the Tofu Manufacturing Process (Tofu Seizo Kotei no Hyojunka in Kansuru Kenkyu), Watanabe, Tokuji et al. Tokyo: Food Research Institute, 1960. The first comprehensive scientific study of the tofu-making process. Contains many graphs and tables. This work played a key role in the modernization of Japanese tofu shops.

Tales of Tofu (Tofu o Kataru): A classic work on tofu cuisine in the provinces written in the early 1920s. Serves as an introduction to the previous work.

Tofu Cookery (Tofu Ryori), Tsuji Kaichi, Tokyo: Fujin Gaho, 1962. A fine collection of recipes by one of Japan's great masters of the art of Tea Ceremony Cuisine.

Tofu Cookery (Tofu no Ryori), Tokyo: Gurafusha, My Life Series; No. 15, 1973. An artistically done volume containing many full-page color photos and recipes of Japan's favorite tofu dishes.

Tofu Cookery: One Hundred Favorites (Tofu Ryori, Hyaku-sen), Tokyo: Sankosha Katei Buhen, Maruhi, 1972. A collection of 100 tofu recipes, each illustrated.

Tofu, Soybean, and Miso Cookery Throughout the 12 Months (Tofu, Mame, Miso Ryori: Ju-ni Kagetsu), Tokyo; Joshi Eiyo Daigaku, 1969. An excellent collection of traditional and modern tofu recipes, many with color photographs.

Wonders of Soymilk, The (Tonyu no Shimpi), Yabuki Teisuke, Tokyo: Sanrodo, 1974. Written by the president of Japan's well-known Luppy Soymilk Company, this 160-page volume discusses soymilk from every conceivable point of view, with particular emphasis given to its value as a medicinal and health food.

Zen Temple Cookery (Shojin Ryori), Tokyo: Fujokai Shuppansha, 1972. Written by the head temple cooks of four of Japan's best-known Buddhist monasteries: Eiheiji, Sojiji, Daitokuji, and Tansenji. A comprehensive work with many illustrative photographs.

Glossary

The following Japanese-style ingredients, referred to in the recipe sections of this book, are generally available in the West at Japanese food markets and at a growing number of natural and health food stores. For local addresses look in the Yellow Pages under Japanese (or Chinese) Food Products or Oriental Goods.

Agar (*kanten*): A sea vegetable gelatin made from the genera *Gelidium* and *Gracilaria*. Sold in the form of flakes, bars, powder, and strands.

Amazaké: Literally "sweet sake." A creamy thick drink with a rich, sweet flavor and virtually no alcohol content. Made from rice *koji* or steamed rice overgrown with a fragrant white mycelium of *Aspergillus oryzae* mold.

Azuki beans: These small red beans (*Vigna angularis*) are cooked with glutinous rice or used to make a sweet filling for confections.

Beefsteak plant (*shiso*): This fragrant herb (*Perilla nankinensis*) is prized for its versatility: beefsteak buds and blossoms (*mejiso and hojiso*) are garnishes, beefsteak seeds (*shisonomi*) are a condiment, green beefsteak leaves (*aojiso*) can be used like mint, and red beefsteak leaves (*shisonoha*) are used in making salt plums, pickles, and confections.

Beni-tadé: Also called *akamé* or "red bud," these tiny purple leaflike sprouts are used as a garnish for chilled tofu.

Bonito flakes (*Hana katsuo*): A popular garnish and basis for soup stocks made by shaving hard-as-wood, dried fermented bonito (*katsuobushi*).

BRACKEN FERN (*warabi*): The olive green young fiddlenecks of *Pteridium aquilinum*. Parboiled and served as a delicacy.

BREAD CRUMB FLAKES (*panko*): Similar to bread crumbs except that each particle has been rolled under pressure to form a tiny, thin flake. Used in deep-fried breadings.

BURDOCK ROOT (*gobo*): *Arctium lappa* has a long, dark-brown tapering root ½ to 1 inch in diameter and 18 to 24 inches long.

BUTTERBUR (*fuki*): The 4-foot-long, ½-inch-diameter stem of this spring vegetable, *Petasites japonicus*, has a flavor resembling that of celery.

CHILIES (*togarashi*): Japanese chilies (*Capsicum annum*), usually sold dried, are 2½ inches long and fiery hot. See also 7-spice chili powder.

CHINESE CABBAGE (*hakusai*): Splendidly tight and crisp heads of *Brassica pekinensis* are as delicious as they are inexpensive.

CHIVES: Popular Japanese varieties include *asatsuki (Allium ledebourianum)* and *nira (Allium tuberosum)*.

CHRYSANTHEMUM LEAVES (*shungiku*): The fragrant greens of *Chrysanthemum coronarium* resemble spinach or trefoil.

CLOUD-EAR MUSHROOM (*kikuragé*): A delicate variety with a wavy cap, *Auricularia auricula-judae* grows on trees and has virtually no stem. Solid dried, it is also known as Dried Black Fungus or Wood Ear.

DAIKON: The marvelously versatile Japanese giant white radish (*Raphanus sativus*) is often as thick as a man's arm and 18 to 24 inches long.

EGGPLANT (*nasu*): The Japanese variety (*Solanum melongena*), sweeter and more tender that its American counterpart, averages 4½ inches in length and 1½ inches in diameter, and weighs 2 ounces.

ENOKIDAKÉ: This pale white mushroom (*Flammulina velutipes*), has a 5-inch-long stem and a tiny ⅜-inch-diameter cap. Usually sold fresh.

GINGERROOT (*shoga*): The 4-inch-long knobby tan root of *Zingiber officinale* is peeled and freshly grated. Two parts by volume of powdered ginger may be substituted for 1 part fresh grated gingerroot. Gingerroot shoots (*shin shoga*) are a popular soup garnish and red pickled gingerroot (*beni-shoga*) is thinly sliced and served with Inari-zushi.

GINKGO NUTS (*ginnan*): These tender ½-inch-long delicacies from the giant *Ginkgo bilboa* tree are sold fresh or canned.

GLUTINOUS RICE (*mochigomé*): Used to make mochi and a variety of treats, *Oryzae sativa glutinosa* contains no amylase, and therefore cooks to a sticky, moist consistency. Occasionaly known in the West as sweet rice.

GLUTINOUS YAM (*tororo imo*): When rubbed on a fine metal grater, these yams (all of the Genus *Dioscorea*) develop a highly cohesive, glutinous quality. Available fresh in many varieties, including *jinenjo* and *yamanoimo*.

GREEN NORI FLAKES (*aonoriko*): A sea vegetable seasoning made by crumbling the fragrant, bright-green fronds of dried *Enteromorpha prolifera*. Delicious on noodles.

HEMP SEEDS (*asanomi*): The tiny light green seeds of *Cannabis sativa*, about the size of sesame or poppy seeds, are widely used in Japanese deep-fried tofu burgers.

HIJIKI: A stringy black sea vegetable (*Hizikia fusiforme*) sold in pieces about 1½ inches long. Often misspelled "hiziki" in the West.

JUNSAI: A "water shield" (*Brasenia purpurea*), this tiny wild pond plant, surrounded by a slippery gelatinous coating, is used in soups.

Kabocha. Also called Hokkaido pumpkin, this delectable fall vegetable (*Cucurbita moschata*), with its dark-green edible skin, looks like a 6-to-8-inch-diameter acorn squash. Substitute winter squash or pumpkin.

KAMPYO: Strips shaved from the dried *yugao* gourd or calabash (*Lagenaria siceraria*) are used for tying food into bundles or rolls.

KATAKURIKO: Japan's most popular, low-cost cooking starch. Often synonymous with potato starch.

KINAKO: Roasted soy flour; see Chapter 4.

KINOMÉ: The fragrant, bright green sprigs of the *sansho* tree (*Zanthoxylum piperitum*) are plucked in the spring and used as a garnish.

KOMBU: A sea vegetable (*Laminaria* species) somewhat

resembling kelp and sold as leathery olive brown fronds. 3 to 6 inches wide and 2½ to 6 feet long. Used to make soup stocks and in stews.

KONNYAKU: Eight-ounce gray, firm jellylike cakes made from the starch of *Amorphallus konjac*, the devil's tongue plant, a relative of the sweet potato. Konnyaku threads (*ito konnyaku*) and noodles (*shirataki*) are used in one-pot cookery.

KUDZU POWDER (*kuzu-ko*): The white, starchlike powder extracted from the roots of the kudzu vine (*Pueraria lobata*), which grows abundantly in the southeast U.S., is a high quality cooking starch and natural medicine widely used in East Asia. For details see *The Book of Kudzu* (Autumn Press).

LEEK (*negi*): The Japanese leek (*Allium fistulosum*) or Welsh onion is somewhat sweeter, mellower, and faster cooking than its Western counterpart.

LILLY BULB (*yuriné*): These fresh roots, about the size and shape of a bulb of garlic, have a mild flavor and are used in tofu treasure balls. The bulb of the tiger lily (*oni yuri; Lilium lancifolium*) is most widely used but those of the Maximowicz's lily (*L. maximowiczii*) and star lily (*L. concolor*) are also used.

LOTUS ROOT (*renkon*): The sausage shaped roots of the lotus (*Nelumbo nucifera*), which grow in the mud at the bottom of ponds, are 2 to 3 inches in diameter and 5 to 8 inches long. Prized for their crisp texture, they are best when fresh.

MANDARIN ORANGE (*mikan*): Japan's most popular and least expensive domestic fresh fruit, it is available from November until March. Delicious.

MATCHA: Powdered green tea, widely used in the tea ceremony.

MATSUTAKÉ: The most expensive and most delicious of Japanese mushrooms, *Trichloma matsutaké* grows a cap up to 8 inches in diameter.

MIRIN: Sweet sake used only for cooking. For each tablespoon of mirin called for, you may substitute ½ teaspoon honey or 2 teaspoons sake or pale dry sherry. Or you may substitute 1½ teaspoons honey and 2½ teaspoons water.

MISO: Fermented soybean paste; see Chapter 4.

MIZUAMÉ: A natural grain sugar extracted from rice, millet, or barley, it looks like a solid, pale-amber resin and may be softened by heating. Also sold as Millet Jelly, Amé, or Rice Honey. Close relatives are barley malt syrup and sorghum molasses.

MOCHI: Cakes of steamed, pounded glutinous rice, each about 3 by 2 by ½ inches.

MUSHROOMS: see Cloud-ear mushroom, *enokidaké, matsutaké, nameko, shiitaké,* and *shimeji.*

MYOGA: The pinkish white buds of the *Zingiber mioga* that emerge from the plant's base each August are a popular garnish.

NAMEKO: Tiny yellowish-brown mushrooms with a slippery coating, *Pholiota namcko* are sold fresh or canned.

NATTO: Fermented whole soybeans; see Chapter 4.

NIGARI: Bittern or bitterns. The traditional Japanese tofu coagulant extracted from clean seawater. See Chapter 8.

NOODLES (*menrui*): See rice-flour noodles, ramen, soba, somen, and udon.

NORI: A sea vegetable sold in paper-thin purplish-black sheets about 8 inches square and packaged in bundles of ten. The Japanese presently consume about 9 *billion* sheets each year. Other *Porphyra* species are known in the West as laver.

OSMUND FERN (*zenmai*): The slender young fiddlenecks of *Osmunda japonica* are a springtime delicacy.

PICKLES (*tsukemono*): Salt pickled vegetables (*shiozuké*), miso pickles (*misozuké*), and rice-bran pickles (*nukamiso-zuké*) are widely used as seasonings in Japan. Famous varieties include *Narazuké* (Uri melons pickled in sake lees) and *Takuan* (dried daikon pickled in nukamiso).

RAMEN: Crinkly yellowish-white Chinese noodles now widely used in Japan, especially in the form of Instant Ramen.

RICE FLOUR (*joshinko*): Finely ground white rice widely used in the preparation of steamed desserts and dumplings (*dango*).

RICE FLOUR NOODLES: Slender, round, white noodles about 10 inches long; popular in salads.

SAKÉ: Japanese rice wine containing about 15 percent alcohol and widely used in cooking. The lees (*sake-no-kasu*) are used in dressings and soups and for pickling other foods.

SALT PLUM (*umeboshi*): The partially ripe fruit of the *Prunus mumé* (which is actually more like an apricot than a plum), is salt pickled, usually with red beefsteak leaves, and used as both a tart seasoning with rice or in salad dressings, or as a highly alkaline natural medicine.

SANSHO PEPPER (*kona zansho*): A fragrant and spicy brownish-green pepper made from the seedpods of the *sansho* tree (*Zanthoxylum piperitum*), the same tree that bears *kinomé* sprigs.

SEA VEGETABLES (*kaiso*): See agar, green nori flakes, hijiki, kombu, nori, and wakame.

SESAME SEEDS (*goma*): The delicious calcium-rich seeds come in white and black varieties and are usually lightly roasted and ground before use. Substitute one half the amount of sesame butter or tahini.

SEVEN-SPICE CHILI POWDER (*shichimi togarashi*): A zippy blend of ground dried chilies and other spices including sesame, *sansho*, grated dried orange peel, green nori flakes, and white pepper.

SHIITAKÉ: Japan's most popular mushroom, *Lentinus edodes* is sold fresh or dried and widely sautéed or used as a basis for stocks.

SHIMEJI: Small mushrooms with tan caps 1 to 1½ inches in diameter, *Lyophyllum aggregatum* are usually sold fresh.

SHOCHU: A popular and very potent type of inexpensive spirits related to gin and often made from sweet potatoes.

SHOYU: Japanese all-purpose soy sauce; see Chapter 4.

SNOW PEAS (*saya endo*): Also called edible-pod peas, these are the paper-thin type widely associated with Chinese cookery.

SOBA: Japanese buckwheat noodles. A great food.

SOMEN: Very slender wheat-flour noodles, usually served chilled in summertime. Substitute vermicelli.

SPINACH (*horenso*): *Spinacia oleracea* is milder and slightly sweeter than its Western counterpart. Delicious.

SUDARÉ: A bamboo mat about 10 inches square used for rolling sushi and other foods.

SURIBACHI: An earthenware grinding bowl or mortar with a serrated interior surface, the usual suribachi is 10 inches in diameter and 3½ inches deep, and is accompanied by a wooden pestle (*surikogi*).

SWEET POTATO (*satsuma imo*): One of Japan's most beloved and tastiest foods, *Ipomoea batatas* has no exact counterpart in the West. About 1½ to 2½ inches in diameter and 4 to 8 inches long, it has a pale red skin and a light-yellow, richly-flavored meat.

TAHINI: A smooth creamy paste made from unroasted or very lightly roasted, hulled white sesame seeds. Due to the removal of the calcium-rich hulls, tahini is not as nutritious as sesame butter, and some commercial varieties use caustic soda in the cleaning and dehulling process. Contains 19 percent protein.

TAMARI: A type of soy sauce resembling shoyu; see Chapter 4.

TARO: A 2½-inch-diameter root vegetable also known in the West as dasheen or albi; the most popular of the many Japanese varieties are *sato imo* (*Colocasia antiquorum*), *yatsugashira*, and *akame imo*. Rich, creamy, and delicious. Used to make Hawaii's *poi*.

TOGAN: Also known in English as "white gourd," *Benincasa hispida* is a mild flavored vegetable.

TRANSPARENT NOODLES (*harusamé*): This slender vermicelli, made from mung beans or sweet potatoes, is also popular in Chinese cookery.

TREFOIL (*mitsuba*): Prized for its unique pungent aroma and handsome green leaves, *Cryptotaenia japonica* is most widely used as a garnish.

TURNIP (*kabu*): The Japanese *Brassica rapa* is a heart-shaped white root about 3 inches in diameter having a mild, slightly sweet flavor.

UDO: Neither quite celery nor asparagus, *Aralia cordata* is a crisp and tender oddity with a unique hint of lemon flavor that is enjoyed fresh or cooked. The best varieties grow wild.

UDON: Fat, white, wheat-flour noodles similar to a No. 2 spaghetti.

URI MELON (*shirouri*): Also called "white melon," "white gourd melon," or "Oriental pickling melon," *Cucumis melo* var. *conomon* is a pale green fruit shaped like a cucumber about 12 inches long and 3 inches in diameter. Widely pickled in sake lees or miso.

WAKAME: A dark-green sea vegetable (*Undaria pinnatifida*) with fronds about 3 inches wide and 12 to 18 inches long, it is sold both fresh and dried; widely used in soups and salads.

WASABI: A hot green horseradish-like paste made from the grated root of the *wasabi* plant (*Wasabia japonica*) which is cultivated in terraced mountain stream beds. Sold fresh or powdered.

WHEAT GLUTEN (*fu*): Both fresh and dried varieties, sold in a multitude of shapes, are widely used in Japanese cookery.

YUZU: A citrus fruit similar to a citron, lime, or lemon, the fruit of the *yuzu* tree (*Citrus junos*) has a green to yellow, refreshingly fragrant rind which is slivered or grated and widely used in soups, sauces, and tofu or miso preparations.

Note: Monosodium glutamate (MSG), a flavor intensifier also known as Aji-no-moto or Accent, is a highly refined white crystalline powder that differs in structure from natural glutamic acid. When used in more than very small quantities, it is well known to produce in some people the "Chinese Restaurant Syndrome" characterized by headaches, burning sensations, a feeling of pressure in the chest, and other discomforting symptoms. Originally extracted from kombu, it is now produced by fermentation or hydrolysis of molasses or glucose from tapioca, cornstarch, potato starch, etc. We and many others interested in natural healthy foods strictly avoid use of this product.

INDEX

A

Aburagé, see tofu pouches
Abura miso, 41
Aemono, 157-59, 228
Agé, see tofu cutlets
Agédashi-dofu, 192
Akadashi miso, 69, home-
made, 45
Almond ice cream, 307
Amayuba, 371, 377
Ankake sauce, *see* sauces
Apple(s)
Curry sauce with deep-
fried tofu, 236, tofu,
170
Dessert with
Deep-fried tofu, 253
Frozen tofu, 357
Turnover in tofu
pouch, 284
Applesauce with chilled
tofu, 143
Atsu-agé, see tofu cutlets
Avocado, guacamole with
tofu, 148
Awasé miso, 44

B

Baked tofu, 173
Banana(s)
Cream with sesame and
tofu, 209
Ice cream with soymilk,
306
Shake with soymilk, 308,
with tofu, 153

Spread with tofu, 148
Tofu pouches, in, 279
Whip with soymilk, 309,
with tofu, 207, 208
Barbecue(d)
Sauce, Korean, *see* sauces
Sauce with deep-fried tofu,
235
Tofu, 332
Barley flour muffins with
okara, 98
Bonito, 35
Bread with
Frozen tofu, 345
Soy flour, 68, 78
Soy purée, 85
Broths, clear, 36, sweetened
shoyu, 36
Buckwheat noodles (soba),
see noodles
Buddha's chicken, fish, and
ham, 373
Bulgur pilaf with tofu, 198
Burdock root miso sauté, 42
Burgers
Okara, 93
Tofu, deep-fried, 215, 261,
267
Tofu with mushroom sauce,
182
Buttermilk, soy, 307

C

Cabbage rolls, 249, 284
Calcium chloride or sulfate,
see coagulants
Canapées with tofu, 149

Carob tofu frosties, 151,
    ice cream, 307, pop-
    sicles, 307
Carrot(s)
    Salad with tofu, 155
    Sautéed with deep-fried
        tofu, 238
Casseroles
    Deep-fried tofu, cheese,
        and onions, 233
    Tofu and brown rice, 175
    Tofu, mushrooms, and
        onions, 176
Cauliflower salad with tofu,
    154
Chahan, 168, 241
Chapaties with okara, 96
Cheese
    Burger with tofu, 270
    Casserole with deep-fried
        tofu, 233
    Fondue with deep-fried
        tofu, 223
    Frozen tofu, with, 350
    Sandwich with tofu, 162
    Sauce with soymilk, 310
    Sauce with tomato, 50
    Soufflé with tofu, 175
    Soymilk, 308
    Stuffing for frozen tofu,
        353
    Tofu with, 179
Cheesecake, tofu, 210, Gisei,
    213
Chiang (Chinese-style miso),
    69
Chicken, Buddha's, 373
Chinese-style recipes
    Bean sauce with tofu, 180
    Deep-fried tofu, 170
    Dipping sauce, 45
    Fermented tofu dipping
        sauces, 363
    Dressing with tofu, 147
    Sauces with dried-frozen
        tofu, 352
    Tofu sautéed, 183

Chinese-style tofu, varieties
    of, 402
Chirinabé, 206
Chutney with deep-fried tofu,
    221
Clear soups, 168
Coagulants, 62, 110, 129
Coconut with tofu whip, 208
Coffee popsicles, 307
Congee, 51
Cookies, Gisei-dofu, 214
Cottage cheese
    Tangy tofu, 150; uses, 224
    Tofu, 151; uses, 157
Cream, soymilk, 305
Cream cheese
    Dip with fermented tofu,
        365
    Tofu, 152
Croquettes, okara, 95
Cucumber(s)
    Hors d'oeuvre with yuba,
        377
    Salad with deep-fried tofu,
        228
Curds, soymilk, 101-109
Curry
    Dip with deep-fried tofu,
        222, fermented tofu,
        365
    Noodles with deep-fried
        tofu, 242
    Rice and tofu salad, 155
    Sauce with curds, 109
    Sauce with deep-fried tofu,
        236, tofu, 170
    Tofu with pita bread, 161
Custard, with tofu, 212,
        silken tofu, 322
Cutlets
    Breaded, deep-fried, 239,
        tofu, 190
    Deep-fried tofu, 215, 253
    Frozen tofu, 351

D

Dairylike soymilk products,

302, tofu products,
150
Daitoku-ji natto, 72
Dashi (*kombu,* No. 1 & 2),
35-36
Deep-fried tofu, 215. *See also*
tofu cutlets, burgers,
and pouches.
Baked, 233
Broiled, grilled, or barbe-
cued, 243
Burgers, 215, 261
Crisps, 275
Cutlets, 215, 253
Deep-fried, 239
Desserts, 253
Eggs with, 232
Grains with, 240
Hors d'oeuvres, 222
Pouches, 215, 270
Preparatory techniques
(broiling, dousing),
219
Quick and easy, 220
Crisp deep-fried tofu,
220
Grilled with barbecue
sauce, 221
Salads, in, 224
Sandwiches and toast, with,
228
Sautéed, stir-fried, or
topped with sauces, 234
Seasoned broths and stews,
with, 244
Soups, in, 230
Deep-frying, 185. *See also*
croquettes, cutlets,
tempura
Deep-fried tofu, 239
Okara, 100
Tofu, regular, 185
Dengaku
Deep-fried tofu, 203
Grilled tofu, 333
Tofu, 199, 380
Desserts. *See also* cookies,
Gisei-dofu, ice cream,

shakes, puddings, turn-
overs
Deep-fried tofu, 253
Frozen tofu, 357
Soymilk dairylike, 306, 309
Tofu, cooked, 210, un-
cooked, 207
Tofu pouches, 270
Dipping sauces, shoyu, 37
Dips
Fermented tofu, 365
Tofu, 143
Domburi
Fox, with deep-fried tofu,
243
Rice with tofu, 196
Doughnuts, okara, 100
Dow-foo or *dowfu,* 110, 402
Dressings
Fermented tofu, 364
Soymilk mayonnaise, 304
Tofu, 143
Dried-frozen tofu, 339, home-
made, 349. *See also*
frozen tofu
Drumsticks, yuba, 373

E

Edamamé, 67
Egg(s) and egg dishes
Fried with deep-fried tofu,
232
Fried with butter-fried
tofu, 171
Japanese style with tofu,
172, 196, frozen tofu,
350
Omelet(s)
Plain, paper-thin, 54
Tofu and mushrooms,
with, 173
Poached, in tofu pouches,
279, in tofu, 172
Scrambled with
Deep-fried tofu, 233
Okara, 93
Tofu, 172

Silken tofu, in homemade, 322
Tofu pouches, in, 279, treasure pouches, in, 283
Tofu *domburi*, with, 196
Eggplant miso sauté, 42
Enchiladas, tofu-filled, 195

F

Fermented tofu, 358
Fondue with deep-fried tofu, 223
French fries, tofu, 189
Fresh soy purée, *see* soy purée
Fritters, okara, 94
Frosties, tofu, 151
Frozen tofu, 339
Storing and cooking, 348
Reconstituting, 347
Fruit(s)
Cocktail with chilled tofu, 209
Silken tofu, in, 323
Tofu pouches, in, 279
Whips, with tofu, 207, with soymilk, 309
Yogurt, with, 304
Fuku-bukuro, 282
Fukuyose-ni, 355
Furu, see fermented tofu
Fuyu, see fermented tofu

G

Ganmo or *ganmodoki*, *see* deep-fried tofu burgers
Gari, 53
Gingerroot, miso sauté, sauce, 37, 42, sweet vinegared, 53
Gisei-dofu, made from tofu, 213
Glutinous yam with deep-fried tofu, 245

Gô (soy purée), 76
Gohoji-dofu, 140
Gojiru, 84
Gomashio, 53
Gomoku-dofu, 139, 259
Granola, okara, 99, chilled tofu with, 143
Grains. *See also* rice, noodles, bulgur wheat, bread
Deep-fried tofu with, 240
Fermented tofu with, 366
Tofu with, 193, tofu pouches, 280
Gratin, tofu, 176, 177
Green peppers sautéed with deep-fried tofu, 236
Grilled tofu, 325, homemade, 331
Guacamole with tofu, 148

H

Ham, Buddha's with yuba, 373
Hamanatto, 72, *see* savory soy nuggets
Herb, dressing, 145, sauce, 310
Hijiki, sautéed with deep-fried tofu, 238
Hitashi mamé, 67
Hiryozu, 269
Hiya-yakko, 141
Hors d'oeuvres
Deep-fried tofu, 222, 269, 286
Fermented tofu, 365
Tofu, 143
Tofu burger balls stuffed, 269
Tofu pouches, rolled, 286
Yuba, 376

I

Ice cream, soymilk, 306, tofu, 153
Ichiban dashi, 35

Icing, tofu, 152
Inari-zushi, 281
Indonesia tofu varieties, 404
Instant powdered tofu, 320
Iridofu, 182
Irimame, 67
Italian-style tofu meatballs, 174, spaghetti with tofu meatballs, 194

K

Kaiseki ryori (Tea Ceremony Cuisine), 384
Kaminari-agé, 191
Kampyo, 282, 284
Kaori yuba, 378
Karashi sumiso, 55
Kefir, 304
Ketchup and Worcestershire sauce, 50
Kinako, 68
Kinome miso, 41, with *shira-ae* tofu salad, 159
Kinugoshi, see silken tofu
Kitsune Domburi, 243
Kombu dashi, 36, rolls, 250
Konnyaku noodle bundles, 250, with *shira-ae* tofu salad, 159
Korean dishes
  Barbecue sauce, 50; uses, 221, 253, 325
  Miso sauté, 44
Korean tofu varieties, 404
Kori-dofu, see frozen tofu
Koya-dofu, see frozen tofu
Kurumi-dofu, 117

L

Lactone silken tofu, 317
Lecithin, soy, 74
Leeks in miso soup, 167
Lemon
  Miso with white sauce, 309

Sauce with dried-frozen tofu, 354
Whip with tofu and honey, 208
Lotus root, miso sauté, 42, salad with tofu, 159

M

Mabo-dofu, 183
Macaroni salad with deep-fried tofu, 227
Magnesium chloride or sulfate, *see* coagulants
Mayonnaise (dressings)
  Miso, 225, 226
  Soymilk, 304
  Tofu, 145
Meatballs, tofu Italian, 174, 194
Mexican tofu dishes, 183, 184, 195, 242
Milkshake, *see* shake
Mincemeat, tofu, 211
Mirin-shoyu, 38
Miso, 69
  Broiled, 45, 244
  Deep-fried tofu with broiled, 244
  Dressings, 55
  Grilled tofu with, 333
  Mixed, 44
  Moromi, 69
  Nerimiso, 39, 202
  Pickled with tofu, 148
  Sauce, *see* sauces, miso
  Sauté, 41
  Soups
    Curds in, 109
    Deep-fried tofu in, 231
    Gojiru, 84
    Tofu in, 165-67
    Yuba in, 372
  Sweet simmered miso, 39
  Toppings, 38, 142, 221
Mizutaki, 206

Muffins, okara and barley flour, 98
Mushroom(s)
  Casserole with tofu, 176
  Egg omelet with tofu, 173
  Miso sauté, 42
  Salad with deep-fried tofu, 225
  Sauce, 47, 310
Mustard vinegar miso, 55

N

Nabé dishes (nabemono or one pot cookery) with
  Deep-fried tofu, 246, 264
  Grilled tofu, 333, 338
  Tofu, 204
Nabeyaki Udon, 206
Nama-agé, see deep-fried tofu cutlets
Natto, 71
Nerimiso, red or white, 39
Niban dashi, 35
Nigari, see coagulants
Nishime, 251
Noodles, 53. See also transparent noodles
  Basic preparation, 53
  Curds with, 109
  Curried with deep-fried tofu, 242
  Fried with deep-fried tofu, 240, tofu, 194
  Gratin with tofu, 177
  Salad with deep-fried tofu, 226
  Tofu pouches, in, 280

O

Oboro-dofu, 102
Oden, 246, grilled tofu in, 338
Oharagi yuba, 373
Okara dishes, 91-100
  ·yu, 51

Omelets, see eggs
Onion(s)
  Eggs with deep-fried tofu, 233, tofu, 172, frozen tofu, 350
  Casserole with deep-fried tofu, 233, tofu, 176
  Gratin with tofu, 176
  Miso sauté, 42
  Sauce, 46. See also sauces, with deep-fried tofu, 234
  Soup with deep-fried tofu, 230, 234, tofu, 165, 166
Orange juice with tofu purée, 208
Oranda-ni, 354
Osechi nishime, 251

P

Pancakes, okara-potato, 95, okara-whole wheat, 97
Pâté, okara, 99
Patties, tofu, 181
Peaches with tofu whip, 207
Peanuts or peanut butter
  Miso, 40
  Sauce, 109
  Silken tofu, homemade, 322
  Spread with tofu, 148
Peking duck dipping sauce, 45
Philippines, tofu varieties, 405
Pilaf with tofu, 198
Pineapple
  Purée with tofu, 207, 208
  Sherbet with tofu, 211
  Sweet & sour sauce with deep-fried tofu, 238
Pita bread with tofu, 161
Pizza toast with deep-fried tofu, 229
Popsicles, 307
Potatoes

Deep-fried with deep-fried
   tofu, 246
Fried with tofu, 184
Pancakes with okara, 95
Powdered tofu, instant, 320
Pressed tofu, 402
Protein, 3, 14
Prune-tofu purée, 208
Pudding
   Custard with tofu, 207, 212
   Rice with tofu, 212
   Tofu or fresh tofu pud-
      ding, 106
Pumpkin, *kabocha,* or squash
   Miso sauté, 42
   Soup with deep-fried tofu,
      231
Purées, soymilk, 309, tofu,
   207
Puri with okara, 97

R

Raisins in
   Salad with tofu, 155
   Whip with tofu, 208, soy-
      milk, 309
Restaurants, tofu, in Japan,
   379
Rice, brown, 51. *See also*
      sushi rice
   Casserole with tofu, 175
   Domburi with tofu, 137,
      deep-fried tofu, 243
   Fermented tofu, with, 366
   Fried with tofu, 194
Porridge, 51, with tofu,
   197
Pudding with tofu, 212
   Salad with deep-fried tofu,
      225, tofu, 155
   Sizzling, with deep-fried
      tofu, 241
   Soup with tofu, 164
   Tofu pouches, in. 280

S

Salads with

Deep-fried tofu, 224
Tofu, 153
Tofu pouches, 280
Sandwiches. *See also* toast
   Deep-fried tofu, 228
   Tofu, 160
Sauces, basic
   Ankake, 49; uses, 190
   Barbecue, 50, 235
   Cheese, 310
   Chinese, 180, 352
   Curry with tofu, 170, deep-
      fried tofu, 236
   Fermented tofu, 363
   Ketchup-Worcestershire, 50
   Korean barbecue, 50; uses,
      221, 253, 325
   Miso, 239, 309
   Mushroom, 47; uses, 182,
      184, 242; other, 310
   Onion, 46, 163, 179, 234,
      350, 354
   Pineapple sweet & sour,
      238
   Rich gingerroot-*ankake,* 49,
      with sizzling tofu, 190
   Shoyu, 37
   Sweet & sour, 238
   Spaghetti with tofu, 169;
      uses, 194
   Tahini with tofu, 177
   Teriyaki, 49
   Tofu sauces, 169
   Tomato and cheese, 50;
      uses, 184
   White basic, 48; lemon-
      miso, 309
Sausage, okara, 98
Savory soy chunks and nug-
   gets, 72
Savory pressed tofu, 402
Sea vegetables, *see nori,*
   wakame, kombu, hijiki
Sesame and tahini
   Cream with tofu, 209
   Dipping sauce with shoyu,
      37

Dressing, Chinese, with tofu, 147
Salt, 53
Sauce with tofu, 169, 177
Soymilk with sesame, 301
Shake, banana with soymilk, 308, with tofu, 153
Sherbet, tofu-pineapple, 211
Shikishi-dofu, 322
Shinoda-maki with tofu pouches, 284, 356
Shira-ae, 158-59, Western style, 156
Shirozu-ae, 156
Shish kebab, with deep-fried tofu, 244
Shojin ryori (Zen Temple Cookery), 384
Shoyu (Japanese soy sauce), 70
  Broth, sweetened, 36
  Dipping sauces, 37
Silken tofu, 311, homemade, 320
Smoothie, soymilk, 304
Soba, see noodles
Soft tofu, description, 319, homemade, 323
Solidifiers for tofu, see coagulants
Soufflé, cheese with tofu, 175
Soups
  Clear, 36
  Curds in, 109
  Deep-fried tofu in, 230
  Miso soups, see miso
  Stocks, 35
  Tofu in, 163, 165
Sour cream
  Dip with fermented tofu, 365
  Tofu sour cream, 152
Soybeans
  Fresh green, 67
  Roasted, 67
  Sprouts, 67
  Whole dry, 58, 66
  Soymilk (homemade), 399

Tofu (homemade), 127-40
Soy flakes, 73
Soy flour and grits, 68, defatted, 73
Soy flour, roasted (kinako), 68
Soy flour tofu, 137
Soy granules, 73
Soymilk, 288, homemade recipes, 399
Soynuts, 67
Soy oil products, 74
Soy protein concentrates, 73, textured, 74
Soy protein isolates, 73
Soy protein, spun, 74
Soy purée, 76, homemade, 84
Soysage, 98
Soy sauce, 70, see also shoyu
Spreads, tofu, 143, fermented tofu, 365
Sprouts, soy, 67
Spun protein fibers, 74
Squash, see pumpkin
Stew, 246
Stocks, soup, 35
Strawberry, dessert with tofu, 207, 209
Sudaré, 418
Suimono, 168
Sukiyaki, 333
Sumashi, 36
Suribachi, 419
Sushi rice, 52. See also inari-zushi
Sweet potatoes, miso sauté, 42, salad with tofu, 159

T

Taco sauce, 242, with tofu, 195
Tahini, see sesame
Taiwanese tofu, varieties of, 402
Takara-zutsumi, 283

Tamago-tofi, 172, with
    frozen tofu, 350
Tangerines, in tofu purée,
    208, fruit cocktail,
    209
Tartare sauce, tofu, 147
Tekka miso, 42, 43
Tempeh, 68, okara, 94
Tempura, batter, 54, deep-
    fried tofu, 239
Teriyaki, tofu, 180, 204. *See
    also* sauces
Textured soy protein, 74
Thailand, tofu varieties, 405
Tien m'ien chiang (Chinese
    sweet flour miso),
    homemade, 45
Toast with tofu, 160, 161,
    and onion sauce, 163.
    See also 228, 229
Tofu (regular or firm)
    Baked dishes, 173
    Broiled, 198
    Chilled, 141
    Deep-fried dishes, 185
    Desserts, cooked, 210,
        uncooked, 207
    Dips, 143
    Dressings, 143
    Eggs with, 171
    Fried, 178
    Grains with, 193
    Homemade, 127-40
    Hors d'oeuvres, 143
    Pan-fried, 178, 179
    Pickled in miso, 148
    Preparatory techniques
        (draining, pressing,
        etc.), 119-26
    Pudding, 106
    Quick and easy, 141
    Salads, in, 153, Japanese-
        style, 154
    Sandwiches and toast,
        with, 160
    Sauces, 169
    Sautéed, stir-fried, and

        topped with sauces,
            178
    Savory pressed, 402
    Simmered in one-pot cook-
        ery and seasoned
        broths, 204
    Simmering tofu, 205, 382
    Soups, Japanese-style, 165,
        Western-style, 163
    Spreads, 143
    Varieties, unusual, 116, 402
Tofu burger balls, 261, 267
Tofu burgers (*ganmo*), 215,
    261. *See also* deep-
    fried tofu
Tofu cutlets (thick *agé*,
    nama-agé, atsu-agé),
    215, 253. *See also*
    deep-fried tofu
Tofu pouches (*agé, aburagé*),
    215, 270. *See also*
    deep-fried tofu,
    shinoda
Tomato
    Salad with deep-fried tofu,
        224, tofu, 156
    Sandwich with deep-fried
        tofu, 229
    Sauce with cheese, 50
    Soup with tofu, 164
Tortillas with deep-fried
    tofu, 242
Tosa-joyu, 38
Toufu (Chinese-style firm
    tofu), 110, 402,
    toufu-kan, 402, *toufu-
    ru*, 358
Trypsin inhibitors, 76
Tubu (Korean tofu), 404
Tuna, mock salad with deep-
    fried tofu, 227
Turnover, in tofu pouch, 284

U

Udon, *see* noodles
Umeboshi salt plumbs, with
    miso, 45

Unohana-no iri-ni, 96

V

Vietnamese tofu, varieties,
    405
Vinegared rice, 52

W

Wakame
    Salad with deep-fried tofu,
        225, 228
    Soup with miso and deep-
        fried tofu, 231, and
        tofu, 167
Walnut(s)
    Ice cream, 306
    Miso, 40
    Salad with tofu, in, 155
    Tofu (walnut tofu), 117
Wari-shita, 38
Wasabi-joyu, 38
Whey, 101-09

Whip(s)
    Soymilk with fruits, 309
    Tofu with fruits, 207
Whipped cream, tofu, 151;
        uses, 157, 253, soy-
        milk, 305
Wine-fermented tofu, 358,
        363
Wok, 186
Worcestershire, ketchup
        sauce, 50

Y

Yaki-dofu, see grilled tofu
Yaki-meshi, 241
Yakimiso, 45
Yaki-soba, 240
Yanagawa-dofu, 391
Yogurt, from soymilk, 302,
        tofu, 151
Yosenabe, 206
Yuba, 367, homemade, 374
Yudofu, 205
Yuzu miso, 40; uses, 202;
        other, 321

SENDING TOFU TO THE FOUR DIRECTIONS

Many men and women throughout the world today are in search of meaningful work. In industrial and post-industrial societies, "alienated labor" is fast losing its appeal as respect for traditional craftsmanship revives and demand for its products grows steadily. In developing nations, where hunger is often a basic fact of daily life, countless individuals are in need of truly productive labor, labor which serves the fundamental needs of society. Whether in rural village or bustling megalopolis, the traditional tofu shop could serve as a practical yet revolutionary means toward the satisfaction of all these crucial needs.

In any setting, the tofu shop can be set up and operated with a minimum of capital and technical know-how. To make the very best tofu, after all, requires only the simplest ingredients, tools, and workshop to make: soybeans which are or can be made available in bulk at relatively low prices almost everywhere; tools which can be handmade or purchased inexpensively; and a shop which need be no bigger than 12 by 15 feet and which, situated near or even adjacent to one's home, can be operated as a cottage industry, with the work and income shared by the members of one's family or community. Retailed directly or through secondary outlets, tofu products can be attractively priced anywhere in the world, and demand for these high-quality foods is bound to grow rapidly over the months and years ahead.

In Boulder or Boston, New Delhi or New Guinea, the daily practice of the traditional tofu-making art offers more than just the challenges and benefits of self-employment and independence. In its subtlety and depth, it can be an enriching exercise in concentration, heightened sensitivity, and creative self-expression. And like Gandhi's spinning, it can serve as the center of a regular pattern of daily life conducive to clear-mindedness, meditation, and peaceful living.

The obstacles to learning the tofu-making art are perhaps greatest in areas such as India, Africa, and South America, where tofu could make its most immediate contribution to human welfare. These obstacles can best and

About the Authors

William Shurtleff and Akiko Aoyagi Shurtleff spent their formative years on opposite sides of the Pacific. Born in California on 28 April 1941, Bill received degrees in engineering, honors humanities, and education from Stanford University. He taught physics for two years in Nigeria in the Peace Corps and has lived and traveled extensively in East Asia and Third World countries. He speaks seven languages, four fluently, including Japanese.

Akiko Aoyagi Shurtleff, born in Tokyo on 24 January 1950, received her education there from the Quaker-run Friends' School and the Women's College of Arts. She has worked as an illustrator and designer in Japan's modern fashion industry and America's emerging soyfoods industry.

Bill and Akiko have been working together since 1972. They have lived for six years in East Asia, mainly in Japan, studying with top soyfoods researchers, manufacturers, nutritionists, historians, and cooks. Over 500,000 copies of their eleven books on soyfoods are now in print.

In 1976 Bill and Akiko founded The Soyfoods Center, and since that time they have worked to introduce soyfoods, especially traditional low-technology soyfoods, to the Western World. They feel that soyfoods can play a key role in helping to solve the world food crisis while providing high-quality low-cost protein and healthier diets for people everywhere. Their work has led to the establishment of hundreds of soyfoods businesses and their nationwide tours and lectures have drawn widespread acclaim.

If you would like to help in the larger work related to soyfoods and world hunger, if you have questions or suggestions related to this book, or if you would like to receive a free copy of their Soyfoods Center Catalog, the authors invite you to contact them.

THE SOYFOODS CENTER
P.O. BOX 234
Lafayette, CA 94549 USA
(Phone: 415-283-2991)

perhaps only bé met on the national level. The Japanese government is presently taking an increasingly active role in aiding less developed nations. But only very recently have the Japanese themselves begun to recognize the unique treasure they possess in their traditional technologies for utilizing soybeans as food. We would urge the Japanese government to initiate a program whereby Japan's knowledge and experience in this field would be shared with receptive, protein-short countries around the world. A pilot program could be modeled on those the Japanese are now using effectively for other technologies: it might include the invitation of teams of foreign representatives to Japan to learn the tofu-making process in detail; the sponsoring of Japanese craftsmen in setting up schools abroad; and the subsidizing (where necessary) of private entrepreneurs invited to developing nations to open shops operated by host nationals. Similarly, we would urge the governments of developing nations to educate and encourage their citizens to incorporate tofu products into their daily diet.

Since 1976 over fifty new (Caucasian-run) tofu shops and soy dairies have been started throughout North America to bring the present total to 115. In 1978 representatives from these shops plus producers of tempeh, miso, shoyu, and other soyfoods established the Soycrafters Association of North America (SANA), a trade association to serve the burgeoning new industry. To aid in the establishment of tofu shops and soy dairies, we have written *Tofu & Soymilk Production: The Book of Tofu, Volume II* which is now available exclusively from our Soyfoods Center, P.O. Box 234, Lafayette, California, 94549. An easy to follow technical manual, it is based on over five years of research. In cooperation with one of Japan's largest and best known manufacturers, we have developed an illustrated English-language catalog of tofu and soymilk equipment. It is now available from The Soyfoods Center.

These developments now make it relatively easy for people everywhere to start their own tofu shops and soy dairies—and to send these fine foods to the four directions.